The Best of What We Are

REFLECTIONS ON THE NICARAGUAN REVOLUTION

JOHN BRENTLINGER

The Best of
What We Are

REFLECTIONS ON THE
NICARAGUAN REVOLUTION

The University of Massachusetts Press
AMHERST

LC 95–20330

ISBN 0–87023–984–8 (cloth); 985–6 (pbk.)

Designed by Dennis Anderson

Set in Galliard and Gill Sans by Keystone Typesetting, Inc.

Printed and bound by Thomson-Shore, Inc.

Lyrics from "Nicaragua" used with permission.

Words by Bruce Cockburn, © Golden Mountain Music Corp. 1984.

From the album *Stealing Fire*.

Library of Congress Cataloging-in-Publication Data

Brentlinger, John, 1934–

    The best of what we are : reflections on the Nicaraguan revolution
/ John Brentlinger.

      p.   cm.

    Includes bibliographical references and index.

    ISBN 0–87023–984–8 (cloth : alk. paper). — ISBN 0–87023–985–6
(pbk. : alk. paper)

    1. Nicaragua—History—1979–1990.   2. Nicaragua—History—1990–
3. Social change—Nicaragua.   4. Brentlinger, John, 1934–

I. Title.

F1528.B74   1995

972.8505'3—dc20   95–20330

                         CIP

British Library Cataloguing in Publication data are available.

This book is dedicated to the Nicaraguans who struggled

In the flash of this moment
You are the best of what we are
Don't let them stop you now, Nicaragua

Bruce Cockburn, "Nicaragua"

Contents

Acknowledgments ix

Introduction 1

1 Managua Journal, 1985 13

2 Sandino, Revolutionary Prophet 69

3 Condega Journal 98

4 Norma: On Sexism and Moral Change 133

5 Yali Journal 153

6 Necessary Poetry 197

7 Matagalpa Journal 215

8 Where Is the Revolution? 247

9 Politics and Representation 267

10 Managua Journal, 1991–92 285

11 Socialism and the Sacred 347

Notes 361

References 365

Index 369

Acknowledgments

This book is truly the work of many people, both in contributing to the experiences on which it is based and in support of the writing. Most of all, I want to acknowledge the gifts received from the Nicaraguans with whom I lived, worked, and discussed. Their generosity and openness in sharing their lives, their courage and idealism in living their lives, and their remarkable intelligence and understanding have been a constant source of encouragement and inspiration. I am especially grateful to Norma Aburto Altamirano and Katherine and Rodman, Lolín and Joaquina Salgado and Dolores and Cecelia, Elena Pineda and her family, especially Rosa and Francisca and Silvio and José, Enrique, Ana Julia Chavarría, Raúl Quintanilla, Daisy Zamora, Padre Enrique, the Centenos of Condega, the Mendiolas of León, and Consuelo Mendieta. There are many, many others.

In the United States I have been fortunate for being surrounded by a community of supportive friends, whose interest and encouragement have helped immensely. They know who they are, and I hope they know my love and appreciation. I am grateful to Eileen Estrada for much work transcribing interviews and to those who read, commented on, and considerably improved various versions of the manuscript, especially Helen Smith, Sandy Mandel, Margaret Randall, Roger Gottlieb, Paul LeBlanc, Ann Ferguson, Gary Tartakov, Charles Purrenhage, and my dedicated editor, Janet Benton.

And special thanks to Sandy Mandel, my *compañera* and main critic and support during the last years of this work.

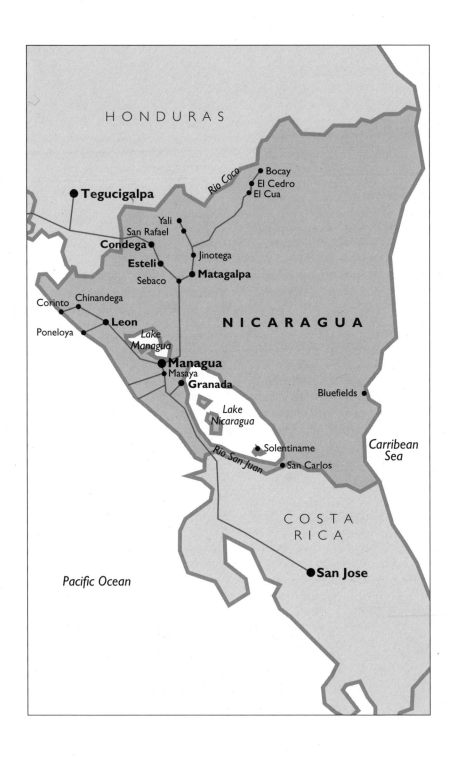

HONDURAS

Rio Coco

Bocay
El Cedro
El Cua

Tegucigalpa

Yali
San Rafael
Condega

Jinotega

Esteli

Sebaco

Matagalpa

Corinto
Chinandega

NICARAGUA

Poneloya

Leon

Lake
Managua

Managua
Masaya
Granada

Bluefields

Lake
Nicaragua

Carribean
Sea

Solentiname
San Carlos

Rio San Juan

COSTA
RICA

Pacific Ocean

San Jose

Introduction

According to the book of Genesis, the waters existed before the earth: "In the beginning God created the heaven and the earth. And the earth was without form and void; and darkness was upon the face of the deep. And the spirit of God moved upon the face of the waters."

Genesis 1:1–2

The waters . . . precede every form and support every creation. One of the paradigmatic images of creation is the island that suddenly manifests itself in the midst of the waves. On the other hand, immersion in water signifies regression to the preformal, reincorporation into the undifferentiated mode of pre-existence. This is why the symbolism of the waters implies both death and rebirth.

Mircea Eliade, *The Sacred and the Profane*

Poneloya is an old, dilapidated resort town on the Pacific Coast of Nicaragua. It is near the city of León, but few people come here. Boarded-up houses face the surf behind rows of coconut palms. A few fishermen beach their boats early in the morning, children walk back and forth to school, and local people pass on errands, but mostly the beach is empty. The Lacayo is the only hotel in town, and at the moment I am the only guest.

The Lacayo is barnlike and smells of old, dusty wood; soft curves are worn into the wooden stairs by sandy feet. Over the second-floor rooms is a roof of beams and tiles that is home to hundreds of bats. A front porch opens onto a beach of dark volcanic sand. In back is a courtyard with toilets

1

and shower stalls and a kitchen where they still cook on woodfires. Each room has a balcony facing west toward the ocean. The railing on the balcony where I sit writing is rotted and renailed at the corners and ends. The green paint of the balcony and hotel has mostly peeled off. It is still shady on the balcony in midmorning, but soon it will be too hot.

Early in the morning the tide is low and the surf and sea are quiet. There are hollowed places where seashells lie thick, winnowed and sifted by the surf. There are flat, low places where the water lies thin on the dark sand and shines like silk. It mirrors the clouds and sky.

Looking down at this sky, blue and perfect in the dark, shining sand, I see the question I would like this book to answer but know it cannot. How does this little patch of volcanic earth, poor Nicaragua, reflect and influence the history that has passed over and laid it waste?

The question is impossibly large, but over the time I have been coming to Nicaragua, six trips in seven years, I have been living and thinking within the purview of that question. It haunts me and others like me who work for a changed society. It concerns relationship and meaning: being part of something larger and redeeming. We think we are building something permanent, a physical thing such as a school or latrine, or, more important, connections between people, a union that will grow and be fruitful to all. We never know. And much of our work, what was completed, seems to have been destroyed by war or hurricane or abandoned by a history that has turned away.

It is one thing for me, a North American here to observe and write and leave, to ask this question. It is something else for Nicaraguans, many of whom gave everything, staked their lives for ten or twenty years, and lost family and friends. Over a hundred thousand died in the last years of the Somoza regime and in the U.S.-sponsored war with the Contras — more than 3 percent of the population. Now the Nicaraguans must try to survive in their devastated country. They must try to think again about the future of Nicaragua and Latin America and revolution.

The question is made more difficult by the collapse of the so-called socialist regimes in Europe, who gave so much economic support and encouragement to Nicaragua and other liberation struggles in Latin America, as well as a context of larger meaning. The world socialist movement, such as it was, for which Nicaragua's revolution signaled a new opening in Latin America and a qualitatively higher form of democracy in the evolution of socialist societies, now seems as devastated as Nicaragua itself. Marxism teaches that hope should base itself on objective conditions. Where is hope to find its way?

There is a host of questions. Sometimes my experience and thinking drift about in pieces of such different kinds that I can only say, "Here is what I saw; this is what I thought."

I had no intention of writing about Nicaragua — I had just come to see what a society in revolution was like — but once here it seemed a natural thing to do.

I had just finished writing a book about a squatters' village in Puerto Rico (in Puerto Rico they call it "land rescue"). Three hundred families rescued some empty pastureland owned by the government and built a community called Villa Sin Miedo (Town Without Fear). The rescuers were poor, landless people who had been pushed around by the economics of land speculation and government projects. Many had been to the States hoping to find a better life; they found instead, as one of them put it, "a language barrier, insults, unemployment, drugs, welfare, and poor education." All the land in Puerto Rico was priced beyond their reach and they didn't want the squalor and danger of the housing projects, which had two- or three-year waiting lists anyway.

They governed themselves and had the only community in Puerto Rico without drugs or crime. They built a one-room clinic and school with their own resources and found volunteers to give them regular health checkups and teach classes for preschoolers and adults. They planted gardens alongside their houses. They elected an assembly and leaders to begin a struggle to legalize the rescue, and many in the government supported them. They built an ecumenical church. They set aside one-third of the land for a cooperative farm. Everyone helped with community projects such as electricity, water, roads, and sewage. They helped one another with food and tools and labor. They built a house for an elderly couple who were afraid to live in their housing project any longer after being robbed three times in two years. The rescuers seemed tremendously uplifted by taking what was surely their right — a little piece of land in their own country — and uniting to build and defend themselves.

But the Puerto Rican government was alarmed by the socialist rhetoric and growing reputation of the community. What if their example spread? Even though the legislature had voted to grant the land, the governor vetoed the measure and ordered the rescuers evicted to protect "the sanctity of private property." A surprise invasion was launched with hundreds of police and shock troops. Puerto Ricans were horrified to see on evening television more than eight hundred people driven by tear gas onto the highway, with nothing but the clothes on their backs, their houses and vehicles in flames.

The town was bulldozed and cleared, and in three days everything was gone — even the gardens and orchards. The government gave the land over to what they cynically called "agricultural use," leasing it as grazing land for racehorses (a large racetrack was a mile down the road).

In spite of this defeat, the community stayed together and eventually rebuilt their houses on land they bought with donations from church and labor groups. Though fewer in number because of years of struggle and suffering, they are still together and still building.

The story of Villa Sin Miedo is an epic drama of our time. Poor people rebuilt their lives and renewed their dignity by creating a new community. Villa Sin Miedo opened a window into the future. I saw real democracy there.

In Nicaragua I witnessed the same kind of struggle on a national scale. Nicaragua, too, is a window into the future. All Latin America has been looking. Many in North America have been watching excitedly and working in support; others have been obsessed by "the threat of communism in Nicaragua." What I saw was a deeply spiritual country trying to become independent and build a new version of socialism. I felt the need and opportunity to learn and respond.

What could be more important for us in the United States to experience than a people who rejected the inhumane order based on individual greed, who reignited hope for a new order, a nurturant community — not just for the rich but for every human being? Now, after the Sandinistas have lost the election and the rule of greed is restored in Nicaragua, we need more than ever to renew this hope.

Later in the morning I hang my hammock in the shade in front of an abandoned house and read and write and think about the past, recent and more remote, personal and Nicaraguan, like a writer who keeps revising or wishing to rewrite what is already said once and for all. Sometimes a cloud passes and it rains softly and briefly, then clears again. I keep listening to the sea. It says, over and over, I am what I am.

A line of pelicans flies low over the water looking for fish, backs flashing, undersides in black shadow. I walk across the dark sand and stand watching the waves, the changes of light, and the white lines of froth. This is perfect, I think, but what has it to do with me? With human life?

The surf is hard and relentless. To the left there are rocks; a little boy and girl with a burlap bag are catching small crabs. Between waves they run among the rocks, then run back or jump up on a rock to keep from getting wet. Acting like crabs. No one else is on the beach. The old man Víctor was out digging turtle eggs this morning. A bowl of the white eggs, the size of golf balls, is kept in a refrigerator behind the bar. Víctor, alcoholic, nearly always irritable, works in the hotel cleaning and serving. He lives on the far end of the second floor, and at night he paces the hall past my room. He walks on the beach every morning and sometimes swims a little in the shallows. Once I saw him lying in the sand on his stomach, his chin propped in his hands, watching the waves almost the entire morning. When he drinks it is for days and very unpleasant. He is up at all hours and yells endlessly in the kitchen at the women who are waiting for someone to cook for. He drinks beer after beer and staggers around the restaurant in a daze until he finally sleeps lying on a bench, a half-empty bottle of "Victoria" on the floor beside him.

Life in the hotel, if it can be called that: the daily hosing and sweeping in the morning, the stacking of chairs at night, the occasional couples or small groups that swim and drink and have a meal, the visits of the beer and Pepsi trucks, the owner trimming his mustache in front of a mirror by the kitchen; all feels like an old movie that has played for decades and runs slower and slower.

Through one of those uncanny synchronicities that abound in Nicaragua, here in this scene of stagnation and slow decay I'm reading *The Bridge on the Drina* by the Bosnian Serb Ivo Andrić. I found the book in Managua and thought this classic history might suit my mood. Andrić describes a student revolutionary whose hopes for a new society are similar to Sandinista ideals: the student speaks passionately of his ideas to a friend; he confidently predicts a socialist revolution. His friend listens but remains silent, and in face of this silence, which is like a wall, the revolutionary's ideas fall to the ground. The silence, Andrić writes, expresses a "dumb, clear and unalterable opinion":

The foundations of the world and the bases of life and human relationships in it have been fixed for centuries. . . . The desire for sudden changes and the thought of their realization by force often appears among men like a disease and gains ground mainly in young brains; only these brains do not think as they should, [and] do not amount to anything in the end. . . . For it is not human desires that dispose and administer the things of the world. Desire is like a wind; it shifts the dust from one place to another, sometimes darkens the whole horizon, but in the end calms down and falls and leaves the old and eternal picture of the world. Lasting deeds are realized on this earth only by God's will, and man is only His blind and humble tool. A deed which is born of desire, human desire, either does not live until realization or is not lasting. (Andrić 1959, 246)

Here in this lonely place by the Pacific Ocean I feel all the force of this ancient, insistent pessimism, so alien to revolutionary hope, so reductive of the desire to make a better world.

What does remain in Nicaragua now that the wind is still and the dust settled? There is no doubt that the struggle for change has led to greater hardship and poverty at the time of this writing, 1992, and to tens of thousands of deaths. Where else has it led? What, if anything, justifies the sacrifices?

In the story that follows — a mixture of narrations and reflections — I try to show the spirit of the revolution and the changes it has made in people through the process of struggle. I look at the revolution as a spiritual journey of a people — divided, to be sure, among themselves and within themselves — attempting to liberate and define themselves anew. Out of this journey much has been created, much has grown. But like any such journey we cannot find a beginning or an end. We cannot make an accounting of it, we cannot measure human suffering and loss of life, or progress and change, as if we were at the end of a day's business. We can only learn that within the struggle for liberation there is a depth and meaning to life we have never known before, and resolve to do all we can to preserve and continue it.

The lines quoted from *The Bridge on the Drina* deny a meaning to human struggle, unless we are chosen as blind instruments of a divine will. The Sandinista priest Miguel D'Escoto says, in contrast, that "humans were created in the image of God. What does this mean if not that humans are themselves creators, with the capacity for creative love? The root and true meaning of democracy is that God made us in his image to be co-creators with him. He left to us the creation of society" (D'Escoto 1991).[1] I come to the Nicaraguan revolution as a teacher of marxism and an atheist. Yet I also believe that "humans are . . . creators, with the capacity for creative love" and that, on that basis, true democracy is possible.

The food in Poneloya is boring and expensive at Hotel Lacayo and the two restaurants along the only street. It's as if a sort of culinary paralysis set in long ago. There is steak, fish, and shrimp, fried, with rice, in

all three places; nothing else can be had. The dinners are beyond my budget, and I eat only breakfast at the Lacayo. It is always scrambled eggs
sitting in a puddle of oil and refried beans and instant coffee. Víctor serves it
with a flourish and a triumphant smile. He used to scowl at me a lot until I
explained to him, "Listen, hombre, you know why I never eat dinner here?
I'm not rich and I'm not getting paid to be in this country. I can't spend that
kind of money for food." I didn't say what I thought of the cooking. He put
his hand on my shoulder and smiled.

My main meal is lunch, which I buy cheap in León. At night I bring food
back from the market: tomato, onion, avocado, mangoes, bananas. I walk
the long, unlit street, brushing past people who appear suddenly like ghosts
out of the dark, to the far end of town where a woman cooks tortillas. Like
many of the Nicaraguans who actually live in Poneloya, she is extremely
poor and lives with her children in a makeshift shed on the grounds of a
vacation house she looks after. Her tortillas are delicious and there is always
a line of people waiting. They are so cheap anyone can afford them—15
córdobas for a large, "family-size" tortilla, when 20 córdobas are worth a
nickel. A five-gallon lard can holds dried corn soaking in water. One of her
daughters turns a metal grinder. Another mixes the flour with a little water
and salt. A boy brings wood for the fire. The woman cooks on a large metal
plate. I buy one, as big as a platter, that smells of fresh corn and carry it with
my vegetables over to an abandoned boat. I cut the tortilla into quarters and
place slices of avocado and tomato and onion on each section and roll
them up.

One night a boy about ten years old comes over and sits with me. I offer
him some of the food. "Do you like avocado?" He shakes his head, no. "Do
you like tomato?" Again, no. The same when I ask about tortilla and onion:
No, no. This is curious to me but I don't say more about it. We sit and he
watches me eat and I ask him questions about his school and how much fish
his father catches and how old are his brothers and sisters. When I finish
this large meal, without leftovers, we say good-bye. I turn around to wave
again and see him on his hands and knees on the bottom of the boat picking
up a few scraps of tomato and onion, putting them in his mouth.

Why spend so much time in a country where you are a stranger?
Why try to write about it, when a basic rule of writing is, Write what you
know?

I often do feel like a stranger here—awkward, oversized, uncompre-
hending. And often Nicaragua feels strange. For example, there are no
street names or house numbers; "From the UNAN bus transfer, five hun-

dred meters south" is the address of the Solentiname Gallery. For a while I had an apartment with two equally usable addresses: "From the Tica bus station, two blocks south, one block up, half a block south"; or, "From the Iglesia San Francisco, forty steps toward the lake."

To be oriented in Managua you need to know that the four directions are *al lago* (toward the lake, which is north); *al sur* (south); *arriba* (up, to the east); and *abajo* (down, to the west). Obviously the system doesn't work at all unless you know where the UNAN transfer is, or a church, or even a certain tree; and some addresses start from where something *was* (which everyone knows, of course). And it is not always clear where "up" and "down" are either, or how far five hundred steps is. I said to some Nicaraguan friends, "Perhaps the new government will do one good thing: put up street signs and house numbers." They smiled and said, "No, you don't understand — we like it this way."

At first I thought Managua must slope downward toward the west, because *arriba* and *abajo* corresponded to east and west. I assumed "up" and "down" meant "uphill" and "downhill." My Nicaraguan friends thought this was very funny. In fact, Managua lies along the southern shore of Lake Managua and is perfectly flat from east to west, and *arriba* and *abajo* are used in all Nicaraguan towns for east and west. In Managua the only slope is southward, as the land rises into hills that have a beautiful view of the city, the lake, and volcanoes to the north. A cab driver finally explained: *arriba* is where the sun comes up; *abajo* is where the sun goes down.

Nicaraguans don't think of their world in terms of a geometric grid. They orient themselves by the lake and the sun. Their world is defined by movie theaters, churches, monuments, hills, and even trees. It is curved and changing, and where something is depends on where you are.

It is interesting to watch a Managuan look at a tourist map of the city. You tell them the place you want to find. You ask, "How do I get there from here?" They become fascinated. They recognize familiar names and places: the InterContinental Hotel, the Plaza of the Revolution, Lake Managua, the barrio called "Central America." They see it as a picture. When you tell them you want to be on your way, they put the map down and say, "From here you go . . ."

Nicaraguans seem not to believe that the world can be charted from a single viewpoint that is fixed and inclusive. My assumption as a gringo traveler is that I can put everything in front of me, on the flat, and get to know it through its geometric connections to everything else. I have a practical motive: to control my relation to the world. And the converse of that is being able to control the world in relation to me.

Nicaragua teaches otherwise. Much of my time here has been "out of my control," as if I were being carried in a river. Here the world is incomplete, in process, cyclical, and open. It is not controllable by gringos.

Nature gives another example of Nicaragua's strangeness. Here the presence of the sun, wind, and rain is so strong that whatever I am doing seems to be defined by nature as much as by my intentions. I have sometimes imagined that I could write about the revolution without mentioning human beings at all. Or include them as parts of nature—as forms of heat, moisture, and force, of dryness and rocks; as hills, as earth smells, as forest colors, as butterflies, as insects that bite, as birds that flock and sing madly, as sleepy iguanas with many secrets, as snakes, as storming wind or water.

Nicaragua suffers enormously from nature, more than any place I have known: its people have recently experienced devastating earthquakes, volcanic eruptions, hurricanes, and either too much or too little rain. Not long after my last stay in Poneloya, the Hotel Lacayo was covered with a snow of volcanic ash; a few months later it was engulfed by a forty-foot tidal wave!

But Nicaraguans love nature openly and sincerely, intimately and comfortably, and they receive great gifts from her: richness of food and fruit and color, of grandeur and sweetness, of gentle, caressing touches. When I am under this spell it is hard even to remember how casual or indifferent I am to nature in the States; how I am able to think of nature as passive, as an object of use, as "private property," as "real estate," as a means of recreation. And even harder to imagine how hip, postmodern intellectuals can say that nature is a "construct," a human invention, defined by science, controlled by technology.

My experiences of the Nicaraguan revolution are always physical experiences—being blown, soaked, dried, burned, shaken, scratched, cut, chilled, filled, touched, caressed by wind, sun, and rain. There is a constant physical exchange. It is sometimes hard, a teeth-gritting trial; sometimes it is incredibly sweet, smooth, and languid. At first it is shocking. But gradually I come to feel a constant, vital metabolism; a direct, conscious, and deeply energetic connection.

What has this to do with revolution? I think it has a lot to do with how people feel about themselves and the world. In one sense the postmodernists are right, there is an interaction, an influence; but surely the influence is mutual. Nature, in Nicaragua, does not appear to be subdued and exhausted, poisoned and in withdrawal. Here it is powerful, fertile, rich, and assertive.

Also strange, to a gringo, is finding that Nicaraguans know us differently and sometimes better than we know ourselves. North Americans often come here because they know something: a skill, a method of research, an advanced technique from a cosmopolitan center in the north. This is good. Yet such people, and also those of us who come to work at simple jobs or to observe and learn, often maintain a sense of self-importance and superiority by which we set ourselves apart. Journalistic accounts of Nicaragua refer to *them* as inexperienced, backward, and naive, in comparison to *us*. And those of us who are critical of imperialist policies very often carry the same attitudes as a basic framework of thought and perception: *we* know how to do things, we "Americans" — whatever we are doing.

True, I am a stranger here, and much is strange to me; yet we are not strangers to Nicaragua. They have known us since William Walker came to Nicaragua a hundred and forty years ago with his small army of *filibusteros* ("filibusters," freebooters). He invaded the town of Granada, declared himself the legitimate government, decreed slavery legal, and was received as a national hero when he returned to Washington. They have known us since 1904, when Rubén Darío wrote his poem "To Roosevelt":

> You think that life is fire
> and progress eruption.
> That the future is where
> Your bullet strikes.
>   No.
> The United States is powerful and great . . .
> You are rich . . .
> You join the cults of Mammon and Hercules.
> Liberty raises her torch in New York
> To light the way for easy conquest.
> But our America, that has poets
> from the ancient days of Netzahualcoyotl . . .
> lives in light and fire and perfume and love . . .
> this America lives and dreams — you men with
> Saxon eyes and barbarous souls — it loves,
> it trembles, it is daughter of the Sun.
> Be careful . . .

(Darío 1980, 47)

When Darío speaks — in poetry — of Nicaragua, he speaks of poets. He refers to nature, to dreaming, to a trembling that is like birthing; and to the threat of revolution. He assumes that nature, poetry, and love form a unity that expresses itself in revolution. And this is how I experienced the revolution in Nicaragua.

I have been trying to understand this unity, not as a complex of ideas, but as a lived reality, a way of being, a deep source that is alive here. I have been drawn to it as by a magnet, and not only to understand it, but as a lover, as someone in need, as someone searching for that unity in myself and my community.

To us North Americans, these strangers who stand in the sun, who create so much beauty, who defy all reason by defying us, live in darkness. But it is a darkness we impose to hide the sources of our wealth and the misery we cause. This darkness covers our own hearts. Our postures of innocence hide a history of terrible deeds and a present of indifference. To acknowledge this would be almost unprecedented. It would require a revolution in values. How could this be done? Nicaraguans have much to teach us (and not only Nicaraguans; I refer to them because of my experiences there). We have to know and unite with them in the struggle to regain our own lost souls.

In his poem "To Roosevelt" Darío said: "You have everything, but lack one thing: God!"

I was often told that the waves in Poneloya are dangerous, and they felt dangerous. The few times I went out I was pushed toward an area of rocks. Often the waves seemed to be coming from three directions at once. But I can easily float in the shallows, and I walk on the beach a lot and collect small seashells of a pure, translucent pink.

The beach is constantly being remade. The surf works it like a potter shapes clay. At times it drops off abruptly into a trough and you step in up to your shoulders and the waves are quick and erratic. At other times it is flat and shallow and gentle near the beach and the waves break farther out in long, high curves that seem to hang in the air before they slowly drop. Their work goes on constantly.

In the night I hear them pounding like thunder and when the late-afternoon thunderclouds come, I can't tell sometimes which is thunder and which is surf. They make an almost continuous crashing. I sit at my table astonished. I want to hold my ears. When the thunder is near, the close, crackling explosions feel as if they are going to crush the roof onto my head. The light often goes out, and the air is so full of electricity I expect these dry old boards to sizzle and burst into flames. I don't feel like touching anything. I nearly always get a slight shock, anyway, turning the light on or off—you have to screw or unscrew the hanging bulb. I close the slatted balcony doors and light a candle for the time it takes the rain to pass.

The little room with its two narrow metal beds and table and chair feels cozy and pleasant in the light of the candle. The walls are one board thick. They are really partitions reaching just above my height, then slats that continue up to the roof to discourage bats from flying in. A few manage to enter through the balcony doors; a few others crawl through the slats and roost among the tiles above the door, spotting the floor and anything I leave there. I don't mind them, though, because they eat mosquitoes.

It is strange in the darkened wooden room. A strange place to be, I think, like an old-fashioned garret in a Gothic novel, the thunder crashing in the style of a Hollywood horror flick. If this were such a movie I would be crouching wide-eyed in terror, expecting any moment to be crushed or burned alive. As it is, I feel happy. The thunder gives a sense of boundless energy and anticipation. I read Neruda's poetry written on the coast of Chile and feel closer to him, to his poems expressing loss, written at a time very like this one:

> In the end there is nobody, no, no voice or mouth,
> no eyes, hands, or feet; everyone has gone . . .
> only the sand opens with a shudder . . .
> The whole sea opens, all silence . . .
> the blind perfume of the earth opens
> but there are no roads
> no one comes back, only
> the silence that sounds
> with the song of a bell.

(Neruda 1970, 334)

When the heavy rain and wind pass I open the balcony doors. The air is fresh and cool, and the sun is setting behind the dark clouds. The storm doesn't end, it passes like a moving city at war. I sit on the balcony or the beach and listen to Thelonius Monk play "Sweet and Lovely" through my earphones and watch the clouds over the sea, dark and light, flash and silence, as they move farther out above the water.

In 1933, Augusto Sandino, in a prophetic mood, said to the Basque journalist Ramón de Belausteguigoitia:

The earth has been in continuous evolution since the beginning of the world. But here in Central America is where I see a formidable transformation. I see something I have never spoken or written about. . . . In all of Central America, in the lower part, it is as if the water will penetrate from one ocean to the other. . . . I see Nicaragua engulfed in water. An immense depression and the coming of the Pacific. . . . Only the volcanoes showing above. . . . As if one ocean empties into the other. (Belausteguigoitia 1985, 177–78)

In the night I often wake and hear the surf rolling and pounding. Sometimes it crashes with a report like a cannon, followed by a loud grating of stones. In the early morning it wakes me. I hear this land tossing in its sleep, stretching and turning, moaning in its agony and desire.

|

Managua Journal, 1985

In July, in Nicaragua, it rains in the afternoon and cools down. Darkness comes strongly and quickly. I am ready to sleep by nine, tired from the heat of the day, and I like being up early to get the privacy and quiet. The houses in this barrio are built wall-to-wall, and the facing rows of houses are close, separated only by an *andén* (an extra-wide sidewalk), and there are always radios and kids playing and calling back and forth.

My space, partitioned from my daughter's, opens onto the front patio where I go out early in the morning to write in my journal. A few people pass but don't notice me sitting behind the low wall. Everyone is resting inwardly at this hour. The sun shines gently on the mango trees and tops of houses. The sky is light, soft blue, and the clouds are touched with yellow and pink.

Soon — always too soon — Lolín comes out to start his car. The patio has room for the car, the hammock, and a couple of chairs. Lolín adds water, checks the oil, and runs it to make sure the battery is up and charging. A morning ritual. If I'm still in bed, this noise and the exhaust through my window wakes me. He checks his car like an airline pilot because it's his living — he sells fire extinguishers for a small factory in Managua and drives hundreds of kilometers every day.

The car, a twenty-year-old Mazda station wagon, needs everything. The tires are worn and go flat, the radiator and muffler leak, the hoses leak, the windows don't work. Parts are expensive or impossible to get. But every day he's driving, and Saturdays they go thirty-two kilometers to Masaya to market and to see his mother; Sundays there's usually a drive for a picnic. The car is also available for the barrio — they tie a loudspeaker to the top and announce meetings or rallies or work in the communal garden.

I get up and go back to the kitchen for another cup of coffee. Joaquina has hot water ready and is whipping pancake batter. Their two teenage daughters are dressing in a room off the kitchen where the four of them sleep. Joaquina is lecturing Cecelia for putting on her newest clothes to wear to school. The morning noise has awakened my fifteen-year-old daughter, Kathy, who makes angry sounds and stays in her bed on the other side of a curtain by the kitchen.

Behind the kitchen is another open patio separated by high walls from the houses in back. There is a lime tree and a mango tree, a clothesline, a little chicken coop, and a wooden table with leather chairs. I sit down to finish writing. Against the house there's a shelf for toilet articles and a broken piece of mirror. The girls come out to fix their hair and brush their teeth. Cecelia dives for a green mango she sees lying on the ground. Lolín shaves, scraping his round, dark-brown face hard and fast with the razor. When he finishes, he comes over and puts his hand on my shoulder. Asks if I'd like to go to the beach this Sunday.

Kathy and I are in Nicaragua on a trip arranged by a Spanish school. After one month she will go home, and I will stay another month to travel. The students live with working-class families, who give us breakfast and dinner, attention, and love. So we can learn about the revolution first-hand. It is my first visit here.

About twenty-five North Americans arrive at the Augusto C. Sandino airport and get on buses waiting to take us to the barrio. Barrio Máximo Jérez was its old, prerevolutionary name; it is now Barrio Ricardo Su, after a young Sandinista martyr. It is pitch-dark when we arrive because the electricity is down, but we can certainly feel the heat — it is like a moist oven. The buses stop beside a small building where a group of people are standing around a lantern. Someone reads a list of names. Kathy and I go with Dolores, who guides us to her house with a flashlight. Tired and sweating, we drag our baggage in.

The Salgados are there to greet us, and we smile at each other and they give us fruit drinks. I try to remember some Spanish. There are posters of Daniel Ortega and Carlos Fonseca on their living-room walls, and paper Santa Clauses and decorated spruce trees left from Christmas. On top of the black-and-white TV are photos sent by internationalists who have visited here: a young German couple, a couple from Wisconsin, a guy from New York. In one, the Salgados are standing together, posing seriously, Joaquina and Lolín about the same height, their faces broad and brown, Joaquina Indian-looking, with a serious, inward expression, and Lolín Afro-Spanish, soft and rounded. Their two girls resemble Lolín, except Dolores is skinny.

I pull out some photos. There is a country house in Massachusetts sur-rounded by deep snow. A woman who is my ex-wife and my daughter's mother and still a good, close friend; she is talking intently to someone and resting her elbows on a picnic table on which there are bowls of food and bottles of beer and wine. My three sons, all young men, one with long dark hair, one with short blond hair, and one with dark curly hair and a beard. My mother, her Irish face round and pinkish, her expression pleasant and gentle, with her thin, bluish-gray hair and plastic-frame glasses; my German father, with broad forehead and receding hair, wearing gold-frame glasses and a tentative smile that doesn't quite fit his severe, longish face. Everyone looking very white and well-to-do.

Cecelia brings out a cigar box full of photographs. There is a large photo of Joaquina's half brother Rafael in an army uniform. He looks to be about twenty-five. "He's my brother but also our son," Joaquina explains. "My mother and father divorced, and she married and had more children when I was older. Then her husband was killed — somebody robbed and killed him near the Honduran border — and she became too sick to care for her children. Rafael was seven and Carmencita five when they came to live with us."

There's a picture postcard of Jinotega, a mountain town in the north where Joaquina grew up, with cypresses in front of the cathedral. Joaquina at age twelve with her mother and two sisters, their arms around one another. The family when the girls were babies. The images begin to blur and my daughter has obviously had enough, so I point at the box and say "Tomorrow, please," and they say "Of course." They show us where we'll sleep and how the toilet flushes (a stick tied to a string hangs out of the tank).

I have the luxury of my own space under a front window with wooden slats I can open for a breeze, if there is one. The bed is an iron cot with a thin mattress. There is nothing else in the small space — I will live out of my bags.

I lie under a sheet in the warm night, amazed to be here. Nicaragua. The Sandinista revolution. 1985. Reagan and the Contras, his "freedom fighters." At the airport a large sign said, "Welcome to Free Nicaragua."

My worry is having Kathy with me, because a lot of people think the United States is going to invade. Before we left, the New York Times (June 4, 1985) ran a front-page article on U.S. military policy toward Nicaragua. "An intelligence officer whose opinions have been solicited by members of the National Security Council" said that an invasion of Nicaragua would be "as easy as falling off a log." The article surveyed military opinion. "United States intelligence sources have told their superiors in Washington that major Nicaraguan installations are lightly defended" — only with 57. mm and 37 mm antiaircraft guns—so "if proper tactics and ordnance were applied to those sites, they'd never know what hit them." Another high-level U.S. official said, "It is difficult to find anyone, friend or foe of the Nicaraguan government, who is confident the Sandinistas will not make a miscalculation that could lead to a military confrontation with the United States." Daniel Ortega, the Sandinista president, had just made what all the U.S. press called a "miscalculation" by traveling to Moscow for economic aid, and as a result the U.S. Congress voted to continue aid to the Contras. Even search-and-destroy operations against Contra bases next to the Nicaraguan-Honduran border would be considered "provocations."

I decided an invasion was unlikely. Reagan was certainly determined to destroy the Nicaraguan revolution, but I didn't think he had enough support in Congress or the military for an action that would cost "American" lives (Latin American people resent the appropriation of the word "American" by North Americans). Still, I couldn't deny the possibility of an invasion. The acclaimed Grenada invasion of 1983, a military spectacle puffed up with lies and medals, could have been a dress rehearsal for an attack on Nicaragua.

This thought slipped into memories of packing late last night; of dozens of errands and letters and last-minute visits; of the sight of Miami Beach that morning from thousands of feet up, with its hotels and white sand and sparkling blue water, home to Cuban and Nicaraguan exiles; and of the run-down Sahsa airliner stopping in Belize and Honduras, where I stood in the doorway to feel the hot, humid air and saw banana plantations near the runways. The airport here was actually pretty, a new building with flowers and bougainvillea bushes. "No photographs!" they said. A rooster on the other side of my wall is also awake—he sounds about six inches away.

In the middle of a dark sleep I hear a cat screech, and something jumps onto my chest and crashes through the slats of the window. A light flashes on over the top of my partition. The light goes out, and I fall back into the darkness.

The next morning I wake in bright sunlight with a headache. It is eight o'clock and I have been hearing noises for a long time—roosters, a car starting, the shower, someone calling. I'm in the middle of a world that is bright, busy, and awake. I shower, get dressed in a headache fog, and walk to the back patio. Dolores (age eighteen, but looking fifteen) is there, wearing a faded yellow T-shirt saying "¡Viva la Revolución Cubana!" She brings us *café con leche* and *nacatamales,* pieces of pork and chopped vegetables in a paste of cornmeal steamed in banana leaves. They are the traditional Sunday breakfast here. Cecelia (age thirteen) sits down with the half of her *nacatamale* she's been saving. Kathy gives me a look that says, "I have to eat this mush?" and I shrug as if to say, "Better try it." I'm so queasy I don't want mine either, although it turns out to be delicious.

Everyone comes to the table and we talk a little, me struggling in Spanish and really wishing to go back to bed with my coffee. We look at the Sandinista newspaper, *Barricada,* with a big picture of Reagan on front, who is angry as a llama, it says, because some U.S. soldiers were killed in a restaurant in San Salvador.

"He will use this against Nicaragua," Lolín says. "It is a 'provocation.'" He explains that it will lead to more U.S. aid to the Salvadoran military, and to more U.S. Marines in El Salvador ready to attack Nicaragua.

"But of course the presence of U.S. Marines in El Salvador is not a provocation to anyone," I add.

"The cat does not provoke the mouse," Lolín says. "The mouse can provoke the cat, and get eaten. But how can the cat provoke the mouse? What is the mouse to do, attack the cat?"

"Well," I say, "Reagan tells people in the U.S. they are in great danger from a mouse." This leads to some jokes about Mighty Mouse, and we agree that Reagan's head, if we could look inside, would be running Disney cartoons.

The sun is beginning to reach over the roof onto the table, and sweat is pouring into my eyes as I drink my *café con leche.*

Lolín planned to take us on an outing. We drive across Managua and out to the country. Managua is shockingly poor. The roads are potholed and trashy, the vehicles — even the taxis — are old and dilapidated, and the shopping areas are badly in need of cleaning and paint. We pass many vacant lots, some with squatters' shacks. I had heard that Managua was devastated by an earthquake thirteen years before and had never been rebuilt because Somoza embezzled most of the international aid; but I wasn't prepared for this bleak and bombed-out look.

Many people are on the streets, nicely dressed and good-looking people, walking, waiting at bus stops, on horseback, crowded on the backs of leaning pickup trucks and jammed into buses, on motorcycles and motor scooters, some of which carry a man, a woman, and two or three little kids. Men are selling coconut milk, and children are selling newspapers and Chiclets and cigarettes. At intersections young soldiers stand about, next to encampments with canvas tents and deep trenches, tanks and artillery partly hidden in them. Ah, these are the sitting ducks the Pentagon spokesman was talking about!

As we leave the city, we pass a hill with the letters FSLN (Sandinista National Liberation Front) on its side, visible for miles, and begin to climb to a higher altitude. Immediately the air is cooler and there are more tropical trees and flowers. Ignacio, Lolín's boss, has a little farm of about twenty-five acres where he and his family — including his son's family, and his wife's sister and her family, and some others — are spending their Sunday in the fresh air of the *campo*. They show me the fields, where bananas, beans, corn, and fruit trees are growing healthy and big. Ignacio has a rifle, and we stride around looking for a monkey he wants to shoot. We don't see the monkey, and when I take aim at a tree we find the gun won't fire anyway. We return to chairs and hammocks under a large tree, and I soon have a plate of chicken and rice in one hand and a beer in the other while I try to follow the conversation. It is one thing to use my rusty, meager Spanish one-to-one with someone whom I can ask to repeat things, quite another to be listening to a chattering, laughing group. After a second beer I give up, pull my chair off to the side, and lie back to catch some sleep. As I close my eyes I see Kathy and Cecelia and some children throwing rocks, trying to knock mangoes off a tree.

In my dream I am missing my classes at the university. They have been going on for two weeks, and I still haven't shown up. "Where is he?" the students are asking. Many are no longer coming. I decide I must pull myself together and go. I enter the university building and walk past the room, barefoot and wearing jeans rolled to the knee. I peek into the room. Students are waiting in their seats, reading and lounging about. I hope no one looks out and sees me. I hurry home and change clothes. I return and go to the front of the room to begin the class. There isn't much time left, but at least I have made it this far. I have a big book in my hand. What is it? What does it say? I have no idea. I have to start.

My first night out in Managua I was robbed at gunpoint. It was half past eight, and a friend and I had just left a poetry reading at Comedor Sara — which turned out to be packed with North Americans and Europeans drinking beer, eating Sara's chicken and rice and beans, and holding forth in highly rhetorical terms about the Nicaraguan revolution. I could have been in New York in the East Village. When we heard about another reading, one with Nicaraguan poets, we left and walked a couple of darkish blocks onto a busy, well-lit street. I had noticed two men walking in front of us, because they would slow a moment and then speed up. Suddenly they turned around. One pointed a gun at my friend, and the other, a short, nervous guy, yelled over and over, "Your money or he'll kill you!"

I was totally amazed. I hadn't come to Nicaragua for this. I had all kinds of valuables in my leather shoulder bag — lots of money in cash, a camera, a tape recorder, my passport. That afternoon a woman who works in Managua had said she always feels safe on the streets at night here. I noticed the streetlights and the passing cars. This is absurd, I thought. So when the short guy tried to take my watch I jerked my arm away and said "No!" and pulled my shoulder bag behind my back with my other hand. My friend, meanwhile, under the influence of the gun, was handing over his watch and wallet and said to me, "Give them what they want."

I have a vivid image of that gun — it was a .38 revolver. (I saw it again later at the police station, in a plastic bag with my Swiss Army knife and the four bullets that were left.) When the gun was turned on me I let him pull my watch off and fish the knife out of my front pocket. Then I took the loose bills out of my back pocket and dropped them on the ground in front of me as if I were handing them over. While the short guy was bent over picking them up, a jeep stopped beside us and a man and a woman in uniform jumped out; the robbers started running in different directions. The uniformed man, who was wearing a pistol, started chasing one, and I ran along with him yelling, "He has a gun!" A couple of seconds later the robber, who was running in the shadows under some trees, fired two shots. A woman screamed and people started yelling. I ran back to the jeep.

An army truck loaded with about twenty soldiers saw the excitement and pulled up. They jumped out and formed a line and readied their AK-47s. The woman soldier was pointing and yelling, "He's over there!" The short robber had climbed into a fenced backyard and they quickly caught him, his hands bleeding from the barbed wire and my friend's watch in his pocket. The other one escaped that night, but the police got his name and address from the first one ("We used psychological techniques," they said). By the next morning, he and an accomplice who had been circling the block in a car were picked up with the stuff we had handed over.

The police knew about them. They had been robbing internationalists — who are rich here, and easy targets. The week before, they had robbed a man from Denmark; the week before that, a German. In back of the pickup truck, on the way to the station, the robber and a policeman, who held a gun on him, had a shouting match: "I didn't do anything!" "You are a bad example to foreigners!" I was sitting so close to the robber that our arms touched when the truck hit a bump.

Inside the police station was a large, open area with some wooden benches, a Ping-Pong table, and several rooms off to the sides. One had bars and the robber went in there. The others were offices and a kitchen. The place looked shabby. Revolutionary graffiti was on the wall. A bunch of tired-looking men and women were sitting on the benches watching a movie on television.

The police seemed like kids. The police force had been completely reconstituted after the revolution, in 1979, and now most were young men and women who had been fighting with the Front—"los muchachos" ("the boys"), they were called, because so many were young. Their offices and manner surprised me. They had no visible equipment except for two typewriters. There was one telephone on the wall by the entrance, and they had no radios in the station or in their cars. Young police wandered in and wanted to hear our story. They would sit or lie across the bare, wooden desks, sharing cigarettes and a bag of sweet bread, joking and chatting. Most wore khaki pants and short-sleeve khaki shirts. One wore jeans and a short-sleeve sports shirt open almost to the waist, a small revolver tucked into his belt. Except for the weapons, it felt like they were college students hanging out in their dormitory.

The policeman in charge of our case, Samuel, was twenty-two years old and in his last year of high school, which he attended at night. His assistant was nineteen and also going to high school. This night Samuel was having a turn of night duty. The processing was thorough and very slow. We spent five hours with Samuel: our stories were typed out (using three sheets of carbon paper); we drove back to the scene of the crime and back and forth in the neighborhood while the police tried to find witnesses; we went to another station and looked through volumes of mugshots. They brought us home at three in the morning.

We came back the next afternoon and Samuel was still there, red-eyed but working. He could sleep, he said, after school was over that night. He was to work three shifts and go to school two evenings without a break. "This is impossible," I said, "the schedule you keep." He said, "If you love your revolution, you can do anything." I told this story the next day to my Spanish teacher. She didn't seem surprised. "Revolutionary Nicaraguans need to work *and* study," she said. "Many of the teachers here are studying at night."

The most disturbing part was having to identify the robbers in the lineup the next afternoon. There were three groups of four prisoners. The short one was easy: I'd had a good look at him and he was in the first group. The thin guy with the gun had a mustache, and I thought he was in the second group. I was looking through one-way glass at Nicaraguan men in jail. They stood at attention looking blankly ahead. They faced me, then turned to the side when ordered. One clenched and unclenched his fists. Another licked his lips. I was grateful so many were different: older, bald, heavy, black, or tall.

Some time later a Nicaraguan woman, a schoolteacher, told me, "During the Somoza years crime in Nicaragua was incredible. You couldn't go to the market wearing jewelry, or walk in the street at night. Then it dropped after the revolution. But in the last year or so it has increased. They want dollars. There are more poor people. It's an aspect of the counterrevolution, the sabotage and the economic blockade. But there's not much violent crime. They pick pockets on the buses and sometimes rob people on the streets, but to use a gun is rare." I think she was right. I knew internationalists who were careless on buses and got robbed, their pockets or bags slit with razors.

"I used to be very timid," Joaquina said. "I was very afraid of the National Guard. When I was a girl in Jinotega, I saw a lot of abuses. For example, a friend and I were walking to a dance one evening and a group of Guardsmen were standing on a street corner. They started making remarks to my friend, and when he told them not to speak in a vulgar way in front of me they hit him with a rifle. My friend had to go to the hospital. This kind of thing happened a lot.

"When I was a girl in school, they taught us that Sandino was a bandit and that Somoza was good—that he built schools and roads. What they didn't tell us was that for every córdoba he spent on the people, he kept three for himself. In Jinotega there was a group that protested abuses, the 'Patriotic Youth,' but I never participated in it, I was too afraid. But I had a friend who went into the mountains and who later went to Cuba to study. When he came back, he told me his experiences and this changed my thinking a lot. Before, I used to think only about myself—my clothes, my food, things like that. It was different in those days.

"For instance, in Jinotega there is a coffee festival on the first of May to celebrate the harvest, and in the old days only the townspeople would come and they'd wear a special kind of clothing, blue jeans and dresses with fringe made from feed sacks, especially for the festival. They would elect a queen, who would always be an upper-class girl, like the daughter of a coffee grower. Now everyone from the countryside comes, all the pickers, and this year they elected a simple country girl who is a picker to be the queen. It is the same with me—I have changed. Now I worry about other people as well, a child who doesn't have enough to eat or clothes to wear.

"When we moved to Managua we used to go to mass every Sunday night, and Father Molina would talk about the people the National Guard put in prison and tortured just for criticizing Somoza. Once when the price of milk was raised, he urged people to protest and not to accept it silently. Father Molina was a very great, dedicated man. He applied the laws of God as they ought to be. I also knew a very progressive priest in Jinotega, Father Andrea, who also favored the poor. He and Father Molina were very different from most priests.

"There was a Bible study group that met at the church on Thursdays. They called it 'the holy day,' and lots of people would go to the church on that day, not only to read the Bible but to discuss it and apply it to what was happening here in Nicaragua. I was going to this and taking the kids—María Dolores was two, Carmencita seven, and Rafael nine. This was about 1969. Lolín didn't come because he was working in León. But then the National Guard came to the church to see who was coming. They stood around a tree with their rifles watching everyone, so after that I stopped going. I would only go to the church on Sundays with Lolín. I was so afraid I didn't participate in the struggle for a long time after.

"Later on, some of the muchachos would come to the house. Lolín knew them and helped them with a little money or food or let them spend the night here. They were in hiding because the Guard had their names and was looking for them, just for organizing a demonstration, something like that. Although some of them were going to the mountains, too, and raising money and buying weapons for the boys in the mountains. Two of them, Chino and Cappy, came to the house one night. They had a pickup truck. Lolín knew they were with the Front, but he didn't tell me. I woke up later and they were smoking marijuana and I just thought they were *marijua-neros* and I complained to Lolín about it. Then one night we were going to bed early because we didn't have electricity, and Cappy came knocking on the door, running, carrying a pistol. I didn't sleep the whole night because if the Guard had come and found him, they would have killed us all. Then I knew he was with the Front.

"Later, during the insurrection, almost the whole barrio became in-

Lolín (left) and friend in the *andén* in the front of Lolín and Joaquina's house (photos by author unless noted)

volved. We had a little store then — we sold a few groceries, soft drinks, that sort of thing — and we had two refrigerators and stored milk and meat and cheese, and a lot of it went to the boys who were hiding out here in the barrio. Many people helped, hiding them, feeding them, carrying messages, caring for the wounded and sick. We hid weapons here in the house. We went out and tore up the streets and built barricades. And we took care of people, the old people or anyone who was sick and needed help. We cleaned up the garbage. When there wasn't water, we brought water. So many people were involved I wasn't afraid any longer."

Now, Lolín and Joaquina, middle-aged people with the usual problems and pleasures, think that at any time the United States is going to invade their country. And they expect to fight. Joaquina belongs to the People's Militia and is a sharpshooter with an AK-47 (Russian-made automatic rifle with a clip holding thirty-two bullets). Not long after my arrival, Defense Minister Humberto Ortega announced that two hundred thousand AK-47s or equivalent weapons were in the hands of the population. That was a lot for a country whose total population is 3 million, about the size of metropolitan Boston. Ortega said, "Every house and workplace will be a battlefield." Lolín, a gentle man with a big potbelly, who loves to lie in his hammock after a long day, leads a battalion of the reserve.

Lolín asked me what I would do if the United States invaded while I was living in their house. There was a long silence while I thought about it, as images from movies of planes firing rockets and houses going up in flames passed through my mind. "I don't know," I said. "I hope it doesn't happen. I don't think it will."

Every June 29 in Managua, the people reenact the "Retreat to Masaya." They walk to a large rally, with music and dancing and speechmaking. The whole government leadership is there. Then they walk all night to the town of Masaya, thirty-two kilometers away, where they hold another rally at about six-thirty in the morning. This year some eighty thousand people made the walk, about 10 percent of Managua's population.

You need to know that about six weeks before the triumph of the revolution, in the summer of 1979, the Sandinistas had occupied the eastern section of Managua — poor and working-class barrios that actively supported the revolution. Many families had children in the Front, and many helped in various ways — with safehouses, messages, food, and care for the wounded. Somoza's National Guard attacked these barrios with modern weapons and armored cars and tanks, and even dropped five-hundred-pound bombs to terrorize the population. "Los muchachos" fought back with homemade contact bombs and Molotov cocktails and every sort of old or captured weapon. But the supplies and support they needed wasn't coming. One of their commanders, William Ramírez, explained:

> From the military point of view we were in very difficult straits. We had been resisting for nineteen days and thought we couldn't hold out for more than three more days. . . . So we talked with our fellow leaders, and our comrades in the national leadership around the country, and we decided to leave with the combatants and any of the people in the barrios who wanted to go with us.
>
> It was a very sad decision, and very difficult, because we knew the National Guard would enter the neighborhoods and begin to investigate after we had left, and they would capture people and torture them and even murder them. This gave us a very serious moral problem . . . because we were deciding to abandon the people who had given us food and drink and taken care of us. If we left they would be defenseless.
>
> From a personal and human standpoint our responsibility to them was total, and we had leaders who cried when we were making this decision, but we could also see its correctness from a military and tactical point of view. So we made the decision to tear ourselves away from them, because the only alternative was to stay and resist two or three more days and let the Guard murder all the forces we had been able to create — which wouldn't help anything. These actions touched very sensitive nerves in us. But at the same time, the conduct of the people, those who came and those who stayed, filled us with satisfaction and joy. (*Nuevo Diario,* Managua, June 29, 1985)

They planned the retreat in secret. They explained the situation to the people, prepared them, moved many of their wounded to other parts of the city, and maintained the appearance of continuing to fight. Diversionary attacks were made by combatants in the western sections; then, after dark on June 29, 1979, about eight thousand men and women, old people and children, the wounded and the combatants, made the retreat to Masaya. In the morning, with seven kilometers still to go, at Nindirí, the Somoza air force began to attack them with machine guns and rockets and bombs. But there were very few casualties because of the good order maintained among the people and the good luck of a heavy rainstorm. In the afternoon they arrived. The retreat was a success.

Now, six years later, people are gathering all over the city — especially young people, who are willing to walk all night, but many older people too, and children, and babies in arms — to make the same walk to Masaya. In my barrio we meet at five in the afternoon. There are about a hundred of us, of whom twenty-five are internationalists living with various families while

Managuans at a demonstration

working or studying Spanish. We are wondering what it will be like to walk all night, and we have stocks of cookies and water and limes, and people are buying ice cream from a street vendor. Many Nicaraguans are wearing olive-green camouflage uniforms or parts of uniforms. People in the civilian militia or reserves are wearing pistols or carrying rifles. Flags of the FSLN are flying, and as we start, people begin to shout slogans.

Political demonstrations in Nicaragua have more spirit and are more fun than any I've ever seen. Their slogans have a call and response form. The slogans, or *consignas,* come from all over the group and the mood gets high; everyone is participating. Soon we meet other groups at a nearby school, and the spirit gets higher. We march several more kilometers, picking up more groups and passing some whose place is behind ours, to a large field at the Roberto Huembes Market where the send-off is taking place. A huge crowd has already gathered and more groups stream in behind us. Everyone is excited. People are chanting, singing, dancing, and drumming. Helicopters drop candies from East Germany. Kids build towers of people — six hold four on their shoulders, then three more, and sometimes one more climbs to the top before they all fall.

It is dark when we arrive, and lights are shining behind a podium where the government leadership stands. Daniel Ortega makes a speech. He says the situation now is the same as before the triumph: the same enemy, the U.S. government (but not the people of the United States, some of whom are with us here tonight), which supplied the Somoza tyranny, is now supplying the Contras; and the same people are fighting, as heroic and unified as before. We want peace, but the United States won't leave us in peace. The Congress of the United States has legalized political terrorism by funding the Contras. If the Contras fail, as they will, Reagan is going to invent a pretext to invade with U.S. troops. But even if he drops an atomic bomb on Nicaragua, the United States will never occupy this country again, because the people are holding firm, combative and dignified. "We have an indestructible 'atomic weapon' of our own," he says, "the conscience and heart of the Nicaraguan people." There is much cheering and applause. Then he and other leaders of the Front lead the march through the eastern barrios of Managua.

We walk in rows six people wide. Our group waits almost an hour to start, and then we walk very fast, sometimes running. We pass my daughter and Lolín and Joaquina and the kids, tanks and armored cars. Everyone is shouting slogans in the same high spirit. The streets are lined with people,

Women soldiers preparing stage for celebration of International Women's Day

and bonfires are burning on the corners. Many people are cooking on grills outside and eating as they watch us pass. Vendors are selling food, fruit drinks, and ice cream. People call out to us North Americans. "Gringo! Walk faster!"

In an hour we are in the countryside among trees and fields. The moon is coming up. The people are still singing and chanting and walking with high energy, and some who want to go fast are passing us. It is hot and sticky. My shirt and even the strap of my leather shoulder bag are soaking wet. I save my water because I don't know when we'll get there. We were on our feet for five hours before even starting. A New Yorker next to me says, "This is going to be the hardest thing I have ever done."

I am walking with Michael, who teaches theology in Kentucky. We talk a long time this night. He was ordained as a priest, but is married now and has two kids. I am interested to know why he became a priest, and what he liked and didn't like, and why he quit. He said he had been in a liberal, progressive order, but of twelve who joined when he did, seven have left. They had a reunion a year ago. It was amazing to see them, he said, with their wives and kids.

We talk about the meaning of sacrifice — why eighty thousand people would wear themselves out walking all night. Many people practice sacrifice in some form or another. The Hopi Indians, for instance, practice sexual abstinence and fast for days before engaging in religious ceremonies. Perhaps it is a form of concentration — a way to focus deeply and seriously and to give oneself more completely. Sacrifice as the gift of oneself.

We talk about the religious quality of this revolution, and about Father Uriel Molina, whose parish includes our barrio, who says "Revolution is the Resurrection"; who described a sort of conversion to political struggle he experienced after coming to Masaya, six years ago, to bury a young boy who was killed during the retreat. I recorded his sermon:

They say I substitute the *guerrilleros* for Christ, but what happens is, I see Christ *in* them. "No one has greater love than he who gives his own life."
I want to tell something that can't be seen in any book but that I carry in my heart. The day of the tactical retreat to Masaya, Lupita Montiel, a woman who lost two sons, called me to bury her son. I went, amid vultures and bullets, and when I arrived in Masaya I saw her boy on the ground covered with a mat. I didn't dare remove the mat, because I knew I was going to encounter something terrible. "Uncover him, Father," she said. And thus I discovered her boy of sixteen years split in two by a rocket. I will never be able to forget such an impression, but I will never be able to forget, either, the words this woman said to me, to help me in my com-

mitment as a priest. She said, "I feel proud to have borne a son who is a Sandinista," a pride I knew she carried like a treasure in very fragile vessels.

I returned to the church, head bowed. I thought, a priest who has seen such extermination by the Somoza dictatorship could never go back. I felt I had lost my faith. I didn't understand the sense of my priesthood. I had seen what made more sense than walking in robes: to be a *guerrillero,* a defender of the national identity from a barricade.

I went in and sat alone and meditated, and it was a gray, solemn afternoon, and from all sides I could hear the screams of mothers who had had a son torn from them. And in this moment of bombardment and fire and grief and fear I heard a guitar begin to play, and when I went to look I saw a boy combatant, who could have been the son of Lupita Montiel, a boy of the community. I wondered how he could sing when there was so much destruction and death, and I realized it was the *guerrilleros* who had the last word, not we who hadn't lived their experience.

When I heard him singing it made my hair stand on end. I began to cry, and I cried all night long, and was confirmed in grace which put me in this revolution: to be a priest who knew how to be in solidarity with his people who fight. Without wanting to be anything more than anyone else, but simply to accompany my people faithfully.

He pointed to the large, central mural that was recently painted in the new church. It showed Christ resurrected as a young Nicaraguan combatant. "This boy represents the martyrs of our people, those who had so much love they were able to give their lives. In this parish alone we had two hundred who died."

And he began to call their names. "Ricardo Su. Luis Alfonso Velásquez." Each time he spoke a name the crowd in the church shouted "¡Presente! ¡Presente! ¡Presente!" Soon people in the church were calling out names. And soon they were calling out slogans: "¡Nicaragua Victoriosa! ¡Ni Se Vende! ¡Ni Se Rinde!" (We're Not for Sale! We Won't Surrender!). There was no difference any longer between a religious ceremony and a political demonstration. There was reading from the Bible and the taking of Communion, and prayer, and songs such as this one, sung along with an eight-piece band of traditional instruments:

CREDO

I believe in you, *compañero*
Christ, human, Christ the worker
who conquered death
with an immense sacrifice
to engender a new human
through liberation.

You are risen
in every arm that is raised
to defend the people
from exploitation
because you live in the farm
and the factory, and the school.
I believe in your Resurrection.

Michael and I talk about the meaning of this walk, about reenactments of religious events and pilgrimages, on this country road in the moonlight, tired but happy, and part of such a long stream of people that we have no idea how far we are from the beginning or the end.

We pass country houses where the people stay up to watch us pass; even now, at midnight or one in the morning, the children are standing by the fences and adults are sitting quietly in chairs. They have set up resting places and first-aid stations along the way. At some houses, they are cooking and handing out food and water to marchers who stop. As time passes, the groups at such places are larger. They shout slogans and joke with us as we pass. Some are drunk. They are happy to see Yankees.

Soon the moon is down, and it is dark and the road seems to get worse. Now it is just a wide, rocky path. I lift my feet high so as not to stumble. The procession stalls where there are lots of sharp volcanic rocks and the path is steep. My legs are aching and I feel shaky. Once, off the road to piss, I stumble on a root and almost fall. A branch with briars cuts my ankle. There are puddles and it is muddy and slippery in places. We come to a large stopping place where hundreds of people are resting and sleeping. We look for a place to lie down, but it is muddy and wet and the banks of the path are thick with bushes and every clearing is full of people. No one seems to know where we are or how much farther we have to go. I feel dazed and exhausted.

I become separated from anyone I know and walk alone for about an hour. I am glad not to talk. Finally the dirt road empties onto an asphalt highway. We are not crowded any longer, and there are lights in the distance. I think, wrongly, that it is Masaya. All along the shoulder of this road people are sleeping, some with their heads on the asphalt — so many that it seems as if the road is lined with dead bodies. I see a grassy place and lie down for a few minutes. I am really tired, but the grass is wet and cold and I feel chilled. I walk another half hour and come to Nindirí, where the Somoza aircraft attacked. It is about four o'clock in the morning, and many people are lying down and sleeping because the march is scheduled to start again here at dawn. A mass of people covers the concrete plaza. There seems to be no space, but José, a man from the barrio, calls to me — "Juan, ven aquí." I squeeze in between him, in uniform, and another man in uniform. I am wearing only a short-sleeve shirt and am cold, but it is warm between the two men; my back in on the concrete, and I am close against them, enjoying the warmth and completely exhausted. In what seems like two minutes José calls to me — "¡Juan! ¡Vamos a Masaya!" "Why?" I ask, from someplace far away. "We can't stay here," he says, "it's dangerous."

At first I feel really bad. This is endless, I think. I can't walk seven more kilometers. My legs are stiff and sore; my feet, in sandals, are scratched and hurting; and I have a bad rash in my crotch (Note: don't wear tight underwear on a retreat). And everyone seems to share my feeling. There are no *consignas* now — we walk in silence. We are back on a dirt road that is wide and filled with people as far as I can see. It is light, but too dim to take a picture, as I stand on a stone fence to look.

The day gradually brightens and I begin to feel awake. The area around Masaya is rich farmland, and the hills are green and cultivated. I see corn and beans and freshly plowed, dark-brown earth. The walk now feels entirely different — I can see everybody. Young girls walk holding hands. Many couples have their arms around each other. Little groups talk quietly as they walk. A girl in uniform runs up behind a young man and puts her hands over his eyes. A pretty woman, her arms crossed, carrying only a purse over her shoulder, walks absorbed, as if completely alone on the road. I am startled to see a soldier holding an automatic rifle in the dimness on a nearby hill. Until he moves I think he is a statue. Then I notice others. They are stationed all along the seven kilometers, "guarding" us from the National Guard. I am waking up enough to understand what José meant when he said it was dangerous. No planes come as if to bomb us, but later, in Masaya, helicopters and planes come to drop flowers on the people.

As it brightens we keep walking in silence. Roosters are crowing. People stand or sit outside their houses with coffee cups in their hands. Children stand in doorways, and they too are quiet. I begin to feel better. Every fifteen yards a large palm leaf is stuck in the ground, a black-and-red plastic FSLN flag attached to it. The same flags are attached to cords strung along the road from Nindirí to Masaya. We walk around barricades made of a freshly cut tree — its trunk, branches, and leaves for hiding behind. Soldiers hide with their rifles, some wearing black-and-red bandanas over their faces like "los muchachos" during the insurrection. One barricade is made of stones. As we pass, no one says anything. It is like a religious ceremony, both theater and reality. We pass a long row of parked tanks and armored vehicles with soldiers sitting on top, watching us. No one sleeps alongside this road, but there are little groups resting or caring for someone sick.

As we get near Masaya, people seem to be waking up. It is fully daybreak. I feel more and more excited. It is the number of people walking, I think, and the sense of that power, achieving what they set out to achieve.

Now, entering Masaya, there are banners overhead saying things like "The Same Walk, the Same People, as the Heroes and Martyrs of Masaya." Lots of people are on the sidewalks. It is a regular parade, at five-thirty in the morning. There is talking now, but still no chanting or singing — obviously everyone is very tired. A local group plays music on the sidewalk with guitars and a marimba. We pass a group of men at a table playing cards and ignoring us. We pass more musicians, with guitars and violins. The street is completely full of walkers, and the sidewalk with people watching.

When I get to the central square I see my daughter and Lolín and Joaquina. They got up at three in the morning to drive here. I see my friend Michael sitting on a curb. He didn't stop to sleep and has been here about an hour. The march is to end in a park about a kilometer past the square, but I stay in the square. The marchers pass by for about an hour more. The tanks and armored vehicles come. The tanks are very imposing — their exhaust blows like a wind on the people as they pass. Planes and helicopters fly overhead. Somewhere Daniel Ortega is speaking again.

Michael and I walk to a nearby house where Lolín told us we could get coffee. We were expecting a restaurant. The door is open and we look in to see a very large room with a tile floor and a curving staircase. Two elegant-looking women and a man are sitting around a glass-covered table talking. The man, on one end of a red-velvet couch, invites us to come in and sit down. It feels strange — the people so clean and well dressed, the house obviously well-to-do. My feet are cut and smeared with mud, and I have been sleeping on the ground. We sit on the edge of the couch and ask for water. They bring glasses of water and large cups of strong, sweet coffee. I feel incredibly grateful and in my exhausted state can't quite believe where I am. A soldier comes to the door, says something I don't understand, and sends his little boy running down the hall. We talk a little. They ask us where we are from. I ask the man what he thinks of the Retreat. "It is marvelous," he said. For some reason I feel relieved. "How many people do you think there are?" I ask. "I don't know," he says, "I didn't watch it all. Sometimes I sit here, sometimes I go out to the street and watch."

Later the Salgados and Kathy and I drive to the Masaya market, which is just opening. They want to buy fruit and vegetables. I start to walk with them, then wait by the car and watch people go in and out. I don't want to walk any more that day.

The Retreat to Masaya allowed me to experience the collective energy and inspiration of the Nicaraguans in revolution. The ups and downs of Nicaraguan money—the córdoba—showed me a lot about another part of Nicaraguan life—how it feels to be subjected daily to U.S. domination.

Entering Nicaragua, you had to exchange 60 dollars at the "official rate," at that time, of 1 dollar to 28 córdobas. Someone had already told me the "real rate" was 1 dollar to 80 córdobas, so I figured the official rate to be a tax on foreign visitors. Over the next couple of days I spent most of my 1,680 córdobas. Prices were high, but I assumed my expenses would drop by two-thirds once I exchanged more money at the regular rate.

Then I heard that the government had just begun to trade córdobas at the same rate as the black market, in an effort to control it. The new rate was 1 dollar to 650 córdobas! I realized this would make everything very cheap, but didn't think much else about it. The next day I cashed 400 dollars in traveler's checks to get spending money for me and my daughter for the rest of the trip. The exchange rate is high, I thought, and a trip to the exchange house takes most of an afternoon, so I'll get a lot of money and not have to think about it. I signed the traveler's checks, and a woman at the desk filled out a form which I took to the cashier.

The cashier handed me a stack of five-hundred- and thousand-córdoba notes that was six inches high. I looked at my form—I was getting a quarter of a million córdobas. I thought, she's made a bad mistake (even though I saw her using a little Japanese calculator). A Canadian businessman behind me said, "Are you going to buy a cotton plantation?"

I ran over to the woman at the desk. "There's a mistake," I tried to say in my excitement. "I don't want all of this!" I waved the money and hoped she would take it back. She smiled and said no, and pointed to the book where the transaction had been entered. If I want dollars back I'll have to come tomorrow, she said, because it's near closing time. She pointed to a long line of people I had passed coming in. I hadn't had to wait because I was buying córdobas; they were in line to buy dollars.

I left with enough money stuffed in my bag to live in luxury in Nicaragua for a year. A room with breakfast for a month was 6,000 córdobas (about 9 dollars). A shrimp dinner in Managua's fanciest restaurant was 600 córdobas (less than a dollar). "I'm a millionaire," I thought, "here to learn about revolution. What will I do with all this money? Where will I keep it? Should I buy a motorcycle?"

It was incredibly hot walking back that afternoon, on a busy four-lane boulevard with no sidewalk. A thunderstorm was moving in. I pulled a five-hundred-córdoba note from my stash and stopped at a restaurant for a bottle of beer (now 11 cents). When I finished the beer I was sweating and it was pouring rain.

This was my first exposure to the craziness over money in Nicaragua. What was it all about? Simply put, it was about a very big country destroying the economy of a tiny country by economic exclusion.

The United States had recently imposed a trade embargo on Nicaragua. Nothing could be sold anymore on the U.S. market, where Nicaragua's coffee, tobacco, bananas, fish, and cotton were usually sold. Also, nearly all of Nicaragua's machinery and other manufactured goods had come from the United States. The need for buyers for exports and for parts, replacements, and various imports and credits became desperate. Nicaragua looked for help from other Latin American and European countries, and at first received oil on credit from Mexico and Venezuela; but little by little the United States pressured them to cut off trade with Nicaragua. It could do so because these countries are also subject to economic pressure from the United States and depend upon trade concessions, foreign aid, and World Bank loans.

Nicaragua lost dollar income and had to pay more for imports. Simultaneously, Washington was stepping up its support of the Contra war, which hurt production in Nicaragua and raised government costs. This economic and military squeeze had been building for more than two years when I first came to Nicaragua. Its consequence was that Nicaragua was forced to trade with the Soviet Union, nine thousand miles away, for completely different and inferior manufactured goods. And when Daniel Ortega made a trade visit to the Soviet Union, the U.S. Congress voted more aid for the Contras and our political commentators called him inept for having alienated Congress! Even though Ortega had gone first to several countries allied with the United States.

As a result of this squeeze, the U.S. dollar began to have a magical status. Anyone with income in dollars was automatically rich. Everyone wanted dollars. For certain things, such as airline tickets, you needed dollars. Then, to satisfy those who had dollars and to take in more for itself, the Nicaraguan government opened "dollar stores," with U.S.-made clothes and laundry soap and Hershey's chocolate, imported from Panama. People on the street often asked foreigners to sell them dollars.

Scarcity creates inflation, so the value of dollars in relation to córdobas constantly rose higher. The physical dollars you saw occasionally, the fives or tens or twenties, took on a mystical aura—they emanated power. One felt they lived in a bigger, richer, more comfortable world, a world with fancy computers and Miami hotels and helicopters with rocket launchers.

I carried a ten-dollar bill with me, taped in the back cover of my Spanish dictionary, as an insurance policy. It meant nothing really bad could happen to me. I could ride a taxi from one end of the country to the other for 10 dollars in cash. Once a Nicaraguan friend, embarrassed, confided that his daughter had bronchial pneumonia and he needed dollars to get the medicine from Costa Rica. When I pulled the ten-dollar bill from my dictionary, I felt like a magician. I could bring medicine from Costa Rica with a movement of my hand. No Nicaraguan had that power. It wasn't like lending money to a friend in the States who was broke or poor. It was a difference of worlds, of having access to only one (him) or to both (me). My friend's need and discomfort, my ease and sense of control, gave me a small, clear image of the nature of imperialism.

The drama over the dollar was one manifest consequence of the economic blockade. It went on and on. Before long, the córdoba was exchanging at 23,000 to 1. New money was being made simply by stamping zeros onto old money.

A new act in this drama occurred one Sunday early in 1988, during a later visit to Nicaragua. Daniel Ortega went on television and announced a drastic monetary reform. Its aim was to reduce inflation, stop speculation, restructure prices, and redistribute income. People had exactly three days to exchange all their old córdobas for new ones at the rate of 1,000 to 1. The exchange rate for dollars was set at 1 dollar to 10 córdobas. Prices were set on all basic items and new wage levels were set.

Lolín counted up their and my córdobas and on Monday morning took a bag of about 5 million to the school down the street. He stood in line all day, and when they closed and everyone left, he came home for dinner and went back. He slept in a chair at the head of the line. At ten-thirty the next morning he came back with the new money without a word of complaint. He said proudly, "They've been planning this for a year, and thousands of people knew the secret"—and he was right, television shorts had even been taped explaining the changes — "but no one else knew, not the CIA, not *La Prensa* [Nicaragua's conservative newspaper], no one!" He raised his fist in a victory sign.

The new conversion rate meant a big devaluation of the dollar in relation to the córdoba. People who held dollars weren't rich anymore. And those who held or earned córdobas were suddenly well-off. They all went shopping, as the government expected. Yet the world market soon had its say. In less than two weeks, the dollar was exchanging on the street for 50 córdobas. The government stores were holding prices stable for basic goods, but the problem was, they often ran out. Then people had to rely on the "free market," where prices had gone up fast.

"Scarcity drives inflation" — I learned that in Nicaragua. The córdoba was held stable, officially, for about three months, as its black-market price dropped below 100 to the dollar. Then it was officially reduced to 120 córdobas to the dollar. In two more months it was down to 450 to the dollar. Two years later, to buy a single U.S. dollar, you had to pay 25 million córdobas!

Something else I learned: the real currency in Nicaragua was never controlled by the Nicaraguan government, and it was not the córdoba but the U.S. dollar. Official U.S. policy and the world market made it so.

Through the Spanish school I was able to learn about many of the policies and accomplishments of the revolution and to become oriented geographically in the country. Besides the morning classes, the school arranged trips and talks for the afternoons, evenings, and weekends. We visited places I might not have seen on my own, and important people came to speak to us. We visited the Ministry of Agriculture for a talk about agrarian reform; the National Assembly (Congress), where a Sandinista delegate talked about the constitution that was being written (Nicaragua had never had a constitution) and about an autonomy bill for the Indians and Blacks of the Atlantic Coast; and the Ministry of Culture, where we heard about poetry and painting workshops in the communities, the prisons, and even for the police.

The Sandinistas we met seemed dedicated, intense, and open to questions. They were willing to admit mistakes and limitations, but were insistent concerning their good intentions and the progress the revolution was making. Always they began by talking about the poverty and devastation the revolution had inherited from thirty-five years of the Somoza family's dictatorship. Then they spoke of the added difficulties of the Contra war and the economic blockade imposed by the United States. We got this story in every part of the government we visited. This was the theme: we are a popular revolution; we are poor; we are progressing; we suffer from enormous difficulties; we are locked in struggle with the Reagan government; we don't confuse the people of the United States, who are our friends, with this government; we need your help in our struggle.

One afternoon we drove about fifteen miles northeast of Managua, through a region that was dry and bare and unpopulated, to a green and prosperous-looking farm. It was a prison farm, a new initiative of the Ministry of the Interior.

The prison farm was three years old. Prisoners with a record of good behavior elsewhere could transfer — forty-nine were living there at the time. They had taken a hundred acres of abandoned land in poor condition and were reclaiming it. They had planted fourteen thousand trees! They grew crops and had cattle and chickens, and the government intended for them to become self-supporting. They called it an "open prison" because there were no fences and the guards were unarmed. I even saw machetes leaning against a toolshed.

The program was geared toward rehabilitation. About thirty of the prisoners were in literacy classes taught by other prisoners. They had adult education, music, sports, lectures, family visits, and private rooms for conjugal visits, and some went home on weekends. Two had escaped in the three years of the program.

I later read about the opening of a much bigger prison farm near León. In all there were seven. I knew there were also traditional prisons, and I have read reports from U.S. visitors who inspected them and found that prisoners' rights were generally respected. The Sandinista government abolished the death penalty, established a maximum sentence of thirty years for the worst offenders, and pardoned most members of the National Guard who were captured during the insurrection. A society reveals its values most clearly in its prisons and mental institutions, where it must face its failings and deal with those who "offend" it. I have taught in prisons in Massachusetts, and I know about the conditions and the high recidivism rates. Here the system assumes personal growth instead of punishment. I love the idea that a prison should be a productive and healthy environment that improves the land on which it stands.

One Saturday morning we rode our bus northwest. First we visited the ruins of Old León, devastated long ago by the volcano Momotombo. Then we drove to a nearby geothermal electrical-generating plant, a clean and efficient source of electricity. The generator, which produces about 20 percent of Nicaragua's electricity, is driven by steam tapped from underground next to Momotombo. Eighteen wells reach almost half a mile down and collect superheated steam, 230 degrees Celsius. The wells were dug in Somoza's time with aid from Italy, but were left covered over. (Somoza owned the land and the construction company, and had written a contract giving himself 13 percent of the sales.) Since the revolution, the plant itself was built, again with aid from Italy. The plant was so attractive it could have been designed by an artist such as Fernand Léger, and it is 50,000 dollars a day cheaper than an oil-fired plant. Alongside such innovations, which seem to belong to the twenty-first century, are ox-drawn carts, whole towns without good drinking water, and the capital city draining its waste directly into Lake Managua.

Among the people who came to talk to us about their work, I remember especially Mary Hartman, a Maryknoll nun. She had lived in Nicaragua for twenty years and was asked by the government to head a commission for the protection of human rights. She was very committed to the revolution. "It was made for the poor," she says, "who had no hope before." She praised the government for giving land to the campesinos and said that Nicaragua was the first country in Latin America to implement a 1980 U.N. proposal for human rights programs. After investigating reports of human rights violations, she had concluded that the government was serious about punishing offenders and correcting such policies as the forced relocation of the Miskito Indians. She discussed several cases she said had been fabricated to make the Sandinista government look bad. She noted that Contra human rights violations are systematic and increasing, and she referred us to published sources such as Reed Brody's *Contra Terror in Nicaragua*.

Manuel Calderón, a Sandinista *comandante,* next in the chain of command under Tomás Borge in the Interior Ministry, spoke to us about the economic and human effects on Nicaragua of the Contra war. He's small and thin, with a large mustache, and speaks as if his mind is organized into rows of small, connected boxes, each labeled and full of facts. He even told us how many gallons of gasoline had been needed for government helicopters searching for Contra invaders.

At the time Calderón spoke with us, there were between eleven thousand and thirteen thousand Contras, half at large in the remote mountains of Nicaragua and half based safely outside in Honduras. They were descended from the old, much-hated, and feared National Guard of Somoza—fifty-eight of their sixty highest officers were former officers of the Guard. Scattered and demoralized by the Sandinista triumph, they had been secretly reorganized and retrained by the CIA, with the specific aim of destroying the Sandinista revolution and reinstating a government of the far right that would willingly serve the economic and political interests of the United States. Hence the name "Contra" — that is, *contrarevolucionario*. They were supplied and paid by the U.S. government, sometimes clandestinely and sometimes with overt congressional approval that nonetheless still violated U.S. and international law. Brody's *Contra Terror in Nicaragua* (1985) and Christopher Dickey's *With the Contras* (1985) are good sources for further information.

Calderón's talk was laden with facts and figures. Thirty-five thousand families, 142,382 people, who lived in remote and undefendable areas, had been displaced and required government support. In their attacks the Contras had destroyed 359 schools, 41 health centers, 14 cooperative farms, and 11 child-care centers. The economic loss to the Nicaraguan people was estimated to be 3 billion dollars. Forty percent of Nicaragua's national budget had to be used for the war. Seven thousand civilians (including 3,000 children) had been killed.

"We want peace," Calderón said. "But in spite of our efforts we run into the wall of imperialism. We approved the Contadora agreements; we answered the demands of [our] ethnic peoples and we are the first country in Latin America to grant them autonomy."

In answer to a question about the internal effects of the war, Calderón said, "The war is a reflection of the class struggle between a great capitalist state and a popular government, so it clearly manifests the class struggle within our country. For example, many families send their children out of the country so they don't have to perform military service. Also, the Nicaraguan bourgeoisie is very different from that of Mexico or Colombia — here they have always sold out to U.S. interests, so people's attitudes toward the war are determined by their patriotic feelings as well as their class. When Cardinal [Miguel] Obando y Bravo came back after offering mass in Miami, many church groups and political parties met him at the airport. You heard all kinds of slogans against the government: 'Down with the Sandinistas!' 'Christianity, Yes! Communism, No!' The police were instructed not to interfere, but eleven policemen were injured by these crowds, and we have announced that we can no longer tolerate that."

Asked when he expected the war to end, Calderón said: "We think it will be a long war. So long as U.S. imperialism exists our revolution will be threatened, because it is the antithesis of imperialism. When a point is reached when the countries of the world will not allow one country to plot war against another country, to debate in their Congress whether to conduct a secret or an open war against another country . . ."

The school arranged whatever visits and talks we requested, and we spent one afternoon with Gerardo Alfaro, head of the Conservative party and a National Assembly member, who gave a broad portrayal of the conservative, anti-Sandinista perspective. He said that what his party favored was a capitalist system free of Somoza-style dictatorship. He believed that the constitution the Sandinistas were creating was a good one, if it really did include freedom of expression, political pluralism, and a mixed economy. But these principles, he claimed, were a Sandinista trick hiding totalitarian ambitions. The Sandinistas, he said, are trying to introduce Marxism-Leninism; they are not really pluralists, they just say they are. He claimed that the Contras constituted a legitimate opposition force, and said that if his party were in power, war wouldn't be necessary. He said he believed the 1984 elections (which the Sandinistas won, receiving 63 percent of the vote) were free and fair, although the opposition parties didn't have enough time to prepare for them. He opposed compulsory military service, because the government was drafting people to fight on one side of what was essentially a civil war. He also opposed U.S. involvement in support of the Contras. He disputed all of the Sandinista claims that the revolution had improved the lives of the people. The land reform program, he said, was a fraud, because the campesinos were not given the land individually—it was formed into cooperatives. The health programs had not improved health—you saw lines three or four blocks long in front of the health centers. The educational system had been improved, but it was too ideological. Also, the government was insincere in its claim to protect private property: one member of his party had a large farm worth several million dollars that the government had refused to remove some squatters from.

I left Alfaro's talk thinking that he had told us what he thought, with one probable exception: he had objected to U.S. support for the Contras. I suspected that was not completely forthcoming, because so many right-wing Nicaraguans were courting such aid. The Sandinista government viewed support for the Contras as treason, so, opposition has its limits, and he was watching his step!

Was the Contra war a civil war, as Alfaro said, or a case of U.S. aggression against Nicaragua, as the Sandinistas said? It was organized and supplied and supported by the United States—not by Nicaraguans. The Nicaraguan right was much too weak and divided to sustain a military presence here. Yet Nicaraguans were fighting, and the war represented a division within Nicaraguan society. It was a class war and, though completely integrated with U.S. interests, it was a civil war. So both were right.

How could Alfaro have said there was no political pluralism when he himself was a member of the National Assembly and his own party held fourteen seats won in an election he had described as fair? How can civil war be legitimate in a country that has just held a fair election? And how could he have said there was no freedom of expression when he could speak so openly to us? In Nicaragua there was more political debate, from more differing points of view, than in any country I know. I have yet to see anyone advocating socialist policies on national television in the United States! It is true that *La Prensa* and Radio Católica (Catholic Radio) were censored from time to time, and I agreed with him that this violated freedom of expression. Yet it occurred in a wartime situation, and then only sporadically. It was wrong, but it hardly defined the human rights situation in Nicaragua.

Many North Americans who come here say they oppose U.S. policies against Nicaragua but do not support the Sandinistas, while I *do*. I came here with a positive attitude and it grows stronger. When I had personal encounters with right-wing critics of the Sandinistas, I sometimes wondered if I too much identified myself as a supporter of the revolution to be a responsible observer.

One afternoon I was sitting on the curb at a bus stop. A middle-aged man in sports shirt and slacks, carrying a large paper bag, stopped in front of me.

"Where are you from? Germany? Canada?"

"The United States."

"Are you a communist?"

"Maybe," I said. "It depends on what you mean. Why do you ask?"

"We don't like communists here." He swayed a little as he stood in front of me in the street.

"Really? Everybody?"

"Almost everybody. We don't like the changes that have been going on here."

"Why?"

"It was better before the revolution. Much better."

"Why better?"

"Then you could buy anything you wanted. You had to work, but you could make money and buy a car, a house, food, anything. Isn't it like that in the U.S.? Can't you buy anything you want? If you work hard you can do it. That's why it was better."

"Maybe it was better for you, but what about the campesinos, the poor people? They worked hard and couldn't buy things — they were still poor. Now a lot of people have their own land who never had land before, and the government is helping them in various ways. They have new schools and clinics and things like that."

"They are still poor," he said, "it hasn't changed. Aren't there poor people in the United States? There's always poor people. But they want to make *everyone* poor, like in Cuba."

"I've been to Cuba," I said. "In Cuba everyone has enough to eat and they have the best health care, the best education, in Latin America. I wouldn't say they are poor."

He looked at me.

"I like freedom," he said. "I want to be able to work and buy what I want. They don't have any freedom in Cuba."

He looked at the man standing next to me.

"I like to eat well — very well." He smiled at the man and patted his stomach. "I like a good steak," he said, and smiled and winked at the man.

He looked back at me. "You say they aren't poor in Cuba?"

"Yeah," I answered. "Not really. There isn't poverty in Cuba, not like in the rest of Latin America, not even like parts of the United States."

He looked at the other man. "Did you hear what he said, this crazy gringo?" Pointing his finger at me. "No one is poor in Cuba!" He began to laugh, pointing his finger at me.

I stood up. "Don't point your finger at me. Don't laugh at me. I'm telling you what I think."

"I'm sorry," he said.

He turned to the other man as he started walking away: "He says nobody is poor in Cuba." "You're crazy," he said to me, "everyone is poor in Cuba. Everyone!"

When I come home in the afternoon, Joaquina and Dolores are often sewing together. They have a foot-powered Singer. Working-class Nicaraguans still make most of their own clothes. They also embroider. They talk like sisters or close friends, gossiping and laughing and dramatizing. Quite often the gossip has a cutting edge.

Joaquina always gets me a cup of coffee or a glass of fruit juice. There are many juices I have never tasted—I make a list of fourteen different kinds. Some are from fruits or seeds and some are unusual combinations, like *arroz con piña*—finely ground rice flour mixed with water, sugar, and pineapple juice.

After it rains, Joaquina and the kids sweep the porch and the walk in front, then bring out chairs for the evening and socialize with the neighbors. All over the barrio people sit in front of their houses, lean against the walls that separate the front porches, read the paper, and watch whoever walks by. Babies are carried up and down, or are followed as they toddle. The little kids play games. Sometimes in front of the house fifteen or so little kids run back and forth in a mob, yelling and laughing as they play a running and squatting game. Stickball is a favorite for the older ones. The high-school-age kids gather at night, putting out sexual energy waves.

Thirteen-year-old Cecelia, the younger daughter, is the goat of the family. Lolín has frequent shouting matches with her that end with sounds of spanking and endless sobs. Joaquina and Dolores team up against her. She is fat (though no more so than Lolín and Joaquina) and eats constantly and often secretly. She piles three heaping spoonfuls of sugar on her pancake, looks at me, and puts her finger to her mouth. She is loud and walks around the house slapping her sandals on the floor. She gets into fights with the kids she plays with and comes home screaming in pain. To everyone's disgust she becomes involved with the Evangelical Christians.

There are little conflicts between this household and others. Sometimes it is because "we" are more active in the barrio than they; sometimes it is about proper behavior; sometimes it is unfathomable. My daughter has to have two going-away parties because her best friends, some of whom live next door, are not allowed in this house. And Dolores and Cecelia can't go to the party next door with the forbidden friends, which is more fun and runs later and is so noisy that the people in this house can't sleep.

Kathy had some doubts about spending her summer vacation in Nicaragua, but was persuaded. And she didn't care for the lack of privacy and the seatless toilet and sagging metal cot or even for the Salgados (who had a tendency to dominate her), but at the end of the month she didn't want to leave. Her friends here were among the best she had ever had. For her party they dressed up and bought a cake and danced until I made her come home. They didn't have a car, but at five in the morning they hitched to the airport, beating us by an hour. They hugged and kissed her as long as possible and everyone cried. I have never seen such openhearted affection.

Last night I was lying in the hammock resting, reading the paper. Kids

The author and Sofi, Joaquina, Carmencita, guest, Cecelia, and Dolores

were playing on the *andén,* loudly exploding caps with the heels of their shoes. Other kids were throwing a Frisbee. The radio was playing Cyndi Lauper, "All Through the Night." The newspaper said that the U.S. military has listed Nicaragua along with Cuba as a source of world terrorism. Accordingly, Nicaragua is a "military objective" if it is decided to "go to the source" and "destroy terrorism."

I usually wake early with my unseen companion, the rooster who shares this wall with me. This morning I slept late, heavy and tired, and was awakened by Cecelia's endless shower, the water sounding like it is splashing beside my bed. Then Lolín starts the car. I can lie in bed now, as if I am used to being here. I know the kids who walk by, dressed in blue and white for school, the boy selling newspapers, the women selling tortillas they carry on their heads in cloth-covered baskets. Also I begin to understand what happens when I get too tired, like yesterday. The theme of the day becomes avoidance: how to avoid the sun, the heat, my perpetual thirst, and going someplace on foot. And discouragement: I lose all capacity and desire to speak Spanish; the country seems hopelessly backward; I can't imagine being able to understand anything here; anyway it seems certain that what exists here will only live briefly and then disappear. And irritation: the noise in the barrio is incessant; the heat and humidity never let up, even when it is pouring rain; it is torture to go anyplace because the buses are jammed and taxis won't stop.

But when I am rested everything changes color. The weather changes from oppressive to dramatic. Conditions become bearable and I only see the people, who are beautiful and strong beyond understanding.

Nicaraguans are always impressed, often amused, and sometimes horrified by my size — a six-foot four-inch gringo with big feet, who is not only tall but often tired and awkward. I bang my head in doorways, cut it on the sharp edge of a tin roof, catch my feet on chairs, spill milk when I get up from the table, step on the dog, and kick over bottles. The Salgado's house to me seems held together like a stack of cards. Once, putting on my jeans, whose legs are longer than any they've ever seen, I caught the hem on my sandal, lost my balance, and grabbed the partition, which is held up by only a piece of wood stuck between it and the wall. The partition and I fell to the floor with a crash. Joaquina rushed in terrified to find me on the floor with my pants off, the partition on top of me. She just stared silently (but she wasn't so silent to the neighbors). Another time a friend of mine, not wanting to sit on the seatless and quite dirty toilet, tried to crouch over it; she lost her balance, and the entire toilet (not bolted to the floor or the wall) capsized — the pipe broke, the house flooded, the toilet bowl cracked. We had the pipe fixed and paid for a new toilet, but Joaquina, I heard, will never forgive me.

"Mi casa es su casa" (My house is your house), Lolín would always say. When I hear that expression now, my antennae go up.

During my first visit to Nicaragua there was a growing threat of U.S. invasion, and an increase in Contra attacks in the north, but the most dramatic conflict was in Managua within the Catholic Church. On one side was the conservative hierarchy, led by the Council of Bishops and the newly elevated cardinal, Miguel Obando y Bravo; on the other was the "popular church" or "liberation church," which included many priests but no bishops. How many priests? Four held high positions in the revolutionary government: Miguel D'Escoto was minister of foreign relations; Ernesto Cardenal, minister of culture; Fernando Cardenal, minister of education; and Edgar Parrales, minister of social welfare. A survey of 220 priests made in 1982–83 concluded that — to varying degrees — 46 percent supported the revolution and 54 percent opposed it (*Envío* 1983).

The conflict within the Church goes back at least to 1970 (see Cabestrero 1985, Girardi 1989). It began when a group of students and professors, arrested for political activities at the University of Central America (a Catholic institution), were being tortured and held without trial. Fernando Cardenal, who was then the university's vice-rector, and others occupied the Managua cathedral in protest. They began a fast and made two demands: those who had been arrested were to be made available for public inspection and interviews (to confirm that they had been tortured), and the government was to guarantee that the prisoners would appear before a judge within the time limit ordained by law.

The takeover and fast quickly gained mass support as a Christian action against Somoza. Seventeen other churches were also taken over. Numerous priests, two sons of army colonels, and two sons of the vice-president of the Republic were known to be taking part. A letter supporting the takeover, signed by twenty-two Jesuit priests, was published in *La Prensa*. Other protests had been quickly crushed by the National Guard, and Fernando Cardenal had said he fully expected the Guard to fulfill their violent threats against himself and the other protesters, but in this case it was impossible. The involvement of so many Christians meant the movement could not simply be dismissed as a communist plot.

And it was a success. After three days the demands were met, and the takeover ended with a march back to the university, where the protesters celebrated the emergence of a Christian opposition movement. They had effectively challenged both the government and the passive complicity of the Church hierarchy.

The event opened a split within the Church. Obando y Bravo and four other bishops published a letter that called the taking of the cathedral a disrespectful and lawless profanation of the rules and physical property of the Church. A response, signed by many priests, defended the takeover as a legitimate protest against the injustices of the Somoza regime. Ernesto Cardenal wrote a long, acerbic letter denouncing the bishops, saying: "To occupy a physical building to defend one's neighbor is not a profanation. To occupy high ecclesiastical positions in order to obtain material benefits and privileges is a profanation. To use the Church to be on the good side of the powerful is to abuse religion. Worse, it is to abuse God. . . . The faithful ought to respect and obey their bishops. But the faithful cannot follow bishops who are blind" (Girardi 1989, 99).

In the seventies many priests identified with the FSLN and some became clandestine members, in spite of its commitment to violent revolution.

Priests such as the Cardenal brothers and Miguel D'Escoto decided they could not personally engage in violence but could accept it as necessary under the circumstances of the Somoza dictatorship, which allowed no legal opposition and maintained itself by violence. Archbishop Obando y Bravo, on the other hand, joined forces with Alfonso Robelo, a rich industrialist and landowner and the founder of an organization of anti-Somoza capitalists called INDE (Nicaragua Institute for Economic Development); together they formed a "Commission for National Dialogue" that recognized the existing political parties and the National Guard but not the Sandinistas, because of their commitment to armed struggle (Selser 1989, 33–36). Somoza, however, was not open to dialogue. Later in the seventies, as opposition to Somoza grew stronger, Obando proposed a government of national transition that, "to prevent Nicaragua from falling into a vacuum of power and anarchy," would allow Somoza to step down peaceably and would preserve the National Guard (Selser 1989, 37). In 1978, when the fall of Somoza to the revolutionary forces seemed inevitable, Obando proposed an "Assembly of National Emergency," by means of which he hoped to get the Sandinistas to negotiate with the National Guard.

These efforts by Obando were in competition with proposals from other groups in the opposition movement. In 1978, some prominent businessmen, politicians, priests, and intellectuals formed the "Group of Twelve"; they accepted the Sandinistas as part of any settlement and demanded the complete abolition of the National Guard. They also accepted other parts of the Sandinista program, including recuperation of all property belonging to the Somoza family, a profound agrarian reform, the elimination of terror as an instrument of government, and the creation of a national constitution and army.

The existence of the Group of Twelve shows that the bourgeois establishment in Nicaragua was divided on the issues of revolution, the Sandinistas, and the National Guard. Archbishop Obando became a leader of those members of the anti-Somoza bourgeoisie who were adamantly opposed to the Sandinistas. As this sector became more isolated after the revolution and as many went into exile, the power and prestige of Obando's position as archbishop, and later as cardinal, together with his presence in Nicaragua, increased his importance as a leader of the counterrevolutionary movement (Selser 1989, 43–46, 55–57). In a 1985 interview in Rome, Obando described his role differently. He is, he said, an individual who exercises the prophetic function of denouncing injustice and announcing the good news of Christ. . . . [W]henever there have been violations of human rights we have spoken out. . . . Under Somocismo they called me "Comandante Miguel." Now the Sandinistas say I am with the right. It is like that when one denounces injustice; if the government is on the right, one is accused of being a communist, and if it is on the left one is categorized as reactionary. (Selser 1989, 27)

After the triumph of the revolution, the split within the Church, and between the Church hierarchy and the Sandinista government, became more acrimonious. A basic issue was the participation of priests in the government. In 1982 the Council of Bishops demanded that the Sandinista priests leave the government, and when they refused they were publicly denounced and accused of open rebellion and formal disobedience to ecclesiastical authority. Finally, they were ordered to renounce the exercise of their ministry as priests, in public and private, as long as they held positions in the government. In 1983, Pope John Paul II visited Nicaragua and was openly booed by Sandinistas when he refused to denounce Contra atrocities. A cycle of action–reaction had commenced, and the two sides became further angered by, and alienated from, each other.

I was able to see the fight in full swing, during my visit in the summer of 1985. From the "liberation" side, Father D'Escoto took a leave of absence from his position as minister of foreign affairs and announced a "Fast for Peace" in opposition to the U.S. aggression against Nicaragua. He began to fast on the seventh of July and continued for thirty-eight days before he was finally persuaded to stop. D'Escoto seemed ready to fast to the death if necessary—a government minister! In an unpublished, mimeographed statement he explained his decision:

Two ideas, two experiences of faith, have been maturing in me in my life as a Christian and a priest. As a citizen and as chancellor of Nicaragua, during all these years, these convictions have become stronger and are now making demands on me.

One conviction is what we Christians call "the mystery of the cross." I am convinced that when through our words and our actions we proclaim with clarity that God is father of all and we are all brothers and sisters, and when we denounce . . . injustice . . . we must become willing to suffer the cross, to be the target of the hostility of those who defend the unjust order, the old order where persons are not equal and are not sisters and brothers. This has happened in Nicaragua as a nation that has initiated a project of justice and sister/brotherhood.

On the other hand, I am convinced that violence is not Christian. . . . I do not disqualify as Christians those who have been forced to use violence . . . but . . . the Christian ideal, when it can be lived in its fullness, is an ideal of nonviolence. . . . In

Nicaragua Somocismo and the U.S. aggression have imposed on us the necessity of defense. But I believe that it is necessary to add other methods. . . . I always think of Martin Luther King. . . . [H]e is the greatest saint of our time. We Christians are countering violence with legitimate defense, but we also have the responsibility to make creative nonviolence a key element of the Good News that we proclaim and practice daily. . . . I trust that, little by little, the new order will open up a way and the old order will crumble.

D'Escoto called his fast "a prayer for peace, in defense of life and against the state terrorism of the government of the United States against Nicaragua." By means of the fast he saw himself as joining those who were fighting and risking their lives in combat, and with "all sisters and brothers who carry the cross which has been placed on them by those who attempt to deny us the right to life." He hoped that his fast would "ignite in all of Nicaragua an evangelical insurrection with that strength which emanates from the Gospel and which is indispensable . . . for the coming of the Kingdom." He also appealed to people from the United States: "I ask God to increase the number of those North Americans who have pledged to resist and stop the plans of aggression of their government and to renew the energies of all those in the world who struggle for justice [and] peace and against terrorism."

Soon tens of thousands of Nicaraguans were fasting one day a week in solidarity with Father Miguel. He received a steady stream of visitors, both national and international. Father Miguel is a fat man with a weak heart, and people were afraid he would die. In *Barricada* (July–August 1985), the Sandinista paper, there were daily reports on his health along with photographs of him seated or in bed receiving visitors. Numerous articles discussed the meaning and impact of his fast; and there were statements and interviews of international figures who came to see him, such as Bishop Pedro Casaldáliga from Brazil, who said, "I bring the support of twenty-three bishops of Brazil, and the solidarity of more than two hundred organizations." Cardinal Paulo Evaristo Arns, of São Paulo wrote D'Escoto saying: "Your prophetic gesture denounces the intention to kill the seed of new life planted by the Sandinista revolution. . . . I very much respect your decision to realize this fast, inspired by your conscience as a priest before the reality of death and destruction that exists in Nicaragua as a consequence of the war of aggression the United States has declared against us."

In every town, on Thursday nights, there were prayers for peace and candlelight processions. I walked with a procession in Managua that began at Father Miguel's church in a working-class barrio and ended at the U.S.

embassy. The street was full of serious, prayerful faces lit by candles. The procession lasted for hours. As we walked through the pitch-black streets lit only by candles and fires built on street corners and the small lights from people's houses, the heat and fatigue of the day left us. Each person seemed to glow with an unquenchable flame. It almost seemed that Father Miguel's prayer to "ignite . . . an evangelical insurrection" would be answered.

D'Escoto was accused by many of manipulating the religious sentiments of the Nicaraguan people to gain support for Sandinista policies. In *La Prensa,* Father Miguel and his fast didn't exist. On Thursdays, the day chosen for national fasting in support of Father Miguel, there would be the oddity of front-page photos of workers eating lunch, with no explanation other than a caption saying, "Managua workers enjoying their daily nourishment, needed for a good day's work." What was really happening this summer of 1985, according to *La Prensa,* began in Rome, when the pope, two years after his visit to revolutionary Nicaragua, one that he himself called "disastrous," elevated the conservative archbishop of Managua, Miguel Obando y Bravo, to the status of cardinal.

Before returning to Nicaragua, Obando offered his first mass as cardinal to a group of Nicaraguans in Miami, among them such Contra leaders as Adolfo Calero and Edén Pastora. His Eminence addressed them as "my good brothers who are gathered here." He read a telegram from President Reagan conveying his "best wishes to you and all those who are united with you in the Church of Saint Michael." In his homily Obando urged everyone present to "remain firm in the faith," a statement that became a slogan of the counterrevolution (Selser 1989, 115–19). The Contra station, Radio September 15, broadcasted the following from Honduras:

The cardinal asked his countrymen in exile "not to lose faith." He said that the future of Nicaragua demands, if necessary, even the shedding of blood. . . . Today there is a slogan that the public repeats and that shows the strength of the opposition against the Sandinista government, which is "United in Faith We Are Invincible!" This is the truth spoken by our beloved pastor, His Eminence Miguel Obando, that today more than ever, united in the faith, we will be invincible against the totalitarianism and terrorism of the Sandinistas. (Selser 1989, 119)

In the summer months after his return to Nicaragua, as Miguel D'Escoto was fasting, Obando made more than eighty-five pastoral visits throughout the non–war zones of the country, mostly scheduled to coincide with religious festivals and saint's days, to celebrate his new status as cardinal and to reaffirm his status as leader of the Nicaraguan Church (Selser 1989,

120–27). Daily *La Prensa* devoted front-page articles and commentaries to these activities, which involved "huge, jubilant crowds welcoming their beloved leader." Radio September 15 said, "The Church of Don Bosco was packed with thousands of faithful Catholics who sang out patriotic and religious slogans and came to demonstrate that 'United in Faith We Are Invincible!' " The faithful were led in such slogans as "Between Christianity and Revolution, Yes, There Is a Contradiction!" "Christianity, Yes, Communism, No!" "Obando, Obando, Daniel is Overthrown [*botado*]!"

The revolution that Cardinal Evaristo Arns had called "the seed of new life" was said by Cardinal Obando "to generate hatred and death. It is guilty of dividing families and creating danger for the survival of the Catholic Church. . . . No longer shall they take people away to die like flies for a [partisan] war by one faction. . . . Their sickle is for cutting off heads, the hammer is to crush them" (Selser 1989, 127, 133).

Traveling in Nicaragua is harder than in any place I've been. According to the newspapers, one-third of the buses of an already meager system are out of service because of shortages of tires and batteries. Many times buses won't stop because they are too full. The newspapers often have articles and letters detailing complaints. A meeting of the bus drivers' union gets a front-page story.

I wanted to take a trip from Managua north, to Estelí and Condega, an important agricultural area that lies along the Pan-American Highway. I wanted to see a cooperative farm and visit a resettlement community.

The last bus for Estelí leaves Managua at five in the afternoon, and I was there at two. There was a long line, but I wasn't worried, because a bus leaves every forty minutes. But Nicaraguans are inconsistent about lines. They are supposed to respect them, and many do, but a lot of people just wait around the loading zone and run to the doors when the bus comes. This sets off a rush to get on. If the driver opens only the front door it doesn't matter — they force the back door and climb through the windows.

When it was time for the last bus to Estelí I had been standing in the full sun for three hours and was about tenth in line. The tension to get on was running high. Some people walked into the line in front of me, ignoring my and other people's comments. Others were standing all around the area the bus would drive into. It was very hot and I was soaking wet. To pass the time I was reading stories by Heinrich Böll in Spanish in a weekly literary supplement. He had died recently, and the issue was dedicated to him. The narrator in one story had to get a job for the first time in his life. He tells about the weird questions he was asked and the weirder answers he put on the forms, and how he got the job anyway in a factory of glass and steel, with spotless dining rooms, and lunches and snacks that were free. Where workers could do no wrong. Böll's alienation in prosperous Germany seemed bizarre at that moment. I dreamed of a fleet of Mercedes buses coming to our rescue and large steins of cold beer. When a Japanese bus finally pulled in, I couldn't get on.

The last bus means your last chance for Estelí and points north that day, and a lot of people were determined to make it. The pushing was incredible. I was in the middle of a mass of people, holding my bag over my head, really afraid someone would get hurt. People were coming from every direction, squeezing along the sides of the bus and climbing through the windows on both sides. Since getting on meant pushing Nicaraguans out of the way, I pushed my way out of the crowd. The next bus, the driver told me, was at four in the morning. I would catch that one. I went back home and had a nice evening at a performance of the National Folkloric Ballet.

The performance was in one of my favorite places in Managua—the ruins of the Grand Hotel. The old Grand Hotel is in the center of Managua—or was, since Managua after the earthquake no longer has a center. It was part of a busy downtown area that now features vacant lots, a few shells of buildings with squatters, and a few scattered others still standing and in use. Enough of the old hotel remains on the first floor to serve as a makeshift cultural center. The central courtyard holds a large, open-air stage. Some rooms around this courtyard are home to an art gallery, and the rooms in back are used for rehearsals and storage. It is imaginatively decorated and has the feeling of a Soho loft, with large spaces and plants and old wood, and with artwork hanging on half-destroyed walls. The audience sits on bleachers. The sky was large, the stars bright, and along the street outside the fronds of palm trees lifted in the breeze. The dancers wore traditional folk costumes and moved with great energy; they were startlingly beautiful, men and women alike. And the audience, too, seemed full of fascinating, handsome people.

I was at the bus station at 3:00 A.M., and still I couldn't get on the first bus. But I was behind a group of high-school students who were going north to work in the tobacco fields. They were disciplined about the line and enforced it against line-breakers, and so I was able to squeeze onto the second bus. It was so full people sat three instead of two abreast; and in the aisles, where I stood for the three-hour trip, you couldn't turn or move without pushing.

Even though it was awful getting on the bus, everyone was helpful and friendly once they were on, and I ended up feeling pleased to be with these people. They looked at me, a tall gringo in a straw hat, with good-humored curiosity. They talked to me eagerly. When I asked one person a question, everyone who heard helped to answer. They hurried to pass my money out the window for a plastic bag of fruit juice when the bus stopped along the way.

Traveling north from steaming Managua to Estelí is like going from New York City to the Connecticut River Valley. You enter a high, cool agricultural valley, with dark, rich-looking soil. There are wide, curving rice fields, lime-green and soaking in water; and fields of corn, beans, and sugar-cane; and herds of cattle; and tobacco fields and long drying-barns. There are new projects, such as a group of newly constructed buildings that will become a processing center for fruits and vegetables. And there are the old shacks and thatch-covered roadside stands, and ox-drawn carts loaded with firewood, and barefoot kids, and people walking and hitchhiking with baskets and bundles, and men on horseback, and overloaded buses leaning on their broken springs.

Here, for the first time, I began to feel danger. Since the U.S. Congress had voted new funding early in the summer, the Contras had stepped up their attacks in this area, sabotaging facilities and ambushing people indiscriminately. Just before my trip north, there had been a mortar and machine-gun attack against the civilian passenger boat *Río Escondido*. Since the destruction of the Bluefields Express seventeen days before, this boat was the only ground transportation to the Atlantic Coast. It was carrying a hundred and fifty passengers, mostly civilians; seventeen were wounded and a soldier was killed. Many internationalists were on board — people from Spain, France, and Canada, as well as two North Americans I knew from my Spanish school in Managua. In another ambush a few days later — which especially outraged Nicaraguans — Contras attacked two truckloads of civilians on their way to visit an army training camp for a graduation weekend. Eighteen people were wounded and nine killed, and eight of those killed were mothers. Two days later, on the same road I was now traveling, they ambushed a car carrying six civilians — four adults and two children. All were killed.

The Contras penetrated this normally peaceful area to engage in surprise attacks, and much damage was being done. New government projects were a prime target, many of which were being destroyed. "The mercenaries of the CIA," the Sandinista government said, "want to show the U.S. that they are earning their money" (Carlos Manuel Morales, political secretary of the FSLN, in *Barricada,* July 30, 1985).

Much effort seemed to go into defense. I saw armed soldiers every-where — on hilltops, at clinics, warehouses and banks, and on bridges, street corners, and highways in jeeps and trucks. Also, every community and farm maintained *vigilancia* (guard duty).

By nine o'clock I was in Estelí. I walked from the bus station down a long, narrow street past old-fashioned, one-story houses and stores, seeing all kinds of vehicles, including horses and wagons. I left my bag at a *pensión,* which had cheap, simple rooms, and went to the local office of INSSBI (Social Security and Welfare) to see whether I could visit a child-care center. They called one, and the coordinator said I could come over. I spent the rest of the day there. It was surprisingly easy and comfortable to talk to people and visit whatever places I wanted to see, even though on this trip I didn't have letters of introduction or even a press pass. I told people I was a professor and writer interested in learning about their reality. Everyone was generous with their time.

The building for the child-care center was a house that had been aban-doned by a Somocista. Such houses seemed to provide most of the new buildings for government projects and offices, and made lovely quarters. The center took children from forty-five days to six years old. It was busy and full and impressive in this poor country. For some hundred and sixty children they had twenty-seven workers: sixteen teachers, three cooks, three cleaning people, two laundry workers, a nurse, a purchaser and bookkeeper, and a coordinator. Besides a room in the house for each age group, there was a large room full of cribs and mattresses, as well as a garden with a thatched-roof shelter where the oldest kids sat working at tables.

Before the revolution, the coordinator said, all child-care facilities were private, and only the upper class could afford them. Now this town of about fifty thousand people had three centers like this one. It wasn't enough. She showed me her record book — since January she had had 209 applications and had only been able to accept half. They had requirements — both par-ents had to be working, and mothers who were tobacco workers, nurses, teachers, or in the army were given priority. The worst problem in the school was short supplies — they didn't have enough of anything.

The children played games, sang, drew, and did crafts, like in preschools in the States. There was no political education, but they had begun to learn about their history and the revolution. They didn't stress differences be-tween boys and girls; they stressed equality. The boys and girls used the same toys, enjoyed the same activities, and used the same toilets. The kids had been very affected by these dangerous times, she said. It was a constant strain for everyone.

I asked her if there was anything she would like to say to the people of my community in the United States, and when she began to talk I stopped her and asked if she would write it down as a letter. This is what she wrote:

Brothers and Sisters:

I am a Nicaraguan sister writing from the three-times-heroic city of Estelí. I would like you to know something about the work I and twenty-six *compañeros* perform in a child-care center here.

Our task is to give love to little ones who don't enjoy the company of their parents because they work outside the house, in production or in defense of our sovereign country, or imparting their knowledge to other children of our town, for whatever tasks are needed by the process of our revolution.

Our work is beautiful because we are helping to form the new person.

There are three children in our school who have lost their parents from ambushes by the Contras. They weren't military, they were just workers, but the Contra doesn't respect anyone. We want the happiness of childhood for the children of the revolution, but it is hard to see when your eyes are full of tears for the loss of your parents.

Also we are full of worry that we can't give the little ones what they need and deserve because of the difficulties caused by the economic blockade. We lack many things, such as toys, teaching materials, and medicines.

I tell you all this so you will know the reality of our country and unite with our cause. We know that you don't agree with war, and that from your country you can help us. We thank you for anything you might do for this brotherly people who struggle for peace.

> Children are born to be happy!
> Children are the future of the revolution!

> Edna Valenzuela
> Estelí, Nicaragua Libre

One night at dinner I got into a conversation with Laura and Cathy, two North American nurses who were working in Condega, about an hour north of Estelí. Laura was a midwife, and Cathy was training with her. Cathy's husband was a doctor in the Condega clinic. "Come visit Condega," Laura said. "There are resettlement camps nearby. Condega was the first town in the north to liberate itself during the revolution. It is very Sandinista. I can introduce you to lots of people who were involved. But you may not be able to go tomorrow. The Contras blew up a bridge just north of here — about fifteen kilometers. The road is closed."

"That's why we're here now," Cathy explained. "We have to spend the night. Maybe the road will be open in the morning."

"It had better be," Laura said. "I have two women who are going to deliver any minute."

"Do you have a car?" I asked hopefully.

"No, we're hitching," Laura said. "But it's easy to get a ride."

"Especially for some people," I said, meaning pretty gringas.

"You're right there," she said.

Laura and Cathy were in their late twenties or early thirties. They were here for the long term. Laura was supported minimally by a solidarity group from Boulder, Colorado, and Cathy was supported by her husband John's pay from the Canadian government, also very low. They were obviously happy and excited to be involved. It was the happiness of being part of a revolution, the sense of change, of possibility, of knowing that a lot of caring people have come together and that what each person does is part of it. It gives people a new energy; the blood flows more rapidly; it's like being in love. Laura's and Cathy's eyes sparkled as we talked.

The next afternoon, after the road was opened, I hitched a ride with a German work brigade. We crossed over the bombed bridge. The Contras had placed charges of plastic explosive on the reinforced concrete roadway, making holes in the surface. But the bridge was sound and traffic still crossed, the drivers carefully avoiding the holes.

The Germans were mostly college kids. There were eleven of us in a small, four-wheel-drive pickup truck, plus all of their packs and gear. I sat on the back with my legs dangling off. A jeep was bouncing along behind us. I watched the hills, looking for Contras. Sometimes we passed groups of soldiers. It was wilder and higher and cooler as we went north. The road followed a river. There were lots of tobacco farms.

We stopped in Condega at the Pensión Baldovinas, my first stay there. There were lots of us, but luckily I got a room. I had dinner and talked with a charming French nurse, Maria-Noëlle. I amused her with the pluck with which I spoke bad Spanish. She came with me to John and Cathy's house. It was small but comfortable and had a lovely garden full of flowers and fruit trees. We talked and drank rum until late. Maria-Noëlle had already gone back, because we slipped into talking English. The *pensión* was closed, so I tried to sleep in a hammock in the garden. It smelled sweet and fresh and the sky was full of stars and owls were hooting, but I couldn't go to sleep. A few miles away there had been another ambush, of a truck carrying twenty-nine soldiers. All twenty-nine were killed. It was cold, and I kept thinking about the soldiers and the Contras in the hills.

I decided I wouldn't try to visit a resettlement community. The one nearest Condega is twenty-five kilometers from the main highway, which meant traveling on dirt roads and more danger of ambush. Also, you must have official permission and travel with military protection, and it takes days to get a permit — more time than I had. Besides, I wasn't prepared to take such a risk. Still, I was sorry.

The resettlement communities were being created because large sections of Nicaragua are sparsely populated and impossible to defend effectively. They say a government needs a ten-to-one superiority to defeat and eliminate a scattered, rural-based guerrilla force; the Sandinista army had special disadvantages because the Contras were very well supplied, often by airdrop, and couldn't be pursued into their camps in Honduras. More than a hundred and fifty thousand people had had to move and were no longer producing. They left behind their homes and the cultivated land. The government supported them and tried to help them start again elsewhere, but sometimes it earned their enmity if it forced them to move.

In Managua I had met a group of eight refugees who lived in a resettlement community, farmers who had left their homes in a farm cooperative because of attacks by the Contras. They had come to Managua to collect clothing, tools, and food for the new community. One evening they visited our barrio.

They said that the Contras had attacked them to demonstrate that they weren't safe on the side of the revolution. They destroyed the barns and equipment to show that the agricultural programs weren't working. They destroyed clinics and schools and killed teachers and government workers to show that the revolution didn't care about the campesinos. "But," they said, "we know that in the old days campesinos had to buy milk from rich farmers. Now we have our own land and our own cows."

One woman, eighteen years old, described how the Contras murdered her mother and father, her brother, her two-year-old daughter, and five others because they lived on a cooperative farm. "They murdered my family to make us afraid," she said. She barely escaped and hid in the woods for two days with her dead daughter. I couldn't forget the way she looked as she talked to the people of our barrio. A shy, country girl, she talked very softly, with her head down, looking at the ground. She stood completely still, with one foot placed in front of the other, like a statue. She held her arms at her sides and her hands were tight fists.

As I lay in the hammock among the scent of flowers, hearing owls nearby, I thought: "No one in the United States, or almost no one, would allow crimes like this to happen if they could prevent them. Yet we are paying for this with our taxes. Surely it will help to know what our government is really doing. Perhaps I can help to stop this war by writing. But only if I see what is really happening."

The next morning we learned that of the twenty-nine soldiers who were ambushed, two were from Condega and there was to be a funeral for one of them. Laura and I were waiting by the church in the main square when we saw the procession a few blocks away. We walked to meet it. In front, young girls were carrying bouquets and wreaths. Behind them, six men were carrying the casket, covered by the flag of the FSLN. The boy's mother, her face hidden by a handkerchief, was supported by two women as she walked. Several young women were among the family group—Laura said she thought some were his sisters and one his wife, but she didn't know which. One was crying loudly. His father, separated a little from the women, walked by himself. A thin man with a mustache, he looked around a little as he walked, with an expression of disbelief. The procession was completely quiet. The only sounds were of footsteps and outbreaks of crying.

In the church, the casket was placed on a table in front of the altar. The people filled the rows in the front, and some stood by the casket or next to the front rows of seats. The priest led them in song as they entered—the "Canto de entrada de la misa campesina nicaragüense" (Entrance Song of the Nicaraguan Campesinos' Mass). I had already heard this song many times in Nicaragua. It is amazing to hear it at a Catholic mass, with its proud, lively folk melody backed by guitars, percussion, and accordion. The *Misa campesina* was written by the Nicaraguan musician Carlos Mejía Godoy and is associated with the movement for a "people's Church." One night on a bus in Managua an "Evangelical" was standing in front, Bible in hand, loudly and incessantly yelling, "Glory to God, I am saved, Glory to God." People were becoming irritated by his loudness and the tedium. After a while, someone started singing the "Canto de entrada" and soon the whole bus was singing it to drown him out. It didn't work, but the ride was more fun. I believe this moment reflected a political as much as a religious conflict, because many Evangelicals are reputed to be against the revolution. Many of the Contras, I would learn later, were Evangelicals.

Here in this small northern town, at the funeral of a local soldier, where many of the singers were weeping, the song was another kind of affirmation:

CANTO DE ENTRADA

You are the God of the poor
The humane and simple God
The God who sweats in the street
The God with a sunburnt face
Therefore I talk to you
like I talk to my people
because you are a God who labors
Christ the worker.
You go with the hand of my people
You struggle in the field and the town
You stand in line in the campground
to get your daily pay.
You sit eating there in the park
with Eusebio, Pancho and Juan José
and you complain about the syrup
when they don't put much honey in it.

The priest read briefly from the Bible and they began another song, and then a third, the priest leading them through the words and melodies that most seemed to know by heart. While they sang four soldiers came in hurriedly, late, carrying AK-47s, and took their positions beside the casket. A young woman came in crying loudly, two friends beside her. She walked up a side aisle and stood in front beside a post, sobbing loudly during the service.

KYRIE

Christ, Christ Jesus
identify yourself with us
Lord, Lord my God
identify yourself with us
Christ, Christ Jesus
join in solidarity
not with the class of oppressors
that exploits and devours the community
but with the oppressed
with my people
who are thirsting for peace.

MAN OF CLAY

How I will sing to the Lord
How I will sing
How I will sing to the Lord
I, a man of clay.

He is in the mountains and the sea
He fills the silence
of the nights in bed
and walks the town.
He doesn't see a man's color
and he doesn't see money.
He is the father of everyone
and gives his love to all.

After the singing, statements were made by a young man, a schoolgirl, an older man, and two older women, all representing organizations: the Sandinista Youth, the Sandinista Defense Committee, the People's Militia, AMNLAE (Luisa Amanda Espinosa Women's Association), the Mothers of Heroes and Martyrs. An older woman, crying, read the statement she wrote for the Mothers of Heroes and Martyrs, which said, in part:

Today, all of us join in the grief that is being suffered by so many orphans, and so many widowed women, that with the blood of their parents, or of their sons and husbands, are creating the story that some not very distant day will be on every page of glory: we die but our cause goes on living.

The greatest empire in the world and its slaves want to defeat us, and see us prostrate at its feet. . . . [D]ay after day, Yankee imperialism prosecutes a war without reason or object. . . . [O]ur only crime is that we are free, and the boot of the oppressor can no longer step on our soil. . . . [W]e, the mothers, say this: the revolution will continue to triumph, and the sacrifices that all of the people and Father Miguel D'Escoto have made, will not be in vain. . . . [W]e are mothers who have given our sons to live in a Nicaragua that is always victorious . . .

"Because the heroes didn't say they would die for the country . . . but they died . . ."

Patria Libre o Morir
    [Our Country Free, or Death]
Nicaragua Victoriosa
    [Nicaragua Victorious]
Ni Se Vende . . .
    [We're Not for Sale]
Ni Se Rinde
    [We Won't Surrender]

A crowd gathered around a woman who seemed to have fainted. A girl began to fan her with a straw hat. Someone brought water in a beer bottle. The sounds of sobbing from the girl by the post continued. There was for me a very moving relation between the grandeur of the statements and the anguish of the poor, plainly dressed people in the church. A man shouted: "Eternal glory to the Heroes and Martyrs! Eternal glory to Miguel Ubeda!"

The casket of Miguel Ubeda being carried to his grave

Facing the congregation were vertical rows of high windows, some tinted green or yellow. Under them was a large banner: "Praying and Fasting for Peace." Along one side a row of posts bore large signs with quotations from the Bible:

There is no greater love than to give one's life for one's friend.

(John 15:13)

Blessed are those who work for peace, for they will be known as children of God.

(Matthew 5:9)

The priest concluded the ceremony by leading them in the Lord's Prayer and a final song. The people went out and waited in front while the casket was put in the back of a pickup truck, wreaths and bouquets placed around it. The soldiers walked in front of the truck, and the people followed to the cemetery. Now slogans were chanted as they walked. Several times someone shouted the boy's name: "Compañero Miguel Ubeda!" And the crowd answered: "¡Presente! ¡Presente! ¡Presente!" The funeral became like a demonstration, yet no one was watching or listening; there was no object of protest; there were no leaders. The slogans were simply the people speaking, in this new time, shouting their grief and defiance as they walked to the cemetery:

¡Por Estos Muertos, Nuestros Muertos, Juramos Defender la Victoria!
[For These Dead, Our Dead, We Swear to Defend the Victory!]

¡De la Frontera, No Pasarán!
[From the Border, They Will Not Pass!]

¡Aquí! ¡Allá! ¡El Yanqui Morirá!
[Here! There! The Yankee Will Die!]

¡Patria Libre o Morir!
[Our Country Free, or Death!]

¡Compañero Miguel Ubeda!
¡Presente! ¡Presente! ¡Presente!

At the cemetery the casket was placed on the ground at the end of the newly dug grave. At the other end someone was mixing a little cement with which to seal the concrete lid of the vault. A door in the lid of the casket was lifted, and some of the people looked at the boy's face. There was much crying and screaming. The father walked away from the grave. Then the casket was carefully lowered by ropes into the vault. There the little door was opened again, for a woman who had climbed into the grave. I saw his face and took his picture.

His face seemed very large — it filled the opening in the casket lid. He had the broad, dark-brown face of an Indian. Cotton was stuffed into his nostrils. One felt there wasn't room in the casket for him. One felt very strongly that both his living and his dying was there in the casket.

The door was closed, and the woman was helped out of the grave. Soldiers standing a little apart began to fire their AKs into the air. Soldiers on top of a nearby hill fired answering shots. Near them was the wreckage of a Somoza airplane, shot down during the final insurrection of 1979, when it was about to bomb the town.

The people left the cemetery. All around were low, green, cultivated hills. On some, cattle were grazing. The new health clinic was only a few hundred meters down the road. I walked there to see the facilities.

The health clinic had been built three years before with money donated by Finland. It had a pharmacy, a lab, and thirty-four beds. In the emergency treatment room a soldier lay on a table, a pool of blood on the floor beside him. He had shot himself in the leg. The outpatient room was the busiest. There were lots of women with their kids, waiting to see doctors. This clinic served the entire Condega district, and some twenty-five thousand people had files here. All visits were free, with small fees for drugs and contraceptives.

As we left, John showed me a project he had helped organize, an orchard in the large, bare area around the clinic, with all kinds of fruit trees, including avocados and bananas. I thought, this clinic shows what a revolution is about. True, it is paid for by foreign aid, but most Latin American countries have poured aid down a sinkhole of luxury resorts and condominiums and production-for-export companies that are sucking their countries dry.

I looked at the hills around us and wondered if there were Contras watching as we talked about the value of citrus trees. How vulnerable this clinic looked, standing on a low hill with its chain-link fence and its pair of older civilians on guard. Someone came up and told John that a woman up at the cemetery was in grave condition — Miguel Ubeda's sister. "*Grave,*" John said, using the Spanish word, "everybody around here is *grave.*" We rode in his jeep back to the cemetery.

"People like you come here," he said, "and see all the killing and destruction that is happening. That is important. But what they don't see is the effects on the personal lives of people and the families. It is devastating, for the women, the kids, sex relations, the families. In Nicaragua there's a word

Miguel Ubeda

that gets used a lot for that—*trastornamos*—'we are upset.'" When we got to the cemetery, some people carried the unconscious woman to the jeep, and John drove her over to the clinic. I walked back to the main square and my *pensión*.

John was driving to Managua and had offered me a ride. I stood waiting, overwhelmed with impressions. Everything looked normal and peaceful. There were kids at play in the park. A man walked by, bent over, pulling a two-wheeled cart loaded with firewood. Just behind me in the doorway, one of the women who worked in the *pensión* sat in a chair knitting. The sun was shining, the sky was very blue, the trees in the park were making cool shadows, a group of people on the other side of the park waited for a truck that would carry them into the countryside. I stood in front of the Pensión Baldovinas, my mind full of questions, a North American, out of place, out of time, in this town that seemed to belong to the days of my grandparents. Condega felt like a movie set, strange, nostalgic, fragile, as if it could be rolled up and taken away overnight. And it could happen. But I doubted that the people who were born here and would live out their lives and die here felt that way. Were they condemned to be "extras" in a North American movie?

Down the street in front of a store, a man stood looking at me. He was smiling and he waved. I walked over to him. He had a small clothing store. He wanted to speak English. He had lived in Los Angeles for a year with his sister, who had married a North American businessman. He liked the States. He knew English and liked to study and practice it. We talked a little about the differences between Spanish and English. He was cleaning the rust from a pair of tinsnips made in the States and was about to paint them. "Before," he said, "we wouldn't take care of such things. They wouldn't be important—the market was full of things like this. Now, I was lucky to find these used. I paid only 900 córdobas."

I looked inside his store. He said he had a degree in business administration but wanted to own his own business, didn't want to join a big company. His store was small but clearly aspired to be a "better" men's clothing store. On hangers, protected by clear plastic wrappers, and in a glass display case, there were expensive-looking shirts from France. There were some pants, but not many. His largest stock seemed to be of Lévi-Strauss caps, like those worn in the old days by railroad workers. He had lots of these on the wall behind the counter, with large Lévi-Strauss labels sewn to the front. Behind the counter sat a small wooden desk where he studied English and kept a grammar, a dictionary, and exercise books.

"Business is bad," he said. "Most of the people who buy here are country people, but they can't farm because of the war, and the prices are too high." He wrote down a little table of inflation for me:

> In 1981
> a shirt cost 180 córdobas
> a farmer received 350 córdobas for 100 pounds of beans
>   (almost enough to buy two shirts)
> In 1985
> a shirt costs 2,300 córdobas
> a farmer receives 1,800 córdobas for 100 pounds of beans
>   (not enough for one shirt)

"I have not increased my profits, but they can't afford to buy."

To see how he would respond I said, "Unfortunately, it seems the United States is causing this problem. The blockade has raised the price of everything, and funding the Contras means that the farmers can't produce as much. What do you think?"

He frowned. "I don't know what the cause is," he said. "There are different viewpoints on that."

The doctor drove up and I got into the jeep. I was sorry I couldn't talk to him longer.

Three and a half hours later, back in the flat, hot, desolate city of Managua, by a dying lake, on a long and busy four-lane highway, we passed an army base, the Augusto C. Sandino Airport, scattered run-down factories, occasional bars and restaurants and outlying neighborhoods, empty, overgrown fields, and people walking or hitching or waiting for the bus or a taxi. We talked about our personal lives — about problems with women. The doctor was ready to return to Canada. He had been "public" for so long — his life devoted full-time to others, his house a way station for visitors. His marriage was under strain. I had my own list. I felt a special pleasure in spending time with a man whom I could talk with personally. He drove me to my barrio, and we planned to see each other again.

Everyone except Dolores was in the country at Lolín's boss's farm. She had the radio playing loud while she washed clothes. She took over Joaquina's role, and made coffee while I unpacked. She seemed tireless to me, an oversized, exhausted gringo, as she moved around the house mopping and remopping every inch of floor. I felt a great relief to be back, in the safety and ease of life here. I wondered about the relief I felt. It was a short trip, yet had seemed such a long time. I felt burdened and excited by the images crowding my mind.

I asked Dolores to turn the radio down and wrote out notes for hours. The notes seemed thin and spotty. A strange process, and such a reduction, the attempt to capture experience in words.

I thought of Alberto, the farmer who lived in the cooperative north of Estelí, who had lived there many years, working for an owner who was an officer in Somoza's National Guard, cutting his cane and plowing his fields. Now he and the other members hold title to the land. When I walked up to talk to him, he was sitting on the porch of his new, two-room brick house, shaving with an old-fashioned straight razor. It was Sunday and he didn't have to work; his shirt was off. His wife immediately brought us coffee, and then a plate of rice and beans and meat. He showed me letters he had received from other visitors and his notebooks from the adult education classes. He goes to classes in the afternoons, has learned to read and write, and is now at the third-grade level. He is a strong, broad man, with full black hair and a mustache. When he took me for a walk in the rain to see the fields, he wore a shirt with a camouflage pattern and posed proudly holding his AK-47 beside the tall corn while I took his picture.

Everyone kept asking, "When will you come back?" At first the idea had seemed remote to me. I had come because I felt supportive, and wanted to learn more, to test my feelings with firsthand experience. I was gradually led to another level by the Nicaraguans themselves. The warmth and generosity I felt from the people made a deep impression on me. I couldn't forget the scene at the airport when my daughter was leaving: the tears, the clinging, the clamor to stand by the railing to wave good-bye as she walked to the plane. I couldn't forget Lolín and Joaquina's kindness. The door of their house was open; it felt like a place I could always go back to. And I was very moved by the courage and idealism in Nicaragua. These people, many at least, seemed filled with a powerful spiritual energy. The difficulties they faced seemed minor, really, in contrast to what they had achieved in their lives.

Then, also, many people I met placed an expectation on me. "Will you help us? We need you to speak to your community, to tell them about us, so that support for the Contras will stop. We need every kind of material aid, pencils and paper, medicines and tools. Help us make this revolution." I remember their eyes and strong, clear voices, the touch of their hands: Edna Valenzuela, in Estelí; Luisa Centeno, sitting on bags of rice and corn as she talked to me in her house in Condega.

Revolution to these Nicaraguans was not a political spectacle or a media event. It was their work and their life. It was food on the table and who was alive to sit at the table. It meant life had a future and a modicum of hope. I was made to feel I was a part of this revolution, that I had a role to play. I was someone the revolution needed in its struggle to survive.

This was hard to resist, and I had no desire to resist. I would do anything I could for them. I could write about them, and do my bit toward reducing the ignorance and misconceptions. I could try to involve others and raise money for material aid. I could go back and strengthen in a small way the bonds between them and us.

If you are driving down a country road and pass someone who is stuck and needs your help, you naturally stop and ask what you can do. If they say, "Please, help us push," you get out of your car and join in, pushing and straining with all your strength. It was like that in Nicaragua — just that simple. In the States, "foreign affairs" feels abstract, complicated, and geo-political. The decision to help a foreign country with its revolution looks romantic and quixotic.

In the States I often have the sense of floating in a huge, becalmed ocean. Most people do not believe in change. The privileged white majority is complacent and self-indulgent. The poor, disenfranchised minorities seem despairing. The left is small and fragmented. It was shocking to come back and see again the wide highways crowded with expensive vehicles, the supermarkets and malls, the clean, middle-class order of the community where I live; and in contrast, the hopelessness and danger in the communities of the poor. It was also shocking to reenter the world of corporate-produced media, television and magazine culture and information, with their enticements and narrowed vision.

But was it true that I had a role to play? Or was this a delusion I shared with Edna and Luisa and the others, coming from different kinds of desper-ation: their need for help with a revolution in trouble, my need for meaning and connectedness?

I thought a lot about what to do. Nicaragua is not far from the United States, it is as close to Massachusetts as California, but it is expensive to travel there and it is much farther away in a psychic sense. Yet I began to think of going there again.

What enabled me periodically to leave my life in the States was the en-couragement and support I received from my community of family, friends, and *compañeros* in struggle. Many opposed our government's policies, and many had traveled to Nicaragua before me. The United States may often feel like an untroubled sea, but the reality is very different. The resistance movement, the anger and frustration, the interest in another version of reality — these were strong and encouraging.

I knew that as a professor of philosophy I needed to redefine my role. Philosophical writers have usually thought about the meaning of life in enclosed rooms. I knew the thought-worlds projected in these rooms; I had seen how skewed and alien they were to the actions and experiences of other people in the world. Philosophy, I felt, should move away from the old task of thinking about the self and the world — as if these are finished and there to be known — and toward the task of creative activity and work; toward *remaking* the self and the world.

It seemed to me that in Nicaragua this work was happening and that it was necessary to join in. Of course, it was happening in the States as well in various ways; yet this was partly *because* of Nicaragua. And in Nicaragua you lived in broad daylight. You felt you knew where you were and who you were, much more than in the soft and murky world of corporate, media-tech society. There was a vision there I wanted to hold onto, to bring back and transplant: the realization that people can take control of their lives and change the course of history.

In Nicaragua you felt present in history as it was happening — history as aspiration and conflict over human destiny. In Nicaragua this history had a tangible presence, like the weather. What happened there reached out in time and space. The attention of the world had been focused and concentrated there, like rays of light through a magnifying glass.

This feeling may have been illusory, but it was widely shared by revolutionaries and counterrevolutionaries alike.

2

Sandino, Revolutionary Prophet

When I first came to Nicaragua, "Sandino" was just a name to me. I knew something about the Sandinistas, but I had only the sketchiest knowledge of the man whose name they took. In Nicaragua, I saw images of Sandino everywhere. A huge portrait hangs in front of the government palace; paintings, prints, and posters abound in offices and homes. He is on coins, córdoba notes, T-shirts, and the flag of the FSLN; his image is spray-painted on buildings and fences in every town and village. Always wearing that hat. Always looking small and youthful, yet defiant. Always, when in full figure, with the left foot forward and his weight on the right leg, at rest but unstable, as if ready to move or not quite at ease being photographed. Small and vulnerable, defiant and omnipresent—that is Sandino in Nicaragua.

Another immediate connection I made with Sandino was through quotations I heard or read. These surprised me for their literary quality, their "quotability." For example, in front of the U.S. embassy building in Managua—which, to digress a moment, is a very ominous sight. It occupies an entire city block and sits quite alone, surrounded by vacant lots, a barrio of humble, wooden shacks, and a shabby string of stores. It is enclosed by expensive-looking and threatening iron-bar fencing, very high, topped with brass spearheads, which are themselves topped with coils of razor wire. Like a prison, with lookout towers and guards placed about, a gold-eagle plaque adorns the gate. The French embassy, by contrast, is on a charming, tree-lined street, and has an art gallery and free movies on Friday nights, and there are no fences or guards; you can walk right in. Why not? Anyway, across the street from the deadly presence of the U.S. Embassy is a simple billboard, all white, with the reproduction of a telegram on it:

69

El Chipote Camp, Vía San Fernando
12 July 1927

To Captain G. D. Hatfield
Commander of the Yankee Marines
Ocatal

I received your communication yesterday and I understand it. I do not surrender and I await you here. I want my country free or death. I am not afraid; I count on the patriotic ardor of those who accompany me.

> Patria Libre
> A. C. Sandino

I began to realize that the phrases which I was hearing in marches or demonstrations, or read in letters or official notices — such as "Patria Libre o Morir" (Our Country Free, or Death), "Ni Se Vende, Ni Se Rinde" (We're Not for Sale, We Won't Surrender) — were quotations from Sandino, whose struggle with the Yankees in the twenties and early thirties was a prolific source of inspiration to the Sandinistas.

I also encountered Sandino and Sandinista history through people who knew a lot and cared. For example: Francisco, a Honduran, who came to Nicaragua to join the Sandinistas. He fought in the mountains against the National Guard, and after the victory he went into the army and has been chasing the Contras ever since. He is a machine gunner, decorated many times.

During my first visit, Francisco used to come early to the house to catch a ride with Lolín to the military hospital. He stood outside the gate and waited quietly on his crutches, and if I was the first up I unlocked the gate and brought him a chair. He was already sweating from the exertion of his walk. He usually wore a clean white shirt, dark loose trousers, and black shoes without socks: clothes that friends had given him. He sat slowly and carefully, as if the least movement or jolt sent pain through his body. He was wounded in the thigh and hip, and went to the hospital for physical therapy. Dolores or I would bring him a cup of coffee. He smiled and sat on the edge of the chair and sipped his coffee with obvious pleasure. When I had time, I sat with him for a while.

When I asked him what it was like fighting in the mountains, he smiled and begged off talking about it. "You should read Omar Cabezas's book, *Fire from the Mountain*," he said. "Or this book." Francisco was carrying a book about Carlos Fonseca written by Tomás Borge. He wanted to know if I had read the works of Fonseca and Borge. "No," I said, "but I want to." I should read these men if I want to understand the Sandinista revolution, he said: "Those two were the founders; they fought in the mountains just as Sandino did. Carlos was killed there in seventy-six, and Borge spent six years in prison and more than a year in solitary confinement, but they didn't kill *him*." He smiled and pointed his forefinger for emphasis. "They and a few others were the first, when they were students in the mid-fifties. Carlos and Borge recovered the works of Sandino. They read Sandino and began where he left off."

"You have to read Sandino," he said. "He is the real founder."

Francisco told me about his life in Honduras and the political conditions there and his decision to come here and join the Sandinistas. He saw the Nicaraguan revolution as vital for all Central America, and he didn't want to see the movement crushed. In spite of his wounds, he had no regrets. "Nothing is happening now, in Honduras," he said. "There is no organization; the repression is very great."

At the time I didn't think much about my little conversations with Francisco. I was usually preoccupied with getting ready to catch the bus to Spanish school, and finishing my homework, and the thought of having to sit at a hard school-desk for another long, hot morning. But I retain a clear impression of Francisco on his crutches at the gate to the patio, sitting on the edge of his chair sipping coffee, and pulling himself up and slowly moving around the car to get in. And his words: "You have to read Sandino. He is the real founder."

The Sandinistas have deliberately raised Sandino to mythic stature. If a mythic figure can be one who is revered as a high example of important human values, there is no reason to object. And it seems natural to use the framework of mythic narrative in discussing Sandino. His was a life of suffering and struggle and achievement; it renewed a great movement for liberation; it ended in tragedy. It is a true historical myth.

In 1933, not long before his death, Sandino talked about his youth with the journalist José Román (Román 1983, 43–49, 54–55). In his early years we can see the contradictions that provoked him to become a leader of Nicaraguan resistance. His story has the moral clarity and simplicity of a biblical parable.

Augusto César Sandino was born in Niquinohomo, a village near Masaya, in 1894 or 1895. His father was a well-to-do landowner and a judge; his mother was a field worker on one of his father's farms. Born, as he put it, "a bastard, according to social conventions," and named Augusto César by his father, he lived with his mother in a wooden shack with a dirt floor on the edge of town. I have in front of me a photograph of that shack, a typical campesino *bohío,* windowless in front, with only the door for light, its walls made of sticks and palm leaves plastered with mud. Sandino's father lived with his legal wife and their three children, of whom the oldest was Sandino's half brother Sócrates, in a fine house in town.

Sandino worked alongside his mother as soon as he was old enough to walk. Often they were so hungry he had to steal from someone's farm or garden. Once his mother was put in jail, because of a debt she owed the village mayor, and suffered a miscarriage there. As he told José Román, there was no money for doctors or hospitals, so the boy Sandino cared for her

in that cold dirty village prison. As biological secrets were revealed to me, until then unknown since I was hardly nine years old, my mother's complaints and the fact that she was near death restrained my anger. And with my mother already asleep and I unable to sleep, I lay down beside her on that bloody floor and though only a boy . . . began to ponder things with my child's philosophy.

If law is the voice of God to protect the people, as the priests say, why is it that authority favors the drones instead of helping us poor people? Why does God love Sócrates more than he loves me, since I have to work and he doesn't? Then God and life are pure shit. It's only us poor people who are getting screwed! (Román 1983, 45–46)

When his mother moved from Niquinohomo to live with a man in Granada, Sandino refused to go with her and lived with his maternal grandmother, who was also very poor. He continued working at little errand-boy jobs, in outrage and misery at his position and its unfairness. But he gathered himself together for a brave and momentous act. When he was ten years old he met his father one day on the street and confronted him.

"Sir, am I your son?" he asked.

"Yes, son, I am your father," he replied.

"If I am your son, why don't you treat me like you treat Sócrates?"

He says that tears appeared in his father's eyes; that he took him into his arms and hugged him long and hard and invited him to live in his house. But Sandino remained a second-class citizen in his father's house. His stepmother insisted he eat his meals with the servants in the kitchen rather than with the family. Even so, Sandino prospered. He said that "by hard work and good behavior I made myself indispensable in my paternal home." He went to school and, after a period of rebellion, made the decision to improve himself and became an excellent student.

In 1912, when he was seventeen, Sandino witnessed an event that was

important in his political development. The U.S. Marines invaded Nicaragua to shield a conservative, U.S.-installed government against a liberal
rebellion. The Liberals were defeated in Masaya, near Sandino's town of
Niquinohomo, and their leader, General Benjamín Zeledón, was killed.
Sandino later described Zeledón as his greatest predecessor in the struggle
against U.S. imperialism. The Marines strapped Zeledón's body to the back
of a horse and led it around the town in public display. Sandino said he
personally saw the body of Benjamín Zeledón, which was buried in Cater-
ina, a village near Niquinohomo.

As he grew into adulthood Sandino worked in his father's business, then
founded a business of his own as a dealer in grain. He seemed to be well on
his way toward material success when, at age twenty-six, something happened that, as he put it, changed the course of his life.

Sandino was engaged to be married to his cousin Mercedes, whom he
had loved for many years, when it was rumored he was "having an amorous
relationship" with another woman, a widow who was the sister of a friend
of Sandino's, Dagoberto Rivas. One Sunday, Dagoberto and Sandino
found themselves sitting near each other in church. Dagoberto made rude
remarks to Sandino and struck him in the forehead; Sandino drew his
revolver and shot Dagoberto in the leg. This fight, which occurred just as
the priest was raising the host to celebrate the Eucharist, led to Sandino's
hasty departure from the country.

The first chapter of the historical myth of Sandino ends with his exile. He
didn't return to Nicaragua for five years, and when he came back it was with
a different kind of ambition.

Sandino worked as a mechanic in Honduras, Guatemala, and
Mexico, then as a clerk for a U.S.-owned oil company in Tampico, Mexico.
In Tampico he got a political education. Tampico's oil fields and port were
a center of labor organizing and radical politics. Sandino saw Mexican
workers attempting to unionize, U.S.-owned companies threatening to
shut down production in response, and the workers demanding that foreign companies be ousted and Mexican oil nationalized. Anarchist, socialist, and communist organizations were active, and Sandino probably witnessed their meetings and debates. Although they differed in strategy and
ideology, these revolutionary groups shared a desire to lead the Mexican
workers in their struggle against foreign — especially U.S. — exploiters and
to establish national ownership of Mexican oil.

Sandino also learned that Nicaragua had a reputation among other Latin

Americans for being servile to the Yankees. And he himself was accused of selling out his country while residing in Mexico. He told José Román about a second experience that changed the direction of his life, but this time, "in a transcendent way." He was in a restaurant with a group of friends reading the international news, and told them he hoped to return to Nicaragua and fight for his [Liberal] party. A Mexican friend said, "No, hombre, why would you go there. Nicaraguans are nothing but a bunch of *vendepatrias* (sellouts or turncoats). You're better off here, making money. They are fucked!" (Román 1983, 54–55). Sandino was shaken by this accusation. At first he refused to accept any personal responsibility because he had never had a position of power. Later, he realized that as a Nicaraguan he had the right and the responsibility to protest.

In Sandino's collected works there is another Tampico story. He writes that he was talking with friends about "the submission of our Latin American peoples before the hypocritical or forceful advance of the murderous Yankee empire. On one of these days I told my friends that if in Nicaragua there were a hundred men who loved their country as much as I do, our nation would restore its absolute sovereignty, threatened by that same Yankee empire" (Sandino 1984, 1:79). His friends said in response that perhaps there were a hundred such men, and more; the difficulty would be in finding them. And from that moment on, wrote Sandino, he set his mind to finding those one hundred men.

Sandino never identified exclusively with any one of the various political tendencies he encountered in Mexico.[1] The point of view he created, which came to be called "Sandinismo," combined strands from various tendencies. Yet he most closely identified with the anarchists, led by the great Mexican anarchist, Ricardo Flores Magón. Sandino never met Flores Magón, who died in a U.S. prison in 1922 (he was sentenced to twenty years for publishing an anarchist manifesto opposing the U.S. entrance into the First World War). But Flores Magón's influence in Mexico was tremendous, and Tampico was its center. We see signs of anarchist influence when the thirty-year-old Sandino used anarchist themes to describe himself as a child lying beside his sick mother pondering his "child's philosophy": how the authority of law and the state and the Catholic Church are used to benefit the rich and exploit the poor. Yet there are also aspects of Sandino's philosophy and political practice that reflected social-democratic and communist influences. Among these are his wish to bring about change through a legal and gradual establishment of reforms, in cooperation with liberal constitutionalists, and his intention to create a revolutionary vanguard among his followers.

There are also broader philosophical perspectives that he seems to have acquired from quasi-religious social movements. Sandino was involved in Freemasonry, and during a second trip to Mexico in 1930 he achieved the status of "master mason." He also became a member of an organization, founded in Argentina by the Basque Joaquín Trincado, known as the Magnetic-Spiritual School of the Universal Commune. These more philosophically oriented organizations gave to Sandino a general perspective on history. Unlike the Catholic Church as Sandino knew it, these movements were politically radical—they supported the anarchist and communist struggles against private property and its injustices. Like the Christian religion, though, these movements espoused a theory of progress toward universal justice and the brother/sisterhood of humanity. Sandino is quoted as saying that Trincado was one of the great contemporary philosophers, "the great master of cosmogony" (Román 1983, 88).

However, this is getting ahead of our story. Sandino made two seminal trips to Mexico, and it was probably during the second, in 1930, that he fully developed his philosophical orientation. The first trip ended after he had spent about three years in the Tampico area. His political outlook included his patriotic anti-imperialism, his anarchist perspective on state and church authority, and his commitment to act: "I worked then for the Huasteca Petroleum Company in Tampico. It was May 15, 1926. I had my savings, which amounted to five thousand dollars. I took from those savings three thousand dollars and I came to Managua. I learned what had been going on and I went to the mines of San Albino, beginning my active political life" (Sandino 1984, 1:81). Sandino's first stay in Mexico, and his political education and dedication to struggle, complete a second chapter in the true historical myth of Sandino.

Sandino returned to Nicaragua in the midst of a civil war between Liberals and Conservatives, traditional rivals for political power. To understand his decision we need to know the history of this rivalry, and why Nicaraguans had the reputation of being *vendepatrias*.

The Conservative and Liberal factions had their origins in Spanish colonialism. The Spanish founded two major cities in Nicaragua, each with its own agricultural base and port: Granada in the east, on the edge of Lake Nicaragua; León in the west, near the Pacific. The economies of the two areas developed in relative independence of each other, as did their dynastic families and political identities. Granada became the base of the Conservatives, or "legitimists," who had opposed independence from Spain (gained in 1821, along with the other countries of Central America); León was the base of the Liberals, who favored independence and the creation of a constitutional republic. Yet their differences seemed more dynastic and economic than ideological.

In 1854 the two factions fought a bloody civil war for control of the national government. U.S. interests were deeply implicated on both sides, owing to an important geographic fact, on the one hand, and an ignominious decision by the Liberals, on the other.

In 1848, the United States had acquired California by conquest and gold was discovered there; hordes of North Americans, hoping to get rich quick, wanted to go there. Now Lake Nicaragua is only about ten miles from the Pacific Ocean on its southwestern side, and its southeastern basin pours into the Atlantic via the San Juan River. Thus, the safest, fastest, and cheapest route from New York to San Francisco was down the Atlantic to the San Juan River and across Lake Nicaragua. From there, coaches and wagons carried passengers and cargo to the quiet harbor of San Juan del Sur, and steamships continued north to San Francisco. Cornelius Vanderbilt, who had won a concession from the Nicaraguan government to operate a shipping company across Nicaraguan territory, made a fortune, and Nicaragua became known as a prime site for a transoceanic canal.

Several years later, in 1854, after a military defeat by Conservative forces, the Liberals recruited a North American adventurer, Brian Cole, to travel to the United States and organize a mercenary brigade to fight on their behalf. In New Orleans, Cole found an eager partner — William Walker, who hoped to extend the domain of slavery and white supremacy to all of Central America (where slavery had been legally abolished in 1824). He and Cole easily organized a group of "filibusters" with the financial backing of Vanderbilt's former partners, now rivals, Charles Morgan and C. K. Garrison. The "filibusters" were welcomed in León as saviors of the Liberals, and Walker was made General Walker.

The North Americans were defeated at Rivas in their first battle, from which Cole fled (he was caught and hung by campesinos), but they managed to conquer the town of Granada in a surprise attack. There Walker received fresh supplies of money and arms from the United States, enlarged his army, and turned against his Nicaraguan sponsors. He declared himself president of Nicaragua, decreed English to be the official language, and reinstituted slavery. President Franklin Pierce (1853–57) immediately recognized Walker's new government. Walker nullified Vanderbilt's lucrative concession and wrote a new one for Morgan and Garrison.

Meanwhile, Vanderbilt, who had openly sworn to destroy Morgan and Garrison, organized and supplied an army gathered from the other Central American countries. Walker's ambition was to conquer all of Central America for the slaveholding United States, and the alarming motto printed on his banners was "Five or None" (referring to the five states of Central America). Events in Nicaragua, and Vanderbilt's money, brought together a Central American counterforce sufficient to drive Walker out of Nicaragua, and in 1857 he fled to New York, where he was received as a national hero. When he returned to fight in Honduras, he was captured and shot.

In this way, Vanderbilt defeated his rivals, and the demoralized Liberals signed a peace treaty that gave national power to the Conservatives, who ruled in relative peace until 1893. In that year, General José Santos Zelaya took power for the Liberals.

Zelaya ruled in a dictatorial manner for sixteen years. An economic liberal, not a political one, he was a fervent promoter of progress and modernization. He was able to see Nicaragua unified as a country (England, in order to appease the regional interests of the United States, gave up its claim on the Atlantic Coast area, which became Zelaya Province), and he decreed a series of laws, such as expropriations of Church and small peasant landholdings, that promoted large-scale agriculture, especially coffee production. He also promoted growth of the economic infrastructure — education, communications, and transportation.

But Zelaya made the mistake, fatal in Latin America, of refusing to bow to U.S. interests. First, he negotiated a loan with a British banking firm, thus violating the financial monopoly U.S. bankers wished to impose on Central America. Next, when Washington chose Panama as the site for its canal, and England obligingly withdrew, Zelaya, who had high hopes for ensuring Nicaraguan development by means of a transoceanic canal, made contact with Germany and Japan. In response, U.S. Secretary of State Philander Chase Knox, organized a Conservative rebellion. This was handled through the offices of a U.S.-owned gold mining company, the Rosario & Light Mines, for which Knox was legal counsel. Rosario & Light had already been "provoked" by Zelaya, who had tried to collect their unpaid taxes. Thus, the company contributed 600,000 dollars as a "loan" to the Conservatives to finance the rebellion. A diplomatic note was sent to Zelaya terminating official recognition of his government and demanding his resignation. U.S. warships were sent "to protect the lives" of North Americans employed by Rosario & Light. And when the victorious Conservatives

arrived in Managua, they appointed the chief accountant of Rosario &
Light, Adolfo Díaz, as Nicaragua's new president.

Díaz accepted a set of financial conditions on Nicaragua that ensured
U.S. domination over its economy (following the pattern known as "dollar
diplomacy"). Loans had to be taken out for Nicaragua's "financial stability"
(and for repayment of Rosario & Light) solely with U.S. banks; these loans
were guaranteed by granting the United States legal control over Nicaraguan customs and taxes (a U.S. citizen was appointed tax collector), to
which control over rail lines, shipping, and banking were later added.

The Liberals, led by Benjamín Zeledón, rebelled against these measures,
and President Díaz called in the U.S. Marines. The Marines crushed the
Liberal rebellion and remained in Nicaragua until 1925 to buttress the
Conservative government. Once firmly in power, the Conservatives signed
the 1914 Bryan-Chamorro Treaty with the United States, as a consequence
of which Nicaragua was paid 3 million dollars and agreed as follows:

> The Government of Nicaragua grants in perpetuity to the Government of the
> United States, forever free from all taxation or other public charge, the exclusive
> proprietary rights necessary and convenient for the construction, operation and
> maintenance of an interoceanic canal . . . whenever the Government of the United
> States shall notify the Government of Nicaragua of its desire or intention to con-
> struct such canal. (Selser 1981, 41–42)

The same treaty gave the United States a ninety-nine-year renewable lease of
the Great Corn and Lesser Corn islands and the right to establish naval
bases on them, should the United States so desire.

The Bryan-Chamorro Treaty even shocked members of the U.S. Congress. Senator William E. Borah, chairman of the Foreign Relations Committee said,

> The treaty which we made with Nicaragua did not in any sense represent the ex-
> pression of view or wishes of the Nicaraguan people. As far as Nicaragua is con-
> cerned it was made by a government which we set up, which by force we
> maintained, and which did not represent the views of the Nicaraguan people at any
> time . . . We were making a treaty with ourselves. We were making a treaty with a
> government which was our puppet . . . It is one of the most indefensible transac-
> tions of which I have knowledge in international affairs. (Selser 1981, 43–44)

And former Secretary of State Elihu Root stated:

> It is apparent that the present government is really maintained in office by the
> presence of U.S. Marines in Nicaragua. Can we afford to make a treaty so serious
> for Nicaragua, granting us perpetual rights in that country, with a president . . .

who is maintained in office by our military force, and to whom we would, as a result, pay a large sum of money to be disposed of by him as president? (Selser 1981, 28)

The treaty shocked Augusto Sandino's father as well. Gregorio Sandino, an active Liberal, was jailed by the Conservatives for his vocal opposition to it. This history informed Augusto Sandino's attitude toward the U.S. presence in Nicaragua. Later, in his "Manifesto to the Nicaraguan People," Sandino wrote that the signers of the Bryan-Chamorro Treaty were guilty of high treason.

The immediate events leading to Sandino's return from Mexico began when the United States withdrew the Marines from Nicaragua in 1925, thinking that the Liberal–Conservative rivalry had died out and a truce achieved. This was not to be. A newly elected "unity government," with a Conservative president and Liberal vice-president, was overthrown by the loser, General Emiliano Chamorro Vargas, signer of the Bryan-Chamorro Treaty and a man who presumed the favor of the United States. General Chamorro forced the National Congress to accept him as president. The Liberals, whose candidate Juan Bautista Sacasa had won the vice-presidency, organized a new rebellion and began what was described as the "constitutionalist war." Sandino went to join them, attracted by the historic efforts of Zelaya and Zeledón to break free of U.S. domination and by the Liberal opposition to the Bryan-Chamorro Treaty. He saw the "constitutionalist war" as a new stage in Nicaragua's struggle for independence. Yet it seems that Sandino had little trust in the Liberals. Why else would he go to an isolated gold mine to independently organize his "crazy little army"?

The Nicaraguan poet Daisy Zamora wrote about San Albino, as if in Sandino's words:

> I knew the workers in that mine
> received pay worth just enough to buy their
> coughs, silicosis, and blood vomited
> in the company store.
> I had to pick and dynamite
> and dig into their consciousness
> hard as living rock and harder than the
> hills of San Albino.
> But from these men we mined gold
> more golden than the gold
> that shines in the dawn
> in the green mountains.[2]

At San Albino the miners worked fifteen-hour days, slept on the floors of ramshackle barracks, and were paid with company coupons. Hired as paymaster by the North American owners, Sandino secretly began to organize the workers. He told them about labor struggles in Mexico and the gains of workers there. In a few months he had a group of twenty-nine men.

With his savings they bought rifles from arms traffickers around the Honduran border and had their first encounter with Conservative forces in El Jícaro. But they needed more arms. Sandino went by canoe on the Río Coco to the Atlantic Coast, where he appealed to the Liberal commander, José María Moncada, to give them weapons. Moncada wanted to know who had made him a general. Sandino answered, "My men!" which did not satisfy Moncada. Some prostitutes there, however, helped Sandino find forty rifles and some ammunition the North Americans had captured and dumped in the ocean. He returned with these to his miners in Nueva Segovia.

Within a few months Sandino's army had grown to about eight hundred. They drove the Conservative government forces out of Nueva Segovia, the northernmost province of Nicaragua, and were recognized, reluctantly, by the high command of the Liberal Army. They took the city of Jinotega and moved farther south to reinforce the left flank of the Liberals. Meanwhile, in other parts of the country, the Liberals were also winning.

This time, the United States intervened with a plan to accept the Liberals — obviously the stronger faction — and buy them out. President Calvin Coolidge (1872–1933) sent Secretary of State Henry Lewis Stimson to negotiate a cease-fire. Stimson met with General Moncada and asked him to accept a cease-fire and a continuation of the Díaz government (the United States had already replaced its man Chamorro with the more reliable Díaz, from Rosario & Light) until new elections could be held. The U.S. Marines would take over the defense of the Díaz government and supervise the elections, and General Moncada, it was understood, would be the Liberal candidate (and almost sure winner) for president. The Liberal army would be disbanded, and each soldier would receive 10 dollars for turning in his rifle (those who refused would be disarmed by force). The generals composing the Liberal army would receive 10 dollars a day severance pay, retroactive to the beginning of their service, and would have control over various departments in the country. As an alternative to his plan, Stimson threatened a U.S. military intervention to defend the Conservative government and defeat the constitutionalist army.

Moncada accepted Stimson's plan at a face-to-face meeting in Tipitapa.

To celebrate, Moncada declared May 4, 1927, a national holiday. He counted on the agreement of the generals under his command, and received it from all except one. Sandino commented:

> The fourth of May would be, in reality, a national holiday, [but] not because Moncada had sold the Liberal army, of which he was commander in chief, as if it were a herd of animals; it must be a national holiday because it was on this day that Nicaragua proved to the world that its national honor would not be humiliated, that there still remained sons who would give their blood to wash away the stains that these traitors had left on it. (Sandino 1984, 2:400)

Sandino had shown a remarkable capacity as a general and leader. He was now being offered the usual spoils of war: political office. This chapter in Sandino's story ends with his temptation.

Sandino met Moncada in Teustepe and asked for an explanation of the peace agreement. The commander received him while lying on a hammock. Around his neck, on a white ribbon, he wore a gold U.S. Marine Corps cross. He explained unctuously the terms of the agreement and the benefits Sandino would receive, including the governorship of Jinotega. When Sandino said that he opposed the agreement, Moncada replied that to do so would be madness. The United States, he said, held Nicaragua in its claws like a jaguar holds a lamb: the more the poor lamb struggles, the deeper the claws will penetrate. When Sandino responded that the Nicaraguan people had been fighting for their freedom, not to continue as subjects of the United States, Moncada smiled sarcastically and uttered these words: "why would you sacrifice yourself for the people. . . . [T]he people are not grateful. . . . I tell you this from my own experience. . . . [L]ife is short and the country goes on. . . . [T]he duty of all human beings is to enjoy themselves and live well . . . without worrying too much" (Sandino 1984, 1:98).

Sandino left this interview "feeling profound disgust for Moncada." He had acted loyally and in concert with the Liberals, despite signs of self-serving behavior. But he wrote that "here in the theater of events, I realized that the political leaders, Conservatives and Liberals alike, are a pack of cowards and traitors, incapable of guiding a patriotic and courageous people" (Sandino 1984, 1:79). He discussed the situation with his general staff and instead of ordering his men to go to Santa Lucía, where Moncada was expecting them to turn in their arms, he sent all but fifty back to Jinotega. Then he and his men went to Boaco for another meeting with Moncada, where Sandino and the other generals were expected to sign the agreement. There he acted with caution. He told Moncada he would accept

Stimson's terms, but that he wanted a three-day grace period to make his way north and turn in his arms at Jinotega.

On the way to Jinotega, as he was considering what to do, he thought he heard a strange voice calling "¡Vendepatria!" (Sellout of your country!) At that moment Sandino committed himself to fighting to the death for the freedom of Nicaragua, where the term *vendepatria* is now an expression of ultimate contempt.

When Sandino arrived in Jinotega he circulated a telegram announcing his decision to continue fighting — now against the Yankees — and invited any of his soldiers who did not support this decision to return to their homes. He ordered a large cache of weapons to be hidden in the jungle, and with three hundred men and many weapons he abandoned Jinotega and traveled north to San Rafael del Norte. Soon thereafter, Moncada arrived in Jinotega with a contingent of Marines. He issued Sandino an order to return there and sign the agreement. Sandino responded with the famous words that would become a motto of the Sandinistas in the revolution: "Ni Se Vende, Ni Se Rinde" (We're Not for Sale, We Won't Surrender) (Sandino 1984, 1:111).

What was Sandino's state of mind at this time? He was thirty-one years old. He had worked as a mechanic and a clerk, and within ten months after he returned to his country and began his "political life" at the San Albino mines, he was a successful general with his own army. He had openly defied his superior officer. He was preparing to fight the most powerful government in the hemisphere. His only resource was a small army of peasants who adored him and joined him in what he described as his sacred duty. This army had quickly dwindled to thirty-one men. No matter; he was a man who had found himself.

After deciding to fight to the death for Nicaragua, Sandino celebrated. He married on his birthday; he received his father's blessing; and he wrote his first manifesto. We have his description of these events (Sandino 1984, 2:403–19).

Sandino had met Blanca Aráuz, "a very sympathetic girl of nineteen years" and the telegraph operator in San Rafael del Norte, several months earlier; her home and the telegraph office had become his communications headquarters. When he returned to San Rafael he went directly to the telegraph office. He asked for her, but was received by her sister, who said Blanca was preparing dinner for him. When he found Blanca, she kissed him and told him that her sister had arranged for a mass to be held for the Virgin of May when he safely returned. The mass was held on the third day and was attended by Sandino and many of his troops.

At two o'clock in the morning, the eighteenth of May, Sandino's birthday, the doors of the church were opened for Sandino, Blanca, her parents, and a small family group. Outside it was cold and foggy, but in the church, brightly lit by many candles, there was the warm aroma of incense and flowers, and the perfumes that filled the church reminded Sandino of his childhood.

The priest invited him to confess. "I did so," he tells us, "sincerely."

Blanca wore a white dress and veil and a crown of orange blossoms. Sandino wore a brown riding uniform and high boots of a dark color, his revolver and cartridge belt. "We left the church and in the street I felt renewed," he wrote. "I appeared to be walking on air." They were met outside the church by his officer of the day with ten saddled horses. Along the street they received congratulations from members of his army and the townspeople. The town resounded with the firing of guns.

Two days later, Sandino moved farther north, to Yalí. There he received a telegram from Blanca saying that his father had come to San Rafael, and that he should please wait for him in Yalí. When Sandino heard that his father had arrived, he went out on the street to wait for him. I will quote at length his description of the meeting:

A group of about ten horsemen came into view. In the middle of this group of ex-members of my column stood out the form of an olive-skinned man of medium build, in riding clothes, a blue jacket, a Panama hat with a black band, and a string tie of the same color.

That man was my father.

After an affectionate greeting between my father and me, I invited them to the house where I was lodging.

The first words of my father were the requests he had brought me [from Moncada], also from my mother and relatives, not to offer armed resistance to the Yankee invaders.

He explained that he felt very strongly about the betrayal of the Liberal army, and that if the chiefs . . . had adopted the position that I was trying to take, Nicaragua would be saved from humiliation. But none had done that, and if I wouldn't desist from my position I would eventually succumb fruitlessly as Benjamín Zeledón had succumbed in 1912 when the Yankees attacked the Masaya plaza defended by that general.

I answered my father that the position I was trying to take was no different from General Zeledón's in that time, with this difference: he was the first to lift the stone that with its weight would some day have the power to bring liberty to our people. That I will carry this stone as far as possible, and that when I fall others will come and carry it when it is needed.

When my father saw in me a firm commitment to sacrifice myself, he understood. And at this moment he felt within himself more affection for me. Then he said these words: "If you are resolved to sacrifice yourself, you must do it with all honor. After you have fired the first shot at the invader, you can expect only death or victory. You must never back down on pretext of hunger, lack of sleep or fatigue. It is better to kill yourself than to fall into a shameful betrayal."

I expressed to my father in the best words I could the blind faith that burned in my heart with respect to throwing the pirates out of our country, basing my words on reason, right, and justice. (Sandino 1984, 2:413–14)[3]

On a dirt street in the mountain town of Yalí, Sandino and his father shook hands and embraced.

Not long thereafter, Sandino published his first manifesto, addressed to "Nicaraguans, Central Americans, and the Indo-Hispanic Race." He wrote twelve manifestos during his six-year war against the "Yankee invaders." They were his principal form of communication to the Nicaraguan people and the world outside Nicaragua.

The first manifesto stressed Sandino's roots and loyalties. He identified with other Latin Americans, especially Central Americans, who would struggle for their identity against the North American invader. He believed that Nicaragua should build its own transoceanic canal using capital from many countries so that all would share in its control and use. He wrote:

A man who does not ask his country for even a piece of land in which to be buried deserves to be heard and believed.

I am Nicaraguan, and I feel proud because in my veins flows Indian blood, which for its antiquity holds the mystery of patriotism within it, loyal and sincere.

I am a worker, but my idealism grazes in rich fields of internationalism, which holds out the right to be free and to create justice. . . .

The Liberal revolution, for me and my comrades in arms, who are not traitors, who have not given up and who have not sold their rifles to satisfy their ambition, is now more than ever strengthened because only those who esteem valor and sacrifice are still in [the fight]. (Sandino 1984, 1:117–18)

So ends a fourth chapter in the historical myth of Sandino.

On July 11, 1927, eleven days after the first manifesto, Captain G. D. Hatfield of the U.S. Marines sent Sandino a letter demanding his surrender. Sandino replied with the telegram that now appears on the billboard facing the U.S. embassy in Managua. The next day Captain Hatfield publicly condemned Sandino as an outlaw, as well as any other persons who joined him or remained in territory occupied by his forces. Two days later, Sandino and his men attacked a Yankee garrison in Ocotal. U.S. aircraft responded by strafing and bombing the civilian population of Ocotal — perhaps the first deliberate bombing of civilians in modern warfare. After two more attacks in July, the Sandinistas retreated to El Chipote, an inaccessible mountain site, where they set up a base for guerrilla-style attacks.

In El Chipote they built palm-leaf huts, corrals for horses and mules, sheds and workshops for repairing weapons and manufacturing ammunition, clothing, and boots. After five months El Chipote was discovered by the Marines and was quickly abandoned. The mountain was bombarded from the air and overrun by hundreds of Marines who found nothing but straw-hatted dummies stuffed with hay. Sandino at that moment was in San Rafael, being interviewed by the journalist Carleton Beals.

Sandino's army grew with the success of their hit-and-run attacks and the bitterness sown by Yankee retaliation. Varying in size from two thousand to six thousand members (the latter strength reached in 1931), the force was divided into eight columns corresponding to eight geographic regions. Most of the fighters were poor campesinos, but some, such as Sandino's half brother Sócrates, came from other classes of society and some from other countries, for revolutionaries from all across Latin America came to join the Sandinistas. All served without pay. They swore to fight to the death or until the Yankees were driven out of the country. By 1931 most of Nicaragua was in their control.

Except for their distinctive red-and-black bandanas, they wore whatever clothes they could get; many wore sandals or went barefoot for lack of boots. Sandino complained about how big the Yankees were, because his men couldn't wear their boots or uniforms. For their weapons the Sandino forces had only what they could capture or had brought when they joined. Many had only machetes. In his accounts of battles, Sandino always listed the supplies captured — the machine guns, the Springfield rifles, the ammunition, the horses and mules. In old photographs we see the men posing proudly with their weapons.

In striking ways, the history of the Marines in Nicaragua foreshadowed the U.S. involvement in Vietnam. In both cases a military power in possession of advanced technology made a very destructive and prolonged attempt to defeat a peasant army whose superior resources lay in its spirit, enterprise, and organic relation to the land and its people. In both there was strong domestic opposition in the United States, and both ended with a humiliating withdrawal of U.S. troops.

Sandino is considered the creator of the modern tactics of guerrilla warfare, influencing many later revolutionaries who adopted the same methods: surprise attack and retreat; never a direct confrontation with a stronger force; a people-based network of supply and communication; and fighting the enemy in your own territory. Sandino's soldiers knew every path, while the Yankees had to deal with strange, largely unmapped jungle. Every house, every campesino, was a potential part of a network whose center could never be found.

The U.S. Marines, in turn, invented scorched-earth bombing. They bombed and burned farms and even entire villages and towns in their frustration and desperation. Concentration camps were created for civilians in an attempt to control various areas. The death by starvation of some two hundred people in a single year in such camps was reported in the U.S. press (Sandino 1984, 1:56).

Newspaper reports on Marine losses and atrocities led to a movement in the United States for withdrawal from Nicaragua. Sandinista support committees sprang up in all the major cities of the United States. In Latin America, Sandino and his forces — which the Chilean poet Gabriela Mistral named "El Pequeño Ejército Loco" (Crazy Little Army) — became famous for their heroic and successful resistance to the Yankee invaders.

Sandino's army, though ragtag and ill-equipped, seems to have had excellent generals and organization. The Basque journalist Ramón de Belausteguigoitia, who lived for several weeks in the mountains with them, wrote:

> We could say the discipline was absolute, definitive. I never saw anyone drunk in the camp. At night there was complete silence. . . . [E]ntering camp in rags without even a mule-load of provisions, they maintained an extraordinary composure, sharing rations that never were enough. . . . The respect paid to officers was more than just discipline; there was a profound camaraderie among the officers and men. The form of salute was a strong embrace, and in the sharing of food and clothes there was no distinction among ranks. . . . [T]hey seem ingrained more with the idea of a fraternal community, united by the most intimate feelings, than by military discipline. (Belausteguigoitia 1985, 131)

Belausteguigoitia described Sandino as he stood one day in the doorway of his house watching a column of his troops returning from the field:

His face, darkened by premature lines, reflected an expression completely his own, between profound reflection and intimate sadness. His face seemed less fixed on the privation-marked soldiers who passed him than on something distant and invisible. Sandino didn't have the fierce, inflexible air or nervous tension of a warrior hardened by the dangers and cruelties of battle. His face reflected the mind of a man made for thought and imagination, a spiritual man converted by fate into a leader. (Belausteguigoitia 1985, 76–77)

Sandino was severe in matters of discipline. Any soldier who failed to comply with orders could be executed. Unlike the modern Sandinistas, he did not reject the death penalty. He even defended the use of the infamous "vest cut" by his soldiers — cutting off the heads and arms of Marine prisoners (although he claimed that his men did this only to soldiers, and only after witnessing the cruelty of the Marines to Nicaraguan civilians). Also, unlike the modern Sandinistas, who distinguish North American people from their government, and are friendly to the former even while suffering the attacks of the latter, Sandino condemned all gringos. When (after taking everything of value) he destroyed La Luz, a North American–owned gold mine on the Atlantic Coast, he wrote a letter to the British manager to be conveyed to the U.S. owners, explaining that all U.S. property and citizens in Nicaragua were in danger so long as the Marines remained on Nicaraguan soil; that while he had once thought that not all North Americans supported the actions of the Coolidge administration, he now believed that the vast majority approved; and so, any North American who might fall into the hands of the Sandinista army would be killed.

Sandino showed much tenderness to children. One old photograph shows a group of children, boys ten, twelve and fourteen, "presenting arms to General Sandino." The children belonged to a special squadron called "El Coro de Angeles" (The Angelic Choir). One of their roles was to join in battle as noisemakers; they would light fireworks, bang on pots and pans, and yell and scream to frighten the Yankees. The older ones became regular fighters, and Sandino had a special affection and respect for them. He wrote a story about one, which I will quote entire, called "The Man-Boy":

By a path we call *picado* [i.e., marked by a line of stakes], an intricate path that is known only to locals and guides, there arrived at our lines a boy of nine years asking to speak to whomever was in charge. He saluted me and handed me a hemp bag containing *yuca* and *plátanos* and *chicharrones enchiladas* [yucca, plantains, and enchiladas with cracklings].

"I want to be one of your soldiers," the Man-Boy said, a boy of pure Indian race, in whose eyes shine the indomitable pride of our ancestors. "I want you to give me a gun and bullets so I can fight against the bandits who are killing us in our houses. In my house we know that you are in the mountains, and I came bringing these things to eat."

He was admitted into our forces because I had no way to convince him that he couldn't stand up to the roughness of war, owing to his age. He has taken part in thirty-six engagements and has acquired in our army, instead of rags, a bright and handsome uniform and the knowledge of how to read and write. (Sandino 1984, 1:281)

The stories of Sandinista child heroes multiply in the 1970s and 1980s in Nicaragua. For example, Luis Alfonso Velásquez, a nine-year-old boy who lived in Barrio Rigüero, organized children to demonstrate against the Somoza dictatorship and was so successful he was eventually assassinated by the National Guard. A large central park in Managua is named in his honor. Such stories repeat the references, very common in Sandino's time, to the biblical story of David and Goliath. Many spoke of Sandino as a new David, and likewise of the children, and of little Nicaragua in its struggle against "the giant of the north." And such later figures as Tomás Borge and Daniel Ortega have also been compared with David.

Sandino became a philosopher and teacher to his men, a guide and leader in the creation of a new community. He told Belausteguigoitia that he spoke often about the ideals of justice and told his men it was the destiny of the army to be fighters for justice. He told them that death was a small thing, a transition, and that they must leave fear behind. He believed he communicated with them directly, that their consciousnesses interpene-trated, and that he was a "spirit guide," possessed of a magnetism that drew them to a common destiny. United, they were expressions of a supreme will for freedom and justice, "which can also be called Love, or Jehovah, God, Allah, Creator."

Sandino wrote a "Manifesto of Light and Truth," which he directed to be read aloud to his army, since so many were illiterate (Sandino 1984, 2:159). It reads almost like scriptural writing. Following the established practice in his army, borrowed from Trincado and the "Magnetic-Spiritual School of the Universal Commune," Sandino addresses his troops as "dear brothers." He speaks of "the laws that rule the Universe," and of the "Divine Impulsion that animates and protects our army."

Sandino explained the universe as a process in which God, or Love, which possesses "a great desire to Be," formed a preexisting material world of "ether" and gave birth to "one child, Divine Justice." Injustice, which exists because of the envy and antagonism of men, will gradually be overcome when the majority realize their true spirit.

What is known as the Last Judgment is, in reality, the "destruction of injustice on earth and the reign of the Spirit of Light and Truth or, one could say, Love." But the Last Judgment does not mean that "Saint Vincent must come and blow a trumpet. . . . [N]o. What will happen is the following: The oppressed people will break the chains of their humiliation with which the imperialists of the world have loved to hold us down. The trumpets to be heard will be the clarions of war . . . of oppressed people against the injustice of the oppressors." Sandino concluded by directly connecting the struggle of his army with world proletarian revolution:

> The honor falls to us, brothers, that we have been chosen in Nicaragua by Divine Justice to begin the judgment against injustice throughout the world. Don't be afraid, dear brothers; and be sure, very sure and certain that very soon we will achieve our definitive triumph in Nicaragua . . . and light the fuse of "Proletarian Explosion" against the imperialists of the earth. (Sandino 1984, 2:160)

Sandino was a self-taught man who drew his ideas from trade-unionist struggles, the Mexican Revolution, anarchism, Freemasonry, Zoroastrianism, spiritualism, theosophy, spiritism, and Marxism-Leninism. Yet he was not a passive, simply eclectic thinker. He tested and adapted the ideas of others in relation to his own experience and the conditions and needs of Nicaragua, in order to give an appropriate spiritual depth and historical significance to his war of independence against imperialism. Ideas such as the sister/brotherhood of humanity, world proletarian revolution, and the creation of a society free of oppression and exploitation are common to most of those ideologies, and are at the core of Sandinismo. The idea of a Divine Love which manifests itself in all creation and at present in the struggle for justice, has Zoroastrian and Christian roots, is reinterpreted in modern theologies of liberation, and is equally important both to Sandino and to many modern Sandinistas.

Once a poor, itinerant mechanic and clerical worker, Sandino developed into a great leader and general, entirely on his own initiative, without a single teacher or sponsor. This gives his character a loneliness and sadness one can see in his photographs. Nonetheless, Sandino stands among the ranks of the great modern revolutionaries, being as much thinker and teacher as a revolutionary fighter against injustice.

How was Sandino able to achieve so much? Belausteguigoitia ascribes to him a great capacity for faith, which he describes as "a privilege of an exquisite nature, and not a weakness. Because faith—apart from [being a] belief in specific theological phenomena—is a special sense of the infinite which unites the spirit to the profound depths of time. Not everyone has it, especially in this scientific age, just as not everyone has a musical sense. For me this faith of Sandino is one of his most fundamental characteristics explaining his tenacity and success" (Belausteguigoitia 1985, 149).

Sandino stated on many occasions that the goal of his rebellion was the liberation of Nicaragua from U.S. domination, and he promised that his troops would lay down their arms when the U.S. Marines left Nicaragua. On January 1, 1933, the day that the last Marines boarded ship for the United States, President Juan Bautista Sacasa received a letter containing Sandino's peace proposal.

Three years before, however, in 1930, the Marines had begun creating a surrogate army that would take over their role in Nicaragua. They inaugurated a military academy in Managua and organized a Nicaraguan force called the National Guard, headed by officers of the U.S. Marine Corps. As the National Guard grew to more than three thousand well-armed men, they and the Marines fought together against Sandino. In 1932 the U.S. State Department brought the Liberal and Conservative parties together on two points: their opposition to Sandino and their support of the National Guard as a national police force. At the same time, the U.S. government appointed Anastasio Somoza García to be the first Nicaraguan head of the National Guard.

The choice of Somoza, so portentous for Nicaragua, was the fruit of a long courtship he had conducted with U.S. citizens in Nicaragua. Somoza was born in San Marcos, a small village near the birthplace of Sandino. His father owned a coffee plantation and was able to send his son to business college in Philadelphia, where he learned to speak English facilely (if not well). He returned to Nicaragua before earning his degree and worked as a car salesman, an outhouse inspector for a sanitation program run by the Rockefeller Foundation, an installer of electric wiring, and an electric-meter reader. He inherited a grocery store in San Marcos but lost it gambling. He was caught trying to counterfeit gold coins with an old friend, who later became chief of his personal guard. He played a minor role in the Liberal rebellion and joined the army, but his great accomplishments were his marriage to a woman of high family (which saved him from prison over the counterfeiting escapade and helped him move up quickly in the army) and his English, which enabled him to become secretary to José María Moncada and interpreter at the Tipitapa conference between Stimson and Moncada. Later Moncada appointed him to a foreign undersecretary job, and he became favored by North Americans as an interpreter. He was a tall, handsome man with a reputation as a bon vivant. It was the U.S. ambassador in Nicaragua, Matthew Hanna, who recommended him as head of the Guard. Hanna's wife, according to Sandino, ran the Yankee legation in Managua. She is said to have been "addicted to [formal dress] balls and to young National Guard officers, [and had] chosen one as her favorite partner — Anastasio Somoza" (Selser 1981, 145, 180–82).

President Sacasa and Sandino were well disposed toward each other, and they negotiated a mutually agreeable peace. In exchange for turning in their arms, the Sandinistas were granted an enormous territory in Nueva Segovia on which they could settle and build a communal society. But Sacasa was too weak or timid to control the National Guard, which harassed the disarmed Sandinistas with beatings, imprisonments, and attacks. Sandino lodged complaints and traveled to Managua on several occasions to obtain guarantees for his men, but Sacasa's "efforts" failed to stop the persecution. Finally, when the National Guard was gathering to attack the main settlement in Nueva Segovia, Sandino made his last trip to Managua. He obtained a real guarantee for the safety of his veterans: Sacasa agreed to appoint a Sandinista general as a "military delegate of the president," with jurisdiction over Nueva Segovia, thus limiting the power of the National Guard. That same day, however, the officers of the National Guard were planning Sandino's death.

According to one of the Guard officers, Somoza visited the U.S. ambassador the day after Sandino obtained Sacasa's guarantee and was told that "Washington supports and recommends the elimination of Augusto César Sandino, considering him as it does a disturber of the country's peace" (Selser 1981, 174). After this meeting Somoza held another with sixteen high-ranking officers, all of whom signed a document committing themselves to the assassination of Sandino.

When Sandino left Sacasa's house that night, after a dinner in his honor, his way was blocked by an apparently stalled car. A number of Guardsmen were standing around it. Several soldiers approached Sandino's car and announced that Sandino and his generals were under arrest. They protested, and one member of the Guard who was not part of the plot demanded permission to call President Sacasa. But this didn't stop the soldiers. The call was made, and Sacasa in turn called Somoza. But Somoza had left instructions that his telephone was not to be answered. At that moment he was attending a poetry reading by the Chilean poet Zoila Rosa Cárdenas. Meanwhile, Sandino and two of his generals were taken away by car and shot. At the same time, a house where his brother Sócrates was staying was attacked with machine guns and he was killed. The next day, the National Guard attacked the Sandinista settlement in Nueva Segovia and murdered more than three hundred men, women, and children. So ends the last chapter of the historical myth of Sandino.

With Sandino's army scattered and demoralized, Somoza became the virtual ruler of Nicaragua. Two years later he overthrew Sacasa and made himself president. He began to turn Nicaragua into his private plantation. The San Albino gold mine, where Sandino had begun his "political life," remained in U.S. hands but paid Somoza 400,000 dollars a year in exchange for tax exemption; in addition, Somoza received 2.5 percent of the gold produced. Later Somoza confiscated all properties owned by German immigrants, under the pretext of anti-Nazism, and by 1944 he owned fifty-one cattle ranches, forty-six coffee farms, and eight sugar plantations. He profiteered during the war economy of the 1940s and used U.S. economic and military aid to augment his personal holdings. He acquired ownership of cement works, construction companies, textile plants, and the state air and shipping lines, and he had a monopoly on the sale of pasteurized milk. He owned dozens of sugar, rice, meat, and fish processing plants, as well as factories for making cigarettes and cigars, matches, rum, cooking oil, plastics, packaging materials, footwear, chemicals, and ice. He owned hotels, newspapers, radio and television stations, insurance companies, banks and finance houses. After Anastasio's assassination in 1956, his two sons, Luis and Tachito, continued to enlarge the family empire as president and head of the National Guard, respectively. The Somozas profited outrageously from the earthquake of 1972, in construction, real estate, and confiscated foreign aid, even selling donated blood plasma on the world market. Indeed, they even founded a company that bought blood from Nicaragua's poor and sold it for high profits in the United States. By 1979 the Somozas owned approximately one-third of the land and industry of Nicaragua; according to a U.S. government estimate, their net worth was just under 1 billion dollars.[4]

For twenty-one years after Sandino's assassination, "because of terror and obscurantism," wrote Carlos Fonseca, his name was "just a murmur" (Fonseca 1981, 1:292–93). This began to change when Fonseca, Tomás Borge, and other politically minded students organized a study group. Borge's father had some books about Sandino, and he let the boys read them. The only generally available book had been written by Anastasio Somoza! Intending to prove that Sandino was a rabid communist, Somoza wrote about the years Sandino spent in Mexico studying and associating with leftists. This was the first book about Sandino the students had read, and it interested them very much; they didn't mind if Sandino was a communist!

In 1956 the student Carlos Fonseca broke with the Nicaraguan Socialist party (PSN) because of its failure to appreciate the heritage of Sandino. Like many other socialist and communist parties in Latin America, the PSN was ideologically dominated by the Soviet Union, which saw Sandino as a nationalist—an *independista* who lacked a socialist or working-class perspective. Fonseca's reading convinced him the PSN and the USSR were wrong. Also, Fonseca felt that a Nicaraguan movement could not adopt a Marxist-Leninist ideology imported from abroad. A genuinely popular movement must root itself in the spiritual traditions of Nicaragua: this meant the tradition of Sandino. So Fonseca, Tomás Borge, and Silvio Mayorga founded the Sandinista National Liberation Front.

The Sandinistas took from Sandino a commitment to armed struggle. In contrast to the city-based PSN, which advocated legal, "peaceful" protest against the Somoza regime, Fonseca wrote:

A *popular, armed insurrection* is the central core of the struggle against the dictatorship. The struggle must be of the *guerrillero* type, in harmony with the geographic circumstances of our country and the great material strength of the dictatorship's army, the type by which the glorious General Augusto César Sandino produced so many victories in the Segovias against the U.S. Marines. The Sandinista struggle definitively proved that our people can fight and win against enemies who have a very great material advantage. (Fonseca 1981, 1:112–13)

Armed insurrection proved to be an effective strategy against the Somoza dictatorship. This open defiance and sacrifice broke the stranglehold of terror the National Guard had held over all political opposition.

The Sandinistas differed from traditional revolutionary organizations in another way—they didn't require doctrinal unity. In this, too, they followed Sandino, whose main doctrinal requirement was dedication to the political independence of Nicaragua, and who combined ideas from many sources to arrive at his own perspective. The Sandinista Front, as defined by Fonseca, united the ideals of "the great revolutionaries of history," among whom he lists Karl Marx, Augusto Sandino, Ernesto "Che" Guevara, and

Camilo Torres (Fonseca 1981, 1:141). He emphasizes his inclusion of Camilo Torres, a Colombian priest. Torres fought with the National Liberation Army of Colombia and was the first priest in Latin America to join a revolutionary armed struggle. Camilo Torres movements had sprung up among the priesthood and Christian laity all over Latin America. Because of their doctrinal openness, the Sandinistas in Nicaragua were able to unite with Christians and others to form a large, popular movement.

The Sandinistas also drew upon the historical example of Sandino in their stress upon the spiritual and moral dimension of revolutionary struggle. Fonseca's first published writing was an anthology of quotations from Sandino's scattered writings. He divided the last chapter, "On Morality," into five moral qualities, virtually repeating those qualities stressed in Sandino's first manifesto: (1) disinterestedness, a commitment to struggle without the motive of personal ambition or gain; (2) willingness to sacrifice—he quotes Sandino's words, "Quiero patria libre o morir"; (3) joy of struggle—Sandino writes, "We have been able to open the conscience of our people, a sweet task I have assumed voluntarily"; (4) human solidarity or love of neighbor; and (5) dignity, understood as the refusal to be bought or to yield to fear—"Ni se vende, ni se rinde" (Fonseca 1981, 2:194–99).

These qualities were important to Sandino and to the later Sandinistas because they corresponded to the needs of poor people uniting in struggle. The stories about Sandino show how the poor were drawn to him through these qualities, how the soldiers and their families shared these qualities in the life they led together. A community of struggle grew around him, producing its own food, clothing, and cultural life, and producing itself as a new form of community. The Sandinista Front also grew and reproduced itself as a community of struggle whose strength and attraction depended in part on these moral and spiritual qualities. I don't mean to say that these qualities were perfectly embodied in the two communities; but they were present to a high degree.

Sandino described himself as a "spirit guide." He spoke of a magnetism by which he and his army were united and "interpenetrated." — "The waves flow and are gathered by whomever is disposed to understand." This happens not only among people who are contemporaries; it also reaches across historical time. The members of Sandino's "crazy little army" and the Sandinista Front are united in such a community. And Francisco: wasn't he introducing me to his spirit guides?

A spirit guide is not necessarily a mystical being. It can be anyone who possesses on a high and exemplary level the moral qualities described in Fonseca's little book.

When Francisco told me to read Sandino's writings I made a mental note. Of course, I will read Sandino and Fonseca and Borge. I couldn't understand the Sandinista Front without such background information. "Background" is a journalist's word. I thought I must read Sandino in order to be a responsible observer. I was invited and I accepted — on my own terms, as a busy, somewhat detached North American visitor.

North Americans often have a cynical response to expressions of political reverence. We tend to smile at the image of Sandino in his high-laced boots and riding pants, the romantic *guerrillero* savior and leader with hat and revolver, the "Father of the Revolution." We are nervous about hero worship. For our public heroes are typically rich men claiming to be "of the people"; we have learned with dismal regularity of their hypocrisy and egotism.

I appreciate the validity of this skepticism in a society whose government functions through deception. But I regret the distance it imposes between us and the world; the mechanical dismissiveness with which we tend to greet political enthusiasm. Now, with more experience of Nicaragua, I feel I understand better the significance of what Francisco was offering me — not a proposal to convert me, not a list of books, but something more simple and direct: an entry into his world.

I would go further. I think I see something I didn't see then, or saw but took for granted: a fire that was glowing warm inside him and can spring up burning, the fire that inspires human beings to change their lives and even to give their lives. Fire is a good metaphor because this kind of spirit has purity and force; it destroys the old and strives for the new. It is purifying force. And it can be ignited by contact with others who carry the same fire. Francisco had that spirit, and he was telling me about others who inspired it in him.

It is best to think of different kinds of spirit, rather than of one essential form.[5] The generic idea of "spirit" is of a transcending force, one that breaks the old boundaries and strives for a higher existence. It has been seen in metaphysical terms as a striving against the body and against material existence in the world. It is described in new-age spirituality as a striving against ego boundaries and the constraints of scientific rationality. In fascism it is the striving against ethnic and racial difference, in a blind and violent—because historically impossible—seeking after "purity" of race and tradition. But the sense of spirit I am talking about is not metaphysical or irrational. It does not deny our bodily existence or our commitment to scientific understanding or our racial and historical connectedness. And it is not a search for merely personal well-being. It seeks transcendence, not of the material world and not of difference, but of oppression and exploitation.

Perhaps it can be best understood as part of a dialectical relation, as a response to the moral dilemmas we feel, living in a system that is unjust. Francisco told me how he felt sitting on his hands in Honduras. I understood only too well: compromised and impotent. Spirit is a life force that rejects the unjust status quo and offers the dignity of hope. It demands a new society. Yet, while spirit exists potentially in us, it may lie dormant. It is ignited and becomes actual by contact with other "spirits" who awaken and inspire it, who by their presence give courage, and who by their knowledge and example show us a path on which to journey. Such is the importance of men like Sandino.

"When there are many men lacking decency, there are always others who have in themselves the decency of many. They are the ones who rebel with terrible force against the robbers of their people's freedom—hence robbers of their decency. Such men are the embodiment of thousands, of a whole people, of human dignity. Such men are sacred" (Selser 1981, 207). These words were written in the last century by José Martí, the Cuban revolutionary who is for Cuba what Sandino is for Nicaragua: a historical father of rebellion and new ideals, a "spirit guide."

Martí's words further clarify what is implied by the idea of revolutionary spirit: its relation to community. "Spirit," understood as the passion to rebel against an unjust system, is easily assumed to be a purely moral or idealistic attitude. But "morality" by itself does not fully represent the relation between spirit and community. Individual moral goodness is often understood as difference from others in the world, as self-denial, or as giving oneself to a higher authority (law, or church, or God). When Martí speaks of a person as an "embodiment of thousands, of a whole people, of human dignity," he stresses that the revolutionary spirit is an expression of connectedness and love, that it binds people together.

By contrast, when we feel ourselves to be part of a corrupt system, we tend to disengage ourselves in defense of our moral complacency; we refuse to identify with the sufferings of those in whose midst we live. We refuse to acknowledge that much of what we have is taken from others. Our world is divided and defined by levels of wealth and privilege; seductive, powerful walls of objects, pleasures, symbols, and styles of life induce us by forgetfulness or fear to ignore our connections with others. Revolutionary spirit breaks down walls that separate us, that hide misery from us, that protect us by excluding those who are in need.

The Sandinistas often refer to the old Hebrew prophets as examples of the spirit of revolution. The prophetic writings of Amos and Hosea and Isaiah and Habbakuk are a long series of outcries against exploiters and imperialists and their collaborators—those who are envied and acclaimed for their wealth and splendid works in spite of the violence and injustice on which they are built.

"The prophet's ear," Abraham Heschel writes, "is attuned to a cry imperceptible to others" (Heschel 1962, 7). The prophet, like the revolutionary, has a sense of connectedness that breaks down the barriers created by a system of exploitation:

> Woe to him who heaps up what is not his own . . .
> Woe to him who gets evil gain for his house . . .
> For the stone cries out from the wall,
> And the beam from the woodwork responds.
> Woe to him, who builds a town with blood,
> And founds a city on iniquity!
>
> Habbakuk 2:6, 9, 11–12

Sandino is a modern prophet. His outcry, *Ni se vende, ni se rinde,* will continue to be heard in all future struggles for justice in Latin America, perhaps even in North America. And his example, as a prophet who did not simply denounce the iniquitous status quo but who devoted his life to changing it, joins the examples given us by other great modern revolutionaries.

3

Condega Journal

It's the usual hot, dusty morning on North Highway, and the usual traffic is passing, the people looking and sometimes calling to me from rattly farm trucks, jammed buses with people holding by their fingers on to the back and in doorways, newish four-wheel-drive Toyotas, and army jeeps looking serious and official. I am standing under the sparse shade of a little *genízero* (raintree), just past an intersection, so that not too many people are around competing for rides, and upwind from a very smelly pile of garbage. I step out to the road when a good prospect approaches and hold out my piece of cardboard on which is written "Condega — Por Favor." Often they yell an apology, other times something like "Gringo! Give me dollars!"

I stand there longer than usual — an hour passes. Owing to the garbage, and boredom, I am thinking about vegetarianism. Here in Managua there are two vegetarian *comedores* I know of, both in private houses. They are cheap and the food is special: vegetables in sauces, potato pancakes, cheese enchiladas, lots of fruit and fruit drinks. A few days ago in Poneloya I ate a large, very delicious red snapper, fried, with a sauce of tomatoes, onions, and peppers on top. At one point, as I was nibbling at the inside of the head, enjoying every morsel I could find, I thought, "Will I ever resolve my attitude about eating meat?" Or animals, I should say. Vegetarians always seem cleaner and morally superior, as if they live on a higher plane than the rest of us. One told me, "I won't take my bread away from another person, or dip it in the blood of animals."

Innocence, for me, has never been a very attractive virtue, and not eating something seems a feeble, merely private form of protest. I believe that to fish or hunt merely for excitement or pleasure is a wrongful violation of the life of another. It is important that the fish I ate was caught for food by a fisherman whose living depends on it (as the living of fish depends on eating fish).

How we treat animals may be closely related to how we treat one an-

98

other. Yet I am on my way to Condega, a town that has struggled long and bravely to escape oppression and create a more humane world. Its main industry is a slaughterhouse, one of the largest in Nicaragua. The slaughterhouse and associated industries — a large tannery and dozens of workshops for making boots, baseballs, and other leather goods — are the town's present basis of survival.

I believe that all life is sacred, but I don't know whether that means it is wrong to raise animals for food, or rats for scientific experiments, or to keep cows and horses confined for our use. I know that killing is always sacrifice and should be done only as necessary and with reverence. That says a lot, but is easy. The hard part is deciding what is necessary and then putting it into practice.

In his book *Memory of Fire: Genesis,* Eduardo Galeano notes that according to an old Indian belief anyone who kills receives into his or her body, without knowing it, the soul of the victim. That is easier to believe than to understand. Perhaps in one's heart or soul one responds with horror and pity at the death of the other, even if one tries to harden oneself. If one causes that death and is not forgiven, the memory may live within like a nub under the skin. It may acquire a voice and whisper, "Avenge me."

Where the Pan-American Highway touches the edge of Condega the army truck stops to let me off, and I say good-bye to the soldiers who gave me a ride. A path leads to the center. It dips across a gully, then widens as it passes the houses on the edge of town. These are of wood and stucco and painted white or in pastel colors — blue, yellow, pink. As I carry my bag down the hillside, people sitting in houses or working out back in a garden stop to look at me. A woman is sweeping dirt out her front door. A saddled horse is tied to a flowering tree. A woman walks past carrying a basket of vegetables on her head.

I have a special feeling entering Condega, as though I were walking into a silent movie from another time. In the central square there is a dreamlike stillness. Fifteen or twenty people wait in the shade on one side of the street for a bus or ride. On the other side, women and children sell food — ears of corn, tacos. Boys are shining shoes. Some men are talking in the street, one holding the reins of a horse. Kids are climbing playground constructions, pyramids made from heavy beams. It is shady in the square, and there are flower beds and sprinklers are watering the grass.

On the far side of the square, kitty-corner from the church, is a sign: "Pensión Baldovinas." It is an old, family-run *pensión*. I take a room on the

View of Condega

far side of the inner garden. It has two iron cots with thin, worn mattresses, a little wooden table and a chair, and it costs about a dollar a day. The ceilings are high, being the underside of an enormous, sagging tile roof supported by ancient, dusty beams. The garden is large and full of flowers and shrubs, with paths crossing it diagonally and a bench in the center. Rooms lie on three sides of the garden. In back, where they stack wood, a gate leads to an orchard.

I have the meal that is standard here, rice and beans, salty cheese, an egg, a tortilla, and coffee. The food is just edible. A herd of flies is grazing on the table. The woman who cooks has a little baby who wanders in and out from the kitchen to the dining room to check me out. A feebleminded woman who lives here and does a few chores is mopping the floors. Doña María comes in, a pleasant woman about seventy-five years old who is the owner. She tells me who is staying here: some men who work at the slaughterhouse and who go back to Managua on weekends, two North Americans who are visiting friends, Maria-Noëlle and some salespeople. Of course, I can put my table in back of the garden, she tells me. Of course, I can have another chair.

In the late afternoon I walk around town and take some color photographs. The afternoon light is magical — walls and fences glow with old, worn color, and the flowers give off light. Looking down any street, you see in the background the soft, rounded hills that surround the town, awash in warm yellow light and shadow.

People say hello like they do in all country towns and, in the old-fashioned way, *adiós*. Children want to pose for me. Little boys ride sticks with string attached to the end — horse and reins. They fly little kites. I pass a long, open room full of men playing pool. Some kids pass me on three horses, running fast. An old man and woman stop me and ask to have their picture taken with their grandchildren. They sit side by side, holding hands. A truck full of soldiers drives past.

My way of being in Condega never follows a plan and includes six visits over a period of five years. I know I love Condega, spontaneously and immediately. I know it is an important town in Nicaragua's history and economy, and a very charming town with a pleasant climate. And people tell me, "Get to know Condega, you'll learn a lot about Nicaragua and the revolution."

All of these things attract me to Condega. What I actually do mostly is visit people's houses and workplaces and take interviews; also, I give public presentations of my photography, hang out, and read and write. I look at Condega sometimes the way people look at a work of art, from different positions, focusing on different parts, squinting and free-associating, as if it has an essence to be discovered. This is an illusion, but it leads to interesting experiences.

In the evening when work is over I often go to see Laura, the nurse-midwife I know from earlier trips. She lives with Julia and José Centeno in a little brick addition they built for her. This afternoon there is a bit of a squabble between Laura and her boyfriend. She's had enough of the mice who are living under their bed and behind the bookcases. She's going to evict them. He wants her to leave them, and him, in peace. This little domestic spat creates a nervous flutter among the Centenos and some friends, so we join in and give so much help the problem is dissolved.

All this accomplishment leads to a group decision to buy beer and tacos. We sit around by the front steps eating and drinking as it gets dark.

While Laura and another nurse, Molly, talk about women they saw today and who is about to deliver, I watch people walk by or ride past on horses, toward their evening rest. I perk up to ask Laura what is happening in the countryside — is there much Contra activity?

"Yeah, a lot. Fighting, ambushes, attacks on civilians, everything. Things have heated up so much I can't go into the country now and there's no way to get people in. I'm just hoping nobody's water breaks. It could be very inconvenient."

Laura says Padre Enrique is taking a risk going out to the *campo*, because he's on a Contra hit list. They would like to kill him because he's on the side of the revolution and very popular in the countryside. He goes out often to visit people and hold mass. They killed the priest who was here before him, five years ago.

"How do you know he's on a hit list?" I ask.

"They don't keep it a secret," Laura says. "It's very Contra in certain areas, and the people talk."

José, back from work at the slaughterhouse, stands smoking in the doorway. José grew up in this town; his parents live next door. His entire family was involved in the liberation struggle, and they had to move to Honduras, then to Mexico, during the last year of the insurrection. That last year was so bad only a few families stayed here, they said. The whole town was boarded up. It was a wreck when they moved back in the fall of seventy-nine. They had to restore water and electricity and rebuild a lot of houses.

He asks me if I could send some manuals here when I return to the States. Basic manuals about electric and gasoline motors. They have an electric generator at the slaughterhouse, but it is just sitting there. No one can fix it.

"We need to learn," he says. "We want to learn, but there are no books."

"In Spanish?" I ask, then feel foolish for such a question.

"Yes, in Spanish." (Where would I find manuals in Spanish? New York, maybe.)

José tells me production is way down at the slaughterhouse. There are not enough animals. The campesinos are afraid to bring their cattle in, because the Contras will shoot them if they see them. And many others have left their farms because of the war. The Contras will do anything they can to sabotage the economy. Now, he says, the slaughterhouse is producing less than before the revolution.

Later I interview the director of the slaughterhouse, and he shows me figures that confirm this. After the revolution, production rose for four years—an important fact to note because in the United States the news media always attribute lower production to "Sandinista policies." At the Condega slaughterhouse, production dropped in direct relation to two U.S. interventions: the Contra war and the economic blockade. Three-fourths of all the machinery in Nicaragua, including the electric generator José mentioned, was imported from the United States. Now it is very hard and expensive to get spare parts.

José is a tall, dark, intense man who doesn't talk much. He answers a question, then looks out to the darkened street. There is no electricity tonight, only candles and lamps and flashlights. One of his arms ends at the wrist—a casualty of the slaughterhouse. He takes the cigarette from his mouth with his right hand and flips the butt into the street.

The next morning I hitch a ride with Father Enrique to Venezia, a remote resettlement community about fifteen miles east of Condega. The back of his pickup is loaded with people who live along the road. A sentry at a bridge just out of town stops us from going any farther—the road is closed because of Contras in the vicinity. Enrique and I turn back, but the country people have to walk to their homes.

What follows are a few stories of people I met and places I visited in Condega.

Gilberto Zavala: A Campesino Revolutionary

The Sandinista *guerrilleros* who fought in the mountains against Somoza's National Guard depended for their survival on the support of the campesinos. One such Sandinista, Omar Cabezas, was in the mountains around Condega, and a book he wrote about his experience has become world-famous—the title in English is *Fire from the Mountain*. Cabezas describes how he gained the trust of various campesinos who brought him food and carried messages and warned him when the National Guard was coming.

Gilberto Zavala was one of the first who helped him. I visited Gilberto in the small wood-frame house where he lived in town while he waited for the war to end. Gilberto spoke briefly but proudly of his role in the revolution. He said that Omar Cabezas and some others first came to his house in 1974, five years before the Sandinista victory. When they asked him to help make a change in Nicaragua, he didn't need convincing. He became a courier. Sometimes he walked as far as "eight leagues" (about twenty-four miles) to deliver a message. Four times the National Guard stopped him, but they never took him prisoner because he defended himself, he said. How did he defend himself? With words, nothing more.

Everybody in his village worked for the FSLN at that time, he said, except two or three families, and they came around when they understood what was happening. Before, the peasants had no defense against the National Guard. Once the Guard came and killed a cousin of his and burned seven houses in the village. They didn't burn Gilberto's house then, but later they did, in 1979, and he built a new one.

"People are tired of this war," he said. "People want to work. A lot of people live in Condega because they can't work in the mountains. I would like to go back to my farm." He has fifteen *manzanas* (thirty-two acres) there. He and some others now have a little land to cultivate outside Condega, but he still depends on support from the government.

Roberto Celedón: A Campesino Painter

Roberto Celedón is a painter in the campesino style made famous on the island of Solentiname. Roberto says he learned it in art school in Managua. Having drawn and painted since he was eight years old, he now earns his living as a painter. The Ministry of Culture acts as a dealer for him and many other Nicaraguan painters.

His work is painstaking and slow and of very high quality. He shows me several in progress and one finished, but doesn't have more—they are sent away as soon as they are done. He is glad for people to take photographs of him and his paintings, because he has no camera to record his work.

Roberto's parents are campesinos and the family used to live in the country, but they are afraid to be there now. They had a terrible loss. Roberto's only sister, Marleni, lived in a farmhouse at the time of the revolution; her fifteen-year-old daughter was a messenger for the FSLN until a neighbor informed on her (they showed me a picture of the informer, who now is in prison). One day the National Guard came to the house and killed Marleni, the daughter, and her thirteen-year-old brother. They burned the house and barn and killed the livestock. The rest of the family fled to Honduras until after the FSLN victory, and since their return they have lived together in town. Roberto told me that they worked together with the CDS (Sandinista Defense Committee) to fix everything—repair the houses, get back water and electricity, and gather food and clothing.

"In other countries, like France and the United States," Roberto said, "they tell many lies about Nicaragua. They say there is repression and torture here. They should come here and learn the truth. In Guatemala they

Gilberto Zavala

Boot Cooperative Workshop

have the death penalty and the army is murderous. In El Salvador they have the death squads. But here there is none of that. In Washington they say the people of Nicaragua and the people of the United States are enemies, but that isn't true. Bush and Reagan are enemies of the Nicaraguan people, but the people of the United States aren't. The people of any country are like brothers."

The Emilio Mansón Boot Cooperative: Reenacting the Industrial Revolution

Condega's slaughterhouse employs some three hundred workers. The tannery employs about a hundred and fifty, and shoe and boot-making cooperatives and a baseball glove cooperative employ hundreds more. I also saw private houses with lasts and cobbler's tools, for making shoes at home. The leather is picked up at a central office, where the finished shoes are returned. They call this mode of production a "collective." A "cooperative" is an independent business owned by the workers.

At the Emilio Mansón Boot Cooperative there are nineteen workers, an accountant, and a supervisor. They make shoes and workboots, and run a

The Comedor Infantil

little store. The workers, all of whom are young men, sit shirtless around worktables in groups of four or five. Everything is done by hand except the tops, which are sewn by machine. They have knives, for cutting out the leather, and large glue pots. I feel I could be in nineteenth-century England, at the beginning of the Industrial Revolution, except these boys are working for themselves. The highest-paid makes 20,000 córdobas a month; the lowest, 8,000. The supervisor makes 18,000. A pair of boots costs about 3,000 córdobas.

The Comedor Infantil

Literally it means "children's diner," but the kids all seem to be preschool age. It is the front room of an ordinary house on a side street, where three women serve lunch, in shifts, to eighty children each day. Poor families or working parents can send their kids for a free lunch, paid for by the local government. When I visited, a bunch of kids who had eaten were hanging around and some others were eating. They were neatly dressed and combed. They liked for me to take their pictures. Each child was given a plate of beans and rice with salad, a tortilla, and a glass of juice. When the

children finished they carried their plates up to a woman who was washing
the dishes, handed her the plate, and said "Gracias."

The Ulises Rodríguez Cooperative Farm: Anyone Can Join

Thirty-three families live here, many since before the revolution. The farm had been owned by a Somocista colonel; he abandoned the
farm and fled to Miami. There are about twelve hundred acres, mostly in
sugarcane, corn, and pasture for their hundred and fifty head of cattle. The
members used to be tenant farmers and laborers.

They feel constant danger from the Contras, but have never been attacked. Ten members do *vigilancia* at all hours of the night, men and
women, armed with AK-47s and hand grenades. During the day, anyone
who works in the fields carries an AK-47 and a bag containing two extra
clips of cartridges and one hand grenade.

Thirty-four of the residents are members, twenty-three men and eleven
women. Everything is decided by a "general assembly." They elect officers in
defense, production, education, and finance. The government helps with
loans and technical advice.

What they produce is shared equally among the members. I asked, "Suppose someone works harder than somebody else?" They said, "We don't
worry about that — everyone works hard." Last year each member received
fifty arrobas of corn (an arroba is twenty-five pounds), twenty arrobas of
beans, equal shares of milk, meat and eggs, 80 córdobas a day, 500 córdobas a day for cutting cane, 10,000 córdobas in April, a private garden,
and a house. They sold the surplus and made some improvements in their
machinery. They've built little houses of brick, each with two rooms — a
bedroom and a kitchen — connected by a covered patio. Soon they expect to
have electricity and plumbing for them.

I asked if other people could join and live there if they wanted. They said
anyone could join. "You can join us," they said.

Juana Francisca Hernández: A Woman in Shock

Driving through town in Padre Enrique's truck we passed a
woman standing in the doorway of her house, breast-feeding a baby and
staring vacantly at the fields across the road. She didn't acknowledge the
passing truck. Enrique said the woman's husband and second-oldest son

had been killed by Contras ten days before. This was in the country, east of Condega. She had moved to her cousin's house in town. The next day I walked over to see her.

She is a tall, thin woman, thirty-six years old. Probably she would be pretty, but she was in a state of shock. When she walked, her body was rigid and slightly bent. Her eyes were enlarged and glazed over by a film so thick she couldn't see anything nearby. She seemed to see only into the distance. She moved about the house like an automaton, sometimes speaking to the children, but without expression. She held her baby like a dead thing. When it began to cry she gave it the breast again, but offered no other response. She seemed indifferent to my presence. She answered my questions, but said nothing else.

Her husband was forty-one years old. They have eight children. He was the coordinator of the CDS, and thus a Sandinista, in a small village of twenty families called San José de Píre.

Padre Enrique told me her husband and the oldest son were on the Contras' list — people they seek out who work for the revolution. He said that many communities in that zone, like San José de Píre, are unorganized and don't have *vigilancia* at night. The Contras can find out who tries to organize and then go after them. They want to make an example of them and sow terror throughout the area. They have no future here, and that is their only strategy — to terrorize the people — he said.

About fifty Contras came to their house at one in the morning. They tossed a hand grenade in front of the door, and when the father came out they shot him, stabbed him with bayonets, and disemboweled him in the front yard. Then they began firing into the house. The mother and kids hid in a corner; but the second boy, Benigno, bolted out of the house carrying the nine-month-old baby in his arms and they shot and killed him. Padre Enrique said they would have killed the others, but it was dark and they didn't see them.

I asked to take a picture of her and the oldest son, William.

Ducuale: A Mass in the Countryside

One Sunday afternoon, a group of us walked with Padre Enrique to Ducuale, a little community six kilometers away, for a fiesta and a mass. We walked through the hills on a winding dirt road, in air that smelled like spring.

About a hundred people were gathered by a long tobacco barn, the end and doorway decorated with branches of pine and with white and red hibiscus flowers. It was as festive as a wedding. All around were broad, green tobacco fields and barns and a meadow with cows and horses.

Someone from the church led the people in games. The men stood at a fence along the road watching, but the women and girls loved it. We played blindman's buff, and catch the fox, and dancing games. We played many games, and the people watched or played intently.

The little kids — striking, with dark lips and large, dark eyes — were so shy I couldn't take their pictures easily or talk to them. Everyone was shy. When we changed partners in the dancing games, the teenage girls ducked away from me and it became a game for me to catch one. One I grabbed was so afraid that as we danced she made low, agonized moans and ran off into the crowd when they told us to change partners again.

There was a piñata, the rope hanging from a branch of the huge tree we were gathered under. They gave us large glasses of tamarind and orange juice, and plates of rice, beans, and salad with a tortilla. The kids lined up for a juice different from what they gave us, and they were so excited I went to see what it was. It was *fresco de maíz y arroz* — rice and corn juice, cold and sweet, with lots of solids to eat at the bottom.

Late in the afternoon, Padre Enrique offered a short mass. They set up a table decorated with flowers in front of the barn. There he placed the Bible and chalice and wafers for Communion. The musicians played. We said the Lord's Prayer.

Later, Padre Enrique said, "Living for two years in Nicaragua is like five years in another country. Life here is very intense. I don't have time to read very much. I don't even know what is going on in my own country. But to experience Nicaragua, to learn about these people and from these people, is like reading a book. They have taught me very, very much. For instance, we Argentines are very egotistical and individualistic. In this sense, I have learned a lot here. They will share with you, or give you anything. Their doors are open. You go to a house and they'll give you coffee, a bed, whatever you need. If you are sick, they worry about you and bring you food. If I need to travel in the country, sometimes I ask someone to accompany me — they always come. I see great value in this people — a very simple, courteous, and courageous people — not only with me, but with everybody. They are like a window, an opening to look through, this people, into the heart of Latin America."

Don Leandro Córdobas and Leonarda Centena Fallacio:
Generations of Sandinistas

Don Leandro is eighty-nine years old and she is eighty-five. They live on a hill near the highway. They are the parents of Moisés Córdobas, who was an FSLN leader and much-loved in the town. Moisés had been in the mountains at a remote community, and was ambushed and assassinated by the Contras on his way home. It had been nine months since Moisés's death when I visited his parents.

Don Leandro seemed very old. The whites of his eyes were bluish-red, and the irises were ringed by a blue line. His skin was a beautiful dark brown. He became animated as he talked. He said he didn't want to talk very long — his arthritis bothered him a lot, the back of his neck hurt, his head ached — then he forgot all that as he became involved in his story.

His wife, Leonarda, sat beside him and sometimes she would help him remember something. When he talked she would look at him affectionately and attentively.

Rather than tell about my interview, I want to quote Omar Cabezas,

Don Leandro Cordobas and Leondarda Centena Fallacio

who tells a beautiful story about Don Leandro. Cabezas and Moisés were in the mountains near Condega when Don Leandro paid them a visit:

In the morning Moisés appeared with my breakfast. He always came alone, but that day I could hear someone was with him. . . . We dropped to our knees, Andrés and I, and took cover with our pistols and grenade. But when I finally got a good look down the little trail that led to the crag, I could see it was a little old man coming behind Moisés. . . . Moisés called out to me, "Juan José [Cabezas's nom de guerre] this is my papito," which is a way of saying my papacito, my papá.

The little old man started laughing and offered me his hand very shyly in the campesino manner. I could see he was a very thin man, of medium height, with curly hair. . . . [H]e was like something very old that had suddenly been brought out into the light. . . . He was wearing his best clothes; it was very humble, but he came that day dressed in his best. I said to him, "Aha, compañero, sir, how are you?" "Ah, not so good. You see, sir, I'm old," he said, "and you can't imagine how my stomach hurts me. And my eyes are bad. I'm so old I can't see, I can't take a step without this cane; if I start out for the cornfield, in a few minutes I'm so tired I have to turn around and go home. My body is a wreck." And then he asked me. "That gun, what is it?" "This is a .45," I answered. "And what did you do with the other weapons?" he asked. I answered that we had to be careful, that we didn't carry heavy weapons since we didn't want people to see them. . . .

I did not realize that he was connecting me with the old Sandinistas from his own day, the time of General Sandino. He was asking me about the other weapons, as somebody might say, you know, the weapons we had in the past, what did they do with these? For him the moment he had preserved and which had grown old was an instant that lasted forty years. Then he confided with an air of wisdom and great confidence, "Those were fine animals, rapid-fire guns, very good. General Sandino once sent me to get tortillas for them at Yalí."

And the old man went on talking, and the anecdotes! He had been Sandino's courier. And he talked about Pablo Umanzor, with whom he had fought, and General Estrada, and Pedro Altamirano. . . . [H]e told me he could see it all. . . . "Look, Juan José," he said, "I'm going to tell you something. I can't go with you on this campaign, because look at me, I'm old and what good would I be? . . . But I have many, many sons, plus all my grandsons; here are all these boys." And he motioned toward his son. "I'm giving them to you, to go along with you because we all have to make an effort, we can't let them put an end to it." He was saying we can't let them put an end to it as if it had never been interrupted, as if all this were a continuation of what he had lived through with Sandino. . . .

I don't know how, but that day when Don Leandro started talking like that, about giving me his sons, and about Sandino and the Sandinista struggle, all of a sudden I began to feel that Don Leandro *was* the father . . . and never did I feel more a son of Sandinismo, more a son of Nicaragua than at that moment. I had been a young student who came to Sandino through books . . . but I had not arrived at the root, the true paternity of all our history. . . .

I embraced Don Leandro with a shudder of joy and of emotion. I felt that my feet were solidly planted on the ground; I wasn't in the air. Not only was I the child of an elaborate theory, but also I was walking on something concrete; I was rooted in the earth, attached to the soil, to history. I felt invincible. When we said goodbye he gave me his hand and I remember I took it in both of mine and pressed it tightly. "We'll be seeing each other soon," I said. And he answered, "Yes, I'm old now, but remember, here are my sons." (Cabezas 1985: 216–21)

The Wildest Slide Show on Earth

To make myself useful, and make friends, I had brought to Nicaragua about two hundred slides and a projector (paid for largely by donations from my community) which I later gave to the Matagalpa Cultural Center. I showed photographs of the history of the Puerto Rican community, Villa Sin Miedo, so similar in its way to the history of Nicaragua, and photos of Nicaragua itself: Solentiname, Condega, and Yalí. I made arrangements to schedule these events with the Ministry of Culture and with cultural centers in various cities around the country. A radio announcer in Matagalpa had recorded the text I had written to accompany the Puerto Rican slides, and I intended the program to be an educational and supportive cultural activity.

I had already shown the photographs in Managua and Matagalpa, to rather small but appreciative audiences. In Condega I contacted Emma Centeno, the director of the local cultural center, and she reserved the community center next to the church. On the evening of the event, I walked out of the Pensión Baldovinas with a friend, and found the entire central square of Condega full of people. I had been hearing the noise of a crowd, and once outside my heart sank. "Oh, no," I said to my friend, "something really big is happening. No one will be coming to see the photographs!"

We crossed the street to go into the community center, and I saw Emma Centeno. "What's happening?" I asked. She smiled, and gestured out to the crowd, which had begun to gather near us and which I now realized was mostly children. "They are here to see the pictures," she said. She had gone to the schools that morning and announced it to all the classes. I strongly suspected there was a misunderstanding, and that the children were there to see free movies about Puerto Rico and Nicaragua! Whatever they had been told, they were very excited to be there; but something they had not been told was how to behave.

The gate into the yard at the center was still shut. About fifteen or twenty older men and women were standing patiently by it, waiting to get in. The kids were crowding around. We opened it and a mob rushed in. I was literally afraid some of the older people would be pushed over. Inside, the kids ran and yelled and circled about in the large, empty room, like the eddy of a river. Some chairs were found for the older people, and the kids had to be made to get off them. Three or four hundred children were completely out of control and no one seemed to think it was possible to stop them. The noise level was so high we couldn't talk. Emma shrugged. Alberto, who was going to run the tape recorder, shrugged. We proceeded to try to set up. A wall was chosen to project on; a table and electric cords were found. But when I turned on the projector, kids ran in front of it waving their arms to make huge shadows on the wall; they couldn't be stopped. So, being the tallest person there, I held the projector on my shoulder for an entire hour and a half, trying to keep my ear from being burnt. The heat left my shirt soaked with sweat, and my arm was shaking from the strain of holding it up so long. The recorded narration was quite useless because the kids yelled and screamed at the sight of every image, but everyone had a good time, I think, except me. I made two other presentations in Condega, also to large groups, out of doors, on large, white-stucco walls. The people loved seeing the photographs.

This morning I am going with Padre Enrique for a mass in the *campo*. I have my rice and beans and coffee and hurry over to the parish house. The door is open and I enter a hall that smells of freshly mopped stones and old wood and wood smoke. On the right is an open door into a kitchen where a woman is peeling vegetables. Some chickens are standing around her and she shoos them out another door into an open yard. "The father will be out in a minute," she tells me, and she asks me to sit on a bench by the door.

He comes out of his office looking cheerful and fresh, and says "Vamanos" (Let's go). He is tall and slender, about thirty-five years old, and very good-looking, with a youthful, thin, beardless face, brown eyes, dark-brown hair reaching to his shoulders, dressed in jeans and a T-shirt—not my image of a priest. He's Argentine and served in Mexico for several years before coming here. He is carrying a Bible and the robe he will wear for the service.

Outside, the back of his truck is almost full of waiting people, who know somehow where and when he is going. Others get on as we pass through town. "It is always like this," he says. "There's no transport to the country-side. People walk, ride horses if they have them, or hitch." As we drive through town he says "adios" to people on the street. He makes a detour to pick up Doña Juana, a very old woman who is visiting her son in town.

Condega, he says, is a town of campesinos — everyone except maybe a few commercial people have their origins in the countryside. Condega is a town, a district, and a parish. In the town, there are about eight thousand people, more than normal because lots have moved in from the *campo* owing to the war. There are more than sixty small communities in the *campo* and about thirty thousand people. This morning we are going to the western part, to a place called Albranza Uno, and I am relieved because the Contras don't go there very much.

The countryside is green and growing from the rainy season. It reminds me of Massachusetts, which is also lush this time of year. The dirt road rises and falls among the hills. Much land is cleared, for corn and beans mostly. We cross shallow, fast-flowing streams and many little houses with fruit trees, banana groves, and animals. Dogs and children stand watching as we pass. Every once in a while Enrique stops to let someone off or pick up someone new. The country people are shy, polite, and gentle-seeming.

I ask how he sees religion and politics here in Nicaragua. Are they related, or are they separate?

"The traditional attitude," he says, "is that politics is one thing and religion another. This is very much the view of the bishops and many conservative priests: politics is about life in this world, religion about things 'above' and in the hereafter. But in Nicaragua we consider the Bible and the message of Jesus to be very liberating because it tells us to give life. In the revolution in Nicaragua everything is contributing to create life, to give land to the campesinos, to provide health and education; and as Christians, as priests, our role is to support this process of life.

"Marxism has promulgated the idea that the message of the church, the work of the church, is the opiate of the people. And in many places that is true. But Daniel Ortega has said that in this country, in many sectors, it is no longer true — the religious person and the revolutionary are one. Lamentably, many bishops and priests don't see it like that.

"I have discovered in Nicaragua that among the Sandinistas, even those who don't believe, there is a great respect for religion and for what we are trying to do. We work together. I often go into communities with representatives of the Sandinistas, to gatherings they organize. I celebrate a mass, and afterward we have a meeting on some problem of the community, such as sanitation or vaccination.

"So there aren't the kinds of problems people imagine. Many people on the right, and the bishops, say that the Sandinistas persecute priests. They point to the closing of Radio Católica and the expulsion of Monsignor [Pablo Antonio] Vega. But it is a lie. The Sandinistas have never persecuted anyone on account of religion. What happens is, some members of the church engage in counterrevolutionary activities, and when the government acts against them they call it religious persecution."

I'll interrupt this interview to explain Enrique's references. Bishop Vega, a close associate of Cardinal Obando, made several trips to the United States and Europe to drum up military aid for the Contras. On one trip, sponsored by the U.S. State Department, he met with members of the conservative Heritage Foundation, along with Contra leaders Enrique Bermúdez, Alfonso Calero, and Arturo Cruz, and stated to the press: "The great dilemma of the Nicaraguan Church is how to secure aid for the military that is trying to liberate our people." He added: "As a result of religious persecution by the Sandinistas, three priests have been killed, and we cannot express ourselves through the means of communication."

These charges caused outrage in Nicaragua, where the very survival of the revolution seems to depend on U.S. funding of the Contras. When Vega returned, he admitted that no priests had been killed, saying that his statement had been misrepresented by the press. He was referring to laypersons, he said, also admitting that these people had died under "obscure circumstances," two of them before the Sandinista revolution. But the damage had been done, and Bishop Vega was expelled from Nicaragua in July 1986. After speaking tours in the United States and Europe, he settled in Miami (Selser 1989, 171–72).

In January 1986, Radio Católica was closed down by the government, which cited some fifty violations of its Emergency Law of Media and Communications. The last straw had been the station's refusal to broadcast Daniel Ortega's year-end speech of December 31, a service that the law required. The government did not allow Radio Católica to resume broadcasting until 1988.

The Emergency Law of Media and Communications also required all publications to be registered with the Ministry of the Interior before publication and circulation. This exercise of censorship, which was carried out fitfully and never reached very large proportions, became a major blemish on the revolution's claim to be committed to freedom of expression. The Sandinistas justified it on the grounds of national emergency in the face of U.S. aggression. In another incident, Bishop Bismark Carballo, director of

Radio Católica, had failed to answer several requests to register the Church publication *La Iglesia,* asserting that to do so would be equivalent to accepting government control and that "bishops are answerable only to the laws of the Church." In October 1985, an entire issue of *La Iglesia* was confiscated, although many copies were secretly saved and sent to members of the U.S. Congress as part of the hierarchy's campaign for aid to the Contras (Selser 1989, 150–52, 385–89).

Cardinal Obando himself made several visits abroad and gave statements to the U.S. press and members of Congress that directly supported President Reagan's claim that the U.S.-organized Contras were "freedom fighters." In Rome in 1985, Obando stated that "the situation in Nicaragua is one of civil war, and permanent violation of human rights, among them the freedom of expression. My life is very much in danger" (Selser 1989, 85).

The Church hierarchy also openly opposed the draft and gave assistance to families and youths who wanted to avoid military conscription. The government arrested several priests, on charges of harboring youths by allowing them to pass as "seminarists" living in Church buildings, and it claimed the Church was operating a network for helping draft evaders get to Costa Rica and Honduras. One such priest was charged with possession of a large quantity of firearms. Cardinal Obando used his weekly, nationally televised mass and unlimited access to Radio Católica to invite young men and their families to resist the draft (Selser 1989, 72–80).

Meanwhile, large numbers of priests, like Enrique, are working with the Sandinistas and supporting the revolution. I ask Enrique if it is dangerous for him to be visiting the countryside. I have heard that the Contras are after him. He smiles and says, "Yes. The Contras asked once to meet with me, as if they wanted to talk. But it was a ruse. They would kill me."

"How do they contact you?" I ask.

"They have sympathizers in some communities. In Picote," he said, "there are many Contra sympathizers."

We cross a stream and park under a tree. From here we have to walk, even the four-wheel drive won't make it. A huge pig is sleeping by the stream. A woman is washing clothes on the stones. We start uphill on a narrow, rutted road. Below, in a ravine to the right, is a pickup truck that rolled off this road a few weeks ago.

"You must remember," Enrique says, "that this community was totally abandoned for forty years under Somoza. Poor Nicaragua! How did this community live? Abandoned! In the fields of health, education, and also religion. Abandoned! The revolution has been doing a lot in these fields, very slowly, but it is making big advances. Here in the municipality of Condega over the past four years no fewer than thirty schools have been built. They lack many things, books and paper and other materials, but the work is growing. Also nutrition. Women who are pregnant are receiving milk six months prior to delivery. Children who are undernourished get free milk.

"I support all of this work," he said, "because a community that is educated, that has good health, is a community that advances. Of course, there is still a kind of religiosity that is a little alienated, you understand, because it expects everything to come from above. I am always trying to get beyond that kind of sensibility."

The work of the revolution in the area of basic human needs is the truly human, caring aspect of revolution. We read about war and power struggle and politics. We don't hear about the small but innumerable molecular changes set to work in the areas of basic needs.

I talked to Miriam Centeno, director of the Ministry of Education for the region of Condega. She explained the structure of the new system to me. There are two preschools, sixty primary schools, and two secondary schools. Besides the increase in schools and teachers, the Sandinista government has launched an adult education program, taught entirely by volunteers called *maestros populares* (teachers of the people). They receive training and the equivalent of about 12 dollars a month to cover expenses. This education is very practical: the math is geared toward learning how to keep accounts, the science toward agriculture, health, and nutrition. They don't lack teachers and students, she says, but do need more and better books. Also, the war conditions create another difficulty: people are tired. They need to attend classes and study in the afternoons and evenings, but they must also be up at night doing *vigilancia*.

Even so, she says, the program is going ahead. Nicaragua's literacy rate, which was less than 50 percent before the revolution, has been raised to about 85 percent. People are going to the university straight from the adult education program. After achieving sixth-grade level they can enter a special practical program in agriculture, economics, or engineering.

Nicaragua has also started schools that combine study and work. Students and professors live together and run a farm. There is one at Tipitapa, on eighteen acres of land that wasn't being used. There are about seven hundred and fifty students of all ages — preschool to university, and an adult education program.

Enrique and I walk about three kilometers on the rutted, mostly uphill dirt road. We come to a steep hill where the rocky path is like steps. On one side some boys are cleaning weeds from a cornfield with machetes. At the top, with a magnificent view, is a new brick school.

School has just ended, and some of the children and some women are preparing the room. A table in front is covered with fresh greens and flowers, and the ceiling and walls are decorated with strips of green crepe paper, because the mass will be held here. There is one large room. From inside you can see the tops of hills and bits of sky through the serrated arrangement of bricks under the tin roof.

I meet the schoolteacher, a young woman about twenty, who grew up here. She lives a typically Nicaraguan, heroic life. Her pay is barely enough for food. She teaches sixteen children of all ages. Two are preschool age, but come anyway with their brothers and sisters. Four are mentally retarded and have behavior problems. There are six books. She herself studies at a college in Estelí on Saturdays, fifty kilometers away. She is up at five-thirty, walks fifteen kilometers to the main road, hitchhikes to her six hours of classes and, since she can't afford to stay overnight, returns the same day.

Enrique and I walk through pasture down the other side of the hill and cross a stretch of woods to an old-fashioned farmhouse. It has a long, covered porch, facing an orchard, and two fenced yards (one for horses, one for cows). At the far end of the house is the kitchen, with its heavy, smoke-blackened table, benches, and stone cookstove, and all kinds of iron and wooden implements hanging on the walls. Some women and children chat happily with Enrique and serve us coffee and sweet bread, then tortillas and chicken soup. After we eat, we all walk down to a stream with ducks and ducklings and sit on the grass.

All of this quiet rural beauty has an anomalous feeling to me. I ask if they feel afraid here. They say no, the Contras haven't been around here for about a year. Most of the attacks have been on the east side of the Pan American Highway, or south, near Estelí. But there have been many deaths this year. "It has been a very hard year for us," Enrique says. "Many people have died — I'm not speaking of combat, but of noncombatants who are working or traveling." They begin recalling these attacks, and Enrique remembers even the dates. "How many were there last year?" I ask.

"The seventh of June [1987], almost exactly a year ago, I remember, a boy who worked in state security, a very good Christian boy, and a man who was a 'delegate of the Word,' were brutally murdered by the Contras. This was in La Trinidad. In those same days the Contras made various ambushes. In one, four or five military people were killed here, in the ambush of a jeep. The month of June was horrendous," he sighed, stressing and repeating often that word, "horrendous." "In every ambush four or five people died. They killed many in the month of June of last year."

"How many in all?"

"In all, about ten people."

"All military?"

"Yes. No, pardon me, a woman was killed in her house. There was combat and her house was in the middle of it. A woman fifty years old. This happened in July of last year.

"Then, in the month of . . . September, the seventh, they killed Moisés Córdobas." One woman nods and then shakes her head sadly. "Moisés Córdobas was for us a very important man, because he was the political coordinator of the Sandinista Front for the entire region of Condega. He grew up here and was a Front member very young, from the beginning. Everyone knew him. He rode on a motorcycle with a reporter from the radio station in Estelí to speak to a community about the peace agreements reached in the conference, Esquipulas II. After the meeting, the Contras, who were waiting for him, killed him and set fire to the body. This was horrendous. It was in Dromadero, on the road to Yalí. This grieved the people tremendously, and me also, because he was an exceptional man and a friend. He was loved by the campesinos and by everyone here. Many people came to the funeral, from here and all over the country. Moisés Córdobas."

As Enrique repeats the name and pauses, I remember that it is he who holds the funeral services for all these dead. Much of his work is with the families of these dead.

"The twentieth of September they killed a boy fifteen years old. He was a civilian in a civilian car. The Contras ambushed them, killing only him. His name was Wili Moncada Peralta. Many people came to bury him, even from outside Condega.

"After that, in the first days of November, they killed a woman sixty years old, Doña María José Talanesa. This woman was a very good friend. She worked in the Ministry of Education, she participated in the Church, and she had a very high consciousness. She was on her way back from visiting her son in Managua. In the insurrection against Somoza he had received several wounds in his back and had become an invalid. She had made her visit because they were going to cut off one of his legs. She went to Managua to see him and to speak with the doctors. So one Sunday, in the night, between Estelí and Condega, the Contras ambushed a bus and Doña María died there immediately. A group of doctors and nurses on their way to

Ocotal were also on this bus. I think one or two of the doctors were killed, and others were wounded.

"In the first days of December the Contras attacked San Ramón, a community about five kilometers east of Condega. They killed Abrahím Mendiola, a civilian, the father of many children and a very good man. Also they killed Gerónimo Ramos, a member of the militia. About thirty Contras attacked at ten at night; and in this community there were some large drying barns for tobacco, and not much else, and they burned the three barns. This was very sad because the killings and the burning of the barns, which were full, made a very big impression on the people.

"The third of January, this year, they attacked El Arenal. They killed the *responsable* of the community and a boy twelve years old. A boy of five was wounded in both legs, and his father received various gunshot wounds. He was a delegate of the Word, an Evangelical.

"One I forgot to mention happened in November. The Contras attacked a community called Naranjita. They came for a specific family. A woman, her brother, and her two children died. Four died. *Four.* Four died," he continued.

"Why were they chosen?"

"They were thought to be members of the Sandinista Front. They organized the community for defense. The brother had a weapon and was a member of the militia. This was very sad for me, too. But there were others—many others. And the years before—eighty-four, eighty-five, eighty-six—were very sad ones for us.

"There have been so many dead; every family in Condega has experienced a death from the war, and some have lost two. One family has lost three young men. The people's face is sad. And besides the Contra attacks, there is the draft—the boys and men who are sent off to fight. The people are very tired. They continue to struggle, but they are tired. Think about it, more than twenty people do *vigilancia* at the slaughterhouse every night."

We leave the rushing stream and the ducks and walk uphill to the school. I smell the damp earth and the grass and sometimes a sweet scent of blossoms.

The people of Albranza Uno, maybe sixty in all, have gathered in the brick school building. Enrique asks the children to come out front and sing some songs they have prepared. The teacher leads the singing. Their voices are clear and strong.

Enrique asks everyone how they are, the children, the adults, and speaks about how beautiful it is now in Albranza Uno, how happy the rain makes everyone feel, how everyone enjoys the peace and beauty here. A community in which there are children singing is a happy community, he says. Then everyone sings a favorite hymn—"Que alegre la mañana cuando habla de Dios" (How Happy the Morning When We Speak of God).

The mass is a mixture of ritual and the ordinary, and Enrique always encourages people to speak. A woman reads from the Bible. Do they have anything they want to say? Any problems they want to talk about? The people say nothing.

After the mass we go to another house for a meal. It is the same—coffee, sweet bread, tortillas, and chicken soup. Then we walk to a third house and are served the same food again. It is hopeless to try to eat it all, so I call over a young boy and ask him if he is hungry. "Yes." So he sits with me, and together we eat my serving.

On the walk back I ask Enrique why we had to eat three times. Couldn't the families get together? He frowns and says, "They are very divided in this community, and very conservative. The problems are simple ones—one got more sugar than another, one got more rice. Things like that. So they come to the mass angry at one another, not talking to one another. I try to help, but it is very difficult."

"When you say they are conservative, what do you mean?"

"In every way," he says, "the campesinos are conservative. In other places they are more revolutionary, but in Albranza Uno, no. They are very traditional, they don't see the unity of religion and revolution."

"How do you respond to that?" I ask.

"On a personal level, but not publicly. They don't like it if I preach politics. But on a personal level I say, 'If you are a Christian, you need to be concerned about the problems of the community and the question of defense.' In Albranza Uno there is no militia.

"They are very campesino, very closed. They lack political understanding. The Front has neglected them. Of course, the Front has its problems. So many are in the army, so many have been killed, they don't have people to work in all the communities here and develop their awareness. And I don't visit much—at most, two or three times a year. I've gotten to know them because I have been here for four years, but really the contact is very little.

"Not everyone here is aware of what the revolution means, and not everyone sees it in a positive way. And they don't like the draft. The people don't agree that through this revolutionary process there is a great future for Nicaragua. They don't see the importance of defending it.

"To be living in a revolutionary country, to be making a revolution, is something magnificent, right? What has happened is that the people have suffered greatly. Lots of people don't want to take part in defense. Why? I repeat, they don't take account of the significance of living in a revolutionary country.

"If this revolution fails," he says, looking at me intensely, "it will be very sad for many countries in Latin America, and for the world." I am sure he is thinking also of Argentina, his own country, which sent army officers to Honduras to train the Contras. "This revolution is very profound, but not everyone understands this. There are many people with a revolutionary consciousness who work hard and are willing to go to any part of the country. But many, no. They are tired of the scarcity, the economic blockade, and the war. That is all they understand.

"It is complicated; but take an example, the monetary reform [a revaluation of the córdoba and official price changes that had been made a few months before]. A lot of people had very high expectations that there wouldn't be any more inflation. The people don't take account of the fact that inflation is a problem of the Third World, a cancer in all poor countries, right? So people who are not aware of this think we are just back where we were before, without any improvement. In my country, in just a few days, there was an inflation of 100 percent. But people think inflation happens only in Nicaragua. They don't see that Mexico, for example, has 100 percent inflation. So the people are very worried; and if they are not clear politically, the revolution is in trouble.

"We have two very great problems: the war and the economic blockade. How much money does this war cost every day? From Condega alone there are five hundred soldiers, men who are not producing because they are in military service. Think how much it costs just to feed these five hundred soldiers! So think how much it is for the whole country. And we are hardly producing anything! On top of that, the damages from the war and the economic blockade.

"There are things that help to build revolutionary consciousness in the people. People know who the Contras are and what they do and who is paying them—the United States, right? Also, they know about all the international aid Nicaragua is getting. Nicaragua survives thanks to international aid. Here in Condega we have built many schools, a hospital, and cooperatives, thanks to international aid. The people see this aid and are grateful for it. Last year ten women from the United States helped to build a school here. *Women!* People were very impressed that these women left their families and country and came here for several months to build a school."

"I know some of these women," I say. "They are from Massachusetts."

"Yes," he says. "People are very impressed that other countries help us against the United States, and even people from the United States come and work with us. But whether people's consciousness really advances or does not advance is very hard to know, right?

"How the people struggle to survive! Last year there was a drought here. With all the other problems there was very little rain in June and July, and none after that. When people don't have enough food there are repercussions. This year the rain is good, right? Now there is a problem of insect pests. Still, it looks like the harvest will be good. This community depends on beans and corn. If there's no beans and corn the people suffer a lot." He repeats, "They suffer a lot."

I go with Enrique several times to the *campo*. One day we visit a community called Honduras Azul for a wedding. We find the people gathered around a group of new buildings: a *casa comunal* (community center), a school, and a *tienda campesina* (peasant's store). There are about a hundred people standing in groups talking, their horses and mules tied up. The young men look strong and healthy in freshly ironed, partly unbuttoned shirts, tight pants, and high boots; the young women are beautiful, in makeup and dresses the color of geraniums and violets; the little girls are spotless and combed, in bright dresses and knee socks, their hair pulled back in ribbons and held with plastic clips. All friendly and kind and shy. They look at me and smile if I look back. When we leave I shake hands with many people I haven't spoken to, and they are so friendly it is as if we have spent a long time together.

The wedding ceremony is simple. Father Enrique asks if anyone has anything to say. "*You* are marrying this couple," he says. "Everyone in the community of Honduras Azul."

At the end he asks me, the visitor, to say something. I make my tried-and-true statement. "I am very happy to see this beautiful community. I will go back to my community and tell them about the generosity and love of peace of the people here."

Honduras Azul is near Albranza Uno, and it too seems very conservative. Especially the men. The women lead the songs, read the Bible, and organize things. The men stand in back or in the doorways or lean in the open windows.

"This is a very *machista* [sexist] society," Enrique says. "Many people feel that going to church or a baptism is something for women to do. They don't think of men as participating in that sort of thing. Also, they think politics is a job for men. At what cost are women excluded from politics? Even for the Front there are costs. There have been changes in this respect, both in the Front and in the government, but not so much in the Church or the home. Things continue to be very divided — 'You take care of the children and the house. I work in the fields.' This is a very ancient way of thinking, is it not?"

"Do you discuss this with the people?"

"Very little," he says. "I don't raise this kind of issue. People don't come to me about this problem. But I'll tell you something we are doing. One very big problem here is alcoholism. This is a problem with the men. Many men drink, and many young men and even children are drinking!

"So one of our projects in collaboration with the government is recreation centers where young people can enjoy themselves. We want a place where young people can learn the guitar, painting, games, all that, so they do something besides drink and play pool. The Front is planning such a center and we are all working together on this.

"The men have nothing to do but work and drink. The young men see their fathers drinking. Add to this the fears and tensions of the war, right? It is a very old pattern here, an old inheritance — for lack of education, for lack of alternatives — such that men can spend two or three months drinking. The people are poor!

"What institutions take responsibility for this problem? All of them! The Workshops for Popular Theology have developed a program on the problem of alcoholism. Meetings have been set up with all the other groups, the Sandinista Front, AMNLAE, the police, the town government, the Ministry of Education, the Church. It is tremendous. What people don't understand is that this is what revolution is about, to break with these old vices of the past, for lack of education, for lack of *formation*. People are working together for one end here in Condega, and it is very beautiful."

A *despedida* is a going-away party, and Nicaraguans have them whenever someone moves to the States or goes to the university or into the army, or when an internationalist is going home. But when Padre Enrique was returning to Argentina after five years in Condega, there was a *despedida* on a scale no one had seen before.

For two days dozens of women were in the yard outside the parish house kitchen, cleaning and soaking beans and rice, grinding corn and patting out three thousand tortillas, cleaning and cooking chickens and beef, shredding cabbages, slicing tomatoes, squeezing oranges and limes, slicing watermelons. A stage platform was constructed, loudspeakers installed, chairs set up, colored streamers hung, and green branches and flowers cut and tied to lampposts or laid on tables.

About two thousand people streamed in from the villages, however they could get here. Forty-eight of the sixty villages in the parish of Condega prepared cultural *actos*—a poem, a song, a dance, a theater piece, a statement. Country music groups like "Don Felipe and the Boys" performed. Poems were recited, some classic but most written for the occasion: "Father Enrique is leaving, / but in our hearts he will always remain. / He shared our sadness and our joy. / Always our friend, / we know that someday he will return." Whoever could make music had a turn, with guitars, banjos, drums, trumpets, and flutes. Little girls in miniskirts and bright lipstick danced to cassettes of popular songs. Men and women formed singing groups for the occasion, with voices and harmonies that were often hilarious, singing words they had written to the melodies of old country tunes.

The cultural acts began at three in the afternoon. They broke for dinner at about seven and started again at nine. There was much joking and dancing, laughing and speechmaking; Enrique sat with friends and with some other priests from the area on the street in front of the stage, talking, dancing, listening, applauding, and wiping his eyes. At twelve, I went to bed. They told me it went on until five in the morning. Afterward, the campesinos slept in the church or the park or at the houses of friends and relatives.

Someone told me: "He went out to the poor people and talked to them and listened to them. He built a people's church here, a church Jesus would want."

I am at my writing table in the back of the garden. It rained in the early morning, and the sky is mostly cloudy with little breaks of blue and sun shining. There is no sound of vehicles or radios, only children, birds, and sometimes the women who work here calling and talking. The loudest sound is the women pounding tortillas next door. Water is still dripping from the old tile roof. A frog sits on the walk, which shines from the rain.

Yesterday I drove out to the country with Emma Centeno, the young woman from Estelí who is director of Condega's cultural center and cultural organizer for the district. We went first to Palacaguina, a town about

Don Felipe, leader of "Don Felipe and the Boys"

twenty-five miles north of here. Palacaguina was made famous by the Mejía Godoy family, whose sons grew up there: Carlos Mejía Godoy, a musician and composer of the *Misa campesina nicaragüense* (Nicaraguan Campesinos' Mass) and dozens of well-known songs, and leader of the music group "Los Palacaguinos"; Luis Henrique Mejía Godoy, an equally renowned singer, composer, and bandleader; Armando Mejía Godoy, who is a painter; and others I haven't met. I wanted to see if the town was really the way Armando painted it, with rolling hills divided by low walls, the earth red, the houses of red adobe, with roofs of red tile. I wanted to see if I could feel the spirit of Carlos Mejía's music, which is sometimes rollicking and wild in a Nicaraguan country-western style, sometimes tender and lyrical. Using traditional instruments and rhythms, Carlos gave the revolution its music.

The actual Palacaguina was charming and asleep. Hardly a soul was visible. "Everyone is in the country planting," Emma said. In the little central square, she showed me the church and crafts store and found someone to open it. They sold pottery, wooden toys, and woven baskets. I bought a small, finely woven basket and we drove back on country roads.

The landscape was blossoming with the yellowish green of spring. I stopped simply to photograph a lush hillside covered with grass. We passed a coffee-dark field where teams of huge, white oxen, pulling wooden plows, were walking gracefully between rows of small corn plants. I stopped to take a picture, hurrying to get close before the team turned at the end of the row. I called out, "Can I take your picture with the oxen working?"

"Take it," he said, a thin, old campesino in a large straw hat. He stood proudly behind the animals.

"The earth is rich with the rain," I said.

"*Riquísimo*" (the richest), he answered.

"Is there enough rain?"

"Yes. If there were more, we couldn't plow."

I thanked him. He started the oxen and made his turn, the arc of the turn rounding six rows of corn. Soon another pair came, guided by a young man. He, too, stopped for a picture. Then came a third. The campesinos were very cheerful. Emma said that this time of year, when the rain is good, is their happiest.

We rode to Ducuale Grande, a village beside a largish river we had to cross on foot, hopping on rocks. Here was a thriving women's pottery cooperative — eight women were full-time members. They had a studio with three kick-wheels and long tables for hand-building. Emma was arranging a sale in Managua, and they were preparing a large shipment. Pots were drying outside the houses, large pots for cooking, for flowerpots, for water. The studio shelves were filled with bowls, platters and cups, painted in earth colors with designs taken from indigenous pottery, geometric forms, flowers and leaves. It was the most beautiful pottery I had seen in Nicaragua. The clay had been gathered near their village and fired in the traditional manner, using woodfires.

Back in Condega, Emma and I looked at the pre-Columbian pottery in the cultural center. Two long walls were lined with glass cases of human and animal figures, in good condition, the variety and quality excellent, all found in this area, much of it in town by people digging gardens or cellars. "There is an old tradition of native crafts here," Emma said, "and we are trying to continue it."

A fine rain has been falling from clouds that pass high overhead. I stand under a tree and listen to water dripping from the leaves. Maria-Noëlle is playing her flute. The moon hovers above the church. With the electricity off, the streets are dark. Some boys talk on a park bench. A fire and a lantern shine at one corner of the park where a woman is cooking meat for tacos.

I walk to that corner and turn up the street into the dark to a store that is lit inside by a candle. For takeout they pour beer into a plastic bag and tie the end. Farther up the street I pass people sitting on their doorsteps, a family in rocking chairs around a lantern, a girl reading a book by candlelight. There is no television tonight—no *novela* from Brazil. A few blocks from the park a Mexican woman prepares tacos with a hot sauce. I sit on the curb and eat tacos and drink my beer Nicaraguan-style by biting a corner off the plastic bag and sucking. The Mexican woman dresses colorfully, talks expansively, and has the air of a sophisticated person here in rural Nicaragua. We exchange stories about Mexico.

I go back to my room and read the old Japanese poet Bashō, whose book *Narrow Road to the Interior* (Bashō 1991) goes well with Condega. He took long walking trips and wrote a journal and haiku poems, so many that each trip became a book of poems. Another poet often accompanied him, and many of Bashō's stops were at the houses of poet friends, where they wrote poetry together.

The Japanese haiku are seventeen syllables and three lines long. From what is described you must be able to tell the season of the year. Despite such rules, haiku seem very free and spontaneous. They describe a single image without metaphor or rhyme or comment by the poet. Bashō believed that the consciousness of the writer, his or her point of view and spirit, should find its direction through the object:

> The first snow —
> Daffodil leaves bend
> Under the weight.

> The sound of a water jar
> Cracking on this icy night
> As I lie awake.

In these poems (translated by Makoto Ueda [1982, 55, 54]) Bashō allows himself to enter the world, its forces and opposites, which meet and interact: heavy snow, tender daffodil leaves; the piercing cold of winter, his own warm body.

Bashō says about writing:

> Go to the pine if you want to learn about the pine, or to the bamboo if you want to learn about the bamboo. And in doing so you will leave your subjective preoccupation with yourself. Otherwise you impose yourself on the object and do not learn. Your poetry issues of its own accord when you and the object have become one — when you have plunged deeply enough into the object to see something like a hidden glimmering there. (Bashō 1966, 33)

I study Bashō's attentiveness, his search for meaning or relationship in ordinary things. It helps me understand why old stucco walls or the shadows on mountains or the empty dirt streets in Condega speak with so much meaning of the life here.

On his walks Bashō looks for places other poets have written about. Five hundred years before him, a poet stood on the shore and watched the moon rise behind a certain island; Bashō walks to that beach and watches the moon rise. He walks to see a great pine tree described by a poet and attaches a poem to the tree.

Bashō's walks express his detachment from possessions and his search for permanence. The walks are like a breeze that brushes over an eternal world. This world is massive, a huge rock underneath the moss and mist and passing people that are visible to us. But changing things — the stages of the moon, the generations of poets he joins in his trips, and the haiku themselves, of which he writes hundreds — also exist. The haiku are an endless stream of images, as recurrent as blossoming clover, that lead to the eternal. Both the transitory and the eternal are real, yet change orients itself around the eternal like the poets who walk the same paths and view the same mountains and waterfalls. The eternal is what the poet seeks in the tree hundreds of years old, or in the horse quietly eating in a meadow of high grass. The eternal manifests itself in the earth, in humble things, in quiet beauty repeated. It shows most clearly in the tension and opposition between the small, finite thing and the vast, surrounding infinite, as in these famous haiku:

> An ancient pond —
> A frog jumps
> With a splash.

> On a bare branch
> a crow is perched —
> Autumn evening.

> (Ueda 1982, 44, 53)

I have been carrying Bashō's book with me for months and have read it five or six times. I am not sure how to explain this obsession, but I know it gives me rest and a sense of peace in a place where I am constantly moving and under stress. Bashō is like an anchor. His calm presence seems to place my feet gently on the ground.

I am always thinking about change and looking for it. Bashō teaches that the sense of change and the need to change are ancient. He teaches awareness of the past, and shows it merging with the present. Here in Condega this dual reality is very strong — the solid weight of the past, the disintegrative and creative forces of change. I see them merge before my eyes, like waves crashing onto the shore.

Bashō teaches that change is impossible without loss, that creation is a form of death, just as death is a form of creation. He teaches the importance of the permanent, and how to find it in small and changing things. He teaches how to find the insides of things and the connections between things.

Sometimes his strongest message is one of sadness and loss. He seems to see no glimmer of hope. His Buddhist consciousness tries to disdain all things that are created and that decay — each living thing bespeaks futility:

> Loneliness —
> Sinking into the rocks
> A cicada's cry.

> (Ueda 1982, 51)

Yet he knows how to overcome this. He later wrote another poem different in only one word:

> Quietness —
> Sinking into the rocks
> A cicada's cry.

(Ueda 1982, 52)

The contrast of loneliness and quietness is the difference between being separate or being connected. The rocks and the cicada's cry are utterly separate in the first poem, and there is a feeling of desolation. In the second, they are part of a common nature and impart a sense of peace. I couldn't find a clearer example of the changes I experience in Nicaragua: at first, separate and alien and desolate, then deeply connected, uplifted, and part of a common world.

There is another root that Bashō's writing has grown into my life: his attention to the concrete detail, the particular thing, as an image of the whole; and, more, as the mode of presence of the whole. The haiku that describe cold rain and the shivering of a monkey without a raincoat, or the silence of a priest sitting down to tea in front of chrysanthemums, bring the world into the small, particular thing.

This is a deliverance to anyone looking for a satisfying picture of the world — in this case, the world of Nicaragua in revolution. My failure is inevitable. The big picture, however interesting and important, however needed, can be very dispiriting because it is always and inevitably full of blanks. It shifts and changes before my eyes. In trying to grasp the meaning of this world I often feel confused. As a living, striving part of it, I am small.

The mode of being of history, the large story, the massive changes of society, in which I feel confused and insignificant, needs to be balanced by the mode of being of the caterpillar surrounded by budding cherry leaves. Knowledge, ideas, thinking need another kind of understanding: the sound of a flute in a cold, star-filled night.

4

Norma: On Sexism and Moral Change

In a house across the *andén,* Bayardo has the radio up full-volume and sings along as he mops the floors. Sitting on the edge of my bed, groggy and sweating from a long nap, I can see him swinging the mop around the front room at high speed. His twelve-year-old voice is piercing as a bugle, and the noise he and the radio make together is passionate and horrendous.

Tim, a young North American who is here teaching math and computer science, stands idly in front of the house talking to Myrna, Bayardo's mother. He lives with them: the five mostly teenage kids, Myrna, and her husband, Vicente, who shares ownership of the little house and lives in the front room, but has his own social world.

Myrna manages a difficult life. For a long time now, she and her husband have been estranged. Vicente has another house and a "wife" and children in Masaya, where he also goes from time to time. Every morning I see him watering the plants and standing in front to watch people walk by, especially the girls. He is about fifty-five, has a mustache, a potbelly, and the air of late middle-age. His main activity seems to be card games in front of the house, games that become very drunken and loud. Myrna is a Sandinista, the director of a state-run supermarket and the president of her union. He is a conservative, doesn't hold a job, and sits in front of the house at night reading *La Prensa.*

Tim comes over to borrow some cooking oil, and after Joaquina gives him almost half a bottle of the precious fluid I walk back with him. Myrna cuts up potatoes and starts to fry them. She is shocked Tim accepted so much oil. We talk about the price of cooking oil and then about what everyone discusses here, economic conditions. Myrna says she barely makes do because she supports five kids, although she earns what is considered a good salary.

"*He* doesn't give anything," she says, pointing toward the empty front room "A family with two salaries and only two kids can do okay, but it is rough with only one salary, even a good one, if you have kids. A Nicaraguan boy has a couple of pairs of pants and a couple of shirts, but shoes! A good pair of Adidas costs a third of my salary for a month. Domestic shoes are much less, but they don't last as long.

"In fact, a lot of kids are undernourished now. Many young men who are drafted have vitamin deficiency and are sent to health clinics. Many children are dying. The infant mortality rate is *rising* now [in the early years of the revolution, it was falling] because poor babies aren't getting enough nourishment to resist a cold or diarrhea." She is angry now, and stops stirring the potatoes to turn to me.

"This is an agricultural country, we don't have industry here, or we have it but it is shit, but we should have enough food. Many people, even leaders, are going into the countryside to help with production, because we can produce food. We have to have food, especially for defense. People can't fight if they are hungry. They can't work if they are hungry."

I ask her about her son-in-law, who is in the army fighting in the north. Myrna jerks her head back and gives a disgusted snort.

"¿Quien sabe?" (Who knows?), she says.

"Why?" I say, surprised. "Where is he? Is he missing?"

"He's missing alright," she says, turning to stir the potatoes.

"What happened," I say, feeling alarmed. "Is he still in Yalí?"

"No, he's in Matagalpa."

"And your daughter, is she in Matagalpa, too?"

"Yes, but she doesn't see him. He is living with another woman."

"Oh my god!" I am shocked, because I knew them both, and the children, and thought of them as a happy family. "Does he still see her? Are the children with her?"

"Of course the children are with her! Where else would they be?"

"Does he come to visit her and the children?"

She looks at me like I'm an idiot. "She never sees him. I wish she would move back here, but she won't."

"I'm sorry," I say.

Again she stops her work and turns to me. "Here," she says, "it's the same everywhere. Men are always the same. They leave the house and go to another woman. Then to another. They leave their kids for the woman to feed and dress and watch after. And they drink. Alcoholism is a very big problem here. It is a problem in the army, and even with very young kids, kids in school.

"Women don't drink, they stay at home and take care of the house and the kids. When they have money, they spend it on food and clothes. But men?

"See, we have women's liberation here, but not liberalism. Here women have a lot of power — they have good jobs and high positions. I'm a supervisor, and men work under me. I'm president of my union, and I was elected by men. Most of the people under my leadership are men. If a man can drive a tractor, a woman can drive a tractor. Women can do anything men can do, except they don't go out drinking, and they don't have twenty boyfriends."

Her eyes flash and she raises her fist and says, "¡No sirven, los hombres, no sirven!" (Men are useless! Useless!).

Tim and I look at each other with embarrassed smiles. What can we say, a couple of gringo men? Myrna is a passionate woman, lively and intelligent and moving ahead with her life, but very weighed down by the double shift — working outside and inside the house. While *he,* the absent presence in the front room of the house, is off in Masaya with the other woman. I look at Myrna, then back at Tim, and shake my head.

"It's true," she says. "Deny it if you can!"

"Myrna," I say, "I wouldn't argue with you, an authority!"

It is time for me to get ready to go out. I'm going to interview and have dinner with my friend Norma Aburto, who lives a few houses away. She, too, is a single woman with children. As I cross the *andén* I wave to Dolores, who lives next door to Lolín and Joaquina, with her three teenage children. She too is a single mother. She is a gynecological nurse. Her first husband was killed in a car accident. He was drunk. Later, she told me, she was with another man for five years until she saw him pass her house with his arm around a woman on a Sunday afternoon! Since then she has been alone.

Joaquina helps me set up to iron my *guayabera* — a white cotton shirt from Cuba I wear to dress up — and while ironing under her watchful eye, I think about the division of work in this country, and the amount of work most women do in the house: cooking, marketing, cleaning, washing and ironing, and child care. Much more time is spent on housework here than in the States, because almost all laundry is done by hand, and everyone irons their clothes, and many women make clothing for themselves and their families.

In one of my university classes, in a section on sexism, we tried to estimate how much more work women in the United States do as compared with men. We didn't have enough data to make sound general estimates, but it was possible to get a sense of the situation. A survey of married couples in upper New York State who worked outside the home and who had two children, showed that, on average, the women did 42 hours of housework a week, and the men did 14. If we assume their jobs both required 40 hours per week, the total combined work of each couple would be 136 hours weekly, 54 hours (40 percent) by the men and 82 hours (60 percent) by the women. In Nicaragua, the situation seems worse to me than in the States because the amount of time spent doing housework is greater. As Marx said, all social domination is, in essence, freedom from labor and disposal over another person's labor.

Nicaragua is a country in revolution, and one of the central goals of the Sandinista Front, as announced in its "Historic Program" of 1969, is complete equality for women. In my interview with Norma Aburto I hope to gain more understanding of how the lives of women have been affected by the revolution. Despite the problems of exploitation, family desertion, physical abuse, rape, and sexual abuse of children, many still believe that the position of women has improved considerably. Norma Stoltz Chinchilla, a professor of sociology at the University of California at Berkeley, notes in her authoritative study that

> women participated massively in the Nicaraguan revolution in roles that many observers have argued were more varied and significant than in any other twentieth century revolution. They were mobilized at practically every level of Nicaraguan society where opposition to the Somoza dictatorship emerged — in the neighborhoods, the schools, on the farms, offices and factories. They were fully incorporated into the actual fighting forces of the FSLN, not only in transportation, communication and logistics, but in combat and positions of command, something unprecedented in Latin American history. (Stanford Central America Action Network 1974, 422)[1]

Why have women gained so much importance? Stoltz Chinchilla mentions several contributing factors. One is the high level of male unemployment and underemployment that existed in Nicaragua in the decades before the revolution. This in turn led to high levels of alcoholism and family desertion, and to many forms of independent economic activity on the part of women. A moral factor she stresses is the growth of the international women's movement and its influence on Latin American liberation movements. The FSLN recognized the importance of women as a revolutionary force and women's need for liberation from male domination. Long before the revolution, the FSLN helped to organize AMPRONAC (Association of Women Facing the Nation's Problems), which drew masses of women into the revolutionary movement. A new dignity was given to women, even if revolutionary women in safehouses had to struggle to avoid the roles of cooks and cleaners for their male comrades. Dora María Téllez, a Sandinista *comandante,* said:

> Personal relationships have changed. In general I think they have improved. During a revolutionary process ideas change. This is the case with women. Women participated in the revolution, not in the kitchens but as combatants. In the political leadership. This gives us a very different experience . . . [and] . . . tremendous moral authority, so that any man — even in intimate relationships — had to respect them. A man would be hard put to lift a hand to hit or mistreat a woman combatant. (Randall 1981, 46)

Myrna certainly has moral authority, and so does my friend Norma, who is a captain in the army, a *militante* in the Sandinista Front, and head of the CDS for her block. Norma owns her own house in the barrio. I go there often to visit and to use the telephone — not many people in this barrio have one. Norma lives with her daughter Lisette, who is about twenty, her son Rodman, who is starting high school, and Lisette's daughter Katherine, who was one when I first met her.

Norma's ex-husband and the father of her children is a Mexican journalist whom they haven't heard from in years. Norma lived in Mexico when the kids were small, but moved back here because he was treating her badly and she didn't want to be away from Nicaragua. She told me she'll never live with a man again. She doesn't need to, having her own house and job, and, she said, "No Nicaraguan man can accept a really independent woman. A woman would have to stay home, or at least be dominated by him. It wouldn't be worth the struggle and the fights."

Norma's house is especially relaxed and pleasant, and the one or two internationalists who are usually staying there always feel free and at ease, as I did when I lived there in 1991. All the houses in the Barrio Máximo Jérez were allotted the same amount of space, about twenty by forty feet. Norma designed her house so that the main sitting area is in back. She built very high walls and left the roof partly open, covered only by the kind of wire used in chain-link fences. Air is pulled through the house and out through the high opening, which generates a breeze and creates a light and airy sitting area away from the noise of the *andén.* It keeps the house relatively cool, getting rid of kitchen heat and odors. Norma has a little garden with lots of plants under the open roof.

When I arrive Rodman lets me in — he and some friends are playing

Ping-Pong on the porch. Lisette is ironing and watching television. Katherine is crying because Lisette won't let her have an *helado* (a plastic bag of frozen fruit juice) from the refrigerator — Norma sells these to neighbors. I give Katherine a horseback ride on my knees. Soon Norma, whom I am used to seeing in an olive-green shirt and pants, comes out looking very striking and elegant in a dark-purple flowered blouse and dark-brown skirt. She drives us to the restaurant in her Russian-made Lada — a car she gets because she is in the army. She has other privileges, too — she can shop at the well-supplied army supermarket, she has a little Russian washing machine and dryer, and she was able to get Rodman a bicycle. And she has that telephone.

We drive across Managua to a restaurant perched on the side of a hill with a spectacular view of Lake Managua, the volcanoes, and the small volcanic lake that holds Managua's water supply. This was still in the days when with dollars you could eat very cheaply in the fanciest restaurants. We order shrimp and a half bottle of rum, and I run my tape recorder, which picks up music and traffic noise and the sounds of ice cubes in our glasses, along with our voices.

I ask Norma to begin by telling me about her early experience with the Front and how the popular movement developed and finally became a revolution. Norma knew the members of the Front in the seventies, the earliest days.

"We would meet in different homes to study the Bible," she said. "It was safe to talk about politics that way, or in church, which is probably why there were so many study groups. If a group of people had met to read Marx together, they would have been jailed by the National Guard.

"But it was the Bible we read, and there were a lot of courses on the Bible. The groups were simple, just friends, and at each meeting we chose a coordinator whose job it was to prepare a reading from the Bible and to teach it. We also met at church, and every Sunday we went to mass.

"From 1972 until 1978, we read Exodus and the prophets and the life of Jesus. These books spoke of God as a liberator of the people. In Exodus, God led the enslaved and oppressed people to a new land where they could live in freedom. The prophets were always denouncing injustice and urging everyone to live as one family, as sisters and brothers. They envisioned a new life here on earth.

"We applied these ideas to ourselves here in Nicaragua. It wasn't hard to see the parallels. And we couldn't just read the Bible and say, 'This is good.'

Norma Aburto Altamirano and her granddaughter Katherine (1991)

We had to do something. We had to recognize that there was a dictatorship here that kept people in poverty, threw them in jail, killed them. We had to face the realities of hunger, unemployment, and lack of education here.

"In the year of the earthquake, 1972, there were many ways we could help people. We formed 'communities' all over Managua in the poorer barrios, the working-class barrios like Rigüero, Máximo Jérez, México, and José Gómez. A group of students from the university, who belonged to the Christian movement and whose parents were well-to-do, moved into Barrio Rigüero. They, too, had been studying the Bible, and decided that if they wanted to be Christian they had to change their lives. So they began to live with families in the barrio and work for them. Among them were several who became *comandantes* in the Front—Alvaro Barcelano, Joaquín Cuadra Lacayo, Luis Carrión, Alvara Guzmán, Salvado Mayorga, Roberto Gutiérrez, and Francisco Lacayo. Fernando Cardenal and Ernesto Cardenal came to the barrio when the boys worked there. This was how these boys began to understand the problems of the poor. They lived with people who had cardboard for walls. They built latrines and health centers and brought in food and medicine.

"But at some point," she said, "you realize that what you are doing is just charity. It's good, but it isn't changing conditions really. It is at this point that the Front becomes important, because if you join the Front it means you are willing to go all the way. You commit yourself to fighting the dictatorship and liberating the country. And many members of the Front, many, came out of these Church groups.

"The National Guard knew this, or suspected it, and persecuted us. They harassed people on the street and searched people's houses, but there wasn't a lot they could do against us because we were Christians, right?

"Gradually the barrios became more organized and people's consciousness developed. After the earthquake, for example, people couldn't get loans to rebuild their houses, or they could but the interest rates were 15 percent or 18 percent. The president of the Housing Bank, Franco Zelayo, was a Somocista and a thief. So here in Máximo Jérez we elected a *directiva* (board) which worked to get low-interest loans and grants for reconstruction. The money was there, tens of millions had been donated to the government, but Somoza and his people were robbing us and the people knew it. The Front helped in this. When they worked in a barrio they would explain what the Somoza government was doing. Then people would come to the meetings and get involved, the people who were active, the natural leaders, right? And so we formed the *directiva,* and it combined with organizations from other barrios. Fifteen or sixteen barrios in Managua got together and formed a 'Federation for the Reconstruction of Housing,' to fight against Franco Zelayo and his bank.

"People's consciousness grew by stages. There were other issues, other things that people really needed, such as electricity. There was metered electricity for the houses, but the streets were dark and dangerous in the poorer barrios, so we demanded lighting. Then, lots of streets weren't paved. They were full of holes and ditches, and there were open sewage ditches in some neighborhoods, with children playing there, as there are right now in parts of Nicaragua and all over Latin America. And many houses didn't have water. So we fought for these things, talking to people and learning from them. It was a process, a long process, but it grew—the people changed and we changed with them.

"Most poor people, you know, have been taught that life is suffering. They accept it. Their babies get diarrhea and die, their little children get measles and die, they don't have shoes, they can't go to school, and they just accept it. The Church has played a great role in this: 'Life is a vale of tears, just wait and you will be happy in the next life.' But the Christians in the

Front were telling people something different: you don't have to suffer, it is because of the unjust system that you are suffering. For example, they raised the bus fares from 40 centavos to 60 centavos, then again to 80 centavos. Most poor people just accept that. Why risk your life in a demonstration over 20 centavos? But we talked to people and explained what it meant for a family with four or five children to have to take the bus. And we talked about who owned the buses and why they were so old and crowded and wouldn't serve the poor neighborhoods.

"In that way, gradually, people's consciousness grew. Then there began to be other issues, like a rise in the price of milk. And disappearances of campesinos in the north. You know, whenever a member of the National Guard wanted a piece of land they would just take it. They would find some excuse to drive off the families who lived there. And if the campesinos objected they were accused of being friends with the *guerrilleros* and were 'disappeared.' This happened to thousands of peasants. And Somoza was so cynical about this, he would just say that they had never existed. A campesino who lived far out in the mountains and who couldn't read or write wouldn't go to town and register a birth. And the Guard would do the same thing to get titles to land, because many peasants didn't have legal title to land they had lived on for generations. Amada Pineda, a campesina, became very famous in Nicaragua for her denunciations of this. She came to Managua, and we brought her to this barrio to speak.

"Then we held demonstrations for political prisoners. Many of these prisoners were from our barrio, in jail just because they had been in a demonstration or were suspected of being with the Front. And when the Front carried out an attack against the National Guard we explained what it was about. We even had what we called 'journalism of the catacombs'; when Somoza closed a lot of newspapers and radio stations, the journalists came to the church, María de los Angeles, and got out the news from there. In this way, people began to understand what was going on all over the country and why the Front was in the mountains. They could see that their problems and the campesinos' problems came from the same system."

By this time we are eating shrimp and rice and are into our second or third drink of rum. But Norma is holding up very well. In fact, she is in her element. She is happy to have an evening out, away from work and home, and enjoys discussion. At this point, I ask her about the position of women in Nicaragua, and how the revolution has affected the status of women. She pauses.

"You could say," she says, "that the revolution has given women an opportunity. Women are participating massively in the revolution, and this was so from the beginning. Twenty-five percent of the *guerrilleros* in the Front were women. There were women *comandantes,* such as Monica Baltodano, Laticia Herrera, and Dora María Téllez, who directed operations in the Rigoberto López Western Front, one of the most important in the war against Somoza. And Doris Tijerino is Managua's chief of police — Managua is the only city in the world that has a woman chief of police.

"Another important opening was the literacy campaign. I think more than half of the hundred thousand teachers who went to the countryside were women, most of them young women. Then there were health campaigns, vaccination campaigns, cleanup campaigns, *vigilancia,* the militia, the army — women have been massively involved. Women were needed and women responded.

"Activities like these do a lot to raise women's consciousness politically and ideologically, and to break down the old patterns in the home. Now children see a different kind of woman. When mothers are at a meeting, they can't be dedicated 100 percent to their children and the children learn to be more independent. They, too, learn more things. They are used to being overprotected, to having their meals and clothes and everything looked after. My son irons his own clothes.

"In my generation, a woman couldn't leave the house until she got married. Now kids join together and pick coffee in the *campo.* The revolution needs this work, so logically the mentality of young people is changing. Before, the mentality of young women was very limited; they just thought about getting married and having children. Now they think about studying, working, and life in other countries.

"This is a new reality for us, and it is important to communicate this because perhaps women in North America don't appreciate the situation of women in Latin America. They see that we still have a high level of machismo on the part of men here. And this is true. I have experienced this in the army. I have a perfect record in the army, an excellent record. Yet men have been promoted past me, and I have even been told that this is because I am a woman and men have problems being under the command of a woman." At this point, Norma's eyes are brimming with tears of anger. I take up my drink and offer it to hers for a toast: "Salud."

"But really," she goes on, "women in Nicaragua have progressed a lot — we are a new case, considering, for example, the great participation of women in the armed struggle and the army and the ministries. It was much higher than it was in Cuba, for instance. We have learned from them and surpassed them.

"There is a second reason for the importance of women in the revolution, and this is my personal opinion; it is not a scientific opinion, but my own observation. I think that the FSLN recovered the historic struggle of Sandino here in Nicaragua and that we women are discovering the historic importance of women in our country. Women were involved in Sandino's army. Those who first helped Sandino, who obtained the forty rifles for him that had been dumped in the ocean, were a group of prostitutes who lived on the Atlantic Coast. And many women fought alongside Sandino, such as Rafaela Reda and Conchita Díaz.

"The women of Nicaragua have been independent and strong throughout our history. There is a paradox here — a contradiction that arises from the great machismo that we suffer from in all of Latin America. Women are left alone in the house, and most women with children are supporting their children. There is a dialectic here that comes from the high level of machismo." She smiles at me. Norma and I trade in words like "dialectic" because she is also well versed in philosophy. "Men put the responsibility for the children onto the woman," she says. "And the woman," she adds, "is forced to develop herself as an independent person. This," Norma says, "is why you see so many women on the street selling, or with their little stores in the front of the house. And why you see only women working in the Oriental Market or the Commercial Center. They are forced to develop economic independence."

Another dialectical interaction occurs, in Norma's view, between the revolutionary government and those women who have been prepared mentally for a more challenging life outside the household: "The revolution builds more schools and needs more teachers. It builds health centers and needs more nurses and doctors. The revolution greatly increases the demand for all kinds of workers. And because of our strength and independence, we Nicaraguan women are ready to study and improve ourselves. We need this revolution, and we identify with it."

By now we are finished with our shrimp dinner, and the half bottle of rum is gone. My head is swimming a bit and I want coffee, but Norma is still wound up. Something I have learned about Nicaraguans is that they are very articulate, knowledgeable about their country, and they love to talk!

"There is another thing I have thought about," she says. "Again, this is just my personal opinion, but I believe it is true. Our revolution is a reflection of our character as Nicaraguans. It isn't possible to understand our revolution without appreciating our character as a people. We are very influenced by our mothers — men and women alike — much more than by our fathers. For this reason certain historians say we are a *pueblo mariana* [Marian people]. In terms of the Church, a people attached to the Virgin Mary.

"Our favorite festival in this country, the national festival that is celebrated with the most enthusiasm all over Nicaragua, is the Purísima, the festival of Mary, on the eighth of December. It is the festival I like most, because people go out into the streets and visit one another's houses and sing and knock on doors and call out: 'What is the cause of so much joy?' And the people in the house answer, 'The conception of the Virgin Mary!' And the people outside enter the house, and the owner offers something — a gift of fruit or fruit juice or candy. It is a very typical Nicaraguan gesture to offer fruit juice to someone who comes to your house. These things show the national character of Nicaragua. If you enter a house and don't take a glass of fruit juice, we feel bad because we show our hospitality that way."

"I am always willing to go along with that [custom]," I say.

"And the children of Nicaragua," she goes on, "grow up with a certain image — celebrated on a national level — of the loving mother. The child doesn't have an image of the father like that, even though we say 'Christ the loving one.' We are called *mariana* because the image of the mother is so strong with us."

Nicaragua a "Marian" society? This idea stirs up a lot of questions. The revolution here does have, in part anyway, a quality of "Love thy neighbor."

"We are a sensitive people, and this affects the process of the revolution," she says. "We are a generous people. We are frank. We are hospitable. You meet a Nicaraguan and they invite you into their house. And this has affected our revolution. We have forgiven many wrongs committed against us by the National Guard. Many of these Guardsmen, more than half of those who were captured, were sent home to their families, because many after all were very poor and ignorant and had no hope to succeed in the world except by joining the Guard. And we are the first revolution in history that permitted no executions, even of the worst criminals and torturers — we immediately abolished the death penalty. Our leaders have said many times, 'Implacable in the struggle, generous in victory.' The generosity and humanism of our revolution is very important, and it is transmitted to us by our mothers. That is what I think."

I am not sure whether I agree with Norma that Nicaragua is a Marian society, or even if I understand what that means, but I do think that many aspects of the revolution here have a nurturing quality. The image that comes to mind is of the revolution bending over to gather up those who have for so long been neglected, a hierarchical society bending to form a circle instead of a pyramid. Uniting what is divided, healing where there is pain. This tendency is very evident in Nicaragua, though it is still a tendency, and hardly as dominant as my image suggests. It needs to be put in the context of equally evident conflict, of old and new forms of privilege.

We begin to talk about the literacy campaign. I found it powerfully moving and amazing that a society should set as its first priority the task of reversing centuries of cruelty and neglect suffered by those who have been the lowest, the poorest, and the most backward. Such a society is truly confronting its historical bad conscience and the conditions that stand in the way of equality and democracy. By organizing those who have education and who agree to work selflessly for the poor, it brings face to face social groups who have been estranged for centuries. The literacy campaign was six months of healing work in which members of about half the families of the country were directly involved as teachers or students.

Also, the literacy campaign shows how revolution can and ought to be the work of the people themselves, using the resources they have in a process of change that doesn't create new forms of dependence or domination. The goals of social change were part of the process. Nor did the campaign cost a lot, for it was based on people teaching and helping one another. The schools and universities were closed for a semester in order to free students to go out to the countryside where the level of illiteracy was as high as 95 percent. Experts from all over the world were invited to help prepare manuals and to formulate methods that could be applied by volunteer teachers. Experts taught teachers who then taught others in a growing circle that finally included a hundred thousand volunteers. The majority of them lived and worked away from their homes in the countryside, without pay, with only their boots and lanterns and notebooks provided, their food and housing given by the communities where they worked.

Much has been written about this campaign (see Hirshon and Butler 1983), a campaign that received a UNESCO prize for its tremendous effort and success. Naturally, more was taught than just reading and writing: Nicaraguan history was taught, with an emphasis on Sandino and the struggle for independence from the United States; eight hundred thousand Bibles were distributed and used (among a total population of 3 million people); and teachers and students exchanged knowledge and lore about their lives. Because the teachers lived with the campesinos, they learned about a world they had never known. A campesino farmworker wrote a letter to the mother of one of the young student-teachers, saying: "Do you know that I'm not ignorant anymore? I know how to read now. Not perfectly, you understand, but I know how. And do you know, your son isn't ignorant anymore either. Now he knows how we live, what we eat, and how we work. And he knows the life of the mountains. Your son, señora, has learned to read from our book."

Of course, compared with what was needed for deep social change, the literacy campaign was brief and relatively superficial. The lack of resources and the war made it impossible to follow up with a massive program of adult education. But the campaign served to define the character of the revolution and to open the way for future development. It was a genuinely democratic experience, both in its methods and its goals. It made me very aware of our own tragedy in the United States — of our growing illiteracy, functional and otherwise — and it suggests how we could organize ourselves to solve problems.

Norma and I talk about how the idea of Nicaragua as a Marian society joins two traditions: mothering and religion. Religion (if we ignore how in class societies it is used to bond people by class and race, and to perpetuate privileges) is ideally a practice of nurturance. It attends to our need for a higher form of life — for peace, love, and encouragement in Being. Yet because its class function has predominated, the needs associated with religion are usually isolated from daily life, and religious nurturing takes a merely symbolic rather than a practical form. The progressive Christians Norma told me about had to move from the level of charity to the revolutionary level by challenging the economic and political system that perpetuates injustice and poverty. They made the leap from Church study groups to the Sandinista Front. That leap is logical, even from a religious point of view; the traditional belief that "spiritual" needs can be satisfied only in another world fails to recognize moral and spiritual progress in history. It artificially separates means and ends, this life from an assumed afterlife. It divides us into two: material beings with material concerns and ghostly spirits with "higher" concerns. In fact, the needs for peace, love, and encouragement in Being are as immediate, as here and now, as basic to life as the need for a roof over our heads. These "spiritual" needs become directed toward an afterlife when exploitation, poverty, and inequality are felt to be inevitable and irreducible in this life. Revolutionary political activity releases the human nurturing potential that is choked off by the oppression of women and by the class-functional religious institutions.

The mother's sphere is traditionally confined to the home. When the male child matures, he is expected to reject his need for a nurturing ambience. The traditional distinctions between private and public, domestic life and life "in the world," women's and men's work — these confine nurturing to the home. The consciousness that is formed and exercised in life's closest and most intense relationships, both for men and for women, naturally extends outward, and wishes for a nurturing world. Frustrated, it becomes an unhappy consciousness, dividing men and women in themselves and from one another.

Religion gives full recognition to our utopian needs. Religious people and revolutionaries yearn for a radically different mode of existence, for radically different relations among people, and for radically different priorities and values. Yet, most people who express these religious needs in worship accept an entirely different system for their work-life, as if radical change can be dreamed of only in symbolic rituals. Revolution releases these needs for satisfaction in *this* world: it would make exploitation as illegal as robbery, starvation as unacceptable as murder, and equality as normal as the right to the pursuit of happiness.

Over coffee, Norma and I talk about the difference between traditional religious thinking and revolutionary thinking. We agree that the difference is essentially whether humans themselves can create the better world. This is not a difference that can be conclusively resolved by argument or scientific proof; but reasons can be given. We believe in moral progress, and I think our belief, though not proven, is factually supported by history: by the abolition of old forms of domination such as serfdom and slavery; by the evolution of democratic societies; by the gradual growth worldwide of a belief in the dignity and value and basic right to life of all human beings. The happiness of being in Nicaragua is seeing and taking part in a new struggle for progress.

When Norma and I leave the restaurant, we walk to the edge of the porch and look off toward Momotombo, the perfectly cone-shaped volcano on the other side of Lake Managua. The moon is up. The world is resting in a soft light. We are pleasantly fed and slightly drunk from the rum that comes from the sugarcane that is grown in this black, volcanic earth. I think what a perfection there is in the world, simply in the taste of things. I laugh and say to Norma, "How nurtured we are, how well fed by this 'Marian society.'"

From here we can't see the brown froth at the edge of that lake, or smell the black water that pours into it from all over the city. And all we can see of the cardboard and tin shacks around this hill are the lights, some of them colored. We smell only woodsmoke. We hear only the distant sounds of music.

We get into Norma's Lada and drive back across Managua to the barrio.

The values Norma stressed as Marian are, roughly speaking, generosity, forgiveness, openness, love, community, and concern for life. These correspond with what feminist philosophers and writers in the United States have been calling "womanly" or "maternal" values as opposed to "male, patriarchal" values. And while some feminists see the feminine as retrograde because it is often used as an argument for keeping women in the house, others, though aware of that pitfall, believe there is a women's consciousness that it is important to recognize and cultivate.[2]

In her book *Maternal Thinking,* the philosopher Sara Ruddick (1989) defines a way of thinking that is in strong contrast to "patriarchal thinking" and that she thinks is more conducive to peaceful, cooperative living among humans and between humans and nature. Ruddick is careful to explain that she doesn't accept the idea — often found among conservatives — that men and women think differently because of their biological differences. She is well aware of how the theory of biological determinism has been used to legitimize the traditional division of labor. But Ruddick believes that women have learned a style of thinking formed through the practice and responsibility of mothering and passed on from mother to daughter. In Ruddick's view, maternal consciousness is developed through watching after others, observing and caring and encouraging — in mothering activity. Girls practice mothering in their play and in caring for younger siblings, and so learn skills and attitudes needed for later relations to their children and also to men. Boys, on the other hand, practice games in which competitiveness and aggressive behavior are important for success.

Here is a list of prototypical female and male styles of thinking such as Ruddick discusses. Each pair of terms should be seen as representing the extremes on a continuum. And while, to some extent, the average person combines these traits — is both preservative and acquisitive, both humble and proud — the point is that females cluster more on the left side, males more on the right:

Prototypically Female	Prototypically Male
Yielding	Aggressive
Cooperative	Individualistic
Realistic	Willful
Concrete and specific	Abstract and general
Accepting and caring	Judgmental and aloof
Personal and subjective	Impersonal and objective
Preservative	Acquisitive
Humble	Proud

I believe Ruddick is right to speak of a woman's form of consciousness, even though women's consciousness varies across groups — e.g., market women can be quite aggressive and acquisitive, though less so, perhaps, than men who work as salesmen in small businesses. And I believe it is right to stress environment, upbringing, and social expectations as the causes of these differences.

However, Ruddick sees a core tendency in the lives of women, one that she calls "attentive love," which can contribute to social change if it becomes a political force. She defines it as the capacity to attend to another human being with a caring, encouraging, and protective attitude. To give this conception a personal and specific definition, she turns to Simone Weil, who wrote:

> In the first legend of the Holy Grail, it is said that the Grail . . . belongs to the first comer who asks the guardian of the vessel, a king three-quarters paralyzed by the most painful wound, "What are you going through?"
> The love of our neighbor in all its fullness simply means being able to say: "What are you going through?" Only those capable of attention can do this. (Ruddick 1989, 121)

Weil's idea of "attention" adds to Ruddick's more mundane idea a political and spiritual implication. Child care requires attention to a specific human being's activities and needs. It is personal and (ideally) loving. When society allots this activity to mothers, it designates women as the primary bearers and examples of the Christian ideal: Love your neighbor.

Ruddick and others hope to find within the condition of women, ambiguous as it is, a new psychological basis for political action. Ruddick hopes that a political movement that incorporates "attentive love" by giving a leading role to women will be qualitatively superior to political movements of the past, which have continued patriarchal ways of thinking, oppressive to women, children, and nature.

"She is right," Norma said when I talked to her about this. "We women bring a new emphasis, a balance. And in Nicaragua many men have interiorized this way of thinking, more, I think, than in other Latin American countries. Our revolution is based on the philosophy of "Love your neighbor" — it really combines Marxism and Christianity-in-practice, and love of neighbor is stronger among women. Women are able to practice it more in their daily lives."

I agree that "Love your neighbor" seems to have become a part of the revolution here. But I don't believe that "Love your neighbor" or mothering, in themselves, are reliable bases of social change, for I see a connection between mothering and machismo.

The family basis of machismo is the practice of overindulging and privileging the male in relation to the female. (In the United States the word "sexist" is close to the meaning of "macho," and the same points apply.) Using very broad strokes, I would say that according to roles that are standard in a sexist society, the boy is served and he doesn't serve others; the girl serves. He is exempt from domestic chores; he plays with his friends outside while his sister mops the floors, peels the potatoes, and watches after his little brother. His clothes are washed and ironed by his mother and sister. He gets more education; it is assumed that he will undertake some kind of important work as a man, and he gets more attention for his accomplishments (and failings). In short, his upbringing tends to be expansive and encouraging, while the girl's is more limiting and confined. In my own family, for instance, my brother and I went to college and professional schools, and my sister, certainly as talented as we, became a secretary. Maybe the point is too obvious to belabor: in a smoothly running sexist society, the socializers of children must propagate patriarchal values. Yet in Nicaragua, as elsewhere, these socializers are primarily women. Hence the paradox: women have power over the socialization of men, yet men have power in society.

These reflections pose serious questions for Ruddick's optimism about maternal consciousness and the value of "attentive love." When a mother raises her male children to think of themselves as superior beings, to be served by women, she acts as a representative of patriarchal values and humiliates herself and oppresses her daughters. On the other hand, when Norma requires her son to wash and iron his own clothes, when she refuses to devote herself 100 percent to her children, she is educating him in the principle of equality. Her son will probably be more able to work cooperatively with others — especially with his wife — without feeling that his masculinity is being undermined.

Norma's new approach does not come from "attentive love." This is not to say that Norma is not an attentive and loving mother — she definitely is, and seems to be a very successful one. But her political commitment to fairness in distributing work, and a recognition of her own needs and those of Lisette, make her different. Attention and love must be combined with progressive political values, actively lived. Otherwise, attention and love can be a force that works against social justice.

Another aspect of Norma's experience is important to notice. She was able to actively practice her political values as a mother because the revolution needed her outside the home and gave her an opportunity for development in ways other than mothering. Without the revolution, even if she'd had the same political values on a personal level, she might have yielded to pressures to raise her son in the traditional way.

In revolutionary struggle, and after the revolution becomes institutionalized through a government, concrete changes in family life, child-rearing, and education occur that become powerful levers for change in values and personal identity. In nonrevolutionary societies it is much more difficult for adults to modify their consciousness and behavior. They may take part in discussion groups, self-help groups, or other organizations, but if changes in ideas are not joined with changed life activities they are likely to fall away when they come into conflict with an opposing tendency within the person or opposing demands in the world.

The Sandinista ideology of complete equality for women was achieved at a relatively high level during the revolutionary struggle, and after, *in contexts where women were needed for certain tasks.* This is the point Myrna and Norma make when they acknowledge the important role women play in the revolution. Yet Nicaraguan men, including many Sandinistas, continue to lord it over women they work with, and continue to expect women to serve them in the house, because they don't consider equality in these areas to be an immediate revolutionary necessity. For these men (and they are the large majority), in most domestic and interpersonal contexts, their childhood formation acts as a more powerful influence than their ideology and revolutionary experience thus far. This is not surprising, and it need not lead to pessimism, although it is — and should be — sobering to anyone who thinks deep change comes easily or quickly.

What this suggests to me is the fundamental importance of changes in actual practices on a societywide, institutional level and over generations. Societywide changes create a general, public consensus that can strongly influence individuals in the face of challenging situations. Institutionalized changes, such as affirmative-action hiring or the creation of day-care centers, establish new conditions and lead to long-term changes in experience; they help to overcome the inevitable vacillations and confusions in individual people's moods and intentions. And changes that influence growing children are much more profound than those which adults adopt voluntarily in their struggles for personal growth.

Of course, change that begins with the individual is also important. The revolution was made by men and women together — meeting, discussing, and voluntarily creating new ways in work and personal relationships. They were inspired to realize new forms of revolutionary struggle as a basis for new forms of society. Yet voluntary, individual change must be enacted daily over a long period of time and in all aspects of life if the new man and woman are to grow out of the revolutionary process. It must become *customary*.

The idea of the new man and woman has a deceptive simplicity. It suggests totality, when in fact change happens bit by bit; and it suggests immediacy, whereas contradictions in ourselves are more problematic than we can resolve in our short lives.

Our personal tendencies and decisions, and the establishment of social practices, reinforce each other; neither is sufficient alone. Nicaragua is a *pueblo mariana,* and this contributes importantly to the revolution. Yet established, revolutionary practice guided by political principles is needed, or the Marian tendencies in Nicaraguans will simply replicate oppressive traditions — as they have in the past.

5

Yalí Journal

I'm in Nicaragua for my third visit, for one short month, and I'm staying at the Salgados to adjust to the climate and do the footwork needed to get a press pass. This morning I am sitting in the hammock reading while Lolín tops off the Mazda's radiator with water. For the last couple of days an army vehicle has been parked nearby in the *andén*.

"Whose jeep is that?" I ask him.

"Avilio's," he says. "He's married to Patricia. He's back from the mountains for the holidays. Come here, I'll show you something."

We walk out the gate to the jeep. He points at what are obviously bullet holes in the front fender, and I see more in the passenger-side door. "He's been ambushed four times in this jeep. Different sections have been replaced and all the windows, several times." We begin to count bullet holes and, at twenty-five or so, Dolores calls us for breakfast.

"I would like to meet him."

"He can tell you a lot. He's in the war zone, and doesn't come down to Managua very often, maybe twice a year."

"Where is he?" I ask.

"Yalí," he says.

"I've been wanting to go to Yalí. Maybe he can help me visit a resettlement camp. I know there are several around Yalí."

"Talk to him," he says.

I don't see Avilio, but the next morning, Sunday, Lolín says, "You can meet Avilio today. They're coming to the beach with us." I gather that Lolín has been arranging things.

We load Lolín's car and the jeep with food and all the people they can hold and make a convoy to Pochomil, a resort park on the Pacific Coast. Leaving Managua on South Highway, we climb a smallish mountain range where it is suddenly cool and windy, then turn abruptly down toward the west and wind our way into the coastal flats. We pass sugar plantations that used to be owned by Somoza, and signs for Nicaragua's largest sugar refinery, also formerly Somoza's. We pass one of his old plantation houses along a smooth, abnormally perfect road of interlocked stone blocks (manufactured by Somoza's company and sold to Somoza's government and installed by Somoza's road-construction company). After the earthquake many streets in Managua were paved with these blocks.

"This road gave Somoza quick access to Managua from his favorite plantation house and the beach," Lolín tells me when I comment about it. I can see the point, as most of Nicaragua's roads are asphalt and potholed, and this road is like a hand-made object.

Avilio is a young, glamorous Sandinista fighter, or so I think under the influence of Lolín's admiring descriptions of him. About twenty-five, light-skinned, freckled, skinny, handsome like Frank Sinatra way back in *From Here to Eternity,* married to a very pretty young woman, father of two kids, one only three months old, he has fought with "the boys" since he was sixteen years old. The experience of living in the north and fighting for so long seems visibly ingrained in him. He doesn't talk much, just answers questions briefly with a Spanish that is hard for me to catch. The *compas* (short for *compañeros*), or army guys, speak a barely audible (to me), slurred Spanish, with all the s's and many word-endings dropped, the dialect of an inner group. He is wiry and small, and his body twists a little and he winces when he laughs.

Pochomil, a resort developed by the Sandinista government, is lined with thatch-covered beach huts, coconut palms, and restaurants. We play in the surf and swim and drink beer and eat our picnic food and buy fried fish and lie in hammocks. Avilio splashes in the water with the kids, runs into the waves with his wife in his arms, drinks lots of beer, and sleeps. Later, he says "No problem" when I tell him I would like to visit a resettlement camp in Yalí. I just need to contact the Ministry of the Interior office when I get to Jinotega, and he'll clear me with them. He'll show me around anytime I want to come!

The population of Nicaragua is concentrated in the western part, which is flatter and better for agriculture. Jinotega is the last town of any size in the northeastern mountains. Beyond it, there are only villages connected by dirt roads and mule paths until you reach Honduras, going north, or the Atlantic Coast, going east. Jinotega, San Rafael del Norte, and Yalí are Sandino territory. His wife, Blanca Aráuz, lived in San Rafael, and he fought many battles in the vicinity.

Lolín drives me out the northbound highway almost to the airport so that I can start hitching past the main feeder roads. My first ride is with three men who work at the slaughterhouse in Condega; I know them from the Pensión Baldovinas. They drop me where the road forks, in Sébaco, where after only five minutes a farm truck stops and a bunch of people jump on back. This will take me northeast to Matagalpa, further into the mountains. The road climbs into coffee country. It is harvesttime, the best, they say, in years. Along this road I see places where the beans are raked, a few inches deep on drying-floors the size of half a city block, and piles of bagged coffee are ready to be trucked out. I have read about the harvest in the paper every day — how much is picked, the great pickers, the volunteer brigades, and defense against the Contras. Coffee is the main resource for foreign exchange — for dollars to buy any kind of machinery, or spare part, or medicine, or bullet.

In Matagalpa I begin hitching again. It is twelve o'clock, and I hope to find Avilio this afternoon. Soon I am in the pickup truck of a government road inspector with about twenty other hitchhikers, farmers, soldiers, women with babies, grandmothers. We begin to climb the highest mountains in Nicaragua. The weather changes suddenly, becoming cold and windy. We can see halfway across the country, we can see the volcano Momotombo far to the southwest. The mountains are rough, green, and craggy, some with sheer rocks and trees, some with smooth meadows and cows on slopes steeper than I've ever seen cows on. Fields of corn, beans, and fruit trees. We pass through rainforest, and see fast streams cut into rock, and trees with mossy hair on their branches. Exposed trees, many pines, are twisted and bent by wind. Little farmhouses sit on mountainsides, with neat hedges and flowering bushes, gardens and groves of bananas. We pass many people on horses, tourist restaurants with spectacular views, road repair crews, a nursery called "Linda Vista" (Pretty View) with plastic-covered greenhouses, a long convoy of army trucks loaded with bags of coffee, young coffee-pickers lying on the bags asleep or talking or waving to us. A family sits by their house with bags and sacks, hitching and waiting for a bus.

Jinotega, nestled in mountains, has an old, colonial, well-to-do feeling. There is a lovely small park in front of the cathedral, and many large, colonial houses are hidden behind thick walls and heavy wooden doors. I stop at a Chinese restaurant and have a delicious bowl of soup. About twenty soldiers are eating quietly at a long table. An Englishman (or Irishman) nearby, heavy in body and nose, wearing a green jacket and red tie, black-and-white checked trousers, and black, highly polished boots, has just finished his meal and a half bottle of rum. I watch the brilliant-colored parrots in the garden, have a second beer, and congratulate myself—I am checked into a little hotel in Jinotega, it is only two in the afternoon, and I am ready to find Avilio.

At the Ministry of the Interior's office they tell me that Avilio is in Yalí, and that to go there I need permission from the office in Matagalpa. But, I say, Avilio said all I need is a press card, and I have one. No, she says, you need the permit. By then it is after three, and I begin to hitch back to Matagalpa. It is a mile walk to the road, and many others are trying. In a half hour a big troop lorry stops and we get on, helping the women and children and babies. Now it is very cold in the mountains, the wind is blowing furiously, and there are dark rainclouds. It doesn't rain, though, and the truck drops me at the ministry at a quarter to five. I find the right man and he gets on the phone, and Avilio was right—my press card is all that is necessary. But I can't leave Matagalpa now—it is getting dark and people don't travel this late in the north, and I am used up. My bag is in the hotel in Jinotega, and I am feeling tired and frustrated, but I take a few deep breaths and shift out of the "get somewhere fast" mode into the "be where you are" mode.

Following directions to a hotel, I pass a large cathedral, flanked by tall, dark cypresses. There are wide-open doors on the sides and the west end, and it is beautiful in the soft, fading light. People are coming in to pray now that work is over. I relax and am happy I can rest for the night. I sit by the door and read a little from the book I am carrying, poems by Azarias H. Pallais, a Nicaraguan priest and poet who lived earlier in this century. I watch the people and wonder what it is like to work in Matagalpa in a shoe store, say, or a government office, and walk to this cathedral in the quiet darkening afternoon to pray before walking home to the family and the evening meal. What is that young woman praying for, and who is she going home to, the one who kissed the foot of the statue of Mary and stayed for only a couple of minutes?

The nice hotel, with a small restaurant where people are eating with evident pleasure, is full—they direct me to the other side of town where there are some *pensiones*. I go to three and they, too, are full. They say there aren't any others, and it is completely dark.

Traveling in Nicaragua is always hard, I remind myself. But I am afraid of the night here, perhaps because I was mugged in Managua, though Nicaraguans are also afraid of the night. I have never seen such darkness—it is thick and blinding. They have a strange expression, which doesn't exist in

Puerto Rico, for example—*es muy noche* (it is very night). Closer to the equator, the earth is broader and heavier, and you feel it. It is dark earlier and longer, and it is in the darkest part of the earth's shadow. To add to this, Matagalpa's electricity is off!

The streets are empty and dark, but I find a little block with two neighborhood diners lit by kerosene lanterns. Two soldiers tell me there's a room for rent across the street and take me over. It's taken, but they say there's another around the corner. That's only available for four people, but they say there's one up the hill. We walk together up a steep dirt road, stepping over puddles and draining water. The woman says she has a room.

We wait in a long front room while she prepares it. A baby is sleeping at one end. A very old woman, a man, another woman, and two children are watching an old black-and-white TV. The soldiers want to know what I think about their country. Do many people agree with Reagan? Do I think he will invade? Have I been to other countries? One soldier has been to Bulgaria for a year and a half to learn welding. It was cold and there was snow, but he liked it. And he has been in Italy for two days, England for two days, and Moscow for a month.

I see the room. There is a small metal cot, an old lumpy mattress, and a sheet. I ask the woman for another sheet, a blanket, and a light. There is no light, she tells me. I need one, I say. At least a candle. There is no candle. Can I buy a candle? No, everything is closed. Can I go down the street to eat? Yes, but she locks her door at nine o'clock. The soldiers walk back with me to a diner. While I am eating they come back, and one gives me a piece of candle and a box of matches. They wish me good luck. I say, "I am lucky to have met you."

The *comedor* is clean and friendly, and I can read and take my time. The dinner they give me, the same for everyone, is beef roasted on a stick, salad, rice and beans, and a tortilla. I drink *fresco de cacao* (chocolate milk) and coffee, and have some delicious cookies, very light and thin, like sugar cookies.

I am liking Azarias H. Pallais. I like his name, which is so old-fashioned sounding, and his life takes me into an older Nicaragua. It seems appropriate to be reading him here in the lamp-lit diner, even though he lived in the flat, hot, coastal town of Corinto and was born in León. My book has two photographs of him: one is of a toothless old man, unshaven, with watery eyes and a bit of white hair; in the other, taken just after his ordination (1909), he looks as young and vigorous as a cadet (Pallais 1974). He went to Paris, Brussels, and Rome for his education as a priest. He loved Europe, Brussels especially, with its cobbled streets and mossy old buildings, and

Brussels became a mythic ideal for him. On his works, after his signature, he would write: Brussels, Flanders.

He returned to become a priest to the poor who lived as one of the poor. For him, as for many artists and intellectuals I have met in Nicaragua, culture implies a love of humanity and a passion for justice. He had affectations, but he was not an elitist. He wore his cassocks until they were threadbare and ragged. He had no possessions except a few books, he gave whatever he had to the poor, and his doors were always open for poor people to enter and spend the night. He was said to believe that locks and keys were inventions of the devil. He traveled third-class on the train between León and Managua, sitting in the open cars the market people took, and he would carry a Quaker Oats box and beg for his fare. He recited classical poetry in Greek or Latin or Spanish while he walked or rode horseback. He taught classes in literature, and he and his students would hold a banquet for the poor each year on July 19, the date that later became the anniversary of the revolution! He was a socialist, an ardent anti-imperialist, and an admirer of Sandino. About the biblical prophets, he said: "Read them. They are great teachers of socialism."

He wrote this poem in 1917 (I translate freely):

TO THE AMERICAN FLAG
Star-covered flag, that this day soils
the pure air of my country instead of
the star which guides our people
to the freedom-redeeming sun — tell me,
why are your stripes of bright red not
wrapped in chains?

(Pallais 1974, 15)

"The country is in rags," he wrote, "Christ is spit on, and the Night of the United States is coming!" About Benjamín Zeledón, who fought the Yankees in 1912, he said: "With Zeledón died the last of the Nicaraguans." And later he wrote about Sandino:

All pass away except the
implacable Sandino.
For his "little brothers"
God is indebted. Sandino
protests with both hands
raised high.

(Pallais 1986, 27)

The writing of Pallais is terse and full of energy. He hates verbosity and wordy people — writers, professors, politicians — and it is said of him that "the key to his poetry, his concept of the magical, is silence" (Pallais 1974, 8). He wrote: "If you know how to read, and have a soul, you will measure everything with the divine measure of silence."

> Silence!
> I want all talk suspended.
> Only twilight voices, lightly winged words
>   and gaze of thoughtful eyes
>
> (Pallais 1974, 7)

About himself:

> I am much discussed. I am very insincere.
> I am very suspect. The Guelfs and Ghibellines [i.e., proper, upper-
>   class families] say
> I am crazy. Thank you, very much!
> I want to live like Francis Jammes, in the beautiful streets
> of silence; very far from the proud Professors.
> My poems don't have manners
> and can't celebrate official farces
> or public places, or received opinions.
>
> (Pallais 1974, 11)

Late in life, Pallais was going to travel again, to visit his beloved Europe, but Somoza denied him funds he had been promised; he suspected Pallais would speak against him. Pallais was kept waiting several days at the National Palace, without being received, then finally was given news of the refusal: "The funds are not available." The humiliation and depression — he had hoped very much to see Brussels again — caused him to fall sick and he was taken to the hospital, where he died in 1954 at age sixty-nine. The people of his parish in Corinto were raising money for his trip, and were so indignant that Somoza feared an insurrection there. The National Guard took the body and brought it to León, where, against his wishes, he was buried with great ceremony in the cathedral. He had written:

> Bury me with the poor, my dear friend.
> I won't go with the others, at the end.
>
> (Pallais 1974, 19)

But the others took charge at the end. Ernesto Cardenal writes about Pallais's funeral:

At his burial many came from different parts of the country, all telling the same story: that Pallais had been their true father. That being orphans or very poor or abandoned, he had taken charge of them, had paid for their education, for some until they graduated from the university. This was not known by Pallais's family nor by his friends. And no one knew how he did it. (Pallais 1986, 23)

Back in my room with my candle, I feel safe and cozy. The woman brought a bottle of kerosene with a rag wick, so there is enough light to read by, and if I wake in the night I can have light. The walls are white-washed stones, and the ceiling is the underside of the old tile roof. The old stones and boards remind me of my country house in Massachusetts, and sleeping here is like being at my grandparents' farm: the strange, rough bed, the smell of old wood and mice and kerosene smoke, and a rooster very close, roused to crow by some disturbance outside.

The next day I'm off to Jinotega in the back of another fast army truck. It is rough and very cold, the wind like a gale. We stop at a roadside mountain spring. I drink and wash my face, and afterward feel frozen in the wind.

In Jinotega the woman in charge apologizes for the mistake. I can go to San Rafael del Norte, then Yalí, after she speaks to Avilio. I am impatient, and have to wait two hours more! I stand in the sun to keep warm and read the paper through. When she finally says okay, I run to the hotel for my bag and run to the market.

Right away a small bus loads up for San Rafael, where I'm supposed to find the local *comandante*. I sit next to a little boy who looks very sad, with a swollen jaw and a handkerchief wrapped around his head. In front of me a girl holds a large, pink, rabbit-shaped birthday cake on a flat tray, pushing people away who threaten to bump it. The bus fills and the driver begins a slow, gentle trip to San Rafael, over flat, rich-looking farmland. We pass a huge lake that feeds an electric generator; many white herons and the white birds that hang out with cattle; many fields of yellow and red flowers, and flowering trees and bushes.

San Rafael is on the north end of this high flatland, a sleepy outpost of a town. The Ministry of Culture has set up a museum about Sandino in an old Spanish-style house. Comandante Chi-Chi takes me there. The woman gives us oranges from the garden. For a tiny fee you can learn the history and see a lot of photographs — Sandino in the mountains with his little army; with Blanca in a dugout canoe on the Río Coco; in Mexico trying to raise money; with the prostitutes who found him rifles; and, Sandino's last photograph, in the presidential house on the day of his assassination.

In San Rafael the war with the Contras feels much closer. There are lots of soldiers and military vehicles, and the lovely white cathedral that sits high on a hill, with its long steps leading up, seems exposed, vulnerable, and like a mausoleum.

I try to talk to Comandante Chi-Chi about the war and its effects on people but, though he is friendly and helpful, he has a rather official manner. Besides being always busy and not very communicative, he seems to consciously treat me as someone who should be given a certain story. This is true of Avilio and other soldiers I speak to. Yet Chi-Chi introduces me to people and leaves me alone to speak to them, and I am free to talk to whomever I want.

I meet two ex-Contras who were kidnapped and recently escaped, Rafael Blandón Marena and Henrio Celedón. Rafael, twenty-three years old, is a carpenter who works with his father. He is neatly dressed, wears horn-rimmed glasses, and looks very bookish. He was kidnapped for over ten months. His family had heard nothing and assumed he was dead. He wrote them from Honduras, but they didn't receive the letter. This is his story.

Rafael was walking alone on a country road on his way to pick coffee. He was carrying some rice to bring to the pickers. About twenty Contras stopped him, and later they met up with a group of twenty more. They tied him to a tree and the next morning began a seventeen-day march to Honduras. There were twelve other kidnapped civilians. He walked with his hands tied, carrying a pack of ammunition. They pushed and pulled him, hit him in the back with the butts of their guns, and threatened him with a knife. They wanted to know why he wasn't in the army (there is a draft, but his eyes are bad). They marched, he said, day and night, without food or sleep.

In Honduras he stayed at an army camp for about a week, and was then taken by the Red Cross to a refugee camp. He asked for a new pair of glasses and was given them. He asked if he could work in carpentry, because of his eyes, and they let him. For six months he worked without pay in a factory that makes cigar boxes.

One morning the bus that took them to the factory was stopped by the Honduran police, and all the Nicaraguans were taken to an army base. They told them they had to go back to Nicaragua and fight. They couldn't stay because they weren't Honduran. They gave them six weeks of military training, and he went back to Nicaragua with a group of two hundred and fifty Contras. There were four officers who were former members of Somoza's National Guard. The officers didn't talk to the men, he says, or explain anything. They just said, "We will tell you what to do later." What were the Contras doing? They would capture peasants and demand information. If the peasants didn't give it, they would be shot.

The men talked among themselves, he tells me, and agreed they were going to run away when they got to Nicaragua. They wouldn't fight against their own people. They waited. Then there was a battle. It was completely chaotic. This was their chance, and they ran. All of them, he said. They were about twenty kilometers away from San Rafael.

The other boy, Henrio, had been in the same group. "How did you escape?" I ask him. "Like a snake," he says. In the confusion of the battle, they all ran in different directions. He threw away his rifle and hid in a hole. The battle was near his family's farm. "What if they saw this face?" he said, and laughed. We are talking on the street late in the afternoon in this mountain town. The wind is blowing hard and we are shivering.

I ask him about the attitude of the leaders. "Did they have a patriotic attitude, or what?" "How could they?" he says. "They rape women, capture peasants, and sabotage production. Destroy the crops and the houses. Could anyone with a patriotic attitude do those things?"

The next day, in Yalí, I talk to another boy who was kidnapped and escaped. He is only fifteen—Manuel Montenegra Peralte. They took him directly to a military camp, trained him for two weeks, and sent him down with a group of forty-five. I ask him why he deserted them. In the first place, he tells me, when he arrived in this area he tore his boots, and there was no way to fix them. It was cold, he was barefoot, and they couldn't rest. For eight days they ate nothing but raw, green bananas, and they were always threatening to kill anyone who lost his gun or ammunition. "I said to myself: 'I won't leave them unless we go near my home.' But one gets exhausted! Eight days hungry, even though we didn't fight!"

"I didn't see any help coming to the Contras," he says. "Not from other countries, and not from the civilian population. They go to ask for food from people in the country, and they say no. When they know Contras are coming, the men and boys run and hide. Only the women stay. And they say no, even if they offer to buy the food. 'We don't have any,' they say. It's not safe in the countryside now—especially for me because they have my name, and if they found me they'd kill me. But with the Sandinistas there's work everywhere, and all kinds of help. To be safe you need the army to be around. One should always look for ways to help and how to work for the revolution."

I wonder how much I am learning by talking to these army-produced witnesses against the Contras, yet they agree generally with the most reliable study of Contra practices I know, done by Reed Brody, in the fall of 1984. His study was checked and confirmed by Americas Watch, the *New York Times,* CBS Evening News, the International Human Rights Law Group, and the Washington Office on Latin America.

Brody summarized:

> This report is not intended to be exhaustive. . . . [B]y necessity [it] can cover only a small sampling. . . . [I]ncidents that have been investigated, however, reveal a distinct pattern, indicating that Contra activities often include:
> • Attacks on purely civilian targets resulting in the killing of unarmed men, women, children and the elderly;
> • Premeditated acts of brutality, including rape, beatings, mutilation and torture;
> • Individual and mass kidnappings of civilians, particularly in the Northern Atlantic Coast Region, for the purpose of forced recruitment into the Contra forces and the creation of a hostage refugee population in Honduras;
> • Assaults on economic and social targets;
> • Intimidation of civilians who participate or cooperate in government or community programs;
> • Kidnapping, intimidation, and even murder of religious leaders who support the government. (Brody 1985, 21–22)

Who are the Contras? Through years of visits to Nicaragua, and through reading, I gradually began to feel I understood. I have learned that like any group of humans, they aren't all the same.

The Sandinistas always described the Contras as members of the old National Guard and CIA mercenaries. This was partly true, but misleading. It is well documented that the CIA funded and organized the remnants of Somoza's old National Guard in order to create the Contras. A 1985 U.S. congressional report states that "46 of the 48 positions in the FDN [National Democratic Front] military leadership are held by ex–National Guardsmen. These include the Strategic Commander, the Regional Command Commander, all five members of the General Staff, four out of five Central Commanders, and all 30 Task Force Commanders" (Brody 1985, 19). An excellent study by Christopher Dickey, *With the Contras,* which details the process by which the Contras were organized and trained, and describes many of the key leaders, shows clearly how the Contras evolved out of the National Guard. But the Contra leadership was not simply a mercenary group. They were Nicaraguans who had enjoyed privilege and power within the Somoza regime, and they wanted to regain those benefits. Many of them were criminal members of a criminal system, but there were also "patriots of the right" who sincerely believed that the Sandinistas' rhetoric (and policies) concerning a mixed economy and protection of private property hid a secret agenda of "communist totalitarianism" (Dickey 1985, 76–77, 268–69).

Yet, for the most part, the fighting members of the Contras were not former Guardsmen or mercenaries (Brody 1985, 133). They were Nicaraguan campesinos, kidnapped or recruited, many of whom had complaints against the Sandinistas and harbored a counterrevolutionary ideology. They cannot be described as mercenaries for the simple reason that many of them were never paid. They were usually well supplied, and the officers were undoubtedly well paid — at least relative to Nicaraguan standards of life. And the men were promised they would be paid, would get land and so forth, after "The Victory." But it is just not plausible that those Contras who joined voluntarily were recruited primarily as mercenaries: the hardship and risks were all out of proportion to the potential reward.

I heard different stories about how much and how regularly Contras were paid. Some said they were not paid at all. One ex-Contra soldier — not an officer — said he and others received 150 U.S. dollars a month, and the officers 300 to 400 dollars a month and up. One officer told me he got 50 dollars a month; another said he got 200 dollars. They may all have been telling me the truth. Maybe the pay was erratic and varied from place to place. Yet some did say they fought for no pay because they believed in the cause — the Sandinistas had in one way or another incurred their hatred.

The Sandinista State Security officer in the zone of El Cúa–Bocay told me that the great majority of the Contras were kidnapped or tricked. "They gather groups of campesinos here in Nicaragua and take them to Honduras for training and indoctrination. Some of the campesinos are very ignorant and easy to manipulate. The majority who go to the Contras can't read or write. They tell them that the Sandinistas are communists and will take everything that they own. They say that communists kill off old people and send the children to Russia. Also, they threaten the campesinos: that if they run away or say they were kidnapped, they will kill them or their families. And they promise money, but they never give them anything — only the officers get paid. Only a minority, perhaps 15 percent, have joined because they are dissatisfied with the revolution for some reason, because of a mistake somebody made, or someone doing something wrong to them."

I later read a series of interviews with ex-Contras. A characteristic one was with Isidro García Díaz. He was among more than forty ex-Contras interviewed by a group working at the Center for International Studies, Managua, in 1990. An analysis and eight of the interviews were published in 1991 in Alejandro Bendana's *Una tragedia campesina: Testimonios de la Resistencia*. Isidro García said:

I lived on a farm of two hundred acres that my parents inherited from my grandparents. . . . [W]e had a few animals and twenty-five acres of coffee . . . and we also grew corn and beans, and we sold everything we produced for the good of the house, because even though one is poor one always struggles to have something.

We were never accused of being Somocistas, or confiscated, or pressured by the CDS (Sandinista Defense Committee). At the beginning the army and State Security were calm, but they changed when the war began. . . . [W]hen the Sandinistas began to see that they were forming the MILPAS [the first Contra groups], that people were leaving in groups of ten, or fifteen, and things were getting difficult, the situation changed. They began . . . [the draft] and then there was no peace or tranquility.

Then the Sandinistas began to take land from the proper owners. . . . It's true that up to 1981 my family never lost a single acre, but when they began to recruit day and night and wouldn't allow us to work in peace my father decided to sell the farm — this was about six months before I left to go to war. . . .

I had agreed with what I had heard from the guerrilla fighters of the Sandinistas [in the Somoza days], but they tricked the people, saying that they were going to share the land, that the campesinos were going to live more peacefully, and they didn't do any of this. Besides, we never really liked the idea — there was no need to give us land because even though we didn't have much, it was enough to work.

When the Sandinistas triumphed, they offered health centers and cooperatives, but we never saw these people. In my zone I never saw a positive aspect of the revolution because I never had anything to do with them. I left my house to go to work, and left my work to go home. . . . In 1981 I was able to connect with some Contra leaders who were cousins of mine. . . . I began to collaborate as a messenger and arms carrier. . . . After that I underwent training for two months in Nicaragua, at Prinzapolka, then four months in Honduras. . . .

In the mountains, the people didn't like the Sandinistas . . . and no one was going to submit themselves to take up a gun against their will [i.e., to be drafted]. If Nicaraguans go to war, we do it because we want to fight for democracy and not because of laziness. I went with the Resistance (the Contras) because I didn't want to be exploited by a regime like the Sandinistas, and so my two brothers and I decided to go to the mountains. Nobody made us, we went of our own accord.

The Sandinistas went around searching everyone. For example, if there was just a rumor that someone was with the Contras, that was enough to kill that person, as in the case of Arístides Gonzáles, who was killed by the Sandinistas even though he was a delegate of the Word in a church we had in La Ulo. The Sandinistas did a lot of bad shit. (Bendana 1991, 82)

Isidro García's interview is confirmed by many sources, including the Sandinistas, who say that in the early years of the revolution the Sandinistas made "mistakes" in dealing with the campesinos. Already in 1980 small bands of Contras were coming down from Honduras to attack workers in government projects. Nicaraguan and Cuban literacy teachers, government workers, and State Security or army personnel were assassinated in isolated actions (Dickey 1985, 94–97). The response of the Sandinista security forces created resentment and fear among those who were viewed as possible collaborators—especially the small or middle landholders who were already skeptical or hostile to the revolution.

It is easy to imagine how the most innocent encounters could lead to open conflict. A Sandinista patrol arrives at an isolated farm. They question suspiciously the suspicious campesino who, they know, has a cousin with the Contras. They get silent stares and a string of no's in response. The Sandinista officer, a twenty-one-year-old urban revolutionary, gives the campesino a little speech on the importance of the revolution and of defending it against "Somocistas." He addresses the man as *compañero*. He ends by reminding him that campesinos who cooperate with the counterrevolution will have their land confiscated and go to jail. For emphasis, he speaks in a threatening voice. The patrol drives away—leaving behind a friend of the Contras. They even sense it themselves.

After my interviews in San Rafael I walk with my bag to the edge of town, where the road to Yalí begins and where Chi-Chi told me to wait for a ride. It is a blustery afternoon. Beside me is a field of grass where cattle are grazing by a broken-down fence. A narrow, rutted dirt road leads into a pine forest. A couple of soldiers who control the road are also waiting. They ask me for cigarettes. We don't talk. I feel tired and dazed. Daylight is going, and we are worried whether the vehicle will come. Then it drives up fast, and the soldiers on board tell us to hurry and get on. It is a blue Toyota pickup loaded with bicycles from the States and a few soldiers. There is room for me to perch on the spare tire while they drive like crazy to Yalí on a high, up-and-down, winding dirt road through spectacular mountain country. Cold air, wind, tall pine trees, rocks, fast streams, meadows, little farmhouses — it feels like familiar country to me, but rougher, craggier, and wilder than the mountains of Massachusetts or Vermont.

San Rafael seems like an outpost, but Yalí feels like an island in an ocean of green mountains. There are no paved roads. There are no private telephones (you phone at the Telcor office), and only a few private vehicles. The farmers ride horses back and forth to their farms, and use oxen or mules to plow. There is no hotel or bar, no restaurant or movie house. There is a general store, and the family that owns it also rents rooms in the back of their old, barnlike house. Up the street a woman cooks meals for visitors. The population is about two thousand.

The truck stops by the central square in front of a low building of town-government offices. They unload the bicycles, and soldiers and kids begin to ride. The hills are touched by clouds broken by blue sky. The light is soft, the shadows long, and the old painted walls and tile roofs of the buildings glow with color. The hills are dark green and shadowy.

I walk around taking color photographs. The central square is being rebuilt. There are newly poured concrete park benches and sidewalks and, in the center, a platform where a group of sculptures will be placed. A little building for a community center is going up on one side, and on the other is the shell and steeple of a new church. The government provides the materials for the park, but the rest is paid for by the people and their labor — some paid, some voluntary. It is surprising to see these projects going forward here.

Yalí is very much in the war zone because of its sparse population amid the thick mountain country. It cannot be adequately defended. On the nearby hills I see tents where soldiers are camped. I noticed a camp on the road from San Rafael. It isn't hard for the Contras to penetrate, and there are frequent ambushes on the roads. It is comforting to see the defenses and the barracks in town with a few dozen soldiers.

Avilio comes out of a meeting to greet me and show me where to stay. I meet William, a young soldier who will help me in the morning. I am not used to such official attention, but glad to have it here.

William takes me to the store where they rent rooms. Men and children stand around in front, by a row of tied-up horses. Behind the store I pass through a hall, my head down because of the low ceiling. A lot of merchandise is stored in the back rooms, and various family members are keeping books and sorting things in one part and cooking and eating in another. An old deaf grandmother is sitting in a rocker. A very handsome young man plays guitar with some friends.

Up some stairs is a hall with a few rooms. Mine has a metal cot and old bedframes leaning against the wall, and nothing else. It is thick with dust, like a country barn. Down the hall from me is a sculptor from Managua, Aparicio Artola, who is making the statues for the square. We are the only guests. Up the road is Idiliana's house, where we eat. Farther up is the house of a family who have a small farm out of town. The father asks me up for coffee when he sees me sitting on Idiliana's steps after a meal. Above his house is a very steep hill where kids fly their kites next to an army tent. The kites are very small—about ten inches square. It is moving to see them playing there, the soldiers watching. By the path at the foot of this hill is a sign saying, "Danger! No Passing!"

Early the next morning I take a tour arranged by Avilio. William introduces me to Rosa Emilia Blandón, who takes me around to meet some of the townswomen—those who have lost sons or husbands to the Contras. It is a sad tour of this pretty country town. The dirt streets lead four or five blocks in any direction from the central square, past small wood-frame houses with gardens and yards full of chickens and pigs and flowering trees and bushes. The women we meet are busy cooking or sweeping or sewing. They still make most of their clothes here, and many women sew to make a little extra money. And they are taking care of their kids. They talk to me with children on their lap. I can go from house to house without seeing any men.

I talk with Catalina Romero, who seems about fifty. She has five children between twelve and twenty-six years old. Her husband was killed by the Contras a year ago. He worked for UNAG (Unión Nacional de Agricultura), the Sandinista organization for promoting cooperative farming.

"We have always worked for the liberation of Nicaragua," she tells me. "In UNAG he was struggling to help the farmers live better, with any problems they had, like needing water, or more land. If they needed houses, or if there were health problems, he helped them.

"He was driving to Las Colinas," she says, "he and another *compañero*. They had been buying baskets for a brigade of coffee-pickers. The Guardia [she means the Contras, the descendants of the old National Guard] met them on the road and killed them both, and burned their truck. It was terrible. They cut out the heart and the eyes and the genitals of the other one—the poor man." She has begun to cry and she cries for the rest of our short interview. She talks in short, disconnected sentences.

"They are so cruel, more cruel than I want to know or remember . . . You know, we have to live . . . You know, we have faith in God that you are going to help us . . . Our life is sad . . . One has a husband, and then one is in the street . . . One is poor and stays poor, with nothing, and one's children are dead.

"It is true that I am taken care of — the government has given me a house and some land to plant. I work at home, and with AMNLAE and the CDS. But life is sad. Everything the poor people do or begin to do — people who haven't hurt anybody — is destroyed by them. They kill them and it comes to nothing . . . our faith and hope is in you and your people . . . that you will help us. Because our life is very sad."

She is a small, dark-haired woman, wearing a housedress and a sweater at eight o'clock on this cool morning. She dries her eyes to pose for a photograph; then she calls to her son, sitting nearby, so she can have a picture of him also.

"Es triste la vida de nosotros," she repeated. These words mean "Our life is sad," but in English the words are too flat, too matter-of-fact. It was to say this, to make this simple statement, that she had gone to the trouble to talk to me about something she found so painful.

I am seen as practically an official emissary from the United States; as someone who may communicate to the opposition, which will change government policy, it is hoped. In the Nicaraguan news media and in the official speeches of leaders such as Daniel Ortega, the point is frequently made — based on U.S. polls — that most people in the United States don't support the Reagan-Bush policy against Nicaragua, that the U.S. Congress is divided over this policy, and that despite establishment-media support for Reagan's claims that the Contras are "freedom fighters" trying to "restore democracy" in Nicaragua, there is widespread public skepticism. Facing the military, economic, and diplomatic power of the United States, most Sandinistas at this time believe that the war, the state of emergency, and the stagnation of the economy will continue until the people of the United States defeat the Reagan-Bush policy. So every North American who visits this country is treated with great seriousness and respect and given an importance that I only wish was justified.

I talk to one woman, then walk along the dirt street past the little houses to talk to another. It is a bright, sunny day, the air sparkling clear as it can be only in a mountain town. When the road climbs a hill I can see the whole town, the mountains around, and flowering trees above the tile roofs. A man on a horse passes by, in from the *campo*, leading a procession of donkeys with white bags of coffee tied to their backs.

I talk to Cándida Rosa Aguilar, whose four grandchildren are orphans.

Their mother, who was thirty years old, was also ambushed on the road to Las Colinas. She was with a group of nine in a pickup truck, riding to the farm cooperative to pick coffee as volunteer workers. All were killed. Many were mutilated; the Contras kill horribly, to terrify the people. People had their eyes and hearts cut out, and tongues and breasts and genitals cut off. They were shot and stabbed over and over.

The mother had been a teacher in the adult education program. Her husband had been killed in combat by the Contras, about a year before. The four children — Marta Lizette, eight, Nuvia Salvadora, seven, María Luisa, six, and Arlen Urana, four — with their large, dark eyes and shy smiles, seem to me the most beautiful children I have ever seen. The government is building the grandmother a little house. She lives on a pension, and because she has a bad hip and can hardly walk, she gets a lot of help from other women in the town.

I meet Marta Mendoza, twenty-five years old, the mother of a one-year-old baby and a daughter, six. She is a schoolteacher, and the primary school where she works is directly across the street from her house. She is small and shy. Her husband was one of the nine ambushed on the way to Las Colinas. He was twenty-seven. His picture is on the wall behind her chair: a good-looking man with thick, wavy hair, strong dark eyes, and a thin mustache. He looks very young in the picture — he could be a high-school senior. His name is William Rivera. He was director of the regional agrarian reform program and a member of the FSLN, and he had fought with the Front against Somoza. He was wounded near the Honduran border, just before the FSLN triumph, and in 1979 he went to Cuba for six months for surgery.

Every woman I talk with is very grave and sad. I become so upset I can hardly ask questions. Marta Mendoza sits stiffly as she talks in a strong, controlled voice, although her eyes are full of tears. There are long silences. I can't think of anything to say. What am I supposed to ask her? How it feels to be alone with your children, your young husband having been mutilated and killed a few kilometers from your home? How it was, having your baby one month after his death? It seems cruel to ask her to talk, to give details, to make the effort.

I meet Isidra Mesa, fifty-two years old, whose husband, Doroteo Tinocua, also fifty-two, was ambushed last year. It took me a moment to realize that it was he who had been with Catalina Romero's husband when the two were bringing baskets to Las Colinas for the coffee-pickers, that he was the man Catalina said had been mutilated. Isidra is very shy, but agrees to talk in

Cándida Rosa Aguilar and her grandchildren

a back bedroom, away from the others in the house. Only her granddaugh-ter, Concepción, comes in, and sits in her lap as we talk.

Her husband, too, worked for UNAG, promoting cooperative farming. "He worked to get the campesinos whatever they needed — tools, land, medicine — so they could farm in peace." There are shortages, and every-thing is expensive. The morale of the people in Yalí is good, she tells me. The problem is, this is a country town, and the people can't work in the country without being attacked by the contra.

This is her house, and she receives a small pension from the govern-ment — 10,000 córdobas a month, or about one-third of the average teach-er's salary in Managua. Also she gets basic foods at reduced prices. She lives here with her daughter and grandchildren. Her daughter's husband also was killed by the Contras. He was one of the nine ambushed on their way to pick coffee last year.

When she tells me this, and I realize that in this house two husbands were lost last year, only a month apart, both suffering horrible deaths, I feel I can't do this any longer. Isidra's daughter is in the kitchen working. I can hear water running and movement. What is she thinking, I wonder. I

Marta Mendoza and her children

should ask to talk with her also, but I can't. I want to leave. Isidra is kind and generous to me. Her voice is very soft and quiet, like a river. But she doesn't really want to talk. She answers my questions briefly, and is so shy I hesitate to ask more. I am unprepared for this experience. I feel like an intruder. She is pleased that I take a picture of her with her granddaughter on her lap.

I sit on a bench in the central square for a while, watching the slow noontime activity of the town. A woman sells food on the sidewalk under a tree, boiled yucca and fried pigskins and cabbage salad served on a banana leaf. Across the street, rice is being unloaded from a large truck. Farmers are putting the bags on their horses and riding off to the country. The blue army pickup truck drives past loaded with soldiers. Two boys shovel dirt in the park, spreading it evenly from piles it has been dumped in. Only one has a decent shovel; the other boy, who is using a narrow piece of wood, begins to toss the dirt aimlessly, then onto the other boy. They begin to have a dirt fight.

I walk up to Idiliana's for lunch. We have almost the same thing for every meal — beans, rice, tortilla, a piece of salty cheese, cabbage salad with tomato. I alternate between feeling very tired of it and pleased to be eating good, healthy food. I think about what Wittgenstein said when he was visiting the States and his host asked what he liked to eat. "Anything," he said, "so long as it's always the same."

At lunch I meet the sculptor Aparicio Artola. I have seen a large casting lying on its side by the park. He says he has a studio set up in a building behind the municipal offices, and he invites me to come by. He would like me to take pictures and send them to him at the university in Managua, where he teaches. He is here on his vacation — in Nicaragua, the long school vacation is from January through March — the coffee-picking season. I will get to know his work better in Managua — he always takes part in the many group shows held there. He is primarily a painter, in a style very like certain German Expressionists: strong, unmixed colors, broad strokes, figures painted with childlike freedom, women and men in states of emotional agony. Aparicio is a real artist. Here in Yalí I find him hard to talk to: a silent, broad, strong, young man, almost suspicious. But I find out later from friends of his that he is "just that way," quiet, introverted, standing apart from groups and other artists, stewing inside, and creating really good, authentic art.

At Idiliana's I meet another craftsman, Luis Rivera, a furnituremaker, who in contrast is friendly and easy to talk to. He becomes my best friend in Yalí, and invites me to stay with him next time I visit. I hang out in his shop, a long shed by a little stream under a huge, spreading tree, along with his child and his ladyfriend, and we talk about carpentry. I try to learn about the different kinds of wood he uses while he works on a bed for someone in town. He does his sawing and sanding by hand. His only power tool is a wood lathe driven with a big belt. With this he makes decorative spool shapes for the legs of his furniture. He wants me to send him a part he needs to repair his electric circular saw, and a manual for carpentry, so he can learn new techniques.

Avilio has promised to arrange a visit to the resettlement cooperative, Las Colinas, and I keep checking with his office to find out about that, but I haven't heard from him. I walk over to the church and ask to see the priest. After a short wait, I'm invited in. He is polite but not friendly, older and conservative-seeming — Father Miguel Angel Vásquez. He has been the priest for the region of Yalí for thirteen years.

I ask him to describe conditions here, and the morale of the people. He answers:

> In the first place, there was a very great rise in the morale of the people after the triumph of the revolution. However, since the beginning of the counterrevolution, about 1981, there have been problems. Groups formed in favor, and others against, and began a struggle, we could say ideological, with political conse-quences, which has created a very disturbing situation in the entire northern re-gion. The government has worked hard and demonstrated much sincerity, but the other side scorns it and puts the government in a very difficult situation with its at-tacks, all kinds of terror, and the fear it creates in the people.
>
> No one knows where this situation is heading. While they talk a lot about peace and order, on the other hand we hear of more aid being given to the counter-revolution. Many want to work, but can't energize themselves. Many place their confidence in the government, but the insecurity and uncertainty of the situation creates, one could say, a paralysis. There are hopes, but no one knows when this is going to stop. And that is the situation we are in and will stay in until God disposes otherwise.
>
> As for social problems, we have many needs here in housing, health, and educa-tion, because the north is a very large sector, and almost all the schools have had to be closed. Many people have had to emigrate, many have been evacuated, and the town here is overcrowded. There is very little food for so many. We have a lot of sickness, and the people crowd in long lines seeking medicines, and there are none. There is only one doctor for the entire population.

I spend my time talking to as many people as I can — among them, a young woman who is the director of the CDS for the town; and Marta Mendoza's mother, who is also a schoolteacher, and very active in the wom-en's organizations. I visit a Sandinista-founded orphanage in a new building, with maybe twenty children and several women cooking food in big pots. I meet Pablo Moncada and Norma Valenzuela, who have twelve children and have lost two sons to the Contras in combat. A third, a beautiful boy with dark eyes and dark, wavy hair sits in a wheelchair in their kitchen, paralyzed from the waist down. They are hoping he can go to Cuba for an operation. I walk up and down the streets taking pictures and looking into people's houses. At night I invite myself into someone's living room to join a family and neighbors in Yalí's evening entertainment orgy — the *novella* on TV. It comes from Brazil and is something like *Dallas* — the loves and intrigues of the rich. I am tired and can't understand much of the dubbed Spanish that doesn't match the lip movements of the actors. They give me a refresco and I end up flirting with a pretty neighbor.

At nine o'clock Yalí is closed for the night. The brightest lights are the stars. As I start to walk back in the dark, I hear a whistle. It is Avilio, up the hill, standing in front of his office. I have the feeling he always knows where I'm at. If it is safe I can go to Las Colinas tomorrow, he says. He asks me how my day has been and if it is worth my trouble, coming here.

In my room, amid the dust and the stacked metal bedframes, I light a candle, take out a book, and begin to feel afraid. At dinner, when I told Luis, my carpenter friend, that I would be going to Las Colinas, he looked at me gravely. "The road is dangerous," he said. "Have there been ambushes lately?" I asked. "Not for a month or so," he replied. "How often are there ambushes?" I asked. "About every month," he said.

It is like playing Russian roulette, I think. If the cylinder stops at a certain point, I will die tomorrow. It's stupid to take chances like that. But Nicaraguans use this road every day. The Contras don't kill everybody — only soldiers, or government workers, or people they have listed as active in the revolution. Others they capture, or threaten, or leave alone. They wouldn't want to kill me, probably, a U.S. citizen, but maybe they would, as a message to people coming here: "It is dangerous, stay away, we don't want the likes of you." Anyway, I'll be traveling with military. If they ambush them tomorrow, I'll be in the middle of it. It *is* dangerous.

Is it stupid to be doing this? No, it is important to go, just like it is important for the government worker or the soldier. Suppose no one went: the Contras will have accomplished exactly what they wanted.

If it is safety I want, I should have stayed home, I tell myself. The Nicaraguans are trying to make a beautiful revolution here, in the front yard of the imperialist power. It isn't safe, but it may be the most important event of this historical moment.

I am not drawn to thrills or personal danger. But there is a place beneath politics and talk that I feel I must touch in order to know this people and their revolution. Just to see its peaceful side is not enough. Nicaraguans live a conflict carried to its uttermost. Their war is not a distant image, a threat, a strategic game, but enters their house like an ugly, screaming guest and lives there, in their kitchen and bedroom, brutally imposing its insane version of life. It flies into their hearts like a prehistoric bird driven mad by hunger.

The next night, after the trip to Las Colinas, I wrote in my journal: "I was literally afraid I was going to die — to be writing seems unexpected, like a gift."

We leave town in the blue Toyota pickup, me and about nine soldiers. We stop outside town on top of a hill. Someone opens a small jar of jam, and they share the jam and some rolls. There is a large view of the hills around. We talk about the States. Is it hard to get work there? How much do people earn? I tell them about the high wages; then about how much things cost, to balance it out. It is early afternoon, the safest time I figure, but I ask whether we are the first to go on this road today. They say no, there have been others. Everyone seems a little nervous. They fix their ammunition belts and ready their AK-47s. A thirteen-year-old, who they say is their mascot, pulls a hand grenade from his vest and checks it. They are more cautious and battle-ready than I was expecting. I ask if they expect to see Contras. They say no, but there are lots in the area. This vehicle was ambushed three weeks ago.

Finally, I see the reason we are waiting. A jeep comes with five or six others; it has the officer in charge and people who are more experienced-looking. Except for one guy sitting up front, our truck is full of kids — thirteen to nineteen years old.

We stay a certain distance behind the jeep. We go in spurts — sometimes very fast, sometimes slow for bumps or to cross streams, or with caution. We stop to wait for a soldier to run down a hill to meet us. Three soldiers walking toward us climb in. We stop and unload some bags of rice, cornmeal, and boots. Some soldiers get out. We slow down, and I see a soldier on a hill waving to us. Then the men in the jeep call back to us. They are pointing at something. On the slope by the road a huge snake, about ten feet long and thick as a man's arm, is slithering awkwardly, flopping, up the slope away from the road.

Later the jeep stops and everyone but the driver gets out; they walk ahead. The guys in the truck get out and walk. This is a thick, bushy stretch, and you can't see more than a couple of feet in. I stay in the truck and think, "Well, if they are here, maybe I'll get a picture." I take a picture of the guys walking. Everyone gets back in a few hundred yards up the road.

The road goes up and down small hills. There are many little farms and houses and, strangely, I am surprised to see so much normal-looking life. Kids and women and men watch us with grave faces as we pass. A few times, but not often, someone waves or smiles.

They show me the site of the most recent ambush. The Contras were on both sides of the road, where there are thick bushes, high on the left side, low on the right, only fifty yards past a little house. Far below are big, open meadows. A seventeen-year-old, sitting high in the back corner of our truck, and the thirteen-year-old next to him were in the truck at the time. They point, and laugh, and the thirteen-year-old makes firing motions with his AK-47, like a kid playing war.

I am glad there is a jeep in front of us. The guys in the truck don't watch carefully. They talk, look vacantly at their feet, or at the distant countryside. Only sometimes do they seem to be alert. I am the only one really watching.

On the road to Las Colinas

For three weeks now, they've made this trip every day without an ambush. Maybe they're getting lax. I want to tell them, "Hey, pay attention, you're working!"

Las Colinas looks fragile and makeshift. It consists of some rows of small wooden huts with zinc roofing, some without siding but covered with black plastic, and one unoccupied row of just roofing on tall wooden poles. I don't see gardens — only grass and a few trees around the huts. It looks more like a refugee camp than like the farming cooperative I had expected; and in fact, that's what it is.

Resettlement camps like Las Colinas are built because of the military necessity of bringing together the scattered campesinos in the mountain country. Santo Eladio, a political organizer in Las Colinas, told me: "The Contras can force the peasants to give them food and information, such as where we are and where we can be attacked, but if the people are here [the Contras] don't have that social base. It weakens and demoralizes them. As a result, the Contras attack the cooperatives."

The best hope of the government is that the peasants will experience the benefits of community life and cooperative production, and will want to maintain the communities when the need is past. The minimal hope is that the camps will be productive and will lessen the cost of supporting the displaced peasants during the counterrevolution. In Las Colinas, and most other resettlement camps, neither of these hopes is being realized. This is hardly surprising — wartime conditions are not conducive to making radical changes in one's mode of life. It is also probable, though I have no evidence of this, that some of the people in Las Colinas would have preferred staying on their own land, even if it meant cooperating with the Contras. The army may have coerced some of them into coming here.

The effect of the war on the cooperative effort is dramatically shown in Brody's *Contra Terror in Nicaragua*. An attack on Las Colinas itself, in April 1984, two years before my first visit, is documented there. Those interviewed estimated that four hundred Contras surrounded the cooperative with mortars, grenades, machine guns, and rifles:

> The attackers soon had the cooperative encircled, and after two hours, they sent in one company to take it by assault. As the cooperative's defenders retreated, three of them were killed, but the others were able to make their way out, as were most of those in the bomb shelter.
>
> When the army arrived, at about 9:00 A.M. and the people returned to the cooperative:
>
> "They [the Contras] had already destroyed all that was the cooperative: a coffee

drying machine, the two dormitories for the coffee cutters, the electricity generators, seven cows, the plant and the food warehouse.

"There was one boy, about 15 years old, who was retarded and suffered from
epilepsy. We had left him in the bomb shelter. When we returned . . . we saw . . .
that they had cut his throat, cut open his stomach, and left his intestines hanging
out on the ground like a string.

"They did the same to Juan Corrales who had already died from a bullet in the
fighting. They opened him up and took out his intestines and cut off his testicles."
(Brody 1985, 71)

It was Doroteo Tinoco, the husband of Isidra Mesa, who had given this
affidavit, and who was killed and mutilated on the road to Las Colinas a
year later.

Through the cooperative the government provides housing, food, land
for cultivation, and social services; they are building a little school, and
expect classes for children to begin in a few months. (There is no adult
education program.) A *comedor infantil* provides meals for seventy children
each day, and a nursing team visits weekly.

Yet none of this attention can erase the fact that the people are essentially
refugees. "The great problem," Eladio told me, "is organizing the people to
work and build a [new] community. Some come here, take a house for a
while, and then leave — for example, for Jinotega or Managua. [The war has
swollen Managua to such an extent that it is now home to one-third of
Nicaragua's population.] Many others are just waiting to return to their
farms in the countryside, and don't work like they would at home."

The officer in charge of the patrol I am riding with tells me we have to
leave by four o'clock, and so I am able to talk to only a few people. I settle
down with an older couple, and a few others gather around. I remember
seeing the man on the bus from Jinotega, a beautiful old man of seventy-six
years. "They killed my son and my nephew," he said, "so the army told us to
come here."

They are from La Rica, and in that whole area there were maybe thirty
families and more than eight hundred Contras. So all the people of Rica
Arriba, Rica Abajo, Chamato, Santa Elena, Prisionero, and La Constancia
have moved away. "All but one family, and God help them," his wife said.

"We have our own farm there," he said, "of twenty-five *manzanas* [sixty-
two acres]. Part of it he inherited from his father, and he bought the rest
from the inheritance of his brother. He was born on that land. "We have
faith that soon this will be settled, and we can go back to our own land," he
said. "We left everything," she said, "the house and tools and crops — and

brought only what we could carry . . . some clothes and some food. We had all kinds of fruit trees, and grew corn and beans and coffee."

This old man says he knew Sandino. He met Sandino when he was thirteen years old. More: Blanca Aráuz is his cousin!

"Tell me about Sandino," I said.

"The basic policy Sandino fought for," he said, "was called 'transaction'— that the Liberals and the Conservatives could settle their disputes between themselves. Because he was Nicaraguan, and they were Nicaraguan.

"The Conservatives were in power, and they were the guilty ones. They would come to a house with their rifles. If the family was sitting at the table eating they would say, 'Who is in charge here?' And no one would take a bite (proving *they* were in charge). And they would carry the food away, leaving the family hungry.

The old man at Las Colinas

"This is why we said . . ." and now the old man recites a long, war poem in rhyming couplets. I give a sample, without the rhyme:

> I am with the defenders who fight
> for the second independence
> with blood, and not with flowers.
> The Conservatives have no conscience
> Because they betray their country.
> In the century of light
> the fighting at Las Cruces
> Telponeca and Ocotal
> is just like at Santa Clara
> and Feroz and Cara Cara:
> We defeat the invader.

When he finishes we all laugh and applaud the old man's memory.

"That is the reason the army fought with such high morale," he said. "Tell me if that isn't true."

The soldiers have been saying we have to leave. I am disappointed — I had expected more time. It is always this way when I do something under the sponsorship of the army. Long waits, then they give me a couple of hours.

To me the ride back is more frightening, because the boys in the truck are even less interested in watching out, and because my fantasy is that the Contras would have seen us pass on the way in, and have set up an ambush for us. I watch enough for everyone.

When I am back, the tension I feel becomes almost physically painful. The traveling and the people here, even the idyllic country, the soft hills and mountain light, the smell of woodfires and horse manure and flowers — everything seems charged with energy, so intense I feel as if I'm in the grip of a strong fist. The mountains hum like a tuning fork. I don't wonder that people in Las Colinas won't work. It is like the priest said: they are paralyzed. Who would want to work there or live there? Whatever gets built is a magnet for destruction. Las Colinas is hopelessly vulnerable. It will be attacked and destroyed again a year after my visit.

Death has made his home here. He lives here openly and powerfully. Not the death I have known, of accident, or literature or film, and not universal death. Not my father's death, the violent and bloody suicide of an old man sick of life, a death of resignation and despair. This Death is a destroyer, a death of rampage and cruelty. This Death tears holes in people and leaves them heartless, tongueless, and sexless; opens their bellies and cruelly exposes their baskets of life. This Death orphans children and leaves women and men desolate and weeping.

It is Death I feel held by. He holds me, he holds everyone here, tight in his hands. He tosses me into the air like a ball and catches me. If he wishes, he can let me fall away into the darkness. It is this playing with life that fills the air with a weird, high-pitched tension. Death stands on the hill above the town by the sign that says "Danger! No Passing!" He gazes across the town with patience. He kicks a stone and watches it roll down the hill.

He will not take everyone, but he will take more than a few, and someone close to everyone. What he is doing seems random, but there is a purpose. He wants to terrorize and paralyze the community, so that people will give up on life. So that, grateful simply to escape, they will go back to the old ways. The ways loved by Death and appropriate to him.

And this Death comes from my country. He is a paid emissary of the White House.

I spend the next morning talking to Cecilia Oliva. She gives me coffee and cookies and sits in her front room telling me the story of her son Jaime, who was killed about six months before. I ask hardly any questions. She talks very rapidly and very reflectively, pausing often, going over some details more than once, and once or twice changing the time so that it isn't always clear where she is in her narrative. It's as if she's living in the world of her story, moving about in it on her own, and if I ask her a question, she exits to explain to me the place where she is. I wonder how she is able to know some of the things she tells me. She says she talked to people who know. Yet I still wonder. I have added to the confusion, because what follows is my story — a retelling of hers.

Jaime Oliva Morales, twenty-six years old, is the supervisor of adult education in the zone of Yalí and a teacher of adult classes in history, geography, mathematics, English, and art. He leaves his office one June morning and jumps on his bicycle. It was a mistake, he thinks, leaving his math book in El Camelote. He taught there the day before yesterday, and Enrique had wanted to borrow it, promising to bring it into town yesterday. Jaime pedals fast by the park to get a good run on the hill. There is no other book, and he needs it for a class this afternoon. He doesn't mind really, being out on a day like this, clear and warm, everything sparkling after the rain. He would like it if he could work outside, he thinks, work with the land on a little farm of his own. He would grow fruit trees and

Cecilia Oliva

plant a vegetable garden and a bit of coffee. Have some animals. This morning, when he stood on the back porch of his house brushing his teeth and looking at the fruit trees, he said to his mother, "Look, Mamá, how well the avocados are doing. Look at the bananas. The rain has been good. We won't go hungry this year — we'll have plenty of food. God is protecting us, Mamá."

Jaime's mother, Cecilia, is an attractive, bright, high-spirited woman who has had six children with five different men. Jaime is the oldest and the head of the house. The youngest, Orlando, is seven years old. Cecilia never married, or even lived with a man except for one brief try. She doesn't like drinking and won't allow it in the house. Once Jaime came home drunk with some friends and she wouldn't let them in. Since then, when Jaime wants to drink, he comes in quietly and alone and goes right to bed.

They live in a new brick house that Jaime built himself. He tore down the old, leaky, wooden one a year ago, and in two months he and a friend had finished the walls and rafters and put on the roof. Later, Jaime installed water pipes and electric wiring and built shelves and counters for the kitchen. Last week he and a friend drove a truck to Estelí for more bricks to finish the kitchen floor.

Jaime is good at building and proud of the house. Very few people in Yalí have a brick house. He likes making things. He went to Granada to study electricity and he likes electrical work — creating a plan of electrical wires and outlets and switches on paper and then making it happen. More than anything, though, he wants to work on the radio. He has a good voice — people have said so. He loves planning programs and playing music and talking to people. Sometimes, in Matagalpa, he stays with his father and helps out there at the station.

This is going to be my last year here, he thinks, as he rides through the countryside. I have been here long enough. I want to make more money. He begins to run songs through his head, humming and singing. He is always a little nervous in the countryside, and he sings as he rides.

He pedals fast because he wants to be back by twelve. His mother doesn't like it when he's late. His oldest sister, Ampara, who works as a nurse at the hospital, comes home at one. After breakfast they leave together and walk into town. He is in awe of Ampara and a little in love with her. She is tall, about six inches taller than he, and black and very beautiful. Jaime is light-skinned and on the small side. On their walks to town they talk about whatever is on their minds. Sometimes they walk holding hands. Jaime feels comfortable with women, and they with him, and he has a lot of women friends. But it never seems to go beyond friendship. More than a few women have wished Jaime would get more serious, but it hasn't happened.

Only once did Jaime want to get married. This was to a Cuban woman, a teacher, who came over after the revolution. Jaime was eighteen and working in the big literacy campaign. He became the coordinator of the campaign for the whole area. She was older than he, married and divorced, and had two children. She taught secondary school here in Yalí for two years. Jaime was crazy about her, and they even lived together a while. Then she went back.

Jaime wrote to her. He decorated his room with pictures of her that he painted himself. In those days, he painted a lot. He copied pictures from magazines and calenders. He painted lots of girls and gave them the pictures. He painted Che Guevara and Daniel Ortega. When he went to the mountains for the literacy campaign, he painted a picture of each member of the family. But the Cuban girl forgot Jaime. She wrote only one letter after she got back, about how her children and parents were getting along and about conditions in Cuba. She didn't answer Jaime's letters.

That morning, while Jaime and Ampara are having breakfast, Cecilia says, "Jaime, are you going out to the country today?"

"No, Mamá, I have classes in town today."

"The Contras are close to Valcón," she says.

"Don't worry," he says. "I'll be back for lunch."

When they are walking out he says it again, "I'll be back for lunch, Mamá." He is smiling when he leaves the house, and he and Ampara begin to sing a popular song.

Cecilia stands in the doorway and watches them walk down the hill. She feels strange, as if chilled, even though she is wearing a sweater. She shivers, standing in the morning sun.

He usually says "adios" when he leaves, she thinks, as she watches them turn the corner.

She doesn't feel quite right this morning. She does some clothes behind the house on the concrete washstand, pulls weeds in the garden, and transplants some flowers to the front of the house. But she does the work automatically, as if dreaming or unconscious. She thinks about when she was a girl living with her father on the farm in Granada. They had quantities of flowers and flowering bushes; and she's not a farmer, she likes living in town, but she always loved her father's farm. Even working on it. She misses the gentle, rich farmland, and the volcanoes so large and near and the huge lake, Lake Nicaragua, and the islands where they would go sometimes on Sunday. She misses the trips to the markets in Masaya and Managua. She always feels confined here in the mountains; it is so far from everything, and so rocky and cold. She shivers thinking about it.

She thinks about the good-looking farmer who came to Granada to see his uncle and the fiesta where she met him because she knew his uncle's family, and how he looked, tight jeans tucked into beautiful black cowboy boots, black sombrero, black mustache, and brown eyes so liquid under the heavy, almond eyelids. Jaime's father. When she knew she was going to have his baby, she went to Yalí looking for him. She found him, but also found he had a wife and children. She stayed in Yalí so her family would think everything was all right, and maybe because she wanted to. Jaime's father moved to Matagalpa twenty years ago, and it is just as well; things were never comfortable with him nearby.

She stands in front of the house, leaning against the doorframe and looking at a mango tree across the road. A memory passes through her mind. Jaime is standing where she is now and they are talking. An old man from the country rides by on a donkey. He is toothless and half-blind probably and passes without a look, his dark, sullen face half-hidden under his hat. When the donkey pauses and looks toward the house, he swears at it and hits it with a stick.

They watch him and the donkey picking its way down the hill, and Jaime bends his knees and starts walking around in a circle in front of the house, beating and cursing an imaginary donkey. He becomes so loud that Olivia is embarrassed.

"Don't, Jaime. You shouldn't laugh at people like that, it's wrong."

"Oh, Mamá," he said, "hush." And pretends to slap her face.

"Don't do that to your mother," she said. "Not even with rose petals."

She goes in and brings up the fire in the kitchen and begins to cook a fresh batch of *ojuelos,* a large, thin, crisp sweet bread you spread jam or honey on. She keeps a basket of them by the front door covered with a white cloth and sells them to neighbors.

She puts *gallo pinto* on the stove to warm up and a pot of chicken soup she made yesterday. The food is ready before twelve. At twelve she usually turns the television on and she does so today, but turns it off right away. She doesn't want to watch television. She feels a little dizzy and goes into her bedroom to lie down.

She wakes to hear Ampara's voice as she comes in the house for lunch. She's talking to someone—a man.

"Ampara!" Cecilia calls. "Is Jaime with you?"

"No, Mamá," she answers. "It's Ricardo. I brought him home for lunch. Are you sleeping, Mamá?"

Jaime is nearing El Camelote, riding fast down a steep hill when he first hears gunfire. It seems far away, though, well beyond the next hill, and he slows down but doesn't stop. He decides to go on to the top of the hill and have a look. If he sees some *compas,* he'll find out what's happening and whether it's safe to go on. If he doesn't, he'll turn around.

He begins to feel more nervous as he crosses the little stream at the bottom and begins to walk his bike up the hill. The firing hasn't stopped, it keeps erupting and it sounds closer. He recognizes the rattly, high-pitched sound of the *compa* AK-47s, the lower-pitched, heavier sounds of the Contra FALs, and the explosions of grenades. He realizes it's stupid to go farther and is about to turn around when two men suddenly crash down onto the road from some bushes above him. He knows right away, from their newish olive-green uniforms, that they are Contras. They are nervous and angry, and one of them hits Jaime in the head with his riflebutt, sending him and his bicycle into a ditch.

"Son of a bitch!" one calls out, raising his rifle at Jaime. The other stops him.

"Be quiet, idiot!" He gestures toward the road behind them.

An ambush has been set, to protect two platoons fighting on the other side of the hill. A dozen Contras are holed up in the bushes above them, with an M-60 machine gun in place. They are expecting *compas* from Yalí to come charging down the road any minute. They are in a hurry and Jaime is in trouble. They can't turn him loose and they can't shoot him.

They throw his bicycle into the woods, smooth the road a little, and one of them, a kid, is told to take him over the hill to the nearest platoon on the other side. Someone throws a piece of rope down from the hill above, and the older one ties Jaime's hands behind his back.

"Get going!" he says. "Run!"

Jaime begins to run up the hill, the kid running after, poking his back with his rifle.

"Run faster, son of a bitch, faster!"

When Jaime thought he couldn't run anymore, they reached the top of the hill and ducked into some trees to catch their breath. Now the shooting was much louder. They looked across to the next hill. Some men were running across an open space and entering the trees near the top. The road took a turn to the left. Down the hill, as far as they could see, there was nothing on the road.

"Let's go," said the boy.

"Look, amigo, let me go here, please. I'll go into the woods. I won't come out. I won't speak to anyone. Just let me go, hombre. I have my mother to take care of, I have my brothers and sisters. Please, hombre, let me go."

"Fuck off," the kid said. "They'd kill me if I let you go, son of a bitch. I'll kill you myself." He readied his weapon, an AK-47, and gave Jaime a kick on the side of his leg. "Get going!"

Jaime and the kid run down the hill, Jaime in front, running carefully to keep his balance, the kid behind cursing him and urging him to go faster. Ahead, the firing continues and grows louder. As he runs toward the fighting, the trees and vines alongside the road seem to grow higher and higher, to be closing into a tunnel of green-and-black shade. The world is blurring green and black, and Jaime feels terrified. He begins to feel a blackness rising in his stomach to meet the blackness in the trees. The blurring green begins to whirl. He steps into a hole and falls. The fall knocks the wind out of him and scrapes his face. The kid is furious.

"Get up, shitface, and run, or I'll kill you!"

Jaime stands, vomiting. He wipes his mouth against his shoulder and bends his head, shaking the tears and vomit away from his face. He can't believe it, but his glasses are still on.

He knows he should get control of himself. He knows what he must do. They won't release him and they never take prisoners. His only hope is to be taken back to Honduras, "kidnapped" or "recruited." He'll have to cooperate. Not cause any problems. Become one of them.

Cecilia sends Ampara and Ricardo back to town to look for Jaime. She sits in her chair by the door, waiting. She feels drugged with sleep and fear.

"Don't worry, Mamá," Ampara says. "There's fighting out near El Camelote and the *compas* have gone out, but Jaime isn't going out today."

Cecilia doesn't feel better, she only feels that Ampara doesn't understand. As she sits in her chair rocking, her eyes closed, her hands clasped in her lap, her mind turns sluggishly as if beginning to whirl. She remembers her dream. She was in the country looking at the Granada volcano, and she felt the earth move. There was a sound like thunder, but it kept sounding louder. The volcano began to turn, slowly, with a huge noise, as if tearing itself away from the earth. A wind came up, blowing fierce and loud. She watched horrified as the mountain began to turn faster.

She gets up and goes to the garden in back. She had planned to plant some seeds. She begins to work, clearing a space, preparing the earth. While she is doing that, Ampara comes back.

"Mamá," she says, "be calm. They said that Jaime went out today to El Camelote. He left at nine. He must have got stuck there because of the fighting. He'll be back. It's two o'clock now. The *compas* are still out, and nobody has any news yet."

The sounds of combat stopped around three o'clock. The *compas* came back just as it was getting dark. They had some wounded and one dead. No one knew anything about Jaime. No, they hadn't seen him. The Contras had been caught in a pincer movement, then managed to squeeze out and escape. But they took heavy losses.

Cecilia went to the Red Cross to see if they had any news, but no one was there. She went to Telcor to call her second son, in Estelí, but it was closed.

Cecilia and Ampara, the boy Rolando, who is twelve, and the younger ones, Raúl, nine, and Monica, seven, sit quietly in the house that evening. There isn't much talking. The younger children begin to fall asleep about nine o'clock. Ampara lies down a little later. Rolando has been crying all evening, so Cecilia lies down with him. To soothe him she strokes his hair.

She must have dozed off as well, because later she wakes suddenly. It is about one in the morning. Her scalp is tingling, and the back of her neck is soaked with sweat.

Jaime is in the room. She can't see him, but she knows he is there. He is standing close to her, next to the bed. She waits without saying anything, then tries to say his name, but nothing comes out. She works her mouth but can't make a sound. He takes her hand and squeezes it hard, so hard it hurts. She wants to pull away from the pain but doesn't dare. With his other hand he touches her forehead. He runs his fingers lightly down her face and body all the way to her feet. With one hand he holds onto her hand tightly, with the other he holds her ankle. He whispers, "Mamá, give me water. Please, Mamá, water!"

She is about to get out of the bed when he lets go of her foot, but he puts his hand over her eyes and presses with his fingers so she can't open them. She becomes frightened. She tries to call out, "God, let me open my eyes so I can see him." Again she calls, and this time her voice works, "Let me open my eyes!"

Then the pressure of his fingers disappears. She opens her eyes and sits up. She sees him—he is standing near the door, barely visible. She gets up to go to him. As she moves toward him he disappears again.

She walks through the house looking for him. She is crying now and calling his name. She knows now that he is dead. "It was then he died," she later said. She looks at the clock. It says one-fifteen.

She walks out into the backyard crying. A half-moon is shining weakly overhead. The trees and plants glow softly, their leaves glowing brighter as the breeze lifts and turns them. The plants seem congregated around the house like a waiting crowd, expectant and awake. She sits down in the old rocker she keeps on the porch. She gets up and walks down to the garden among the plants and touches them as she cries, drawing the leaves through her fingers, smelling their green odors and the smells of fresh earth and damp. She leans against a banana plant and looks up at the porch where Jaime was standing this morning brushing his teeth. Finally she goes into the house for a sweater and comes back and sits down in her chair on the back porch, watching the moon as it recedes to the west. She sits on the porch until it begins to get light. Then she comes in and makes coffee and wakes the boy. "Get up now," she says, "we're going to look for Jaime."

It is ten at night when Jaime and the group of Contras stop their forced march at a farmhouse somewhere north of El Camelote. Lamps are glowing inside the house. A fire burns outside, and a large pot of hot water is steaming. A woman is cleaning chickens. Some Contras are in the house, others sit on the steps and porch, or against trees or on the ground. Some have strung hammocks on the long porch and among the trees. Jaime can smell coffee. A lot of them are chewing on field rations courtesy of the U.S. government, protein bars and crackers, sardines and chocolate. They don't seem to notice Jaime being tied to a tree facing the porch.

The man in command, Martín, has been inside the house studying topographical maps and talking to the farmer who lives here. He comes out and orders a head count and sends most of the men to camp on two hilltops that overlook the house.

The rest sit around eating, drinking water, and passing around a bottle of rum. Jaime asks for water and a couple of men look over at him, but no one responds. Some men come out of the house carrying pieces of chicken. They stand by the porch rail as they eat, throwing the bones to the dogs.

The Contras talk to the campesinos on the front porch. Jaime can easily hear them and make out their faces. He knows the family, but not well, and he's always known they side with the Contras. He vaguely recognizes the toothless, half-blind old man, sitting in a rocking chair on the porch, his hat over his eyes as if asleep. The commander questions the farmer about Jaime.

"We found him riding a bicycle on the road," he says. "He says he heard the fighting and came to join us. Do you know him?"

The farmer looks across the dimness toward Jaime. "Sure, I know who he is. He's a Sandinista. He's a teacher. He lives in Yalí and teaches in the country."

"I see," Martín says. "A teacher. Too bad, hombre, too bad for you," Martín says across the yard to Jaime.

"Take care of the teacher," Martín orders the kid who had been leading Jaime with a rope tied around his neck.

The kid walks over to Jaime and squares himself off in front of him. The yard becomes silent except for the dogs chewing bones.

Jaime says, "Please, hombre, can I talk to the *comandante*? Can I have some water?" One of the Contras on the porch laughs.

"I'll show you the water you're going to get," says the kid.

The men on the porch stand by eating chicken and tossing the bones to the dogs as they watch the kid.

Cecilia and the boy walk over to the barracks to look for Marco, a friend of Jaime's. No one is awake, so she bangs a long time on the big wooden door. Finally someone answers, and tells her Marco sleeps in a house on the other side of town. She goes to this house and wakes the woman, who says Marco isn't there.

They go to the house where the telephone operator lives and leave money for her to wire the boy in Estelí. Then they go to the CDS office, this is about six-thirty in the morning, and get them up. They give her some sedative pills to take.

"So I don't run around and do something that will scandalize people," she thinks.

She takes some of the pills and goes home, but nothing changes. Ampara is up. The boy goes out for milk. They drink coffee and milk and they pack some water and a little food, and she and the boy walk back into town to look for a ride to El Camelote. They find a pickup truck that will be leaving soon.

El Camelote is nothing but a crossroads with a campesino store and a health clinic. A few horses are tied up in front of the store. They ask about Jaime, and the people say the fighting was east of town. They didn't see any Contras here, and they didn't see Jaime yesterday.

They walk east a short distance and turn north on a side road. A little way down this road, on the banks of a stream, they see papers lying on the ground, many torn into pieces. They are Jaime's papers. Cecilia gathers them all and puts them in the bag with the food.

A little farther on they come to a farmhouse. Cecilia calls and a woman comes to the door.

"Did you see Contras?" she asks. The woman shakes her head no.

"Did you see Jaime?" she asks.

"No," the woman says.

"If your boys are Contras, please tell them to let him go," Cecilia says. "If they haven't killed him. Please, leave him with me."

"My boys haven't done anything," the woman answers coldly. "Don't be looking around here — there is nothing here. Go on back home."

Cecilia and the boy go on, certain now that Jaime has been brought this way. She asks the same questions at every house. By early afternoon she comes to the house of a woman she knows well, a friend, who asks her to come in to rest and take some coffee. The woman says, "You should go back home. He may be alive. He may be back there in Yalí."

"No, I know he is dead," Cecilia says. "He came to me."

"Perhaps you dreamed it," the woman says.

"I was awake when he touched me," she said. "How could I have been sleeping at such a time?"

The woman persuades Cecilia to turn back, and gives the boy a ride on her horse to the main road.

"I will look for him," the woman says, as she climbs onto her horse. "If I get news of him, I'll come and tell you right away."

When they get back to Yalí Cecilia goes to the Red Cross again, but they have no news. Then, on the street, she sees some men from El Camelote standing by their horses. She knows them.

"Did you see Jaime?" She asks. They answer no.

"Did you see Contras?" "Yes," they say.

"And Jaime wasn't with them?" She almost screams. She notices that the toothless old man who rides a donkey is with them.

A campesino, whose name is Horacio Ubeda and who later went to jail, says, "Jaime wasn't with them. No one was with them. They passed my house and stole my chickens, then they went on. But no one was with them."

He looks steadily at her with dark, cold eyes. His face is thin and pinched. She knows he is lying from the coldness she sees. She stands her ground in front of the men.

"I know they took him," she says.

Another man says, "We didn't see him, Doña Cecilia. But if we hear of him, I'll let you know. I'll look for him myself."

"Listen," Cecilia says. "You are rich people, you have a farm. We are poor, we don't have land or animals. All we can do is work for the government. We have to. I ask you, please leave him alone if he isn't dead. I need him. Please leave him for me."

The men nod and say nothing. Cecilia turns and walks home.

The next day, Saturday, Cecilia goes into town several times to ask about Jaime. She speaks to everyone she meets from El Camelote. She decides to go to regional headquarters in Matagalpa but can't find a ride. She tries to telephone but can't get through. But she doesn't go into the country again.

People tell her, "Don't go. Someone will find him. Or he's alive. He's with them."

The next morning, Sunday, the woman from El Camelote comes to her house.

"They found him this morning dead. Hanging in a tree. There was no truck to bring him, but they have sent one."

Cecilia waits until she knows the truck is back, then goes to the Red Cross. The women there don't want her to go in—it is terrible, they say. But she won't be stopped so they let her.

He is on a table, covered with a sheet. When she pulls back the sheet she doesn't recognize him. She knows him by his clothes, a pair of dark-red pants. He seems very small and white and deformed.

"He is a monster," she thinks, "a monster." He is crawling with worms. On the table by his feet are wooden clogs with nails in them.

"He is like Saint Sebastian," she says to the woman standing in the door. He has forty-two stab wounds. His stomach is cut open from one side to the other, and his genitals are cut off and his tongue cut out. His fingers are broken. She takes his hands in hers—his fingers are very soft, like a doll's fingers.

"He is so pale, he has no blood," she says. "They drank his blood. They think it gives them more."

The next day, Cecilia watches over him. Few people come because the smell is unbearable. The next day they bury him.

After the funeral, which was very large, Cecilia stays at home. She sits in her chair by the door. Always a talkative, active woman, she speaks to people who come by, and friends often come and she gives them coffee and *ojuelos* and talks not very coherently about her memories. The friends usually end up sitting quietly and nodding as she talks.

"Why did they do that to him?" the friends say. "He was such a good boy, so hardworking, so serious. He never did anything to anybody."

Cecilia looks at them from far away and nods.

Cecilia has begun to talk to the dead. Her father has begun to come and visit her. He sits in another rocker beside her, and they talk about old times in Granada. Then her older brother comes, a favorite of hers, tall, with a big mustache and a large sombrero. He was killed riding a crazy horse. Then Jaime begins to come, looking like his old self, in his glasses and clean shirt and pants, and some of his friends come as well. They sit around and talk and joke together. Cecilia just listens. Cecilia begins to look forward to these visits from the dead, on the mornings and afternoons when the children are away at school, or even at night. They are not frightening, these dead, they are pleasant, clean and healthy-looking and well dressed. They gather in the room or at the door. The old dead sit quietly and when they do talk, which is little, it is about old times. They only mention the war in passing, if at all, and it isn't clear which war they mean, the present one or the one before, Sandino's war.

Four weeks after the funeral, it is Cecilia's birthday. That day Ampara prepares a meal and invites some of her friends and Cecilia's friends. Everyone eats and tries to be happy, but it is difficult. Cecilia pulls away from the people and sits in her chair by the front door. Many of her dead drift in, smiling, to offer congratulations. Inside the house a young friend of Jaime begins to play a guitar. The dead are smiling and their faces are bright. Then Jaime comes. He is carrying a large cake. He had ordered it, and brings it with his own hands so it will be a surprise. It has her name and "Feliz Cumpleaños" written in pink.

He stands next to her holding the cake and says, "We are going to celebrate the birthday of my mamá, because she is fifty-one years old." He is in high spirits. He turns to Cecilia, bends, and kisses her forehead and says, "None of them can believe that my mamá is fifty-one." She looks at them. They nod and smile.

Someone passing the house looks in and says, "Who's having a birthday today?"

Jaime answers, "She is, the mistress of the house. She is the reason for the joy in this house."

Avilio has to go to San Rafael for a meeting and has offered to give me a ride. I need to leave because I am going to a poetry marathon in Ciudad Darío that is to be held tomorrow, January 16, the anniversary of

Rubén Darío's birth. I talk with people until my time runs out, then hurry back to my room. Avilio's jeep is parked in front, waiting for me. I grab my bag, and we leave for San Rafael. This is a dangerous road, but I am not so worried. I feel I am leaving danger behind me, and Avilio has a Czech automatic rifle beside his seat and it is a beautiful, clear day and farmers are on the road on their horses.

Avilio doesn't know Cecilia or her son Jaime.

We don't talk much as we drive. It is bouncy and noisy in the jeep, and I am dazed from talking to Cecilia. He tells me that nearly all the farmers are against the Contras, and inform the army when they see them. I feel an unreality about this trip. There is so much I don't know.

I want to take a picture of Avilio, so he stops and poses in the woods as if he is hunting Contras. Again, it is like a kid playing war; the pictures come out looking silly.

He drops me at a place where I can have lunch and wait for the bus to Jinotega. Several other people are waiting at the *comedor* for the noonday serving. I sit with them in the front room of the low stucco house, which

Young soldier photographed on the road to Las Colinas one year before his death

has a sink for washing up. Soon we move to the tables in the next room and they bring a lunch plate. Myself and three neatly dressed farmers in cowboy boots and straw hats; also some men and women who seem like office-workers. Everyone shy and quiet. The same food as always.

At nine-thirty that night, four rides later, I am sitting in a crowded restaurant in Cuidad Darío, drinking cold beer and eating a fried-chicken dinner. I sleep ten hours that night, and wake thick and stiff as the dead.

A year later I visited Yalí again. When I went to see Cecilia Oliva and give her some photographs, I learned she had sold the house in Yalí and moved to Estelí to be with her second son.

I had photographs of various people to distribute. One was of a young soldier who had been riding on the jeep with me when I went to Las Colinas. He is posed squatting with his rifle across his legs. He is very young-looking, maybe seventeen, and smiling sweetly.

"That's my brother," said a little boy when he saw the picture. "His funeral was yesterday." He stared at the photograph and began to cry.

They said the family had no picture of the boy. I said I would take it to his mother, but they said no, she was indisposed: "Take it to the father. He has a little stand for selling leather goods by the church." I found the stand, a shed, stocked with belts and harnesses and a few saddles. He was a small man, with a mustache, and looked quizzically at me as I handed the photograph to him. Then he looked as if he were seeing a ghost. "I took that photo a year ago, on the road to Las Colinas," I said. "Take it, it is for your family."

6

Necessary Poetry

While Death roamed the mountains sowing fear and horror, many of Nicaragua's poets were in Ciudad Darío singing defiance and hope. This didn't seem inappropriate—it felt natural and even necessary that poetry was responding to the life struggles of the people.

I have attended a lot of poetry readings in the United States, most in university settings. The audience is usually university students of literature or creative writing, professors, and a handful of people from the community—poets and poetry fans. These quiet, sedate gatherings are the remnants of poetry in a society that considers it a waste of time. They are poetry's remaining niche among lives crammed with work and television culture, a television one can watch for a year, on all channels at once, and never see a poet reading his or her work.

In such conditions, what are the unwanted poets to do? They turn away and retreat into themselves. They find the few out-of-the-way places where they can earn a marginal living. Their loneliness and unemployed sensitivity, their joking cynicism and private lives, become the themes of thousands upon thousands of depressing songs. Adrienne Rich writes: "art produced in an exceptional, rarefied situation like an artist's colony for the few, can be rarefied, self-reflecting, complicit with the circumstances of its making, cut off from a larger, richer, and more disturbing life" (Rich 1993, 63).

Is poetry really necessary? In her essay "Poetry Is Not a Luxury," Audre Lorde answers: "For women, then, poetry is not a luxury. It is a vital necessity for our existence. It forms the quality of light within which we predicate our hopes and dreams toward survival and change, first made into language, then into idea, then into more tangible action. Poetry is the way we help give name to the nameless so it can be thought. The farthest horizons of our hopes and fears are cobbled by our poems, carved from the rock experiences of our lives" (Lorde 1984, 37). This conception can be applied to any oppressed people, or anyone struggling "toward survival and change." Poetry projects dreams that arise from our deepest needs. No won-

Young poet reading

Nicaraguan poetry audience

der it shrivels and goes dormant in a consumer society, where all dreams are transformed into dreams for *things*.

Poets are organic beings; they need a nurturing environment as much as any human being, as much as plants need soil. As the poet in each of us needs the courage to imagine, and deeply feel our needs. Even in the United States, poetry springs up like desert flowers among certain groups, on certain occasions. It happens when people come together in refusal or desire, and one of them is a natural poet who speaks out to them and for them. It happens when the poet is part of a community.

Nicaragua is known for the number and quality of its poets and artists. Is this a national aptitude for art, or the stimulus of the revolution? I can't answer, but Rubén Darío (1867–1916), Nicaragua's national poet, said long ago that in Nicaragua, of every ten inhabitants, five write verses.

Darío is considered by many to be the greatest poet of Latin America and the founder of "modernism" in twentieth-century Spanish poetry. In Nicaragua his birthday is the occasion of a day-long poetry marathon sponsored by the Sandinista government. Ciudad Darío, his birthplace, has a museum in the house where he was born (as León has a museum in the house where he died). The poetry marathon, in which some thirty poets recite, takes place in a little park with an amphitheater that holds four or five hundred people.

I have never seen an audience like this at a poetry reading—families, old people, children, the people you see in the street or at the market. Every seat is taken, and people stand in the back and on the sides and crowd around the stage, applauding, serious, laughing, listening with great attention to poetry all day in the full sun, most staying until it is too dark to read from the page. I watched this event in two different years, wondering how it is possible. I felt a similar wonder when I saw the weekend literary supplements of the three newspapers, devoted mostly to poetry. Do people actually read all this poetry? I asked, and found that many did. Sometimes someone would ask me if I had read such and such a poem in the newspaper, and would urge me to do so. I came to be familiar with many of the better-known poets, and was amazed that there were so many who were truly interesting and important, and that many Nicaraguans knew who they were and had read them. A Nicaraguan friend and I had a discussion about this.

"Why do Nicaraguans read poetry so much?" I asked.

"The answer is easy," he said. "Nicaraguans are lazy. They like talking but they hate reading. And poems are shorter and easier to read than long speeches or essays."

"Well," I thought, "may the whole world be lazy."

The Nicaraguan people's interest in poetry was not just stimulated by the government, it was shared by it. President Daniel Ortega, Vice-President Sergio Ramírez, Minister of the Interior Tomás Borge (all of whom write verses), and other ministers and high officials come to the readings. Many of the best poets of Nicaragua come, and there is a sense of family involvement between poets and government, of a common purpose between poetry and revolution. This is not hard to understand, in light of Audre Lorde's explanation of the necessity of poetry. But it is an unforgettable experience to see heads of state listen respectfully to hours of poetry reading. In an opening address to one of the gatherings, Tomás Borge argued that poetry is of basic importance for the revolution because it synthesizes the intrinsic qualities that are vital to the success of the revolutionary process: freedom and quality. Darío, he said, inspires for his authentic national voice and his anti-imperialism, but even more for the high quality of his art. Beauty in poetry and art, Borge said, is beauty in the face of the revolution.

As minister of the interior, Borge headed the police and ran a prison system known as one of the most progressive in the world. He also writes good poems. A group of his poems was published in an issue of *Poesía Libre* (Free Poetry), a journal of the Ministry of Culture. They were written in 1977–78 from a Somoza jail, where he was tortured and held in solitary confinement. This one is called "Nicaragua":

> I love you from here, Volcano
> Broken pottery jug
> Canoe among cannibalistic fish
>
> From my solitude I love you
> Tornado, Mirror
> threshed in the din of this valley
>
> I love your fine thighs
> your eyes that teach, your
> teeth that weep fireworks
> I love your famous sad
> poets, your joyful dead
> who refuse to die.

(Borge 1986, 4)

Minister of Culture Ernesto Cardenal is Nicaragua's greatest and most famous living poet. He was born by Lake Nicaragua in the town of Granada, educated in Mexico and the United States, and influenced by certain North American poets, especially Walt Whitman and Ezra Pound. He became a Trappist monk and lived in Kentucky under the spiritual guidance of Thomas Merton. He founded a spiritual community in Nicaragua, on the islands of Solentiname. There he became intimate with the poverty and need of the Nicaraguan peasants, and began projects with them — painting, poetry, and crafts — that gradually transformed the islands culturally and economically. He wrote long narrative poems, using Pound's "collage" style, about the history of Nicaragua, its native people, its country life and flora and fauna, its history of struggle with the United States and the Somoza dictatorship. In 1973 he visited Cuba for three months and "converted" to socialism. He wrote one of the best books ever about the Cuban Revolution, *In Cuba*.

He joined the Sandinista Front and became a sort of cultural ambassador of the revolution. He continued in that role as minister of culture, and complained then that he spent most of his life on airplanes. Indeed, many of his poems from the 1980s were written on airplanes or inspired by perceptions he had when flying:

From the round window, everything is blue
the earth bluish, blue-green, blue
                                    (and sky)
        everything is blue
blue lakes and lagoons
            blue volcanoes
bluer the farther away the land
            blue islands in a blue lake.
        This is the face of the liberated land.

                                    (Cardenal 1983, 294)

Ernesto's poetry is descriptive and plain; his language is simple and everyday, his phrases short, his ideas direct and explicit, his meaning clear — qualities he drew from the objectivist style of the North Americans. His poems respond to ordinary things, yet they make great leaps and connections, showing "the ordinary" to be worthy of awe:

Everything else blurred and I saw only this raised hand
like when the camera zooms in to focus on a single detail
a palm and five separate fingers.
What does this hand say to me?
It showed me the most human of human organs
and the most perfect member of the human body
by which we passed from monkey to human.
Did we develop it hanging from branches?
A planar space with five cylindical elongations agile as
acrobats?
            The hand saluted.
That which carved the first flint
which made skyscrapers, books, cloth, tractors and violins
and also these floats,
a palm and five fingers
which made primal people think and speak
discover fire
made these revolutionary floats
made a revolution.

                                    (Cardenal 1983, 297)

Ernesto's poems speak of animals, birds, iguanas, sea, and sky; he sees nature as a creation and as teeming with creation:

It was in the Pacific
        Facing the coast of Nicaragua
We were fishing for red snapper
in the blue sea with the blue sky
        the sea like blue ink

and suddenly two turtles, coupled
one mounted over the other
    making love in the sea
like they have been doing since the beginning of their
    species
the same act in the sea for millions of years
for love

(Cardenal 1985, 72)

At the poetry marathon, Ernesto read first — only one poem, because, he said, "We are many who want to read today." His newly written poem addressed a common experience at that time in Nicaragua:

EMPTY SHELVES

I went into a supermarket yesterday
and saw the empty shelves. Most of them empty.
I felt a little sad among the empty shelves
but even more I felt joy for the dignity of our people
who are patient with the empty shelves.
Before, these shelves were overflowing with things of all
colors, necessary and unnecessary
like it is in other countries.
It's the price we pay — a little people fighting against
    a Colossus —
the storeroom full of heroism, but the shelves empty.
It is the price of independence, and why we
have thousands of little Sandino-cubs running free in the
    mountains.
And just as we lack rivers of pretty merchandise
we also lack women sitting on the curb showing their sores
or children with eyes white as marble holding out their
    hands.
The children play in their neighborhoods, and most are
    tranquil.
And the police don't go into the neighborhoods with
    nightsticks to hit people
or with tear-gas bombs or fire hoses, wearing anti-riot shields
because of the empty shelves . . .

Dr. Fernando Silva is the director of a pediatric hospital in Managua called "The Mascot" (named in memory of Manuel de Jesús Rivera, who at age twelve was killed by the National Guard, and who was buried with the rank of FSLN lieutenant). I interviewed Silva in the hospital where he works. He is very proud of it. The parents can live with their sick child there; they can eat and sleep there and help with the nursing care.

Everything is free. He showed me the "milk bank" he started, where mothers may donate or take out milk for feeding their babies.

In addition to four novels and seven books of poetry, Silva has written a manual on the health care of children, full of pictures and stories and poems. At the marathon he read from that manual. He introduced himself by saying: "I am a poet of the people, and I talk to the people. Also, I am a doctor, and although I left La Mascota to come to you I didn't leave my mind, or my heart, or what I do and see and live. So I am dedicating this poem to mothers, as a message about something very serious in Nicaragua. It is about diarrhea—how to cure it and how to prevent it." (Diarrhea, caused by parasites or germs that thrive on unsanitary conditions and a lack of pure drinking water, is the principal cause of infant mortality in the Third World.) Dr. Silva's poem:

DIARRHEA

It's not what he ate last night that made sick
    the child
and it wasn't the little piece of sweet roll you gave him
or that he had yesterday's milk unboiled at noon today.
No. It's the dirt.
The nipple that was left on the table for the flies
and even worse it's the garbage
garbage inside
garbage in the street
    wherever. And besides
most important
you quit using the breast for the still-small baby . . .
there you have the cause of serious diarrhea . . .
    the child is undernourished
    and then he gets diarrhea
a liquid bowel movement in an undernourished child
is more serious than five bowel movements in a well-nourished
    child.
Nothing is better than the breast
    give him your breast, girl
    what more would he want
you only take it from your blouse
    and make the little face comfortable
he will stick to you just here . . .
Is there anything easier, simpler, more comfortable
    than giving your breast to your child
even at night
    there's no need to go looking for anything

only turn over and put him to the breast and you will
     be relaxed
and the child too . . .
the thing is the child should always be well fed
because being malnourished and being very small
he will get diarrhea easier and also complications
and worse when the mother lets it go
thinking it's not serious
     a malnourished child with diarrhea
run run run
there is the ORV (Oral Rehydration Unit)
it is necessary to carry him there
     don't wait like when they come for immunizations
     don't let anyone say wait a while
say, I can't wait, my child has diarrhea . . .

In an interview Silva told me that in the time of the Somoza dictatorship, poetry was an important form of resistance. There was much despair, but the poets stood together like family:

We created from within ourselves, almost clandestinely, and in our works there was a preoccupation with the value of Nicaragua, and with being Nicaraguan, and [with the fact] that this country did not deserve the dictatorship.

And after the revolution there was great joy and enthusiasm in poetry. It was as if after a long, sad, boring day, I am standing on the street and see a beautiful woman passing, and I say, "How beautiful! How wonderful! I want to serve her! I want to give her everything I have!" Our poetry combined love and friendship and struggle, and pleasure in ordinary things: "What a wonderful table I have! Do you see my glass? I can drink from it every morning! I raise it to my mouth, full of water! See my shirt? I am so happy to have this shirt!" Even the most ordinary things entered poetry, because the revolution made them interesting. It brought them back to life.

Everything became the subject of poetry, and poetry became accessible to everyone. We don't say poetry is difficult to reach: it isn't necessary to discover what goes on in the dark night of my despair. Everyone is concerned with the subject of poetry, and that is why the poetry workshops began with such enthusiasm. The workshops produced a very pure, very exact, and very direct poetry, like ancient Chinese poetry. But most important, the poetry workshops gave everyone the opportunity to be close to art. The people took in poetry like fresh air to someone gasping for air. [Silva raised his head and sucked in air like a newborn child.] They read poetry, they wrote, they discussed, and they incorporated their life into poetry, as if for the first time they could breathe fresh air. (Silva 1987)

Daisy Zamora studied psychology at the university, took part in the popular insurrection of 1978, became program director for the clandestine Radio Sandino prior to the FSLN triumph, then worked with

Ernesto Cardenal as vice-minister of culture. At the poetry marathon, she read from a new series of poems she was writing about the life of Sandino. Her poems that follow are in the voice of Sandino:

THE BATTLE OF LAS CRUCES

The commander of the Marines was
Lieutenant Colonel Bruce
who was offering to all comers
$10,000 for my head.
But we ambushed them
on the road to El Jícaro
and we gave ourselves in recompense:
A United States flag — maps —
official documents — Captain Livingston —
some Marines — and the head of
Lieutenant Colonel Bruce which
we sent to the invaders.
A little before they received the first
charge Bruce was heard to say
"Don't be afraid, mule,
there are no bandits here."

BLANCA ARÁUZ

I knew her from the beginning of the war.
I loved her, and drinking coffee and talking
through the afternoon and sometimes all night
until dawn we knew we thought alike —
one body, the same thought.
We were like two lanterns beside
the Coleman lantern that lit
the whitewashed boards of the telegraph office.
Even though we were not together.
Even though we passed five years apart —
she in San Rafael, I in these mountains —
the two lights search for each other
across the swamp, across the night and
the trees, each to throw
its light on the other.

Later, speaking to Daisy Zamora in her home, I asked how she felt being a poet now in Nicaragua. She said:

Life is always hard for a poet, for someone who is born a poet, because there is a sensitivity to experience that means you live unsheltered and vulnerable. And now in Nicaragua there are difficulties — material difficulties, such as not having enough time to write. The big change is that now I have basic tranquillity as a poet. My work, and my worth as a poet, is recognized in this society.

After the literacy campaign the Ministry of Culture encouraged a special program, a sort of literacy campaign for poetry, for all the people of Nicaragua, because poetry has always been an important tradition of our people, though mostly an oral tradition. So, as they learned how to read and write, we started to establish poetry workshops in the places where they had the literacy campaign. This was very important because we socialized the means of literary expression. We gave the people the means of expressing themselves. This was another big change for poetry in Nicaragua. We never intended to make everybody a poet, but we wanted to create a public for poetry, and the possibility for anyone to write poetry.

We undertook an almost person-to-person campaign in all the towns and villages and cities of Nicaragua, and let it be known that there was a Ministry of Culture, and what that meant for people, and it was very impressive that almost everybody started taking the best house of every town, let's say the abandoned house of the town Somocista, and turned it into the House of Culture for the town. And the first thing they would have would be a poetry workshop.

So I don't feel any contradiction between my being a poet and the world I am living in. I have a very special feeling — it is difficult to describe — the consciousness that you are living an important event in history and that you contributed to it and are going on with it. That is very important to my life. (Zamora 1986)

In her introduction to a recently published poetry anthology, *La mujer nicaragüense en la poesía* (Nicaraguan Women in Poetry), Daisy Zamora writes that it was only during the struggles of the sixties and seventies against the Somoza dictatorship that women's voices broke into Nicaraguan literature. Until then, the Nicaraguan poets who were recognized had been almost exclusively men. And these new and disruptive voices, she says, can be identified distinctively as voices of women. Poems, she adds, are not male or female; but their authors are. And the experience and consciousness of women involves certain constant themes. Indeed, "In a society that is oppressive to women, to assert oneself as a woman, to be human, to think and act, to praise one's own sex, is subversive" (Zamora 1992, 42). As an example, she refers to a poem by Gioconda Belli:

AND GOD MADE ME WOMAN

And God made me woman
with long hair
eyes
nose and mouth of a woman.
With curves
and folds
and soft valleys

and hollowed my insides
for a workshop for human beings.
Delicately wove my nerves
and carefully balanced
the number of my hormones.
Composed my blood
and injected me with it
to irrigate my entire body;
ideas were born
dreams
and instinct.
Everything created softly
with hammer-blows of breath
and drillings of love
the thousand and one things that make me
woman every day
for which I wake proudly
every morning
and bless my sex.

One quality of Nicaraguan women's writing that Daisy Zamora cites as characteristic is a close identification with the subject, as if it becomes a reflection of themselves, especially of their bodies. At the poetry marathon, Claribel Alegría read a new poem that exemplifies this quality. Alegría grew up in El Salvador, and for many years she has been observing and documenting in her poems the suffering of the Salvadoran people. But having a Nicaraguan father, she also feels Nicaraguan, and has been living here since the revolution. They introduced her as "Salvadoran and also Nicaraguan." She said, "My poem is called 'Unicornio cimarrón' [Wild Unicorn], and it is dedicated to my Nicaraguan niece, Rita Alejandra, and to all the children of Nicaragua." Her poem is a very complex merging of images, of the unicorn and the horse, repression and revolution, and her memories as a girl:

More than the rider, the horse
Cloppety, Cloppety, Clop.
I saw you dance in Managua
on the back of a truck
hammering with your hooves
the rise and fall of History.
Zeledón on the plains.
Sandino entering a mine
on his little white donkey.
The Somoza dynasty

sowing chaos and death
and guerrillas in the mountains.
Prancing on the bodies
they threw in the street
the 19th of July
celebration of the victory.
Cloppety, Cloppety, Clop.
The rocking horse
of the roving photographer
in our neighborhood
had a torn mane
and splintered hooves,
and I climbed onto it,
the little horse of my childhood,
feeling brave as a Valkyrie and
asked the man to take my photo.
The box camera

Daisy Zamora reading. Seated to her left are Fernando Silva, José Coronel Urtecho, and Ernesto Cardenal, poets; Daniel Ortega, President of the Republic; and Sergio Ramírez, Vice President (left to right)

covered with a black cloth
only showed a girl
with an innocent smile.
After, it was a black colt
on the volcano of Santa Ana.
A bird frightened it
I gripped its neck,
my father on his horse
that reared on its hind legs
yelled for me to stay low
and hold hard with my knees,
I closed my eyes
Clippity, Clippity, Clop
while I flew among vines,
the cinch-clasp pressed against me.
On the tapestry
the shining unicorn
rested its head
on the silk lap
of the wide-eyed virgin.
I dreamed of you when I was a girl
and ran away afraid,
wild unicorn
Cloppety, Cloppety, Clop.
It is my childhood,
my dream,
my people who rise up,
broken loose and neighing.
You are life and you are death.
Four winged horsemen
announce the end of a world.
The sky parts in two,
your outline barely visible,
you sow triumph, you sow chaos
Clippity, Clippity, Clop
your mane flies in the wind,
your face is sharp and pale,
there is hope, destruction
with lips half open
you run toward the dawn.

At the marathon, young poets from the poetry workshops read alongside the famous writers of Nicaragua. It is impressive the support these young writers receive — they are published regularly in the newspaper supplements and in *Poesía Libre*.

But there was also conflict and frustration. A style of poetics called "exteriorism" was being propagated, and some young poets said that workshop leaders from the Ministry of Culture were teaching it dogmatically. They felt that it didn't apply to all poets or all kinds of poetry, and at best should be taught as guidelines rather than rules. The concept of exteriorism was defined in an important anthology that was assembled and introduced by Ernesto Cardenal in 1972. He called it "the principal tendency in Nicaraguan poetry . . . the kind of poetry we prefer."

> Exteriorism is not an ism or a school. It is as ancient as Homer and biblical poetry (in reality it has constituted the great poetry of all time.) . . . [I]t is created with images of the external world, the world we see and touch. . . . [I]t is objective: narrative and anecdotal, made from elements of real life and concrete things, with proper names and precise details and exact dates and statistics and facts and quotes. In sum, it is *impure* poetry. Poetry that for some is closer to prose than to poetry. . . .
>
> Interior poetry, in contrast, is subjective poetry, made only with abstract or symbolic words, like red, skin, ashes, lips, absence, bitter, dream, tact, foam, desire, shadow, time, blood, stone, weep, night. . . .
>
> I believe that the only poetry that can express Latin American reality, and reach the people, and be revolutionary, is exteriorism. Therefore, I thought it was important to present Nicaraguan exteriorist poetry in this anthology. (Cardenal 1981 [1972], vii–x)

This definition, which tries to legislate how art can achieve certain results ("be revolutionary"), is bound to be mischievous. How could poetry be rid of "the subjective," or of the words listed in Cardenal's description of "interiorism?" What about all the great subjective poetry of such revolutionary poets as César Vallejo, Pablo Neruda, and Federico García Lorca? Cardenal's own poems violate his rules. I share Cardenal's preferences, but believe he should simply define a certain tendency in poetry, an interest in the external world in contrast to subjective self-absorption, not try to draw a line between "objective" and "subjective" poetry — every great poem is both. Also, one can say what one likes or prefers without trying to enthrone a certain style as the *only* way to "express Latin American reality."

Unfortunately, a lot of the workshop poetry that was granted publication, though interesting and (as Fernando Silva said) often as exact and direct as classic Chinese poetry, also tended to be flat, formulaic, and uninspired. Here is an example from a poem read at the marathon by a young soldier from the islands of Solentiname:

> Solentiname was the people discussing scripture on Sundays.
> It was catching turtle and iguana for communal lunches.
> It is Elvis and Donald, with bloodied heads, thrown in sacks
>   in a launch and taken to Managua (we haven't heard from them)

> It was the noise of the kids in boats on their way to school
>   scaring the ducks who flew away shitting.
> It was the music of Elvis and William and Adancito on Sundays.
> And the paintings of the peasants full of life.
> It was our swearing Patria Libre o Morir . . .

This poem, which continues for about thirty-five lines, is full of concrete detail and has authenticity and interest, but if I were a young Nicaraguan poet who could *sing,* I would be very upset to see my work rejected by *Poesía Libre* to make room for this plodding assemblage of facts and proper names!

Other workshop writing is much better. This short poem, though dry and literal as can be, seems almost to rise off the page for its sense of emotion and drama that is present but unexpressed:

> In the park of your town
> the swans are cement.
> The old carriages creak
> along the street.
> Birds are in the trees
> and dry leaves fall
> on the benches.
> At night the wind cries
> and the leaves, changed to copper
> sway in the raintrees and laurels
> by the nests
> and the immobile swans reflect
> the moon and many-colored stars.
> At dawn
> the leaves fall
> and the birds sing again
> and next to the swans
> rose-colored butterflies
> dry themselves in the sun.

Written by a sixteen-year-old girl from a workshop in Ciudad Darío, this poem describes "the world we see" in simple, concrete words, but her perceptions are so acute and alive that a powerful sense of place, desire, and human relationship is invoked. The "objective" and the "subjective" are merged. The poet, Gretel Cruz, read another poem at the marathon, in a strong, clear voice, that literally brought the audience to its feet:

> A human needs
> a sun
> the night
> a sky
> a window

a sun-god
   cosmic energy.
a night
   with the Pleiades
   and dark, abysmal pulsars
and a window
to throw our five senses through
to the sky!

Gioconda Belli worked in the clandestine "urban front" of the FSLN during the 1970s, left the country several times to avoid arrest, and wrote two prizewinning books of poetry (one being the prestigious Cuban "Casa de las Américas" prize, for her book *Linea del fuego*). After the FSLN triumph she worked with the new government in its information office, a job so demanding that she often felt she must give up poetry or, rather, as she put it, decide to "make my work the best poem I could write." But she did continue writing, and in the eighties she published two novels in addition to poetry. To me, she is one of the best poets of Nicaragua, and the most exciting moment of the marathon for me was her reading of a new, long poem entitled "Nicaragua Water Fire." Here is an excerpt:

Nicaragua my love my little raped girl
get up now straighten your skirt
walk behind the assassin follow him
down the mountain up the mountain
no passing say the songbirds
no passing say the lovers who make love
who make children who make bread who make trenches
who make uniforms maps for the soldiers
Nicaragua my love my Black Miskito Suma Rama
maypole in the lake of pearls
hurricane winds beating San Juan down
no passing and rain on the sombreros
who walk stalking the face of the beasts
and doesn't let them rest pursues them tears them
from the breast of the country tears pulls them
the bad weeds
don't let them seed here
we want corn rice beans
that seed in the earth where the farmer
guards his wooden house his title (from agrarian
   reform)
no passing those devils talking of good times
to those who saw ranches burn

and neighbor assassinated in front of wife and
    children
Nicaragua my little girl
dance learn to read speak with people
tell them your story go in airplanes to sing your
    story
walk over the whole world your story on your back
talk until blue in the face in incomprehensible
    newspapers
yell it strongly furiously . . .

During this time the revolutionary government in Nicaragua, under attack by the Reagan-Bush government, had to spend half its budget on defense and could no longer build schools and health clinics. Thousands had been killed, there were desperate economic problems, and the people were very tired. Yet the government was sponsoring the most exciting poetry events I had ever seen. And wherever I traveled in Nicaragua I felt a high consciousness of the human spirit of the revolution and its sanctity, as shown in its poetry.

The sixteen-year-old Gretel Cruz offered an example of that consciousness:

Mother:
From the hill I draw
the delicate greenish blue
of the earth below
with sustained words
from the silent river
four hundred meters to the top
until touching the sky with the soul.
The eye draws from above
rows of pines and rows of oaks
(both are like people).
And tomorrow, in other dawns
if what I am writing survives
and some son still remains, my mother
you will send him to the hill
because from above he will plant
pines and yellow oaks
and draw greenish blue and
white, intense and free
our sky and earth.

7

Matagalpa Journal

My fourth trip to Nicaragua was to be a long one, so I bought a used motorcycle. This changed everything. I traveled more and saw the world differently. I also spent a lot of time at mechanic's shops.

Lolín helped me look for one, but he disapproved. "Buy a bicycle," he said. "The drivers here are *caballos* [horses]. I don't want you to go home in a box." We looked at a miserable wreck for 800 dollars and at others too small or too expensive. Finally, in Estelí, I found a used East German IFA, imported (probably donated) for military use — a heavy, one-cylinder city bike. "It's in bad condition," said Eugenio, the mechanic. "Very neglected, and everything dirty. But it's good."

Eugenio worked out of a side room in his mother's house, full of parts and torn-down frames of motorcycles. Two kids worked for him, though he was a kid himself, no more than twenty, but serious and sincere with me. He was short, had dark wavy hair, and squinted as he talked in rapid-fire sentences. He would overhaul the bike for me tomorrow, he said. It would take all day. It actually took two.

He took apart the carburator, motor, transmission, and generator — and cleaned and adjusted them. The tail pipe needed a new brace. The brace attaching the motor to the frame was broken. The spring for the kickstart was broken — the owner had been pushing the bike downhill to start it. These he fixed, but other parts he couldn't help with. Both tires were bad (the rear one had a hole through to the tube), there was no front brake, no taillight, no mirror, no speedometer, the chain needed replacing, and the battery was weak. He said I could get some parts in Managua on the black market. He showed me the problems and which were most serious and how to take care of them.

"It will leak oil around the clutch cable," he said, "but not much. Be careful not to overfill it." I had watched him take off the cable several times and adjust it. "The leak won't stop, because you need a new cable, but ¡*no hay!*" he said, squinting up at me (an expression heard often in Nicaragua:

"There isn't any!"). Then he showed me how to check the oil and said, "When it's below the hole add a fourth of a liter, no more!" He repeated for emphasis: "a fourth of a liter, no more!"

Eugenio was the best mechanic I met in Nicaragua. Some overcharged me, or stole gas from my tank, or were poor workers, but most were good. I knew several in every town I stayed in. But when I could I stopped in Estelí to get Eugenio to do something.

Whenever I rode the bike I was happy. I loved the view from all sides, the fresh air and the wind, the smells, the closeness to things: smoke from fires burning in the fields; fresh-turned earth; women washing clothes in the rivers. I lived inside Cardenal's poem:

> In April, in Nicaragua, the fields are dry.
> It's the month of brush-burning . . .
> and of fields made blue by the smoke
> and the dust clouds of the tractors uprooting trees;
> of riverbeds dry as roads
> and the branches stripped like roots;
> of suns blurred and blood-red
> and moons huge and red as suns
> and the far-off brushfires, at night, like stars.
> In May come the first rains.
> The tender grass is reborn from the ashes.
> The muddy tractors plow the earth.
> The roads fill with puddles and butterflies,
> and the nights are cool . . .
>
> (Cardenal 1983, 57)

Everywhere there were campesinos cutting brush with machetes or planting or hoeing. There were carts loaded with firewood pulled by oxen, kids beside the road watching me and waving, roadside stands with watermelons and cantaloupes. Several times I slowly threaded my way through a herd of cattle that lumbered toward me with long curved horns. Near certain rivers and lakes kids stood holding strings of fresh fish. In other places, boys were holding iguanas or armadillos high by the tail. A man sat in a chair, cages of green parrots beside him. All tried to wave me down. A man stalled by the road yelled for "un poco de gasolina" (a little gas).

The weather was strong and dramatic. Either the sun beat down hard and I felt my arms and face burning or the wind blew fiercely, pushing me sometimes from one side of the road to the other, or pushing my body forward like a sail. Or a gray raincloud moved down from a mountain toward the road as I hurried to beat it. The drops wet my shirt and beat against my face like pellets of hail. Or sometimes I ran into a downpour and had to take off my glasses and go very slow to see. In the mountains of Jinotega it was cold and windy in the rain. The passing trucks soaked me with a cold, heavy spray. My motor died from the water. I pushed the bike through streams of muddy water flowing across the highway until I reached a peak and could coast the remaining eight kilometers to Matagalpa. When I left the rain, the air felt warm and my clothes began to dry in the wind.

Nicaraguan roads are surprisingly empty, especially at night. My Nicaraguan friends were always shocked when I said I was going to travel at night. Perhaps it is the habit of being at war. Even buses don't run on the highways at night. But Nicaraguans are like birds: there is much movement in the late afternoon, and by dark they are settled where they want to be.

I loved the road at night. I didn't have to deal with the sun, and the world was quieter. Usually the wind had fallen, and I could see the stars behind dark, looming hills. And then, twice, there was a looming horse standing on the road asleep.

Distances in Nicaragua are short. You can ride from the Honduran to the Costa Rican border in seven hours. Yet, there are great changes in the landscape. In the north the mountains are close and high and intensely green and checked with cultivated fields. Near Estelí you drop to the broad valley of Sébaco with its rice fields and vegetable farms. Next is the poorer, drier land from which I could see the lights of Managua fifty kilometers away. The great mountains of Matagalpa and the coffee country are to the east; to the west, across Lake Managua, is the flat, hot cotton and sorghum country of León and Chinandega and hundreds of kilometers of Pacific beach. The rich farmland of Masaya and Jinotepe is south by Lake Managua, where you meet a chain of lovely volcanoes that reaches to Granada and down through Lake Nicaragua, dotted with islands; then come flat banana plantations and cattle ranches and Costa Rica.

I was getting to know Nicaragua in a special way — as a changing expanse of rich and beautiful earth. The love and astonishment I felt for the land also gave me a new understanding of imperialism. Campesinos pointed to this earth and told me, "It's rich, Nicaragua, very rich. We're poor, but not Nicaragua. Nicaragua is rich."

I crossed this country as if sailing in the bright, clean air. Sometimes I thought about bugs. I kept my mouth closed except when I was singing. There weren't many bugs, as Nicaragua has so many birds. But there were many butterflies. When I came into a flock of them, often yellow ones, I would dodge my head this way and that as if at the receiving end of a shooting range. But sometimes they would catch on the side of my helmet and get in my ears. This was a hazard—butterflies in my ears.

When Eugenio finished with the IFA, I drove to Managua and found a helmet, one tire, a chain, a brakelight, and a rearview mirror—all used. I loaded the bike and drove to Matagalpa, where I planned to base myself for a couple of months. Facing a little park where boys sit on benches waiting to shine shoes was the San Martín, a pensión where a lot of internationalists stayed. It was cheap and the woman who ran it, Blanca, knew everyone. There was a room on the second floor in back, away from the television and next to a porch, with a writing table and chair. I looked out onto pigeons, mountains, and lines of fires where campesinos were burning fields.

Unlike hot, sprawling, destroyed Managua, Matagalpa is cool and pleasant and a true city, with a large cathedral and several streets lined with stores. It felt different from when I had first come here, in the dark, on my way to Yalí; more like a European city, tucked among high, massive hills.

Also, the circumstances were changed—peace talks had begun. The Sandinistas had launched an offensive against the Contras in December and January and had driven large numbers of them into Honduras. After years of war the result was clear: the Contras could not gain control of even a part of Nicaragua, and had to negotiate. The Sandinistas were offering amnesty and aid in resettling; they demanded that the Contras accept the Sandinista government and give up armed resistance in favor of elections and legal forms of opposition. The Contras were demanding a new government and army. A cease-fire had been called.

The high command of the Contras and the Sandinistas were meeting in Sapoa, a town near the Costa Rican border. The night before I left Managua, the Sandinistas had called for a vigil for the negotiators. Norma and I drove with a truckload of residents from Máximo Jérez to the Masaya highway, by then closed to traffic and filled with people. There were bonfires and fireworks, puppets and clowns; people were gathered around music groups of many kinds. The vigil began at about eight in the evening and lasted until five in the morning, when Humberto Ortega (minister of defense) and other Sandinista negotiators left for Sapoa. Thousands of people were lining the road to the southern border. We walked to a main intersection jammed with people dancing and playing games. We danced to

"Soul Vibes," a reggae group from the Atlantic Coast, and watched the National Folkloric Ballet.

At about one-thirty in the morning we heard sirens and saw a motorcade coming. Daniel Ortega was driving the first car with Brian Wilson beside him; Brian's wife, Holly, and Kris Kristofferson were riding in the back seat. Ortega drove slowly and talked to people as he passed, looking very pleased to be there. People were running alongside and shouting greetings and slogans: "¡Para una Paz Digna!" (For a Peace with Dignity!)

At the main intersection, Ortega and Brian Wilson on his crutches (he lost his lower legs when protesting the movement of a military transport train in California) were lifted onto the bandstand. With many interruptions by the people shouting slogans, Wilson thanked them for their warm welcome and promised that more and more people in the United States would go to the streets and demonstrate for a just peace for Nicaragua. Then Kris Kristofferson sang "Nicaragua, Nicaraguita," a lovely, sentimental ballad, and the crowd joined in. Daniel Ortega stood by looking relaxed and pleased; he said only that he hoped the people would still be there, wide awake, at five-thirty when Humberto and the others were to drive past. Feeling tired, and wanting some rest before driving to Matagalpa, I walked back home, high from the energy of the people and the hope for an end to the war. The air was warm and the stars bright in the dark, dark sky.

A few days later, on the television at the Pensión San Martín, I watched Ortega award Nicaragua's highest honor to Brian Wilson: the Order of Augusto C. Sandino. I had met Brian Wilson a year and a half earlier in Massachusetts. It was the fifth of October, the anniversary of the Peace Pagoda in Leverett, Massachusetts. Wilson was there with three other veterans: Charlie Litky, George Mizo, and Duncan Murphy. The veterans were fasting, and every afternoon on the steps of the Capitol in Washington they held a vigil. They began the fast on September first (Mizo and Litky) and the fifteenth (Wilson and Murphy), shortly after Congress approved 100 million dollars in aid for the Contras. The veterans were calling for a national peace movement, and they were committed to fast until they saw a significant growth in protest by those U.S. citizens (estimated to be 62 percent) who were against U.S. policies toward Nicaragua. In an open letter to the North American people, the veterans said:

This band of thugs that the president of the United States calls "freedom fighters" has consistently used terrorism to intimidate and control the poor of Nicaragua. The Contras' record of crimes against humanity are well documented in reports by Amnesty International and Americas Watch. For arming, funding, training, and directing the Contras the United States was recently condemned by the World Court, whose jurisdiction we had accepted until Nicaragua filed its case.

We are here because we want to make it absolutely clear that if our government insists on supporting proxy killers, if it insists on violating the sovereignty and right to self-determination of other nations, if it insists on violating our own constitution and international law, they are not going to do it in our name.

Three of the veterans had served in Vietnam, one in the Second World War. They had seen the effects of war. They stood for very clear moral priorities: human lives are worth protecting; resources should be used for life, not for exploitation or death; political leaders who act against conscience should not be obeyed. I didn't see how such principles could be denied.

The veterans had organized brigades to work and witness for peace in northern Nicaragua. I made ready to join them for part of my time in Matagalpa.

It was a slow time in town because Holy Week was near, when everything comes to a stop; I saw to more repairs on the IFA and wandered about. I visited the Center for Popular Culture in Matagalpa to meet artists and find out about cultural programs, and I arranged to give a talk about Villa Sin Miedo, Puerto Rico.

In Matagalpa I found more conservatism than in Condega or Yalí. Matagalpa is a commercial center for outlying coffee plantations, and there was more impatience here with the war and the economic constraints of the central government. I heard lots of grumbling, and for the first time met people who yearned for the old days, the Somoza days when, they said, the United States sponsored and supported everything.

"There was plenty of gas, transport, and every kind of supply. And you could work," a man told me. He made his living trading in milk and cheese, but couldn't repair his truck for lack of parts, and couldn't keep it in gas when it was working. And, more surprising, I heard a U.S. invasion referred to in positive terms. I was eating lunch with a friend; at a nearby table four men were drinking beer and talking about the peace negotiations at Sapoa. I was eavesdropping and then joined them for a few minutes.

"They will accomplish nothing in Sapoa," one man said, and the others agreed; and so it seemed, because the Contras were divided. The Reagan-Bush administration supported the hardliners, who wouldn't accept a Sandinista government and wanted a military victory or at least a prolonged "low-intensity" war. The Contras who supported the talks were probably going to lose out. One man asked me if I thought the United States would invade Nicaragua and install a "Contra" government. I said I didn't think so. But one man added: "It's the only thing that will get us out of this mess."

"No," another man said, "an invasion would be horrible. It would be from airplanes, and those bombs would be worse than the Managua earthquake."

No one responded.

Perhaps another reason I perceived greater conservatism here was the advent of Holy Week. I often sat in the cathedral to read and rest; I was fascinated by the comings and goings and by the way the Church orchestrated the holidays.

One late afternoon I sat near an almost life-size plaster Christ carrying the cross. He was white-skinned and wearing real clothes — a white gown tied with a narrow red sash, and a red velvet cloak. A richly dressed Christ, indeed. In front of Christ there was a life-size statue of an altar boy, also white-skinned, also in real clothes, pale blue and dark red, carrying an offering box.

A constant stream of people stopped and made the sign of the cross. A dark little girl, very Indian-looking, touched the face of the altar boy and felt his clothes, then went to the Christ and felt his velvet cloak. A woman and two schoolboys knelt, then got up and touched Christ's velvet cloak. It became dark in the church, and the face of Christ, thin and bearded and full of suffering, looked beautiful in the shadows.

The next day there was Christ crucified, surrounded by candles and oil lamps. A small old man knelt to pray. He wore a short-sleeve dress shirt, striped; Christ wore a plain white robe. When the man got up, he reached across the rows of burning candles and touched Christ's bleeding foot; he turned and walked out limping. He was very thin, and looked worn and tired. One shoulder was narrower and higher than the other. He carried a machete wrapped in newspaper. Others stopped to pray in front of this image; all touched the bleeding foot.

Every day new images of Christ, new scenes, appeared in the church. Every day, several times, they swept and mopped the floors. There was a constant and not unpleasant smell of ammonia.

In Matagalpa there was no evidence of a liberation Church.

One afternoon I saw about two hundred people coming out of the cathedral in a funeral procession to the cemetery. A pickup truck carried the casket and piles of flowers. The boy, José Alberto Mendoza, eighteen years old, had been a soldier in the Sandinista army. He had been killed one day before the cease-fire began.

I joined them for the long, slow walk across the city. It was four in the afternoon and the sun was bright and strong; the people sought the shady sides of the streets. I remembered the funeral three years before in Condega, where the people walked alongside a pickup truck shouting slogans angrily and defiantly in their grief. But in this group, though some talked among themselves, most walked wordlessly, looking ahead or at the ground. One heard only the sound of their steps. They seemed to carry a silence with them that soaked up the noises of the city and drew people to windows and doorways as they passed.

It took an hour to reach the last turn and start up the sloping road to the cemetery. It is a majestic place, on the side of a hill overlooking the city. There's a high portico with many columns, and rows of tall cypress so dark they seem black, and large family crypts among the graves. It was beautiful in the softening light and long shadows of afternoon.

A man carrying a spade on his shoulder met the crowd, and they followed him. The casket was carried to the grave and the people sat in silence on the stones and crypts, alone or scattered in small groups. Only the mother was crying out loud. She said over and over, "My beautiful little boy."

The family sat together on a raised grave. The father, a fat, kindly-seeming man, looked straight ahead with a frown, his arm around the mother. The boy's brothers and sisters sat looking out at nothing.

A young man stood by the casket and read a short poem and a statement in a strong, loud voice: "With this death we affirm again, yet again, our commitment to defend Nicaragua from the counterrevolution, and we affirm again, yet again, our unity with the Sandinista National Liberation Front. Patria Libre," he shouted, and a few answered, "O Morir."

After a silence, a man near the grave said, "I have to say you are not speaking for this boy. He had no ideology. He was a boy who died for his country, that is all."

After a moment the young man responded by shouting again, "Patria Libre." No one answered, "O Morir."

The young man stood by the grave for a while, then sat down a few yards away. Friends joined him. Soon the older man also came and sat beside him. He put his arm around the younger man and said, "I just wanted to say what was true." The other didn't answer or look up, or pull away, either. They continued sitting in silence.

The casket was lowered into a concrete container and a concrete block was placed on top, with fresh cement between. Then the men began to shovel the dirt on top, taking turns with the shovel. After some hesitation, I took a turn. When the grave was filled the women and girls came forward with white and light-blue flowers, the long stems tied in bundles. A few red ones were placed at the head of the grave. The women stuck the flowers one by one in the dirt, doubling the lower part of the stem to give it strength. They continued until the grave seemed a thick bed of flowers.

A few people began to trickle away, but most sat or stood silently as the afternoon changed into evening.

The children and I became silly making verses:

Terrabona, Terrabona
Que bonita la tierra
Terrabonita, Terrabonita
Que tierra la bonita

We were in a remote mountain village called Terrabona, sitting around Denis while he drew the house and tree across the road. The heavy tile roof was bending, the earthen walls were cracked and worn. A bare tree nearby, about the same age, reached a gnarled branch toward the house. Denis and I had come here for a day's outing. He is an artist from Matagalpa, and likes to visit old places and draw and learn about the customs. The children had been with him for hours. I was tired and sunburned from walking around town and talking to people, and it was almost time to go back. Except I didn't want to leave. It was Holy Saturday and there was to be a procession at five o'clock. And I had fallen in love with Terrabona.

We ate green mangoes from the tree we were sitting under, and the kids were giving one another rides in a pullcart with wooden wheels. The village was coming alive from the afternoon heat. A group of cattle with long, curved horns lumbered past, driven by a small boy on a horse. A group of horses passed, no person with them, as if on some business of their own. Families were walking in from the country to see the procession: we said, "Good afternoon." A man came out of the house Denis was drawing and, with a machete in one hand, climbed a huge raintree covered with orange flowers. He cut a large branch, climbed down, dragged the branch across the yard, and stuck it in the ground beside the road.

Terrabona is three long dirt streets wide, and six short dirt streets long. On every street, for the Holy Week processions, they had planted the leafy green branches of a certain bush about every ten feet, which gave a holiday feeling to the dusty town. And in front of some houses, people had placed wreaths of flowering hibiscus or bougainvillea, or little altars with a plaster Christ on the cross and flowers all around.

On my walk I passed a house where two women were tying a string of green branches and flowers across their porch. I was thirsty and stopped to ask where I could buy something to drink, and ended up sitting on their porch with them and my two guides, Jaime, age fourteen, and Donaldo, age fifteen. Jaime and Donaldo were happy to have me for something to do on the long holiday afternoon, and they led me around town, telling me who lived in what house and a little bit of town lore, such as where their girlfriends lived. Both were neatly dressed, small, and slender. Both are "cheles," as they call light-skinned people in Nicaragua. (There are many *cheles* in Terrabona. I saw redheads, and little girls with blue eyes and blond hair. Many of Nicaragua's *cheles,* they say, come from the U.S. Marines who occupied the country from 1912 to 1933. But there have also been German immigrants.) The women gave us a large pitcher of *pinolia,* a rich and thirst-quenching drink made with very finely ground corn flour and cacao, and pastries filled with mango jelly.

Jaime's family lives across from the church, and he said yes when Denis and I asked a group of kids if they knew of anything old around here. "There is an old stone wheel behind my house," he said, and we went to see, hoping it would be a Mayan calendar.

Jaime's house was part of a family compound. From the street we entered a high-ceiling room with a few cane-backed rocking chairs. A radio was playing the Beatles. An old woman, Jaime's grandmother, was sitting in one of the chairs, tapping her hand to the music. Green crepe paper was strung across the ceiling. We passed through the kitchen with its huge pots, woodfire and high cement cooking hearth. The backyard was fenced into sections, and we passed over low gateways from one section to the next. Some girls were washing clothes on a concrete washstand; horses and cows were in one section; there were lime, orange, mango and papaya trees, worktables and hanging laundry, and kids and chickens and pigs. We gathered around the stone wheel, an old millstone. When we expressed some disappointment, Jaime's mother told him to bring out the jaguar's head. This was a real treasure, a Mayan stone carving, very worn, but the eyes, ears, and mouth were clearly distinguishable. It was found in a place about thirty minutes away by horse.

Terrabona is isolated. You leave the Pan-American Highway in a desolate area, by an electric line, a dirt road, and a sign: "Terrabona, 18 Kilometers."

But the distance doesn't express the two hours it took on my IFA, over steep mountains on pitted, rutty roads of volcanic stone.

At first, Terrabona felt desolate, perhaps because it was at the end of the dry season. The streets were dusty, the trees were bare. We asked where we could get some breakfast, and found a small *comedor* in the front room of a house. A very fat man holding a baby greeted us from a rocking chair. It was a relief to sit in the shade and drink some juice. A little girl kept trying to herd some baby chickens out of the room. The man told us about Terrabona as he rocked and cuddled the baby and as his wife fixed rice and beans and eggs.

Terrabona is famous in Nicaragua for its festival of San José (Saint Joseph). Before Terrabona existed, the man said, four families lived in this area. A girl, walking near what is now the edge of town, found a small statue of San José on the ground beside the road. She took the statue home. That evening her father stuck the point of his knife into it — perhaps to see what it was made of — and fell over dead. The statue was old and worn, and her uncle decided to paint it. When his brush touched it, he fell dead. Now the statue is in a special altar of the Church of San José. The festival begins on March nineteenth and lasts a week. They give away food and drink in large quantities, and people come from all over Nicaragua and even from other countries. The people who give away the food are called *priostes* (stewards). They save, perhaps all year, and give an entire cow or pig, or more if they are rich; for this they are blessed. It is a festival of giving because San José went around Bethlehem asking for food and lodging for the pregnant Virgin Mary, and was refused. Here in Terrabona, everyone gives.

There are many wonderful things in Terrabona. In the mountains nearby, a huge rock rings like a bell when you strike it. It can be heard all over the valley. The place is called Cerro de la Campana (Hill of the Bell). Then there is Piedra de la Goya (Goya's Rock), from which a woman jumped, trying to kill herself; she flew safely to the ground.

We heard the church bell ring and some announcements over the loudspeaker, and said we had to hurry or we'd miss something. The fat man, still rocking the baby, said, "*Con calma, con calma.* Give everything its time. Life is better that way."

The church was busy with preparations — girls sweeping, women arranging flowers, boys hanging a curtain from the ceiling to hide the statue of Christ on the cross. Christ in his all-glass casket would lie in front of the curtain, this being the day before Easter and the Resurrection.

I sat in a pew with the priest while he directed the hanging of the curtain.

He turned out to be an Irishman from Gary, Indiana. "What is it like here?" I ask.

"The people are very independent, very much apart," he said. "For example, they don't like the government, you won't find more than a couple of Sandinista activists here."

"Why?"

"Because of the repression."

"What repression?"

"The draft. They don't want to join up, and they just won't. There is almost 100 percent noncooperation here; not violent, just passive refusal. And the Sandinistas have come and taken some of the boys. So the people don't like them."

"Are there any other kinds of repression?"

"No," he said, "they don't like the war or the economic situation, but they don't see the government at fault there.

"But I think the government retaliates against the community economically," he said. "I can't prove this, but there have been times of real shortages. For example, in December and January there were shortages in basic foods—beans, sugar, things like that—and I think the government was holding back food from this community, although this is only my opinion." (I wondered: does he know that such shortages existed all over the country last year, and that Nicaragua had to import beans because of drought?)

I asked, "If the people only dislike the government because of the draft, why don't they support the draft because they like the revolution?"

"Well," he said, "you'll have to ask them about that, I really can't say."

I asked whether I could talk with him more today, and whether he could give me someone's name I could talk to, an articulate person who knows the community well. He looked at me strangely.

"Sometimes internationalists come here," he said, "and talk to people, but the people just tell them what they want to hear, not what they really think. They won't talk to a stranger—they are very independent and suspicious."

The priest told the boys to stop for lunch; then he excused himself, saying he would talk more later. But later he napped, then had a long meeting until the procession. I wondered about this priest. If San José came to his church, would he invite him to lunch?

In Jaime's house, when I asked out of curiosity if there was a place to spend the night, his mother brushed her hair back from her eyes, smiled, and said that there wasn't a hotel or *pensión*, but her sister next door had spare beds where we'd be welcome.

Most of the people in Terrabona farm and raise cattle in the surrounding valley. The houses seem neither rich nor poor. They are usually two rooms: a kitchen and a bedroom. The larger ones also have a sitting room. The walls are mud or brick, the roofs red tile. They have large yards for animals and gardens. The boys showed me a tall, wonderful tree — the *guanacaste*. Its fruit is dry and rattles and is shaped like a dark-brown human ear. The seeds inside are brown with a white stripe, and would make nice beads. The campesinos use the pulp to wash clothes. The boys and I walked every street, and they told me who lives in the house with the beautiful carved door and who has the orchard full of heavy-laden orange trees.

We stopped to talk to three young campesinos standing in front of a store. One lives about ten kilometers west, in a place called Ojo de Agua (Eye of Water). He and his family own a fifty-acre farm. Another lives fifteen kilometers east, on a cooperative farm in a place called Altavista (High View). "The cooperatives are best," he said, "because you can produce more. We have a tractor and irrigation equipment, and we couldn't afford them as individual producers."

The first man said, "My farm is small, and it isn't necessary to be part of a cooperative. I don't like the idea of joining with others."

The third man, who lives in Terrabona, said, "That is the way it is here. Some farm cooperatively, and there are several kinds of cooperatives, and some independently, and some live and work on state-owned farms. Each thinks their own way is best, or if they don't they can change over to another way."

I asked, "What is it like here in Terrabona? Are the people with the process?" (That's how you ask whether they support the revolution.)

"Yes, of course," the second man said. "Before the revolution, the whole area where I live was owned by a Somocista — about nine thousand acres. The families around there couldn't survive. Many went to Honduras, some from my own family. Now we have legal title to the land, and it is much better, even with the war and the economic blockade. We have shortages of tools and supplies such as fertilizers, and many people are afraid to be in the countryside, and production is low. We think it is important to fight and defend the land. But fighting is not what we want. We want to produce and better ourselves." The three campesinos seemed to agree about that.

It began to be hard to continue this conversation because two older men, quite tipsy, came up and wanted my attention. One kept interrupting and making jokes. I couldn't understand his Spanish, and when we asked him to be quiet he imitated my posture (folding his arms across his chest), listened with feigned wide-eyed interest, and whistled. Soon we all were laughing. And when he raised his shirt and started exposing his belly button, we had to break up entirely.

The procession started late, but Denis and I stayed for the beginning. Loudspeakers played march music while perhaps a hundred people gathered in front of the church. They came dressed up. I didn't see Jaime or Donaldo. By self-selection, some of the town joined the procession while others stayed home to watch. The church had spent a lot of money to bring in a band from Matagalpa for all of Holy Week. There were six players, and they played well, a slow processional type of music.

In front walked several small girls in identical yellow dresses and bright-red lipstick, carrying large bunches of flowers. Behind them, women carried more flowers. The people carried large puppets of Mary and Joseph, and a cross decorated with streamers. Some men were bearing the glass casket of Christ on a wooden platform. His plaster body seemed small and thin and delicate. He was wounded and scratched, and those spots were painted red.

The freckled Irish priest from Indiana was at the back of the procession in dark sunglasses and long robes. He walked slowly and gravely, not looking at us as he passed.

On the way back to Matagalpa we were happy. It was cooler, and the ride was mostly downhill.

The veterans arrived from the States at Pensión San Martín, then left for El Cedro cooperative. I had to wait three days to give my talk, then go to Jinotega to take a transport truck. Again I crossed the cold and windy mountains that stand like a wall between the two cities.

That night in Jinotega I heard rain pouring on the roof of my hotel, the first rain of the year. It was still raining softly in the first light as I walked to the market. The sunlight was coming over the mountains, filtered by clouds and mist. A woman was tending a fire, heating a pot of coffee and another of milk. A man pointed over to the truck. People were running to get on. I downed my coffee and grabbed my bag.

The truck had low sides, with side-rails and cross-rails. Soon every surface was covered with people packed tightly against one another. More people got on, more bags of this and that. Men threw bags of rice onto the heads of people jammed together in the truck. The bags slid to the floor and people stood or sat on them.

The mountains east of Jinotega are high and steep. Sometimes I felt giddy when the truck rounded a turn and a valley opened to view. Far below I could see the road crossing cornfields, the corn like fine hairs, a hawk circling over. The road snaked through the fields, passed out of sight around a woods, and appeared again crossing a river.

Half an hour later we crossed that river, only a few inches deep in the dry season. The air smelled of cold mountain water. The driver chose the down side, where the stones were more even. He stopped, shifted down, and crossed, the stones grinding loudly under the wheels. He shifted further down and began the long ascent. In the truck we moved and resettled.

At first the people talked and ate their food and the mood was jolly. We were lucky to have a place in the truck. Then weariness set in. I was sitting high on a side-rail, a two-by-four, good because I could see everything, but exhausting after a few hours of bouncing and balancing. A few inches under my shoe was the dark, braided hair of an old woman. Next to her a young woman was nursing a baby. The woman sitting behind me held my sleeve. The man in front of me had to move his hand when I moved mine. Near the end, after most of the people had jumped off at various villages and cooperatives and we seemed quite thinned out, I counted fifty-seven people still on the truck.

This was my deepest trip into the mountains. The truck was the only public transport from Jinotega northeast to San Juan de Bocay. After Bocay there are just mule paths to Honduras or points east and south.

The countryside felt peaceful. The Sapoa peace talks and the cease-fire were still going on. There has been violations, but people were feeling safer and more hopeful. Last year a truck like this one was blown up by an antitank mine, and forty-five people were killed. We passed its ruined shell.

After eight hours of bouncing and straining, the truck rolled into El Cedro. It looked surprisingly cozy, with neat rows of newly built huts. A baseball game was under way. Some oxen were pulling a cart. A group of army tents sat on a hill across from the cooperative. I saw some of the veterans standing around a newly constructed latrine. A banner hung in front of one hut: "Veterans for Peace." There was pasture and woods and a river.

The army camp was there to protect the cooperative. El Cedro is near Honduras, and a logical place for the Contras to try for a permanent base in

Nicaragua. If they succeeded, the United States might recognize the Contras as the legitimate government of Nicaragua, formalize relations, and increase support massively.

Consequently, El Cedro has been attacked a lot. First built in 1982, it was destroyed by Contras in 1983. Eight members of the cooperative were killed. They rebuilt on the other side of the river in a more defensible position, but were still attacked repeatedly. In 1985, the health clinic, many of the rebuilt houses, and more than half of the cattle were wiped out, and ten members were killed. In March 1987, the Contras overran the cooperative, burned houses, and killed five members before the Sandinistas drove them away. In all, forty-nine members of all ages, out of a population of three hundred, had been killed by Contra attacks. The health clinic had been shelled and burned four times. Its fifth incarnation was standing, rebuilt by a Veterans' Peace Action Team (V-PAT).

Every few months a new V-PAT came to Nicaragua and worked in El Cedro, chosen because of the remoteness and danger. In one of their public statements the veterans wrote, "The U.S. government is destroying schools and clinics and houses and killing innocent people here. We are here to build. In Vietnam we gave mind and body to serve in a genocidal war of destruction. Here we give our minds and bodies for life." The veterans seemed connected, serious, loving, and hopeful. I felt close to them automatically. Besides, I too am a veteran and an older man.

This group was building latrines. They had chain saws for milling lumber; the cement came in by truck. The next day I joined them in the work. We dug rectangular holes eight feet deep. Over the hole a concrete slab was poured and then the seats, walls, and roof were built. The soil was dense, heavy clay, and the sun was very hot in these mountains. After work we cooled down in the river, which has a pool deep enough to dive in. At night in El Cedro we lay in the dark on the floor of our hut, and each person spoke about the day and how he or she was feeling; then we spoke about our lives and why we were there.

Jim said that for ten years he didn't talk to anyone about what he went through in Vietnam. Finally, after a divorce, he began to face his feelings. He lives in the Southwest, a few miles from an enormous air base, in a community supported by military money. Every week, he and three nuns stand at the gates of the base and hand out leaflets. He said that with what he knows about Vietnam, the arms race, "Star Wars," and all that, he can't do nothing.

John described an experience he will never forget: a cop dragging a black kid through revolving doors, then cracking his head open outside. He saw this when standing in the lobby of the Conrad Hilton Hotel in Chicago during the 1968 Democratic Party Convention. He was there for a party, dressed in a suit and tie. He said in Vietnam he thought a lot and decided to devote his life to two things: helping bring people together and sharing abundance with people who didn't have. After the war, he worked in Chicago teaching poor kids in a special school. His aim was to teach them how to teach themselves.

"Nothing will change if no one tries to get rid of the dictator," he said. "We play a small part. Do you want to end the war? You can if you put yourself in the way. The authorities don't know what to do when they are challenged by the truth."

Another of the veterans deserted and went to Canada after being in Vietnam for a few months. "I knew I would be killed if I stayed," he said. "All the people who told me I should go [to Vietnam] were staying safely at home." He is a skilled electrician, mechanic, and boat builder. In California, he had a successful well-drilling business, which he sold to support his kids while he lived in Nicaragua. He had been working here for a year, and would stay several years more.

Another veteran, a woman, works as a secretary in Hawaii. She was doing a census and a history of the cooperative. Another veteran was a potter from Kennebunkport, Maine. Still another was a lawyer from Seattle.

Fred was the spokesperson and leader of the group. He was a tall, good-looking man of forty. He had spent the past seventeen years recovering from Vietnam. He was in light-weapons infantry and spent a year in combat. He wouldn't talk to me about it, but said it was like the movie *Platoon*. For fourteen years after the war he was "smoldering" — he had a small construction business, did a lot of drugs, and went from woman to woman. Then he began to travel in Central America, where he met and lived with a politically savvy German woman. He learned Spanish and got a degree in Latin American politics. He went through a drug and alcohol rehabilitation program. He studied to become an emergency health worker, to bring that skill to Nicaragua. When he heard about the V-PAT project, he contacted them, and they made him permanent organizer.

At least two-thirds of El Cedro's population are children. One household was all kids, nine in all. A boy of fifteen, a girl of fourteen, and a girl of thirteen took care of the others.

Even the very small children worked — sweeping, watching their younger brothers, and sisters, moving animals from pasture to yard, gathering and chopping wood, carrying water. Or played intensely — running games like tag, pulling games like tug-of-war, and stickball with sticks and rocks. The younger boys played cowboy; the older boys played baseball, using a tennis ball which they hit with a stick or with a rock in their fist.

At the river, little boys soaped themselves all over and dove and swam like sardines. They lined up in a row and the kid at the back would swim to the front between their legs. The girls and women bathed in a different place.

Walking back from the river, I saw three boys resting by three bundles of wood. They were holding a big snake someone had killed. I helped one boy load wood onto his back — he was smaller than his bundle.

Outside the school you could hear the children loudly saying their letters in unison.

Walking past a house, I heard a bunch of kids inside singing a nonsense song they repeated over and over. It would suddenly stop. Then they would laugh.

The veterans' meals were like animal feedings. At exactly 7:00, 12:00, and 5:00 o'clock we walked in a group over to Esperanza's house, a woman who cooked for us and some of the military stationed there. We passed in a herd through rows of huts; we narrowed our ranks to cross planks laid over ditches; we passed children playing, and pigs and chickens strolling; we milled around Esperanza's front yard and porch until she called us. We washed our hands in water and peroxide, and drank water with iodine. We were careful about parasites because so many veterans in earlier groups had become sick.

The food was always the same: beans and rice and tortilla, three times a day. The helpings were large — and if someone wasn't feeling well and didn't eat everything, someone would finish for them. The veterans had brought peanut butter, but it ran out. They had brought spices like lemon-flavored garlic salt, which got used up. We stood on the porch watching the sun set and the chickens climb onto the clothesline posts for the night, like work animals gathered for their evening grain. We were hungry, and we ate a lot and were very satisfied. The rice, beans, tortilla, and sweet coffee became more and more delicious.

One evening the doctor, here for a vaccination campaign, sat with us in candlelight and talked about the history of this region, called El Cúa–Bocay. "This area is very fertile," she said, "but it is jungle and mountains and while the Miskito and Sumo Indians lived along the rivers, very few others lived here until early in this century. The serious migrations came when campesinos were driven off their holdings by big landlords — owners of coffee plantations in Jinotega and San Rafael del Norte and, in the western areas, U.S. capitalists, who invested in cotton plantations. The poor campesinos were attracted by the abundance of land. But when I first saw El Cedro there were only three houses.

"The area has always been known for revolutionary struggle. Sandino fought here and gathered troops from among the peasants. Many Sandinista leaders were born here. And many people are descendants of U.S. Marines, here to fight Sandino. People with names like Moore, Rand, and Dawson came to be vaccinated today."

The doctor, María Felicia de Salón, is an Argentine who fled the right-wing government of her native country; she lived for two years in France, then came to Nicaragua after the FSLN triumph in 1979. Her husband teaches high school in Matagalpa. She and her husband are paid with money from the World Council of Churches. She has a degree in medicine and a master's in epidemiology. She worked out of Managua until Ambrosio — her "soul mate" — was killed in an ambush. She volunteered to take his place.

"Doctors and teachers are targets," she said, "because they are hard to replace. It may take years to replace a trained person." The Contras tried to ambush her twice. Once, in November 1986, she was in a truck near El Cúa bringing vaccination supplies and salaries to health workers. "Someone jumped into the road in front of the truck; we didn't know he was a Contra until we saw his face full of hate and he started firing. There were others on the hill above us. The driver was wounded in the shoulder, but he started driving backwards. A woman in back was thrown out and kidnapped, and two women were wounded. The driver drove backward to the nearest village, using only one arm. That saved us. I was attacked on the road to El Cúa one other time, but the Sandinistas were near and drove them away."

A report on the religion of El Cúa–Bocay, prepared by the Ministry of Agriculture, noted that before the revolution there were no schools, no health clinics, no banks or technical assistance for the campesinos, no electricity, no construction, and no year-round passable roads (except by mule). By 1988, however, there were thirteen schools, forty teachers, two health clinics, three health posts, a doctor, several nurses, and twenty-five other health workers. There were two agencies representing the national bank and fifteen agricultural technicians, and the town of El Cúa now had hydroelectric power; some six hundred and fifty houses were built in 1985–86 alone, and the roads were passable all year.

"I love this revolution," María Felicia said. "I have never seen a government that could engage in self-criticism like the Sandinistas. This revolution has a dignity that is shown in many ways—for example, abolishing the death penalty and [setting up] the system of open prison farms. They have a very Christian vision, they are very forgiving, as in giving amnesty and pardon to political prisoners. I don't understand how they can be so forgiving. For example, Tomás Borge pardoned the man who tortured him and his wife. . . . It would cost me a lot to meet the man who killed Ambrosio, but that is the way the revolution is and the way we have to be."

We took an afternoon off and drove with María Felicia to San Juan de Bocay. She knew every house and stream. She pointed to a place where Sandino had camped with his army; to a red-and-black bird called the sandinista; to the shell of an ambulance that had held eight health workers and her beloved Ambrosio.

Bocay was like an old western town, with rows of small, wood-frame houses and stores with horses tied in front. A carnival was in town, a few patched tents and a rickety merry-go-round. We bought a watermelon, drove to the far side of town, and saw the Río Coco and the end of the road.

The medical workers had organized a vaccination campaign in El Cedro. The cooperative was called to a meeting. They sang the national anthem, the health workers and cooperative members performed a "sociodrama" about hygiene, and the doctor gave a talk. She was upset.

"Two people died here this month," she said, "an infant with diarrhea and a woman with tuberculosis. How can we let this happen? There are cures for these problems. Speak out if someone throws garbage out the door. The veterans have built latrines, now the people must use them. The mothers and fathers must set an example for the little ones."

Later she said: "These deaths are also casualties of the war. There is not enough soap, medicine, transportation; there are not enough health workers."

After dinner there was a dance. Light was provided by a bottle of kerosene with a rag wick, placed in the center of the floor. Two guitar players made music. Most of the community danced, even the little kids. There were two kinds of dance: *suelto* (which means loose or free), where the partners don't touch, and *amarrado* (fastened), where the partners hold each other close.

That night, I woke to the sound of moaning from a nearby house. It was Bernardo, having intense stomach pain. This was the third night we had heard him. It didn't seem to have a physical cause — the doctor had checked him. She decided it was shock. He was the father of the baby who had died from diarrhea.

In the mountains the days are bright and hot, the nights cold and black. Each is twelve hours long. We usually woke at six to the rhythmic pounding of tortillas. The sound came from every house. Outside a man split firewood; another sharpened a machete on a stone. Woodsmoke poured from under the roofs of the houses.

Each family group, sometimes three generations and ten or twelve people, had a house. There were forty houses in El Cedro, as well as storage buildings and a school and a clinic. They had about five hundred acres of land, and each family worked a few acres for private consumption.

Some members of the cooperative were ex-Contras. They carried guns, did guard duty, and had a house, like everyone else. Some had family, brothers or sons, in the Contras. Such families were divided much as families were in the U.S. Civil War. It was a strange experience to be among people who had suffered so much from Contra attacks, and see so many ex-Contras and families of Contras. I began to lose my image of Contras as the Other, in spite of the fact that I had mostly known them through the atrocities they regularly committed.

Every month there was a meeting of ex-Contras in this region who had taken advantage of the amnesty and gone back to their homes. There were about forty men at this meeting. They lined up in rows and gave their names. Some had been on the truck from Jinotega with me; some were from El Cedro. They were obviously not too happy being observed and photographed by us veterans, and lectured to by Pablo Blanco, the director of the Sandinista Front in this zone, who was about half the age of most of them. Blanco said: "You are the first to work for peace; for a man who accepts the amnesty and leaves the counterrevolutionary forces is a lover of peace. It is U.S. imperialism that has divided us. We want peace, not because we are afraid but because the war is wrong. We want to stop the bloodshed and suffering, plant our crops, build our houses, and live together as one family. The only strange faces here are these North Americans [he pointed to us veterans, and everyone laughed]. All of us are brothers."

The head of zonal security, Marcos Montoya, went over some rules: "Don't travel without getting a permit. If the Contra ask you to go back, don't do it. They will come to you first because they know you, but remember the sacrifices your families have made because of the war. If you have any difficulties, come and talk to us. We have the goodwill to help. If you need work or land, go to the *compañero* here from UNAG.

"You have had years of combat, and you know what it is like to fight in the mountains. If you have any contact with the Contras, talk to them. We know they are afraid. Tell them that we respect the amnesty law. We hope to have more of you at our next meeting."

The peace talks in Sapoa had ended; the Reagan government opposed the Sandinista terms, and the Contra leadership was divided and trying to consolidate its position. Some favored negotiations; others, in line with U.S. policy, were taking a harder line. But here everyone was excited and hopeful because a battalion of Contras was nearby, and their officers had had a peace meeting with Sandinista army officers. They had arranged it between themselves. The armies themselves were getting together and talking about peace. We found out the details because Fred was invited. He described the meeting to us that night.

"Manuel came by at four in the morning," he told us, "and said there was going to be an important meeting between the Contras and the army. He wanted me to come as a representative of the Veterans for Peace. Then he went off, and I didn't think much more about it until he came again at one. I had one minute to decide. I ran for my camera and film. We walked into the jungle and met an entire company of BLI [light infantry battalion], a hundred and fifty heavily armed men. They were the escorts for a captain, a lieutenant, Luis Quant [regional representative of the Sandinista Front], Manuel [head of UNAG for the region], and me.

"I was really excited. Everything was crystal clear, I could smell the flowers on the coffee trees, I watched the faces of the soldiers. It was as if I saw everything at the same time. We were walking on a very narrow trail. The soldiers were in all sorts of uniforms, new and old, and many were wearing the red-and-black bandanas of the Sandinistas, and many were wearing rosaries. They looked intense, competent, aware and seasoned, the kind of soldiers I knew from Vietnam. They were walking into Contra territory, protecting their commander, and they seemed aware that this was a historic event. I was glad they seemed so competent, because I was free to mull over my feelings, which were almost overwhelming and continued to be overwhelming.

"We walked for several kilometers on this trail and crossed a river, and

A family in El Cedro

Soldiers and their families in El Cedro

they told me to wait because they weren't sure the Contras would want me to be present. Manuel and I sat and talked. I asked him how he had arranged the meeting. I knew he was a UNAG promoter, but this was something more momentous than helping cooperatives in the war zone. He told me that the Contra *comandante* was his brother-in-law. They had always been close friends, and a few months ago they had exchanged letters. Then he got a message that the man would like to meet with him about family matters, because he hadn't seen his wife and family for three years. So they met and talked and began to express their feelings about the war. They discovered they felt the same.

"Finally Manuel said he didn't want to wait any longer, so we walked along the path by the river. It was incredibly beautiful. The sun was at a perfect angle to the river, which often broke into rapids, and it was one of those lush, narrow river valleys with high mountains on both sides and a lot of beautiful trees, banana trees and those pink flowering trees we see a lot. We walked way up onto a ridge to the nearest army outpost. The soldiers said we could wait there. They had binoculars and were keeping an eye on a hillside that was covered by the BLI force surrounding this little house that was barely visible up on the hill. We waited about two hours until someone

A meeting of ex-Contras in El Cedro

waved his arm and we walked up this incredibly steep walk. I was hot and sweating and excited. A guy on a horse met us and followed us up. I asked Manuel what I was supposed to say. Just tell them who you are and that you represent Veterans for Peace and that you're happy to be here. Take your pictures and relax, he said.

"I don't know what I was expecting, some kind of armed fortress, but it turned out to be just a little wooden house owned by a small farmer in an isolated spot with a tremendous view and a forty-foot waterfall just around the hill from the house. The scene was incredibly picturesque. I expected people to be tense and armed to the teeth. What I saw was the usual handful of Nicaraguan kids running and playing, and Contra and Sandinista soldiers standing around talking to one another. I couldn't always tell which was which! But mostly I could, because the Contras had newer camouflaged uniforms with 'U.S.' stamped all over them, and some of the *compas* I recognized, like Juan and Víctor and some of the guys we see all the time at dinner. It felt almost like a picnic. I couldn't get it through my head: these two sides have been trying to kill each other for eight years!

"Anyway, they invited me inside the house and I shook hands with everyone and explained who I was. When I told them I didn't have a flash we went outside to take the pictures. It turned into a hysterical picture-taking session — everytime I got ready to take one, about five or six people would crowd in, putting their arms around one another and shaking hands — it was not anything like I had expected. These guys acted like they knew one another! Even though there must have been a lot of animosity, there seemed to be a feeling on both sides that this was an opportunity for a peaceful settlement. They said there will be another meeting on the first of May. So I took the rest of a roll and then a roll of thirty-six in about ten minutes. I got Manuel to take my picture shaking hands with the Contra commander. This guy was real handsome, with curly black hair down to his shoulders, brand-new uniform, real proud and authoritative, but very relaxed and smiling. Everybody sort of milled around the house, about forty or fifty on each side. It was beginning to get dark, so as it was breaking up everyone was yelling back and forth — let's get together, let's have a beer in Matagalpa, punching each other on the shoulder, hugging each other and smiling. I could hardly talk, I was so choked up. I felt like this was the most momentous occasion of my life. It was the first time in my fifteen months in Nicaragua I have seen a real step toward peace; and it was not from the big leaders, but from the guys who have been slogging in the mountains for years, shooting at one another, launching grenades at one another, at their cousins and brothers-in-law!"

After Fred talked, Marcos came in to give us his impressions. He seemed just as excited. He said the regional officers on both sides were going to take the news of this meeting to their higher officers.

"We looked at the situation with those who were actually fighting," Marcos said, "and we said we didn't want more war, that we are brothers who are killing one another and we can't continue this bloodshed, our own and that of the civilian population. They said there is no need for war, there is plenty of land in Nicaragua for everyone, so it would be better to lay down these weapons and pick up machetes. They said it had been years since they had seen their families or had been able to see the lights of a city and sit at a table in a restaurant and drink a beer. They said the high command doesn't have to deal with the bombs and bullets. They are not living in the mountains. We are the ones who are suffering.

"This was a very historic, emotional meeting," Marcos said. "We were very satisfied to see one another face-to-face, and we understand that we want to consolidate our relations and put an end to the bloodshed. This was a gigantic step for Nicaragua, and also for all of Latin America, because it was we the people of Nicaragua showing the Contra leaders and the U.S. government that we want peace."

I was dying with frustration to see another meeting between the army and the Contras. The images of the Contras I had absorbed were becoming more real and complex, but were still very stereotyped, very simplistic.

When the veterans left El Cedro, I rode with them to Matagalpa and sent off some mail. Then I hitched back to El Cúa, near El Cedro, to the first anniversary commemoration of the death of Ben Linder, a North American engineer who had helped design and build a water-powered electric generator in El Cúa. Ben had lived and worked there for two years; before that, he had worked as a clown in the Nicaraguan circus. He and two Nicaraguans were measuring the waterflow of a stream when they were killed in a Contra ambush.

Lots of people from Managua and Matagalpa had come. Ben's mother and father and sister were in El Cúa and spoke about him and his work, as did members of the families of the Nicaraguans. The Linders had spent the past year traveling around the United States, speaking and raising money for the electrification project Ben was working on. They had collected 150,000 dollars for it. A machine shop was going to be built in El Cúa, to manufacture parts for hydroelectric generators. It would run on electricity from the El Cúa generator. A retired machinist from Seattle had come to work and train Nicaraguans.

El Cúa is two rows of houses alongside a road that follows a fast-moving river in a narrow valley. It has a market, a bank, a clinic, and an army post. I had arranged with the regional commander of the army to be present at the next meeting with the Contras. I had nothing to do but wait.

I was tired from so much moving around and sleeping on concrete floors and sagging beds. Also, I was homesick. It was the beginning of May, and I imagined tulips and forsythia and lilacs and apple blossoms in Massachusetts. In El Cúa, too, there was a sense of spring. It was the beginning of the rainy season, and the hills were a fresh, light-green color.

The doctor, María Felicia, lent me her little house in El Cúa. It was only a few feet from the river; there were banana trees outside and rose and hibiscus. I could sit in her doorway and look at the river. Campesinos crossed on horseback going in and out of town, leading donkeys loaded with bags, stopping to water the animals, making silhouettes in the soft evening light.

Soldiers at rest camp

Women washed clothes in the river. Everyone bathed in it. A soldier took off his boots, stripped to his undershorts, waded out, and soaped all over. Two little boys with him jumped and fell in, over and over, splashing each other and laughing. I lay in the shallow water with my feet against a rock and let the current massage my neck and back.

I boiled potatoes and cabbage on María Felicia's camping stove and made avocado salad and drank cups of hot, boiled water. It felt luxurious to be at rest, listening to frogs and crickets and Abdullah Ibrahim on the cassette deck. Lightning was flashing outside constantly and gently, heat lightning without thunder, like a muted display of fireworks. You could see jagged lines of fires on the mountains. The river's voice was gentle and probing, like fingers on my body.

For all of the early morning hours, I kept coming back to the same dream: men were throwing rocks at one another in front of my house. They were scattered about the yards, and up and down the street. There was no issue between them, and they didn't seem to be divided into sides; there was just a compulsion to do it. I went into my house because rocks were also thrown at me, at anyone outside. I kept the lights turned off. A Vietnam veteran we call Country Fred came into the house. In real life, Fred used to get drunk at a bar near where I lived and would stop by to sleep because he couldn't make it home. He would come into the house and call out, "John! It's me, Fred!" I would get out of bed and toss a sleeping bag down the stairs. I could see him standing there, one hand on the stairpost, swaying slightly, a sweet smile on his face. "You know where the couch is," I'd say. "I'll see you in the morning." But he was never there in the morning. The only sign was the sleeping bag rolled up on the couch. Now here he was in my dream in Nicaragua. We stood by the windows, Country Fred and I, and watched the men throwing rocks at one another.

     I stopped by the office of Luis Quant, regional chief of the Sandinista Front for El Cúa–Bocay. He said that army–Contra meetings were happening elsewhere, all over the north: Bocaycito, Pedernales, Waslala, Quilali. There would probably be more in this zone. He was very pleased about this. It felt like the war was crumbling from the inside. "The Contras don't understand the amnesty law," he said. "Their officers never explained it to them. These meetings are good because we tell them about it and reassure them. They learn they can lay down their arms and go home in peace." He said the campesinos are very happy these days because of the cease-fire. The rains are coming, and they will have the confidence to plant.

Down the street is a house where meals are served and a few rooms are rented. There I met Clifford, a North American who has lived here for three years working on the electrification project with Ben Linder. He was middle-aged, a very thin, unshaven, grungy-looking, and happy man. He was in the process of buying a little cabin and a piece of land. We walked over to look at it. It had about three acres with bananas and a few citrus trees, right by the river. He wanted to live there forever.

We went up to the little dam above El Cúa, which he had to empty so they could repair some leaks. For a couple of days there would be no electricity. We drove a few miles into the hills, then walked, following a concrete flow channel. It was jungle as soon as you were in the woods. All kinds of ferns and flowers and birds. Sometimes the screams of monkeys. It was easy to drain the dam. He cranked up the metal door and it emptied like a bathtub.

Clifford and I went to visit Don Cosme, the old man Ben Linder had lived with. The house was at the edge of town and painted red and black "so the Contras will know who lives here," he said. He had pastureland in back of the house, and horses and cows. He said he had spent six years with Sandino's army. He wanted me to take his picture holding his AK-47, this sprightly, skinny man, seventy-two years old, who started crying when he talked about Ben Linder. "He was my son," he said, "and the second son of mine killed by the Contras. They attacked this house, fifteen of them, and killed my Alejandro."

I was reading *Hemingway en Cuba* by Norberto Fuentes, published in Cuba and Nicaragua. It has lots of photographs and uses only Cuban sources — interviews and materials obtained from the Hemingway museum there. Fuentes mines and sifts all this material with great care and patience. He talks to everyone: Gregorio Fuentes, the fisherman who ran Hemingway's boat and who was the inspiration for *The Old Man and the Sea;* old Havana friends; fishing and drinking buddies.

I see a new side of Hemingway, through this Cuban, socialist writer. Hemingway was much loved in Cuba. He had good, colloquial Spanish. He knew lots of working-class Cubans and generously loaned or gave money to many people. He willed his boat to Gregorio Fuentes. He was friends with the great socialist filmmaker Joris Ivens, whom he met during the Spanish Civil War. He donated money to the Cuban Communist party. He loved his house and his dogs and cats, and claimed to have eighteen varieties of mango trees on the grounds. He had many guests there. One of Fuentes's stories was told by Hemingway's gardener:

"One day the *maestro* was sitting by the swimming pool, his feet in the water. He told me: 'Sit down here and take off your shoes and put your feet in the water.'

"We sat side by side. He put his arm around me. He looked at me and said, 'Hombre, this morning Ava Gardner swam naked in this water!'"

According to Fuentes, Hemingway respected the Cuban Revolution and left his house and much of its contents to the new government, contrary to stories published in the United States that claimed the property had been confiscated. Certainly Hemingway is respected in Cuba. His books have been republished many times there; when I went back to Matagalpa I bought a copy of *For Whom the Bell Tolls* in Spanish. His house is maintained exactly as it was, including the magazines on the coffee tables and the liquor bottles at the bar. An annual Gulf Stream fishing competition is named after Hemingway.

Hemingway is often criticized for the pessimism of his writing and for its "formalism" — its preoccupation with style. Ralph Ellison wrote that Hemingway avoided dealing with social reality: "Artists such as Hemingway were seeking a technical perfection rather than moral insight. (Or could we say theirs was a morality of technique?) . . . [I]t conditions the reader to accept the less worthy values of society, and it serves to justify and absolve our sins of social irresponsibility. With unconscious irony it advises stoic acceptance of those conditions of life which it so accurately describes and which it pretends to reject" (Ellison 1964, 38–40).

Ellison is right, I think, yet Fidel Castro, in an interview with Fuentes, offers another perspective. Hemingway is his favorite author. He has read and continues to read all of Hemingway's works, and has read his favorite, *For Whom the Bell Tolls,* several times. "The first reason he attracts me," Fidel said, "is his realism. His writing is clean and clear and always convincing."

Fidel especially likes Hemingway's writing about the sea, ". . . the Gulf Stream, eternal and powerful. . . . I too know and admire this silent landscape flowing inexorably along the coast of the island. . . . I think I understand Hemingway's feelings when he navigates through these waters. . . .

"Also Hemingway is an adventurer in the genuine, beautiful sense of the word — one who doesn't conform to the world around him and who assumes he must break with convention and change the world. . . . [H]e has great audacity and courage." Lastly, speaking of *The Old Man and the Sea,* Fidel said, "I want to tell you about . . . how Hemingway has been among us here in these years. He has been with us because really his works don't speak of men who are so hard they have been dehumanized. . . . [T]his is a point about which his critics have erred. The confusion arises because of the iron will of his characters. A man who confronts adversity must do so totally. The end will not be written, victory will not always be gained. What is important is to try, to struggle. This is the message of Hemingway that has been present here in Cuba in the middle of the revolution. A revolutionary wants to convert dreams into reality, is one who lives in the belief that they can destroy us a thousand times, but never conquer us. This is the message that captivated us in the revolution, the message proclaimed by all people who have struggled and in the literature of all epochs: 'A man can be destroyed, but never conquered'" (Fuentes 1984, 523–26).

This is excellent and true, but there is something more that Fidel leaves out. Hemingway was a physical and mental wreck by age sixty-two, an alcoholic and a suicide. Why? He had a "successful" life. His childhood was privileged, emotionally secure, and relatively normal. I don't know the answer, but I think a key symptom of his misery is that for most of his adult life he depended for happiness on killing animals. Fuentes writes that in one month he caught fifty-three large marlin, and in one season almost two hundred. His house is full of animal trophies, as if impalas and kudu and buffalo had broken through the walls and were standing alive and at attention.

Hemingway was happiest in his early years, fishing and hunting in Michigan. As an adult, those boyhood pleasures lost their innocence, and he foundered morally and politically. He lived among aristocratic "sportsmen," whom he often despised. He acted the patriot during wartime, yet he didn't love his country. His writing was unanchored—it often veered uncontrollably from the romantic to the sentimental and sickly.

I had spent a week in the house by the river when Captain Zamoro came by to give me bad news: the meeting they had expected to have with the Contras had been canceled. Comandante Marlin had been ordered to pull back to Honduras. Alfredo César, head of the FDN, had ordered Contra troops not to meet with civilians or Sandinista troops. Evidently, he and Enrique Bermúdez (former National Guard colonel and now military chief of the FDN) were firmly in control. Their terms for peace: defeat of the revolution.

I learned later that three Contra *comandantes* who opposed the Bermúdez-César line had been arrested by the Honduran army and flown to Miami, where the CIA ordered them "retired." Voice of America radio began accusing the Sandinistas of violating the cease-fire. It charged that they were blocking food supplies from reaching the Contras and were heavily rearming their own troops.

I had wanted to see Nicaraguans uniting in spite of Bermúdez and César, Eliot Abrams and Ronald Reagan; uniting to build a new society in peace. But this was not to be.

8

Where Is the Revolution?

What is revolution? Where does it exist? My *Penguin Encyclopedia* defines revolution as "a sudden change of government (or of the entire political system) . . ."; the *American Heritage Dictionary* defines it as "a sudden political overthrow . . . A forcible substitution of rulers . . . Seizure of state power." Reports in the popular news media conform to these definitions; they focus attention on the political arena — who is and who is not in the government and what happens within the government.

This was not how Nicaraguans spoke about their revolution. They spoke of working for themselves instead of being exploited by others; of justice and caring for the needs of all; of loving and caring for nature. They spoke of education, housing, health care, and culture. They spoke of a new life, creative spirit, healing, practicing love for one another. They stressed the need for continued struggle with the deficiencies and conflicts inherited from the past. They saw the revolution as process, as moving through time from the past into the future.

They also spoke of the revolution as the creation of a new kingdom. This meant new government and laws, based on new principles. In this regard they agreed with the dictionaries: a revolutionary government was needed to create and defend a new order. But a change in political power was not all; there was a need for fundamental change, and struggle, over privilege and power in all areas of life. There was a need for changed values.

The narrowness of the dictionary definitions is shown by their use of the word "sudden." Revolutionary changes in people's lives take time. It may be better to speak of evolution, rather than revolution. Yet, as Ernesto Cardenal writes,

> Evolution comes in leaps . . .
>   evolution is Revolution
> Revolution is not illusion
>   the caterpillar weaves around itself a new home

from which it emerges with colored wings
with which it flies off to the sky

(Cardenal 1983, 215–16)

Social revolutions involve vast numbers of small changes in people's relationships. These culminate in disruptions and reconstruction, and are followed by more slow, molecular changes.

Everyone who came to Nicaragua to observe the revolution indicated, by the focus of their attention, where the revolution lived for them. For me, the political arena—the government—is like an outer skin or cocoon. It is important and necessary, but the heart of revolution is where people remake their lives: in their work, their homes, and their communities.

The Luis Hernández Farm Cooperative

I hit rain on my motorcycle, coming back through the mountains, and everything I had was wet. I wrote my notes in Matagalpa, in the Pensión San Martín on a cold and rainy evening, wrapped in a sheet. The day before, when the afternoon rains came, I was working at Luis Hernández in the women's garden, on my knees searching for the beet tops among strange tropical weeds, some with roots growing from the stem and visible above ground, some with such deep, strong roots that pulling them brought the beets up with them.

The women in the cooperative worked in the garden in the afternoon. Some hoed peppers, one sprayed cabbages, one tied tomato plants, one picked beans. Later I joined the bean picker because I could reach the high ones on the stakes. The bushes were loaded. I'd pull a handful of five or six pods and toss them onto a piece of plastic. I'd watch the sky. High in those mountains it was like being among the clouds. It was mostly sunny, with large white clouds and several thunderclouds, and everything green, green, green. The Sandinista *guerrilleros* in the mountains wrote that they sometimes felt they were going insane from the color green.

There was thunder for about an hour, always moving closer, becoming heavy and deafening, monumental, like a tour in some tropical thunder museum, filled with the sounds of birds and screaming monkeys who hate the thunder.

When it began to rain we stopped working and wrapped the pile of green beans—about thirty pounds—in the plastic. A young woman, Myra, carried it on her head as we wound our way along a narrow path, up and down and across streams. At a steep spot, slippery from the rain, she slipped and almost dumped the beans. I carried them for a while, and then slipped also, sliding in the mud but holding the beans secure. "Oh, Señor Juan! Oh, Señor Juan!" they said, laughing and embarrassed. At the cooperative the women divided the beans. These were green beans, not the black beans that grow on low bushes in the large fields and are the main staple of the campesino. These are eaten fresh, as is the rest of the produce from the women's garden. Such a garden is unusual in the mountains of Nicaragua; it was promoted by three Basque internationalists.

I met two of the Basques, Jon and Araxo, at the San Martín. I heard them talking and typing on the balcony outside my room, writing a proposal to UNAG for help with a flower-growing project. In their view, the cooperative needed more products to sell for cash. Araxo was typing and Jon was dictating, his hands covered with pus-swollen blisters. I loaned him antibiotic cream, and they told me about the cooperative and invited me to visit. It is on the other side of Jinotega, about twenty miles into the mountains.

A few weeks later, I half drove and half pushed my motorcycle up their mountain on the steep, muddy, rocky paths; my heavy city bike wasn't made for off-road riding and I was exhausted. When I came to a group of one-room houses perched on the side of the mountain, I saw Vidal, the cooperative's president, herding some cows higher up. They were scattering. He ran up the side of the mountain, throwing rocks at them and leaping like a dancer on clouds. When he came back to show me where to put my things, he wasn't a bit out of breath. The Basques and the others were at Corinto (a state farm next to theirs) for a big fiesta. "Let's go!" he said.

Vidal showed me their fields of beans and corn and where the coffee was planted and where the next farm began. The land was high and offered large views.

"We have nine families and 265 *manzanas* [about six hundred acres]," he said. "Five years ago there was nothing here. Now we have our houses, and three years ago we put in the coffee *beneficio* [mill]. We've only had coffee for three years. Last year's crop was twice as big as the one before, and this year's will be bigger."

We passed a dead ox covered with buzzards, many circling overhead. It had died of some sickness, and this left them with only three oxen as work animals. They have no tractor or truck. They carry produce down the mountain by oxcart, with the animals hitched at both ends, the paths are so steep.

"We have seventy cattle," Vidal told me. "We have cows for milk, and each family has its own pigs and chickens. We have the new school. It has two rooms and two teachers. Children come from around the area. But we need more people. See these fields? They are filling up with weeds. We don't have the labor to clear them."

Corinto is much bigger than Luis Hernández — with about five times as much land and more than fifty workers. There are large barns and corrals, obviously decades old — the farm had been abandoned by a Somocista and was taken over by the state. At the fiesta, the people ate and danced (outside in a horse corral), competed in horse races and greased-pole climbing, and listened to speeches by officials from UNAG and the FSLN urging people to work hard and not be discouraged by the war. We straggled back to Luis Hernández as it was getting dark.

Vidal and his wife Manz had five children, ages four to thirteen. Manz drew extra rations from the cooperative, because she cooked for the Basques. The Basques were very affectionate with the children, and the younger ones often sat on their laps, sharing their food. We had rice and beans and coffee, and the most delicious tortillas I ever ate in Nicaragua, very light and tasting of fresh corn.

After dinner Vidal and I stood outside the house. He had turned on the generator so the houses would have electric light for their allotted two and a half hours a day. Just below us was the new brick school. To the left was the *beneficio,* where coffee was shelled and cleaned. We looked into the wide valley below with its scattered lights and at the stars overhead that seemed nearly as close.

"We all think alike," he said, "all the members of the cooperative. It is just like that boy said who spoke to us today. It is simple. The revolution has taken the power away from the Somocistas and given it to the campesinos.

"I used to work for Somoza. It was his own farm, a big one near Sébaco. He didn't live there — one of his managers did. I rented the land for 300 córdobas a *manzana* [about two and a half acres] for each harvest. I had to provide everything — the seed and fertilizer and insecticide. I hired oxen to plow and a mule to carry the crop in to market. I had to sell to a dealer — there were no guaranteed prices like we have now — so I had to take what they offered me. Sometimes I made nothing. Nothing!"

Vidal is a husky man with a thick mustache and an easy smile; he radiated optimism and energy. Here on this mountain, his hand stretched toward a view that reached north to Honduras, and he seemed to be speaking to the world.

The school in the Luis Hernandez farm cooperative

"The big difference," he said, "is we own the land. We have credit at the bank and can build a house for anyone who will move here. We need more families. And we need peace."

The war was one reason for the shortage of labor. One member was away doing his reserve duty, and Vidal would have to go soon. New people were reluctant to move into the war zone. At night the men stay in a little shelter above the cooperative, and two have to stay awake at all times. That leaves them tired and takes away from their work. They've been lucky, though; they have never been attacked by the Contras.

"We have a future," Vidal said. "We can get ahead and our children can get ahead. When we have peace in Nicaragua, everyone will dance."

All nine families at Luis Hernández had been day workers or tenant farmers. They came with nothing or next to nothing — a few tools, a horse. One of them, Juan Carlos, was standing here with us. His daughter was on his shoulders. He pointed to the lights in the valley and said, "Look! There are houses there where the lights are shining!" Juan Carlos asked me to hold her while he helped a newborn calf trying to nurse. I remembered showing my children books with pictures of farms on mountains, whose lights shone beneath the stars, where calves were born and struggled to nurse.

This work and this future, I thought, is what my government is bent on destroying. It is Vidal and Juan Carlos (the *"responsable de producción"*) talking about tomorrow's work plan. It is a revolution that created something unheard of among Third World countries, among poor people: under-population relative to economic opportunity. "We need more people," Vidal said.

At night the Basques and I sat in their cabin and talked in candlelight about our countries and the revolution here. They were friendly and welcoming. Araxo and Jon were a couple. He was tall, thin, and rather severe; she was gentler, but also serious, with striking dark eyebrows over deep, green eyes. Both she and Jon put in long, hard, farmwork days. As did Pulo, the third in their group. He was more lively, humorous, and energizing. He was the classic Basque or Spanish anarchist: a small man with a thick mustache, dark gentle eyes, and a deep voice, very talkative, and always teaching the children. He seemed like a man who dreamed much and was happy dreaming.

The Basques were here because the revolution gave them a way to do projects that were real and tangible, to work for a new society. They made a commitment to stay for a year and a half, and they came with certain political ideas for the projects they promoted. For example, they were concerned about the patriarchal family structure among the campesinos. Each family lived separately, and before the women's garden only the men worked together for the cooperative. In this cooperative, only the men were members. They met in the mornings, they spoke at the assemblies, and they elected the officers. The women, the Basques said, stayed in the house doing work private to each family.

The Basques hoped to change these patterns by creating women's projects. They noticed that the women shared few activities together, and had no place to discuss things and help each other with problems. The women's garden was created not only because of dietary and economic considerations, but also because it would give the women a cooperative way to contribute. The Basques also began a project to build a communal laundry. The women carried their laundry to a stream where they washed the clothes on rocks in the traditional manner; the Basques were working to get the government to provide materials so that a laundry facility could be built by the water pipe. There, too, the women could come together more easily.

The Basques were also very concerned about the children. They felt the campesinos treated them like lower-class citizens. Often, for example, the adults ate first and the kids got what was left. And a boy was in a class above a girl: the girls worked more, yet the boys ate ahead of the girls and got more. But those were problems they felt they could do little to change. They concentrated on health, cleanliness, vitamins, things like that. And they tried to treat the kids equally.

Cleanliness was a big issue. The houses had dirt floors; chickens were always inside under the corn grinder or the table looking for crumbs; pigs sneaked in the houses and had to be driven out. The kids ran barefoot and seldom washed their hands. They got parasites and then, in the rainy season, they had colds.

In the morning, walking up the muddy road to the field where the milking is done, I had to laugh at the six or seven little girls carrying plastic bottles or pans for the milk, themselves laughing at my presence, as they played and chattered and ran to keep up with me. Flor dropped the lid to the milk can on the muddy path and ran to a ditch to wash it off with rainwater. It was calving time, so the families got little milk: one liter for each family, although Flor got three because the Basques ate with her family. The man who milked brought the pails to the fence where we waited,

Fetching milk

took a coffee can off the ground and used it for a dipper. I couldn't help but notice bits of dirt in it. When Flor came back to the house, Manz poured the milk through a strainer.

Manz served a cup of coffee right away and smiled but didn't answer when I said thanks. She brought scrambled eggs and some of her delicious tortillas. She had a pleasant, quiet manner, a round, gentle face, and a beautiful smile. The kids had her smile. Flor or Coco (the two older daughters) ground the corn. The younger boys, Chepe and José, wrote in their schoolbooks or played, or went out to drive the cows or gather firewood. The girls swept, washed dishes, fetched water and milk and supplies from the storehouse, such as coffee or corn, and cut firewood for cooking. Orlando, the older boy, was beginning to work in the fields, and when he came in he sat at the table and was served like a man.

Besides problems of male privilege and health there were conflicts about cooperative work. Some took off too much time to cultivate their private plots or to go to town. One member drank. Some women wouldn't work in the garden, but were suspected of taking from it on the sly. Such problems were taken as proof, by anti-Sandinistas in Nicaragua, that campesinos won't work cooperatively. "They don't like cooperatives and are not cut out for them," one told me. Yet cooperatives are something new; one of the dramas of this revolution is the contradiction between the old ways and the new. Indeed, there is a struggle between the old and the new in each of us.

One morning I watched the co-op members at a meeting in front of the *beneficio*. It was six o'clock. Everyone was there. First they went over the logbook to see who had worked which days. I looked at the list of names. Most seemed to be working four or five days a week. Some more, some less. That day, they distributed the profits from the sale of the coffee crop: 60, 70, 80 dollars—crisp U.S. dollars in fives and tens and twenties. They counted and held the bills as if they had never seen such money before. Jon said later, "They shouldn't have paid out the money. They should have saved it for investment."

After the distribution, they discussed Luis's request for support during the time he would be in Cuba to study farm administration. Cuba was offering him a scholarship that would pay for everything, but he wanted the cooperative to give him full work credits for the six months he would be away, for his wife and two kids. He was going into Jinotega that morning and was wearing a clean dress shirt and new jeans with the label showing. He said, "I am going to talk to UNAG today about rations for my family

An early morning meeting of the cooperative members

while I'm away. I want to know what you have to say. Can I say I have the full support of the members?"

The discussion moved slowly. At first no one said anything. Each man seemed separate from the group, and I couldn't tell if they were in their own thoughts, or bored, or half-asleep. Then Alfredo began to talk. "We have a problem," he said. He was leaning against an empty drying rack for coffee beans, idly shaving the frame smoother with his machete.

"There is too much work here for too few people. We have a new member" — he pointed to one of the men I hadn't met — "who left off working for an hacienda because here you get a share of production, you're not just working to benefit someone else. But Vidal leaves soon for the reserves and Enrique is away in the army, so the rest of us have to work even harder. Roberto is building his house, and Carlos is sick. Still, the revolution needs many kinds of work. It needs production and defense, but it also needs us to study. We have to help with that also."

Some other men spoke. They agreed, but felt that Luis was asking for too much. In the end, they agreed to give four months of work credits for his wife and children.

A Family in León

I met Angelina at "Indio Viejo," a *comedor* run by a women's cooperative. Some had been prostitutes before the revolution. After the FSLN triumph, they said, Tomás Borge had come to speak at some activity and proposed they start a *comedor*, promising that the government would find them a space. They were five or six women and some of their daughters. They made delicious beef soup full of vegetables; their meals were cheap, and the place was popular and had a fine spirit. Mamá, the *coordinadora* and chief cook, sat with me one afternoon to tell stories and sing songs she had written herself. One was about her son fighting in the mountains; another was about her husband, who had left her for another woman and never helped with the children.

Angelina worked for a nearby optician. People shared tables and asked what you were doing in León, and when I said I wanted to meet people and learn about life here, she invited me to meet her family. She cocked her head sideways and spoke loud, short sentences like machine-gun fire, smiling as she waited for a response. She was twenty-eight, had a seven-year-old daughter named Tanya, and was separated from her husband. She made almost nothing at the optician's, but it was better than the housework job she had before. And she hoped to advance herself. She had quit school after the fourth grade. Why? She blushed and pointed with her finger: "Because my head is too hard. But I can read and write my name, and all that." Later she said, "I'm alone. I work only for my little girl, for food. If there is anything you can do to help us, clothes or anything, please do."

On that trip I spent one evening with her family. It was large and confusing, full of brothers and sisters, uncles and aunts. We sat around in a group, and they talked a little about themselves. Tanya was very sweet. They were proud of themselves and their family. The uncles were shoemakers who worked at home but belonged to cooperatives that sold their product and supplied them with materials. Holding their finished shoes, they posed proudly for a photograph. One aunt sold *refrescos,* or fruit drinks, and she gave me samples of the different kinds — cacao, fruit salad, orange. They talked about the revolution, which they said was wonderful but had also created problems. For example, they had to use inferior dyes because of the blockade, and they couldn't get fine leather. But they survived, Juanita said, because "if any one of us has a problem, we come together and little by little we solve it."

On my next trip to Nicaragua, which was in 1988, a year and a half later, I spent more time in León and made many visits to Angelina's family. After another year and a half of war and blockade, the economy of Nicaragua was much worse — production continued to fall, shortages spread wider and deeper, and inflation was astounding. I wanted to see how they were managing.

They lived in Laboria, an old working-class barrio of León, in a century-old house, stucco with a tile roof, built by their grandparents. The older members of the family, all in their fifties and sixties, were born there: the sisters, Juanita and Yolanda, and the brothers, Jorge and Rafael. Their father and grandfather were carpenters and masons. "We were always poor," Rafael said.

The house was simple, though large, a typical Nicaraguan city house. There were two front doors, and the house was divided among the family. One door opened into the room where Jorge sat at his work. There were a couple of rocking chairs and a table, where Yolanda ironed clothes. There were two bedrooms on this side, shared by seven adults and four children.

In back was an open-air patio, also divided. Here they cooked and ate and washed clothes, and Rafael had a small table for his leatherwork. Farther back they had the garden and a few fruit trees, chickens, an outdoor privy and shower, and the shed where the younger Jorge had a lathe. Young Jorge had lost the use of his legs from polio; he balanced on his crutches and made bedposts and legs for tables and chairs.

The other front door opened into the space for Juanita and her husband Leónidas. She sold *refrescos* and a few other things from the front room, which served as a store and a sitting room. There was only one bedroom on this side, then the patio again, with another sink, a gas stove, a wood-burning stove, and a large dining table and chairs. Beyond the patio, they had built an addition, consisting of two bedrooms and a modern bathroom. Their two daughters lived there and went to the medical school at the University of León. Their son was studying at the university in Managua.

In all, eleven adults and five children lived in the house. When I came to visit, it seemed always the same — the adults were working in various parts of the house, and I would move from one to another to talk. Jorge sat at a narrow table that held jars of tacks and glue and pieces of leather and rubber. He was sixty-two and had been separated from his wife for ten years. Besides his son, Jorge, he had a daughter who lived in Managua. He was brown-skinned, lean, and sinewy. Usually, four or five pairs of shoes were sitting there for him to repair for people in the neighborhood, but for his main income he made four new pairs of shoes a week. He sat at this spot and worked intently from seven in the morning until six or seven at night. There was a tension in him, I thought, because he worked for two, himself and his crippled son. The younger Jorge was bored and distressed for lack of work. He hung out at the park down the street or on the sidewalk in front. Later he got some work assisting another carpenter.

Because he sat near the door Jorge could see the kids playing on the street and the people passing. He didn't talk much. His brother, Rafael, always quit much earlier than he and sat on the steps to read the paper and talk to people. He was more relaxed. Jorge listened while continuing his work. Rafael told him what was in the news (Jorge can't read) and when someone stopped to talk, Jorge would listen. Sometimes he would stop a moment and look up and rest his arms and hands, nod and smile, then turn his head back down to the work, hammering the leather to make it soft, trimming the back of a heel and sanding it smooth, sewing the sole to the upper with wide motions of his hands.

Rafael, three years older, liked to read and talk about ideas. He specialized in making women's dress shoes, but didn't do that now because of the shortage of materials. Instead, he made little leather "booties" for fighting cocks: one type that holds a metal talon, another type for protection. He subscribed to a cockfighting magazine. In a good period, he would make three or four times as much money as Jorge, because these little products were sold for good prices in Mexico to the *galleros* (gamecock owners). He seemed to work less than Jorge. Sometimes he was away in Managua visiting his children. Often he was sitting in front when I would come to visit. "I became a shoemaker because I couldn't study," Rafael told me. "In those days it cost a lot to study. Now it is different. I have three children in Managua, and all of them are studying—engineering, business administration, and theology. I help support them."

Their sister Juanita was usually working in the kitchen in back, or if it was morning she'd be at the market. She did the buying for the house because the other sister, Yolanda, "is not intelligent," they said; she couldn't read or count and didn't know, for instance, the ages of her children. Juanita seemed more than anyone to be the head of the house. It was she I talked to most. She was pretty and had been a great beauty, to judge from her wedding photographs. As she explained their hardships to me, she sometimes seemed on the verge of tears. She never rested, she said, except after lunch when she lay down for fifteen minutes. She was at work from five in the morning until eleven at night. I could see that she became very tired. Her

Jorge at work

legs were thickly veined from standing. Sometimes she staggered a little while talking and cutting fruit.

I watched her make "fruit salad," a *refresco* that is about half solid fruit and sells for a little more than the others. She squeezed the oranges and limes by hand on a ceramic, cone-shaped dish — two dozen oranges, a half dozen limes. She cut up two and a half pounds of bananas and five pounds of papaya. She added water to the liquid and mixed in two pounds of sugar. I asked her how much money she made on a batch like this. It would yield thirty glasses, which she would sell for 40 córdobas each. She had her costs all figured out:

oranges and limes	300
papaya	500
sugar	100
bananas	125
Total	1,025

Thus she would earn 175 córdobas for her work and the cost of electricity and ice. How much was 175 córdobas at that time? Very little. The best available laundry soap was a blue bar, imported from Costa Rica, that sold for 200 córdobas each. She and her daughters used five bars a week to wash the family's clothes.

From other kinds of *refrescos* she makes a little more profit. One of the most popular was made from carrots. It took three pounds of carrots and two pounds of sugar to make twenty-four glasses. She made a profit of 320 córdobas, worth a bar and a half of laundry soap.

Juanita belonged to a cooperative of *refresco* venders, and she was elected its coordinator. The cooperatives had an allotment of sugar from the government, so the venders could buy at a low, stable price. But there were problems with the cooperative. Recently the government cut their quota from five hundred pounds a month to two hundred and fifty. This cut her sales in half (since no Nicaraguan would dream of eating less sugar). Other things she used to sell had become too expensive. Crackers, formerly 30 córdobas a box, went up to 500, so she didn't sell them. Cigarettes or rum? She almost never had them. If the government cut her sugar quota again, she would be out of business. "Also there is corruption in the cooperative," Juanita said. "There are people who care more about profits for themselves than for the community, so they buy the sugar for 6,500 and turn around and sell it on the black market for 40,000. If I find this happening I take action to stop it, but it happens."

"The cooperatives are not perfect," Rafael said. "The sort of cooperation that people here are used to is working together under a boss, who takes all the profits for himself. This is the system the Spanish established among the Indians, a system of exploitation. The government provides basic products at a low price and the farmer sells at a low price, but the speculators in the market sell for three or four times more. But little by little the people are changing."

Juanita's daughters, Mercedes and Carolina, were both studying at the León Medical School. They had the good humor and energy of their mother. Carolina, who was four months pregnant, might sit all day in a rocking chair near Jorge, reading a book and taking notes. Then she would wash clothes. Mercedes would come back from classes and immediately begin to study at the dining room table. There was always a clear, even intense feeling of activity in the house. Each person was working at something. For the girls the main work was study, but they also did a lot of housework. When I asked about this, Mercedes said, "Our mother never asks us to do anything, because she wants us to study. But we know what needs to be done, so when we have the time, we do it." "I wash, clean, make *refrescos,* everything," Carolina said. "It isn't different just because I have a profession. And everyone here cares for Aarón [her four-year-old son]. We all have an obligation to help one another." In spite of the limitations and difficulties in their lives, there was harmony and trust, and the mood generally felt pleasant. There was no tension about getting things done, no sense of "not enough time." I came to recognize Carolina's laugh. Mercedes sang as she mopped the floors or washed the sidewalks in the patio.

Juanita's husband, Leónidas, read meters for the electric company and brought home a small salary of 1,400 córdobas every two weeks. Her daughter Carolina received 3,800 a month for her scholarship to study pharmacy, and Mercedes, who was studying to be a doctor, received 2,400. They gave all of it to Juanita. The rest of her household money came from selling *refrescos*. In all, she made about 1,500 córdobas a week from her store — enough to pay for her laundry soap, to give the people in her family (and visitors like me) a quantity of healthy fruit drinks, and to buy perhaps one day's food.

Sometimes money came from other sources. I saw an impressive example when Leónidas took a week's vacation. He spent his time at home, making two pair of men's dress pants for a cousin in Managua. He used a picture his cousin had clipped from a catalog, of fancy resort-style pants with pleats. He did an amazingly professional job, and from each he earned 800 córdobas.

The family economy was complex, yet boiled down to a simple reality — everyone worked and still it was all they could do to have enough to eat. No one drank or smoked, except Juanita sometimes had a cigarette. There were no extras. Consider Francisco, thirty-two years old, the oldest son of Yolanda and a professor in a school of agronomy a few miles outside León. He earned 5,200 córdobas a month and gave it all to the household for food. I asked if he ever ate in a restaurant, and he laughed. Five or six years ago, he told me, he could eat in a restaurant two or three times a month. He couldn't remember when the last time was. "Thank God I'm not married," he said — he was for three years, but hadn't had any kids. Just his transportation to work cost 500 córdobas a month; a pair of blue jeans cost 10,000. He got his lunch free at the school — that is important because lunch is the big meal of the day for working-class Nicaraguans and the only meal with meat. He seemed to camp in the house. He had a small space of his own, partitioned from his sister Angelina and her children. He had a long row of shirts and pants on hangers, a shelf of books, a record player, and a small black-and-white television he kept covered with plastic. Sometimes in the evening he brought out the TV for everyone to watch. But much of the time he was away visiting friends. He was friendly to me, but quiet. He said what almost everyone said: "Life is hard now in Nicaragua."

His father died of a heart problem about twenty years ago. His mother, Yolanda, is considered "unintelligent" and dependent, although in the mornings she does the cooking and cleaning for her family and in the afternoons beautifully irons endless rows of shirts, pants, and dresses. She makes some money by ironing, but depends on her children and Juanita for food money.

If we include the adult children who are away at school, there were fifteen adults and five children in the Mendiola family. Their total income, in córdobas, was about 48,000 a month at a time when the córdoba was officially exchanging for 320 to the dollar. Their income in dollars, then, was about 150 a month, or 1,800 a year. For a family of twenty, this would appear to be the most abject poverty. Yet their lives had no resemblance to poverty as we know it in the United States. They were healthy, lived in a supportive environment, and had a deep sense of pride and security. The biggest difference was in the lives of the young adults — they were working or studying, or both. They had a future because of the policies of the revolution.

This family emphasized the importance of the revolution many times in our discussions. Carolina, twenty-eight, the oldest daughter of Juanita and Leónidas, always wanted to be a doctor. When she was ready to begin medical studies, it was still the time of Somoza and her parents couldn't think of paying for medical school, so she took a shorter course to be a medical technician. After the revolution she worked first in a health brigade during the literacy campaign, then in a health clinic on the Atlantic Coast for a few years, and then in Managua. She received a scholarship from the Ministry of Health to study pharmacy. She felt she could never have advanced as she had without the education and health programs of the revolution. She had a four-year-old son and was pregnant at that moment. Carolina's husband was a doctor in Managua, and every weekend he would drive here and take her and Aarón to his hometown of Chichigalpa, where he had a house. If she needed clothes money for Aarón he gave it to her, but otherwise he didn't support her — the revolution did.

Her younger sister, Mercedes, was studying medicine and hoped to become a psychiatrist. The difference is evident, she said. Before the revolution only fifty students were admitted to medical school in all of Nicaragua, and they had to have money. Now there are some three hundred and fifty admitted each year in León alone, seven hundred throughout Nicaragua, and they don't need money. The students here in León who don't live with family receive free housing — they live in cramped quarters, four to a room — and get very cheap meals. Books and school materials are provided, although the books must be shared and are out-of-date. The medical schools in Nicaragua are as poor as most families.

For some, this situation deserves harsh criticism. I spent an afternoon talking to Máximo Alonso, a leader of the opposition and the León reporter for *La Prensa,* the opposition newspaper. He lives in an ordinary house, newer than the Mendiolas', yet seemingly no richer, even though he receives an income from *La Prensa* of 100,000 córdobas a month — twice the combined income of the fifteen adults in the Mendiola family. He was nattily dressed in black wool pants and a starched, white shirt. He was a dark, angry man, and a wave of sympathy passed through me when I saw his front room full of chairs for a meeting and a set of loudspeakers for the top of a car. I was familiar with being in the opposition.

He hated the Sandinistas. "The Nicaraguan people prefer a capitalist system," he said, "but this government is striving in every possible way to create a total communist system. This means eliminating all private property, all freedom of expression and freedom to organize, and especially here in Nicaragua it means persecution of the Church. The Sandinistas want an end to private property. They don't really care about education and health and all those things they talk about."

Máximo Alonso believed that the only hope for Nicaragua was an invasion and takeover by the United States. He said that the foreigners who come here don't see the reality and that people were afraid to speak out against the government. I wondered how this could be so, because he and several of his friends talked freely and critically with me about the government and the Sandinistas, even though I was unknown to them. He said some Sandinista youth had thrown shit on his porch on the morning of July 19, the anniversary of the revolution.

"They are turning the people of Nicaragua into slaves," he said. "Here's an example. So many men have been taken into the army that they had to bring prisoners — hundreds of them — to work in the Ingenio [a large sugar refinery outside León]. The Ingenio paid them, but the penitentiary took the money for the government, and the prisoners never saw it. They just went back to being slaves. This is the sort of black and ugly thing that all Nicaraguan people reject.

"Now they have seized the Ingenio. [The government's confiscation of the Ingenio San Antonio had just occurred the week before and was big

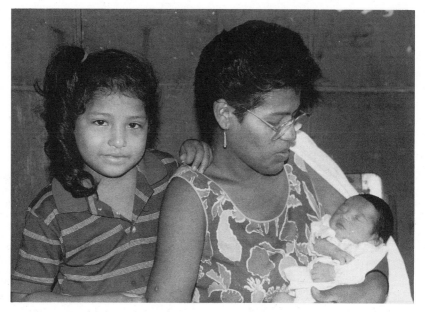

Tanya, Angelina, and Angelina's six-day-old baby

news. The government claimed that the owners, who are opposed to the revolution, had let production fall by two-thirds; the workers had complained to the government that the owners were driving the refinery into the ground by neglect; and, according to the government, the owners were putting money into a bank account in Miami and giving aid to the Contras.] They have thrown off the mask of being democratic. This is a frontal attack against private property. They are lying when they say production was too low, and even if it is it's because there is a shortage of workers because of their war. The truth is, they don't care about production. All they care about is war and building up the army. You know what they will do with the Ingenio? They will dismantle it and sell the parts."

Máximo had twenty-one children. Three were doctors and four were in medical school. Two had been drafted into military service. When he told me that four of his children were in medical school, I suggested this was a benefit he received from the revolution he so strongly opposed. "No," he said, "the schools were better before the revolution, and deserving students could go then as easily as now." His daughter was one of Mercedes's classmates. During our discussion she walked into the room from the back of the house, stopped in front of the mirror for a moment, looked out the

From top clockwise: Jorge, Tanya, Mercedes, Felipe, Aarón

front door, and walked slowly back, repeating the same circuit five or six times. When we were discussing the medical schools she interjected, "The students can't learn anything — there are no books." Later, Mercedes told me that the children of Máximo Alonso are very good students. "They have scholarships. They are reactionary, and everyone knows their views, but there is no discrimination against them."

Two other experiences I had are telling with respect to the medical program at León and its connection with the revolution. The first is an interview I had with a poet who, along with some other young León writers, had formed a poetry group. This poet was also a doctor who taught occupational medicine. "I received my degree in 1982," he said, "and rather than practice I began to teach at the university." He and some others created the first department for preventive medicine, focusing specifically on problems of occupational health. "I went to Cuba to study occupational medicine and brought back some books on the subject from there," he said, "but mainly we are putting together our own study materials based on our experience and fieldwork."

The second experience was of a serious drama in the Mendiola house. I was sitting in the front room watching Jorge work magic on a pair of old shoes when Angelina came into the house carrying her five-day-old baby from a visit to the hospital. I hadn't seen the baby yet and hurried over to greet her. "Let me see him," I said. As she looked down and started to unwrap the blanket, she burst into tears. I saw its left leg, blue and swollen to twice the size of the other. She had to return to the hospital immediately with the baby's things. Juanita went to the hospital with her. Tanya, the eight-year-old sister, sat huddled in a chair and cried. Everyone was afraid for the baby. After a few hours, Angelina came back extremely upset. She had to leave the baby at the hospital. She thought they were going to cut open his leg to release the infection, and she didn't know if she could see the baby. But she hadn't understood. They want mothers to stay with their children. She spent the next five days at the hospital, sitting with the baby and feeding him, and when she slept at home she could contribute to their milk bank. The baby was fed at night without her. They decided to try a massive dose of antibiotics and not to operate. Fortunately, it worked.

These incidents illustrate new forms of democracy and participation and, equally important, that Angelina can receive the full support of a hospital, free of charge, without feeling humiliation for being poor. After leaving León I wondered what I could say about this family. What had I learned? I began by asking how they survived in these difficult times. The answer was a matter of details, of hard work and sacrifice. But there was something more, a reality that is not seen but that one senses in different ways.

The image that comes to mind is of hands and arms intertwined. The family is connected as though in a net that reaches beyond the family to an extended community of people who give and take and hold onto each other with energy and determination and purpose. This is the molecular structure of the revolution.

People in the United States often say that "real" social change must begin within the individual. What one sees in Nicaragua is a dialectic between individual change and changed social and economic conditions. The individual spirit is nurtured by the community, which gives opportunity and hope to the individual, and which itself depends upon the individuals who sustain it. A collective spirit emerges. The inherited poverty of the past and the hard times of the present are lightened. Individuals share the spirit to build and create, to go beyond the given society. This spirit of struggle and hope is the heart of the revolution.

9

Politics and Representation

> Critical practice is often reduced to a matter of evaluation and judgment, or of declaring what is not right in the state of things. Yet if criticism is indispensable to sociopolitical—in fact any—transformation, it is because of its potential to set into relief the frame of thought within which operate the practices we accept.
>
> Trin T. Minh-ha, "Critical Reflections"

Many Nicaraguans have said to me, "When you go back to the United States tell what it is like here, so they will know our reality." Others have said, "You foreigners don't see what is really happening. The Sandinistas lie to you, and the people are afraid to say what they think."

I have read so many criticisms of the government and heard so many people talk freely in Nicaragua that I don't believe anyone there is afraid to speak out. Still, doubts and questions arise over the possibility of writing objectively about the revolution. I have my own interest in being here, which is to document, study, and support a struggle for liberation. When I open a magazine on the flight home, like *Time* or *Newsweek,* I enter a world whose image of Nicaragua is so foreign to what I have seen that my experience feels in danger of being obliterated, or reduced to the idiosyncratic perspective of some middle-aged hippie "fellow traveler."

Being called "eccentric" is not so bad — it puts me in very good company. Yet I feel compelled to come to terms with the establishment media.[1] I want *their* perspective to seem eccentric. In my heroic moments I feel like a guerrilla fighter who is isolated, outnumbered, outequipped, out-everythinged. To survive, I must know the enemy and expose their pretensions.

In self-defense I have studied the magazine articles on Nicaragua in the U.S. mass media. This is a tedious business, but one cause of the tedium also adds interest to the work: the mass media seem to have the same basic message to get across, even a certain way of doing it that is common to them all. Finding this subtext can be interesting.

Any piece of writing, fiction or nonfiction, creates a symbolic, imaginatively constructed world. After a while I began to feel that I knew my way around the world of the mass-circulation newsweeklies. Certain features of this world began to stand out, and once they were identified I could easily recognize them in their various guises. And I could understand why I felt so estranged from the world they created. It wasn't just that I was *for* the Sandinista revolution and they were *for* the U.S. policies. Our difference in perspective affected everything: the subjects chosen, the people who spoke, even physical details in the description of a town plaza.

One factor was so pervasive in the articles I read that it would qualify as what Trin T. Minh-ha called a "frame of thought." I call it "distance effect." A writer creates a certain degree of distance or closeness between herself or himself and the subject, and that distance/closeness is passed on to the reader. In the mass media, writer and reader are "we" (often this "we" includes the U.S. government), and Nicaraguans are "they." Although "we" and "they" are interacting at this particular moment, no real community exists between us. Various strategies ensure that "we" find "them" to be foreign, strange, incomprehensible, even dangerous, in "our" terms.

My tendency, not always the most sensible or realistic one, is to assume closeness. I seek out ordinary people and spend a lot of time with them. I let them into my life and ask to be admitted to theirs. I try to reciprocate their openness and generosity. We often build friendships that continue after my work is over. My aim is to understand people as much as possible in their own terms, which ultimately implies becoming one of them. It also implies that they reciprocate by accepting and understanding me. I know this is literally impossible, but I believe it makes sense to move toward the goal of eliminating the separation of "us" and "them." My presence here is not neutral—I hope to contribute to a movement that will break down traditional forms of oppression between my country and others. I believe that community-building and the destruction of traditional concepts of "them" and "us" is essential to this effort.

The journalists who write for the mass media live in expensive hotels as near as possible to the rich and powerful people whose behavior they scrutinize. Otherwise, they work and socialize mostly with one another. They eat in expensive restaurants and party at upper-class homes or press clubs. They travel in rented vehicles, usually in groups. When they speak to and quote ordinary Nicaraguans, it is nearly always commercial people or others they encounter only briefly: taxi drivers, market women, retail sales workers, or people they meet on the street or at a demonstration or scene of violence.

They keep their distance, physically and socially, as an essential part of their identity as "objective" reporters. They see this as a part of their professional practice. This is correct, yet the way their practice is structured yields a result corresponding to the social interests of those who employ them. It expresses and reproduces the dominant social position "we" have over Nicaraguans.

Their style of working and living implies a certain way of perceiving. It means that the people whose acts and words are considered important, those who (in media terms) have "power and influence" over the course of history, are upper-class businessmen or political leaders. Ordinary people are consulted not in regard to what they do or how they live, but in regard to how they react — as spectators or (dis)obedient followers — to the actions of leaders or the turn of events. Society is divided into an active, powerful elite and the masses, who are portrayed as relatively anonymous and passive.

If the revolution is seen as a sequence of events governed by the decisions of powerful individuals, as a revolution in which the masses are passively engaged as mere followers, can it possibly reveal a new level of democracy?

Writers for the mass media focus attention on *events;* they turn out for press conferences, important meetings between government leaders, demonstrations, violent clashes between groups, and scenes of ambushes or other violence. In all such events, the leaders are doing or are about to be doing something, while the people are passively standing by. The latter are polled by reporters for their immediate reactions, which in these contexts often seem transient and easily manipulated.

On a purely political level such a perspective may appear valid. The Sandinistas and the other parties and factions in Nicaragua all have their powerful leaders whose words and decisions make a difference. Their followers are people whose direct involvement in decisionmaking is at best sporadic and limited.

Yet is it on this level that real social change takes place? To what extent are decisions of leaders the causes and agents of change, and to what extent are they the reflections of conditions in their constituencies? Perhaps the actions of "leaders" are often founded on the willingness and capabilities of their "followers" to make things happen in Nicaragua. Or perhaps the relations among people making a revolution are much more complex and dialectical than either the leader–follower perspective or the constituency–representative perspective is capable of articulating.

I believe that the center of gravity of people's lives is in their work and community. It is there one must look for the sorts of changes that matter, for attitudes and values and understandings formed over time. One cannot expect to find the full meaning of a revolution in town plazas or at the InterContinental Hotel.

The perspective of the mass media turns revolution into a spectacle — a sequence of more or less violent events in which certain "stars" are the main actors and the masses participate passively. Yet this trivializes and dehumanizes the revolutionary process, and distances it from the mass audience of the media. We are not brought into the lives of the Nicaraguan people. We do not experience them as people like ourselves, with the same aspirations and problems. We the audience may watch the media spectacle in order to inform or entertain ourselves, but there is little basis for humane involvement. Through stereotypical images of power struggles and violence, we are, in effect, warned *not* to become involved.

Demonstrations, scenes of violence, press conferences, and so on are public expressions of forces at work in communities and at workplaces. They are not the revolution; they are better understood as symptoms of conflicting interests within the revolution.

The writing styles of *Time* and *Newsweek* reinforce such distancing. I have always been aware of their terse, nervous, sardonic styles, but I never quite realized the power of these styles to shape an image into a caricature. Information and analysis are put into a quickly consumable, entertaining form; the reader is assumed to be an easily distracted spectator whose attention is short and whose true interests lie elsewhere.

In both *Time* and *Newsweek,* the same simple, clear message is conveyed by distancing: relax; we are innocent.

In preparation for an essay I was writing (Brentlinger 1990) I read all the articles on Nicaragua in the mass-circulation newsweeklies from 1980 through 1989. Two examples, one from *Time,* the other from *Newsweek,* will serve to illustrate their perspectives.

An article in *Time,* written for the issue of November 16, 1987, presents a general overview of the revolution and the U.S. role. It is one of their three or four extended treatments of the revolution during the ten-year period of my study. The title, "Nicaragua at War with Itself," establishes the distancing from the start; it almost says "United States not involved." This was a hot issue at the time: the Reagan-Bush administration was carrying on a secret war, and the U.S. public and Congress were divided over the question of support for the Contras and the economic blockade. Perhaps because of this secrecy and deception, *Time* stressed that responsibility belonged to the Nicaraguans. The article emphasizes that the Sandinistas said otherwise—*they* said that the United States was at war with them. *They* show, the article says, "a profound inability to recognize what the Sandinista–Contra dispute is all about: a domestic disagreement over the future of the land."

"The real issues at the root of the conflict have not been addressed," *Time* says. "Nicaragua is at war with itself, as it has been before in a history as violent as the tropical storms that sweep across the isthmus. It is not just a war in the mountains between guerrillas and soldiers, but a much larger struggle among Nicaraguans over the destiny of their country." Thus, the history of U.S. domination of Nicaragua is completely suppressed, and war is made to seem a part of Nicaragua's destiny, like the weather. Yet U.S. interests are felt subliminally in the theme of revolution. Revolution against what or whom? The sub-headline of the article, "A Revolution Still in Search of a Lasting Purpose," tells us that it wasn't against anything! This further distanced the U.S. public: the central problem of the revolution was not U.S. imperialism (which the Sandinistas said it was against!) but an internal one, failure to find a "lasting purpose."

The eight-year-old revolution as a failed effort is probably the strongest image conveyed by the article. The four photographs and the bulk of the text are meant to convince us that the revolution is hated and that it has steadily diminished the quality of life in Nicaragua. Further, the article situates the Nicaraguan revolution among Third World revolutions in general, and portrays them all as dismal failures.

The opening text describes a funeral in a poor section of Managua. Supposedly, the family of the young soldier and his friends blame the Sandinista government for the young man's death. The soldier had been a draft dodger, but was caught and was later killed in the Contra war. A Sandinista official in the procession is lambasted:

"You sons of bitches are killing us like dogs," yells one of the young pall-bearers. "Just leave us alone."

The writer or editor emphasizes this quotation by giving it its own paragraph, then comments: "The outburst was steeped in the emotion of the moment, but it seemed a cry from the heart of a confused and unhappy country." By moving to poetic language to avoid facts, the author neatly manages to make this one cry appear to be representative of the entire country.

Most of the article is concerned with Nicaragua's worsening economy. It gives figures on the decline in exports, the increased national debt, inflation, and a reduced standard of living. Also, the article is sprinkled with negative quotations, giving it the air of an objective sampling of opinion. It quotes two friends of the dead soldier, an intellectual "who was once a fervent believer," another draft dodger, two street vendors, and a woman on the street. All complain about the economy, and most are critical of the government. The draft dodger says, "They have taken all our rights, even the right to toilet paper. . . . People are tired of their empty slogans." "The Sandinistas came to power with the support of 80% to 90% of the population," says the former true believer. "Now they would have to scrape to come up with 40%." A woman holding a baby says, "Medicine is supposed to be free. But you have to wait so long to see a doctor, and the right drugs aren't always to be found."

To further convey the image of poverty and failed revolution, the reporter describes his impressions on first arriving: "The ride from the airport to down-town Managua calls to mind those almost forgotten revolutions in Africa, from Angola to Zaire, where the rhetoric has marched quickly away from reality. An aging Chevrolet Impala with a cracked windshield and an oil light that glows menacingly in the dark rattles down a potholed road. Bouncing headlights pick up clumps of stoic people waiting for buses that arrive infrequently and full. The bus fleet, local wisdom has it, has almost been run off the road because its mechanics are employed fixing the army's Soviet T-54 tanks. Many people resort to walking, and after dark, shadowy figures flit ghostlike through a heavy shroud of exhaust fumes created by engines vigorously protesting the shortage of spare parts."

There is a comic-book quality in the personified images of this paragraph, the aging Chevrolet (with a driver?), the menacing glow of the oil light, the bouncing headlights, climaxed by cars that protest the revolution in Nicaragua! That the only people mentioned are "dark, shadowy figures that flit ghostlike" injects a stereotyped image of Third World people — they are dark and shadowy! — which reinforces the earlier mention of "almost forgotten revolutions in Africa."

Stereotypes become dominant in the article. The writer describes his arrival at the airport: "The traveler is confronted by immigration officers in high, completely enclosed wooden booths with thick glass windows and heavy curtains. Out of sight, the officer rustles mysteriously through what seems to be a thick book. Then he appears to scribble furiously for a minute or two. After a final scrutiny of the traveler's face, the passport is pushed back. 'Welcome to Nicaragua,' says the officer, hitting a switch that opens the electronically operated exit doors. If the Sandinistas do not admit to being Communists or Marxists, they certainly understand the etiquette." The author hopes readers will not recall that an identical scrutiny of foreigners, by computer, is performed by U.S. immigration officers.

The article ends with medieval images of an evil empire: "the armored knights of the revolution continue to clank noisily in the halls of power, shouting anti-U.S. epithets. Only last month, Tomás Borge, the powerful Interior Minister, told a gathering in Managua that the U.S. was the 'enemy of humanity' and vowed never-ending battle. As he spoke, several Sentinels of the People's Happiness, as the ministry's police are called, stared fixedly ahead." Such comic-book imagery creates an ideological perspective in which revolution means a rebellion of the inferior. We in the United States must endure the ultimately self-destructive insults and dangerous antics of these Latin Americans. They are like actors in the garb of rulers and police, shouting slogans and threats. In daylight they posture like children, at night they are dark and sinister.

Compare a synoptic account of the revolution from *Newsweek* (June 6, 1983), which depicts childlike fervor and optimism quickly dashed by reality. Headlined "The Betrayal of the Revolution," the first paragraph says: "July 19, 1979, was 'a day of dreams' for Juan Francisco López García. . . . The bitter war was over, after two years and 40,000 deaths. 'Now we'll have peace and plenty and freedom, just like the revolution promised,' he told his mother. 'Nicaragua belongs to the people.'" A woman is quoted as saying July 19 was "like a religious vision — everybody was loving everybody else." The article concludes by quoting an adamant anti-Sandinista as if he were speaking for all of the revolution's former supporters: "There is no pluralism, there is no democracy, there isn't even much of a revolution. . . . There are only Sandinistas in place of Somoza."

As described in the mass-circulation newsweeklies, Nicaraguan people speak like children, and are as easily enticed. At first transported by "promises," they quickly become disillusioned. Thus, a *Time* article describes a 1984 May Day rally in Chinandega as a "flopped revolutionary road-show." "There is a drastic change of mood," the article says. "Only a few months ago, citizens eagerly rallied by the thousands to listen to the exhortations." Now there is "a deep sense of frustration and demoralization within Nicaragua that affects even the Sandinistas leadership." *Time* refers sardonically to "all the earnest vows swapped in the sticky July heat of 1979, when Dictator Anastasio Somoza Debayle was finally toppled."

In these accounts and many others, the meaning of the revolution to Nicaraguans is reduced to the "mood" reporters observe at a demonstration. We readers become spectators of spectators of spectators. What filters through is the message that leaders act and the people experience the consequences.

In this condescending scenario, we are told that leaders and followers are bonded irrationally by fervor, faith, and utopian dreams. As the people wake to the harsh light of reality, the dreams evaporate, and the unity of the leaders and the people is seen as a cruel deception. The dream becomes nightmare: the Sandinistas are no better than Somoza. They crack down on internal opposition and set off a chain reaction that leads to a police state. And they vent their frustration with an ever more shrill invective against the great father figure of Latin America, Uncle Sam. "The Sandinistas," *Time* says, "by calling on the Reagan Administration to disband the contras, are behaving just like the Somozas and the clutch of tyrants and oppressors before them who always looked to Washington for a solution to their problems" (October 25, 1987).

In the mass media, the Sandinistas rarely just speak. They yell loudly, they blame and complain. "Sandinista rhetoric about the U.S. and the contra threat remains as shrill as ever," says an article in *Time* (May 14, 1984). "For the third time in two years, the Sandinistas were loudly convinced— or so they said—that U.S. troops were about to invade their soil," says another article that same year (November 26, 1984). Note especially the twisted expression "loudly convinced."

In the ideological picture established by these images, the United States and Nicaragua appear as mythic figures embodying simple, opposed characters: the paternalistic power, which can be generous or withholding, protective or punishing; the small, immature, dependent, racially and culturally inferior subject. These images continue a long tradition of racist and imperialist writing: it is Prospero and Caliban become Uncle Sam and Juan Valdez.

Within this framework, revolution means a rebellion that is bad not because it is threatening or unfair; rather, revolution is a naive and self-destructive nuisance. It is contrary to the nature of master-and-slave relations, as defined by Aristotle (1941): "there is one rule exercised over subjects who are by nature free, another over subjects who are by nature slaves. . . . [T]here is a marked distinction between the two classes, rendering it expedient and right for the one to be slaves and the others to be masters. . . . [T]he abuse of this authority is injurious to both. . . . [W]here the relation is natural they are friends and have a common interest" (*Politics* 1.6.1255b5 +).

When U.S. political leaders speak of "our friends south of the border" it is usually in this Aristotelian sense that "friend" is meant. The United States *naturally* exercises authority over affairs in Latin America. If Nicaragua lays claim to its own destiny, it destroys this common interest based on the natural superiority of one and the inferiority of the other; and the consequences are economic chaos and sham politics, built on deception and adolescent posturing. So it is necessary that Daniel Ortega, Nicaragua's Sandinista president and an extraordinary person and political leader, be reduced to "a little dictator wearing designer glasses" by our actor-leader Ronald Reagan.

The artificiality of the perspective of the mass-media newsweeklies is shown by their obliviousness to context and history. U.S. policies and Nicaragua's history under Somoza are irrelevant to Nicaragua's poverty and economic problems: the revolution causes them. *Business Week,* for example, speaks of "shortages, stemming from the government's reluctance to let the market allocate goods and services" (January 24, 1983). They print a photograph captioned as follows: "Nicaraguan citizens form lines outside government supermarkets awaiting food rations." The image is fraudulent. It is a photograph taken by Susan Meiselas only a few days after the victory of July 19, 1979—three and a half years before the article appeared. It shows a line of smiling people, mostly kids, holding buckets and other containers. They are there for free milk, distributed to stem the food shortage that accompanied the collapse of the Somoza dictatorship! Meiselas considered suing *Business Week* for the misuse of her photograph, but was advised not to engage such a powerful enemy in court.

U.S. News and World Report, in the issue of March 5, 1984, quotes a worker in Managua as saying, "The Sandinistas have built up a huge army that is taking the food out of our mouths." Then it comments: "There is no genuine hunger. But shortages are a constant product of a distribution system weighed down by socialist ideology, inept bureaucrats, and corruption." This explanation, implausible on its face—that ideology or government ineptness causes shortages and that corruption could be so serious in a five-year-old revolutionary government—also fraudulently misuses a photograph. Its caption: "Managua residents wait in a long line to buy bread,

beans, and other food. Shortages created by Marxist ideology and ineffi-
cient bureaucrats make this a daily chore." The line they show occurs daily
at a bakery near a busy Managua shopping center called "Plaza de España."
It is frequented by reporters because the shopping center contains a bank
and airline ticket offices. What the reporter didn't know, or didn't care to
say, is that the customers at this bakery are mainly retailers who line up to
buy large quantities of bread which they sell in the neighborhood stores,
where there are no long lines.

The Sandinistas have argued that, besides having to begin with a devastated and impoverished economy they inherited from Somoza, the revolution has been economically crippled by the U.S.-sponsored war and the
economic blockade. Given the history of U.S. interventions, this claim is
hard to deny. Yet specific denial of U.S. responsibility is a major theme of
the articles on Nicaragua in the popular media.

A word on the economics of shortages. The theme of shortages and
rationing was repeated often in the newsweeklies. Indeed, the mere mention of shortages seemed to be enough to condemn the revolution. Aside
from the problem of Nicaragua's inherited poverty, though, shortages can
occur because of a political decision to share a limited quantity of goods
among all. When this happens, it may appear to some that scarcity increases. Those who have plenty of money, and who are accustomed to
buying whatever and whenever they want, suddenly cannot. Their complaints, frequently quoted in *Time* and *Newsweek*, were real enough. But
their perspective is the perspective of the formerly privileged: it is only for
them that socialist redistribution policies "create shortages."

Alongside the popular media there existed in the 1980s another media perspective on Nicaragua, one that had a more limited audience and that actually provided important information. I want now to
characterize this second establishment perspective. Generally, the mass media seemed concerned to legitimize and even represent the government to
its audience. If Reagan called the Contras "freedom fighters" and the moral
equivalent of our Founding Fathers, that is what appeared in *Time* and
Newsweek. They never told us, and sometimes lied about, who the Contras
were. But the *New York Times,* through their Central America reporter
James LeMoyne, did tell us.

LeMoyne has an extensive background of direct experience with the
Contras. In his *New York Times Magazine* article "Can the Contras Go On?"
(October 4, 1987), he wrote: "the administration created a guerrilla force

that suffers from what in Latin America is a fatal defect: being seen as a creature of Washington." He went on to explain that the CIA organized the Contras and selected their officials and military commanders from former National Guardsmen and from civilians who had collaborated with Somoza. The CIA also hired Argentine military men to train the Contras in Texas and Florida. These trainers were famous for their torture and assassination of labor and opposition leaders in Argentina and, according to one Contra member, "knew nothing about a rural guerrilla war. The truth is, a lot of them were Nazis." LeMoyne called the Contras a "rude war machine" with "no political direction other than crude anticommunism," in whom "signs of brutality were . . . evident." He summarizes: "despite recent political and military improvements . . . the Contras remain essentially an instrument of U.S. foreign policy."

This perspective is a long way from the image offered by the mass media. LeMoyne's article not only provides information that is not consumed by the general public, but it is also critical of the U.S. government's policies and interpretation of events. The *New York Times,* in fact, never supported our government's policy and seemed to direct a considerable effort toward changing it. Stephen Kinzer, the *Times* bureau chief in Managua for most of the 1980s, wrote two important *New York Times Magazine* articles on the Nicaraguan situation (August 28, 1983, and January 10, 1988).

In them, Kinzer stressed the historical background of U.S. interference in Nicaragua. He acknowledged its long-standing domination of Nicaraguan society, both economic and political: "in Nicaragua," he wrote, "perhaps more than any other Latin American country, anti-imperialist rhetoric has a firm basis in history." He concludes one article by noting that "American interventions have left an enduring impression in Nicaragua. In many villages, it is still possible to find people who remember their country's occupation by American marines. They saw American military planes bomb Nicaraguan hillsides, watched Sandino lead his defiant peasants against the United States Marines, and were outraged at his murder. Acts like these have left the bitter legacy to which [Daniel] Ortega is heir. He and his movement are, above all, a logical and even inevitable reaction to American foreign policy."

Kinzer did not support the Sandinista revolution, but he did oppose the tactics of the Reagan administration as brutal and self-defeating. Tens of thousands of Nicaraguans had been killed, and billions spent, and the United States was farther away than ever from achieving its goals in Latin America. "My sympathy isn't with the government here, it's with the people," he said in an *Esquire* interview. "They have suffered as much as any people on earth. . . . They've had volcanoes that buried cities; earthquakes; the cruelest, crudest dictators; foreign invasions — it just never stops. Looking at Nicaraguan history, you can't deny the need for revolutionary change: you had a feudal society here. There's a great deal of disagreement, though, on what sort of change that should be. But *everyone* remembers what the National Guard was like, and *nobody* wants to go back to those days . . . and it shows how little the United States knows about what's going on here that we would throw in with the *one* group that most everyone in Nicaragua fears" (*Esquire,* November 1986).

The *New York Times* took the long view of history, a necessary condition of realism, and it favored policies that could succeed in the long run. Kinzer concluded his August 28, 1983, article as follows: "If the Reagan Administration has really decided to destroy the Sandinista regime, that is just what Washington decided about the Zelaya Government in 1909 and the Zeledón and Sandino uprisings that followed. Each time, the Americans were temporarily successful; each time, Nicaraguan nationalism re-emerged more radical than before. The alternative is to recognize that the days when the United States could control events in Latin America are passing, and that Washington must learn to live with revolutionary governments in its own hemisphere."

The *New York Times* favored a seemingly more realistic, moderate policy, which the right saw as "soft on communism." But in fact, as members of the U.S. establishment, *Time* and the *Times* are united in their support of capitalism and in their opposition to socialist movements. Thus, the *Times* favored tolerance of revolutionary movements directed against "feudal," dictatorial regimes, and argued for policies that would turn such revolutions toward "democratic" (meaning nonsocialist) economic systems. *Time* was less subtle and more rabidly anti-Sandinista. Why the difference?

I believe these two organs of the establishment correspond to different, though overlapping, concerns and readerships. *Time* and *Newsweek* have more than ten times the circulation of the *New York Times,* and are aimed at a much broader middle-class and upper-middle-class readership, a group that is at the core of the voting public in the United States. The readership of the *New York Times,* by contrast, is narrower, and might be described as part of the core of the economic and political establishment in the United States.

Most readers of the mass newsweeklies probably don't much care whether Nicaragua is independent and socialist. They don't feel they have a stake in the outcome. They will support our government's pro-Contra policies only if sufficiently "distanced" from Nicaragua's problems and revolutionary aspirations. It also helps if they are made to suspect that the Sandinistas are incompetent and self-seeking. And to provide aid and training to the Contras, or to intervene militarily, Washington needs to arouse fears of a communist menace or appeal to our idealism — we must help the "freedom fighters" win Nicaragua's "civil war." Our mass media always seem to cooperate fully with the U.S. government in this way. For an account of the extent of this cooperation and an explanation of it, I recommend Bagdikian's book *The Media Monopoly* (1992).

Occasionally, the *New York Times* has taken a stand against important government actions or policies.[2] It has been able to do so, I believe, because it represents a constituency that is more interested in the economic and political future of its international investments, and therefore in the long-term success of U.S. government policies, than in the credibility of a particular president and his policies. U.S. businesses with foreign investments require political and, sometimes, military clout in order to protect their interests. This means, of course, that they need the consent of the voting middle class. But they also need the long-range security brought by good relations with foreign governments. They need information and analyses that respect the historical reality and actual conditions of Latin America, and it is not *Time* but publications like the *New York Times* that undertake to respond to that need.

The *Times,* moreover, rises above the racism and contempt for Latin Americans that is so common in the mass media. Its urbanity is illustrated by another important *New York Times Magazine* article during the 1980s. The *Times* asked the Peruvian novelist and presidential candidate Mario Vargas Llosa to write his impressions of Nicaragua after a month-long visit there, and the result was a piece called "In Nicaragua" (April 28, 1985). Vargas Llosa is well known for his public denunciations of the Sandinistas and of Cuba, so his antisocialist credentials were not in doubt. Yet he is a widely respected Latin American intellectual — a contradiction in terms for the comic-book world of *Time*.

The difference between the two establishment media becomes clear if we recall how *Time* referred to the police in Nicaragua as "Sentinels of the People's Happiness" who "stared fixedly ahead" while "the powerful Interior Minister" Tomás Borge shouted epithets against the United States. Nothing could be more remote from my own experience of the police in Nicaragua, or of Tomás Borge, than this caricature. Vargas Llosa, who knows Borge well and admires him very much, writes: "If it is true that all Nicaraguans have a kind of natural addiction to poetic imagery — Nicaragua has a higher percentage of good poets than any other Latin American country — in Tomás Borge this trait has been honed to a perversion. In front of the Ministry of the Interior he has hung an enormous poster that proclaims the ministry 'Guardian of the People's Happiness.' The title of his book on Carlos Fonseca is *Carlos, Dawn Is No Longer a Temptation.*" The police in Nicaragua are not called "Sentinels of the People's Happiness," although Vargas Llosa gives us the factual basis for the *Time* reporter's distortion; and there is quite a difference between the sinister implications of *Time*'s fascist imagery and accusing the head of police of being a fanatical poet!

The issue that concerns Mario Vargas Llosa (and the *New York Times*) is not the validity of the Nicaraguan revolution or their capacity for independence and self-government, which are readily acknowledged; it is Nicaragua's "wavering" between "freedom and totalitarianism." No unduly close reading of Vargas Llosa's article is needed to see that this means wavering between capitalism and socialism. It is on this issue that I find myself at odds with the perspective of the *New York Times*. They identify Nicaragua's socialistic policies with totalitarianism, with a lack of respect for freedom. Why? Because, for them, freedom must include freedom of investment. Ergo, socialism is intrinsically opposed to liberty.

The facts that prove otherwise are ignored by the *Times*. Under the Sandinista government, Nicaragua adopted its first constitution. It guaranteed the rights of free speech, association, organization (including political parties of whatever type), and religion. It established the right to private property, including capitalist property, alongside government ownership and control of state property and central banking. It defined a form of representative government, and it established that free elections be held every six years. Throughout the Sandinista period, with occasional violations that were often publicized and criticized within Nicaragua itself, these principles were followed. So why the concern about "totalitarianism" in a society that permitted more open political conflict, more widely discussed, than any I have seen?

Vargas Llosa says the Sandinistas lack a willingness to share power. They have "the old Latin-American view that legitimate power grows out of the barrel of a gun." They are strongly committed to bettering the lives of the poor, he says, but naively believe they can govern without the support of the bourgeois elements in Nicaragua. He acknowledges the huge Sandinista victory in the 1984 elections, but dismisses its significance with respect to legitimating FSLN policies or as evidence of democracy. He explains: "the organizational structures in Nicaraguan society make it difficult to determine if the figure is a real reflection of the regime's popularity."

The structures he refers to are the Sandinista Defense Committees (CDSs). He says: "The committees have made a valuable contribution to the campaigns for literacy and mass vaccinations, and they played an important role in the success of police operations against crime and drug traffic. In Managua there is no drug problem among the young. It is safe to walk through any neighborhood, day or night, and the U.S. Ambassador has only one bodyguard as compared to the six needed by his counterpart in Costa Rica, and the eight in San Salvador. The chief function of the defense committees, however, is to spy on neighbors." Vargas Llosa gives no evidence for his fantastic claim that spying is their chief function; but his charge expresses a crucial point of *class conflict* over the issue of power within a democratic society. The Nicaraguan parties to the right of the Sandinistas agree with Vargas Llosa. They, too, have claimed that the purpose of the CDSs was to repress dissent and spy on the opposition.

The CDSs grew out of prerevolutionary popular organizations.[3] They were intended to develop the awakening initiative of the people and to create more participation in every aspect of life — work, study, the military and police, and the community. They extended democracy beyond the electoral forms that are traditional in bourgeois societies. Vice-President Sergio Ramírez said about them that "this is the only dynamic which can make a revolutionary process possible, because if the leadership were locked away giving orders, without these organizations understanding the measures which were taken, and without the critical and creative support which these organizations must give, then the revolution simply would not work" (Black 1981, 233).

The mass media in the United States invariably condemned the CDSs: "At home," says *Newsweek* (April 29, 1985), "the Sandinistas have been anything but benevolent rulers. They have set up neighborhood 'watch committees' to spy on citizens." *Time* (May 14, 1985) says: "The Sandinistas, led by their nine-member national directorate, retain an awesome monopoly of force in Nicaragua. They command a combined army and militia of some 100,000, well-equipped by Cuba and the Soviet Union. A net-work of Sandinista Defense Committees gives the regime a pervasive system of surveillance and social control." And even though the election in Nicaragua was by secret ballot, *U.S. News and World Report* (June 3, 1985) published the fantastic charge that there couldn't be a free election in Nicaragua because ration cards, which are distributed through the CDSs, wouldn't be given to people who vote against the Sandinista party.

Vargas Llosa also sees the CDSs as intrinsically totalitarian, because the activity of government reaches into the neighborhoods where people know one another and interact on every level of life. But the Sandinistas argue that this is precisely why they are more democratic, and why Nicaragua has had such success dealing with crime, drugs, education, and health.

One must ask: why is it preferable to keep policing functions in the hands of state bureaucrats, as opposed to the people of each neighborhood? Who is best qualified to give recommendations to people requesting scholarships or state jobs? Abuses occurred, it is true, but complaints were also filed and action was taken to correct abuses. Being imperfect, and of varying degrees of egotism and greed, people will abuse power to some extent in any system. Some Sandinistas were intolerant of, and persecuted, the opposition. Wartime conditions naturally exacerbated tensions and raised the level of conflict within neighborhoods and even within families. But much was accomplished through these organizations. They were relatively unbureaucratic, because most participation was unpaid and voluntary. Whatever bureaucratic privilege and corruption that did exist in them was minor compared to that found in most governments. Neighborhood *vigilancia* was seen as a burden and was discontinued in many neighborhoods, but it effectively reduced crime. Now Managua is less safe because of worsening economic conditions and a decline in the activity of the block committees, but there is no indication it is freer, as Vargas Llosa should believe, except for the thieves.

Vargas Llosa assumes that democracy exists only in its traditional form, as found in capitalist societies, in which the parties, candidates, and legislatures are easily controllable by the wealthy. But this is democracy for the few. The socialist conception stresses participation in community and workplace governance, and more effectively includes the majority.

The CDSs grew out of organizations in which tens of thousands of creative, courageous people from the working classes risked their lives to engage the Somoza regime and its terrifying National Guard in an open struggle for power. In victory, the Sandinista revolution offered to share power with the bourgeoisie, but only as minority participants in a popular movement.

On the economic side, Vargas Llosa's article reports complaints from business owners that the Sandinista "mixed economy" is only a veiled form of socialism. There is no mixed economy, they say, because, to quote Vargas Llosa's paraphrase, "the state decides what we should plant and when we should plant it. We sell only to the state, only at the price it sets. It pays in córdobas and decides when, and in what currency, it will give us money for upkeep and equipment. With the banks nationalized, we have to depend on the state for credit. And we live in the threat that they'll confiscate our land on the pretext that we are sabotaging the economy."

But the Sandinista mixed economy doesn't mean the coexistence of a capitalist system and a socialist system. It means private ownership within an economy that is structured to serve the needs of the vast majority. Vice-President Sergio Ramírez, responding to Vargas Llosa concerning criticisms from the business organization COSEP and its president, a rich industrialist named Enrique Bolaños, said: "Bolaños' problem, and COSEP's problem, is that they haven't resigned themselves to their loss of political power. . . . [W]e have no difficulty reaching an understanding with Carlos Pellas, the multimillionaire, or other industrialists who discuss credits, foreign exchange, stocks, and investments with us. But no capitalist will ever be president of the Central Bank again, or dictate our economic policy, and that is what COSEP cannot accept."

Freedom is relative. Freedom for whom, and at whose expense? As Vargas Llosa admits, the revolution benefited the majority of Nicaraguans, and tore down an unspeakably unequal class system. It reduced the freedom of the businessman, but greatly increased the political power and economic opportunities — the freedom — of the average farmer and worker. The freedom of the businessman received an historic limitation, and the workers received freedoms that the government worked hard to guarantee.

Mario Vargas Llosa concludes his analysis by using a favorite theme of bourgeois ideology: the supposed conflict between equality and freedom. "Tragically," he writes, "liberty and equality are harsh antagonists. At the heels of a revolution, there is a temptation to establish social justice by sacrificing individual freedom; conversely, a desire to safeguard liberty can lead to further exploitation and unspeakable inequality. Real progress depends on achieving a tense equilibrium between the two ideals. No socialist revolution has yet achieved this balance."

Under what assumptions are liberty and equality "harsh antagonists"? Liberty always has limits. There should be no liberty to rob or kill. Why should liberty be permitted to lead to "exploitation and . . . inequality"? It will do so if liberty includes the free exercise of economic power that exists in capitalist societies. Liberty for the capitalist class to hold power is irreconcilable with equality and with the freedom of the vast majority to control their conditions of life.

In reality, it is not "liberty" and "equality" that are in conflict, it is capitalism and democracy. It is different sectors of society that are in conflict over their respective shares of power and the liberty to use that power. And greater democracy and equality in all aspects of society — community, workplace, and government — is the solution to that conflict proposed by the Sandinistas.

In a 1982 issue of *Time* magazine I read: "For the celebration of the third anniversary of Nicaragua's Sandinista revolution, the dusty provincial town of Masaya . . . last week was colorfully decorated with flags and posters. The band played revolutionary songs, and the crowd sang along. But there was little cheer in the speech." This image calls up the same cynical cliché I have seen dozens of times in the U.S. media about Latin America. A dusty, backwater town, with downcast people, their lives filled with empty hopes, deception, and disillusionment. To describe the anniversary rally *I* saw, one would write about the hundreds of thousands of enthusiastic and beautiful people who came from all over Nicaragua to join in an unforgettable celebration: the anniversary of their liberation from a long and humiliating history of external domination.

As I write this, the Nicaraguan government is now in the hands of the counterrevolution. The perspective of *Time* may appear to be confirmed. Yet, did the revolution fall for lack of popular support? Was this the wrong path for Nicaraguan development? Or was it crippled by the slow, suffocating pressure of the economic and military power of the United States, too heavy for a small country to withstand? And what role did the U.S. media play in creating the consensus needed to sustain that pressure?

In the *New York Times Magazine,* Stephen Kinzer wrote that each time the United States has set out to destroy a Nicaraguan regime it has been temporarily successful, only to see Nicaraguan nationalism reemerge more radically — and, he could have said, more strongly — than before.

10

Managua Journal, 1991–92

I was in Massachusetts the day the Sandinistas lost the election to UNO: February 25, 1990, ten years and eight months after the triumph of the revolution. UNO, the National Union of the Opposition, is a coalition of fourteen parties, ranging from the far right to the two communist parties. With its 12 million dollars of campaign funds from the United States, it took 58 percent of the vote against the Sandinistas' 42 percent. My friends and I were taken by surprise. The polls consistently showed a strong Sandinista majority, and we thought anyway that the UNO coalition was such a bizarre collection of political tendencies that it couldn't have much credibility in Nicaragua. We had already circulated posters and fliers and sold tickets for a Sandinista victory dance. We held the dance, but we also held gatherings in friends' houses to talk about our shock and dismay and how to react.

Our feelings were nothing compared with what was experienced in Nicaragua. The day after the election, I was told, people huddled in their houses in shock. There were small UNO celebrations, and some church bells rang, but even the victors seemed at a loss about what to do. This was more than an electoral change of government; it was the reversal of a revolutionary process. The distribution of economic power and property, and the profoundest social values, were shifting once again to realign with the interests of the United States. One campesino said, "It was as if all the mothers in Nicaragua had died" (Mendoza 1990, 23).

Or *would* there be a turning back? In his first postelection messages, Daniel Ortega expressed opposite moods. On February 26, he said in resignation, "We feel proud about having contributed a little bit of dignity to this unjust world, divided between the powerful and the weak. Thank you, brother Nicaraguans!" Then, on February 27, he spoke again, saying that the Sandinistas would respect the electoral process, but since they were the most powerful political force in the country they could continue to govern as an opposition party, "from below."

"Government from Below" became the slogan of the postelection revolutionary movement. It wasn't clear what it meant, but it had credibility. With 42 percent of the population supporting them, even after ten years of war and economic hardship, the Sandinistas were undoubtedly the most powerful organized political force in the country. And that percentage did not fully represent their following. Many who believed in the revolution were opposed to the law of compulsory military service. It was an onerous and hated law, with devastating economic effects, that the Sandinistas would not abolish or weaken. It required two years of active duty, followed by service in the active reserves. Men in the reserves had to leave their jobs and families for three months every year. Also, many Sandinistas were perceived as arrogant, unself-critical, and corrupt; it was said they would benefit from the shake-up that an electoral defeat, or a very narrow victory, would give them. Then, too, there were many basically sympathetic people who felt that Nicaragua could not survive against the United States if the Sandinistas remained in power. What did they have to offer the Nicaraguan people, after all? More costly war, more economic blockade, more funerals; more desperate, courageous sacrifice against hopeless odds. Many Nicaraguans who voted for UNO were still Sandinistas in their hearts. Under new conditions, they might unite to struggle in a new way. And their ability to continue the policies and gains of the revolution was enhanced by a vitally important fact: the Sandinistas controlled the army and the police. There could be no political repression of the left in Nicaragua, as in other Latin American countries.

If I were Nicaraguan, I might have abstained from voting for the Sandinistas. I admit that when I heard the election results I felt relief. The war and the blockade were costing Nicaragua too much, and there was no end in sight. For the United States to blockade poor Nicaragua and to finance the Contras was painless militarily and added little to a national debt the Republicans ignored. Our big country had a new concept for destroying rebellious governments: low-intensity warfare by proxy. It was devastating; it worked.

Perhaps things would improve with a new government. The United States would stop its aggression and might even be generous to a government it had virtually installed. And with the Sandinistas as an opposition force, there could be no return to the Somoza days. The Sandinistas promised a revitalization of the revolutionary movement, and this was my hope.

To return I had to wait until 1991, when I had a sabbatical leave; by then, a year after the election, my hopes had already been dashed. Poor Nicaragua was daily becoming poorer, and politically it seemed that all sides were losing.

I began this trip in California, where some friends helped me find a good 1978 Honda Civic, a cheap, reliable car that got forty-five miles to the gallon. I had always wanted to drive through Central America. I loaded up with camping gear, notes, and books and crossed the border at Tiajuana, drove the seven hundred and fifty miles of amazing desert and coastline of Baja California, ferried to the mainland, and followed the Pacific coast of Mexico to the state of Oaxaca. I ate fish and fruit, and spent a day or two at places I especially liked. I drove through the mountains of southern Mexico and Guatemala. Turned back at El Salvador, I circled east and crossed Honduras. When Hernán Cortés was asked by the king of Spain to describe Central America he is supposed to have taken a piece of paper and crumpled it. This is one of my memories. Mountains and more brooding mountains; single-lane roads; deserts of stones and fields of cactus; jungle and cold and foggy heights; reds and browns in every shade. Gathering impatience.

When I arrived at the Nicaraguan border, I couldn't enter. The customs workers were on strike, one of many strikes under the new government, one of the forms of "governing from below." I waited eight days in a Honduran bordertown, reading my journals and notes in the garden of a *pensión*. I didn't terribly mind the delay. I would be there for at least eight months, and this trip would be different. I wouldn't be rushing from place to place under a time limit. I expected to stay mostly in one place and write.

Once in the country I went directly to Norma's house; she had a room I could rent. Suddenly I was in familiar Nicaragua—yet now it wasn't so familiar. Much had changed in a very short time.

I spent my first days talking with people and reading old newspapers and magazines. The archives of *Barricada*—now declared independent of the Sandinista party—were nearby. Slowly, as if out of a fog, the new reality took form for me.

The vital statistics were almost too bad to believe. Production had fallen even further, and drastically, in both agriculture and industry. Inflation in one year reached 1,500 percent; unemployment, more than 60 percent. An epidemic of layoffs, wage reductions, and evictions had hit the country. All indices of social distress were rising dramatically: infant mortality, deaths of mothers in childbirth, polio, measles, cholera; increased crime, domestic violence, family desertion, and alcoholism.

Every day after my return I read news items in the paper like this one from Matagalpa: "More than a hundred children died last month on state farms because of diarrhea and malnutrition. . . . [A]t one farm, fifty children have entered phase three of malnutrition, and no authority is concerning itself with the situation." A tragedy like this was unthinkable during the Sandinista government. But in the first year of the UNO government, some thirteen hundred children died of diarrhea and measles — easily preventable deaths.

What lay behind these facts? Nicaragua, of course, had been experiencing economic destruction and deterioration since the Contra war and economic blockade began in roughly 1983. The new government had inherited an impoverished country. Yet why had things worsened so dramatically? The average income in Nicaragua was said to be the lowest of any country in Latin America, except for Haiti. The problem seemed to be that the new government was tearing down the old productive forces and not putting anything in their place.

The UNO coalition, led by President Violeta Chamorro and her chief minister and adviser (and son-in-law) Antonio Lacayo, quickly adopted a series of measures designed to placate the Bush administration and show that their priorities were on the side of the wealthy. UNO controlled a sufficient majority in the National Assembly to outvote the Sandinistas on these measures. Having agreed to International Monetary Fund guidelines for loans and aid, which demanded reductions in government expenditures and a restructuring of priorities regarding foreign investment, UNO radically cut all social services and raised their cost. Medical care and medicine, always scarce, have become unavailable or beyond the resources of most people. Schools have been closed, teachers laid off, scholarships cut, tuitions increased, and fees introduced even for primary schools. A poor family with several children is now unable to send them all to school because of these fees. Many students have had to leave the universities. Housing costs have increased dramatically: electricity and water rates have risen by 400 to 600 percent, real-estate taxes have been set at astronomical rates, and land costs have shot up. With other costs so high, and with production down, food prices, even for fresh vegetables and fruit, have risen to levels comparable to those in the United States.

A general strike of health-care workers was called shortly after I returned

UNO government workers painting over a mural in central Managua. Photo by Mauricio Duarte. Barricada, 1991. By permission.

to the country. All hospitals were closed except for emergency care. The mostly Sandinista health-care workers were demanding an increased budget for the health sector, a restoration of recently cut wage levels, and more supplies for hospitals and health centers. Nineteen workers fasted to dramatize the severity of the problem, and did so for more than thirty days until the strike was finally won. A moving and important example of government from below.

But conditions remain truly desperate. Fifty percent of the health centers have been closed. Hospitals are now divided into first-, second-, and third-class sections, according to ability to pay. New epidemics have been breaking out, even of such diseases as malaria and tuberculosis and polio, which had almost been eliminated. The public hospitals lack everything, even sufficient cleaning materials. Some didn't even have antibiotics.

In Matagalpa I spoke with María Felicia, the Argentine doctor I had met in El Cedro. She told me that she and her husband were considering leaving the country because of the poor conditions. "When there was the revolution," she said, "we could sacrifice with the knowledge that the conditions of the poor were improving and the basis for a good society was being laid. Now that incentive has been lost. We are missing things that we used to be able to do without — cultural life, time off for vacations and training in new medical knowledge, better schools for Jorge, that sort of thing. I think we will be going back to Argentina soon. It is even hard for us to keep our son in school now with the increased costs — and my husband is a teacher and I'm a doctor!" Thanks to the successful strike, María Felicia's salary was increased from 135 dollars a month to 250 dollars a month. "But it costs us more than 400 dollars a month to live," she said, "and my husband only makes 73 dollars a month."

The UNO policies have proven ineffective even in their own terms: they have not brought foreign aid or investment. This is partly for political reasons. The UNO government is deeply divided between moderates such as President Chamorro, who favor reconciliation, and the ex-Contras, who want to destroy Sandinista power, especially in the army and the police. U.S. aid has been blocked because Jesse Helms and other Republican members of the Senate have for years been closely allied with the ex-Contras. They accept the anti-Sandinistas' claim that the Sandinistas are too powerful, even though the army and police have been cooperating assiduously — many say too much — with the new government. The mere existence of the Sandinista movement has caused the Bush administration to continue its hostile and punitive attitude toward Nicaragua. The Chamorro government even renounced Nicaragua's claim against the United States for war-damage reparations, won at the World Court in The Hague, in hopes that the Bush administration would grant an aid package. Nonetheless, they received only a small fraction of the promised aid, and much of that was earmarked to service their foreign debt.

Why the increase in unemployment, from 20 percent at the end of 1990 to more than 60 percent? The cuts in social services, education, cultural programs, agricultural programs, and so on — indeed, the dismantling of the Sandinista government by UNO — have meant layoffs in large numbers. The reduction in university students has put more jobseekers in the streets. The army was reduced from eighty thousand to about twenty thousand, in a country where such a reduction is equal to about one-sixth of the entire wage-labor force. The Contras, numbering about fifteen thousand, were demobilized and returned to the countryside, expecting jobs and housing assistance that has not been forthcoming. Many state farms and enterprises have laid off workers because the government wanted to sell these properties or turn them over to their previous owners. Privately owned enterprises are laying off workers in order to "rationalize" production — for example, Victoria Beer closed down entirely, then rehired 30 percent of its workers when it reopened.

The UNO government's policies are intended to attract foreign investment. Yet, because of a worldwide recession, the investors are not coming. Also, Nicaragua is not very appealing to the foreign investor, owing to the poor quality of its economic infrastructure, its outdated plant and equipment, and the organized militancy of its labor force. But the government's efforts doggedly continue, and continue to make life harder in Nicaragua. For instance, taxes have been reduced on all imports of luxury goods, such as cars, liquor, and perfumes, while new sales taxes have been imposed on essential consumer goods, including medicines, clothing, and school supplies.

Paradoxically, the end of the war in Nicaragua turns out to have brought even more misery and death into the lives of most Nicaraguans. The new government has proven to be weak, ineffective, and unreliable; it has fallen pitifully into the grip of U.S. control and international financial constraints. The notion of "government from below" has proven for the most part to be a dream as well. The Sandinistas have struggled mightily, but have been unable to prevent the new government from scrapping most of their social programs. It is amazing in a year's time to see values that insisted that anyone should be able to live replaced by policies that make it expensive and for many no longer possible to live.

A bourgeois social order has come into being almost before my eyes. It is as if the society, amoebalike, divided into two. A much smaller part, the bourgeoisie, exuberantly dominates public life with its flamboyant lifestyle. Now there are many new cars on the streets, even BMWs and Mercedes, because the returned bourgeoisie were allowed to repatriate two cars per person duty-free. Many brought cars to sell, and car prices have dropped accordingly. Now Managua has traffic problems. New gasoline service stations have opened, many open all night. Car dealerships have opened, with large inventories of Toyotas, VWs, and Mercedes. Motorcycles and bicycles are displayed in grand showrooms.

Consumer goods of every kind are plentiful, and new stores are opening all over Managua, especially fancy specialty shops — offering beauty products, women's fashions, children's clothing, home appliances, hardware, copy machines, computers and other previously scarce electronic goods. There's even a Radio Shack, where I could buy fuses for my car radio. The owners of these stores are trying hard to exploit a new market, composed of bourgeois families who have recently returned or are newly prosperous, and although it is a comparatively small market, it dominates advertising and the media. New billboards are up, all catering to the affluent buyer: expensive restaurants and oceanside resorts, liquor, stylish clothing, furniture, and appliances are boldly offered in bright colors beside the bleak intersections largely populated by new cars and street hustlers. There are new nightclubs whose parking lots are crowded with shiny cars and motorcycles, driven by young people wearing Miami fashions. A highly publicized, expensive club for gay men has opened, featuring acts from Miami and San Francisco. Concerts of popular singers from Mexico are advertised in full-page newspaper ads. Previously unheard-of ticket prices are charged — 20, 30, 40 dollars — as much as New York City, as much as half a month's teacher's salary! For the first time, Nicaragua has entered the "Miss World" contest. The finals were held at the InterContinental Hotel, where for 25 dollars a seat you could witness the competition and crowning of "Miss Nicaragua." Advertisements appear for weekends on the Pacific Coast, for special sales of furniture and appliances, and for every kind of plastic surgery (a drawing of a female body maps out the possibilities).

On the surface, prosperity seems to have come to Nicaragua. There is a new busyness, color, and sense of plenty. And the intense drive to exploit the bourgeois market is matched by commercial hustle among the poor. Almost every working-class family runs some kind of small business out of their house, if only selling bags of ice from the refrigerator. Street corners by traffic lights are crowded with peddlers. I have been offered bags of fruit and vegetables, pastries and breads, sweets, Chiclets and cigarettes (of course), every kind of hardware item, car seats, TV antennas, toys, inflatable Santa Clauses, Christmas trees and decorations, parrots, monkeys, fish, even a baby deer. Children wipe off your window. Others, very weak and hungry-looking, simply beg — Managua now has thousands of homeless children. Most anomalous of all, young women sell themselves at night at traffic lights and by the InterContinental Hotel. The number of prostitutes in Managua is said to have increased in 1991 alone from fewer than two hundred to perhaps fifteen hundred. And since this is Nicaragua, they are already organizing and demonstrating against police interference!

The United States has channeled the little foreign aid that has arrived into the hands of the more conservative sectors of UNO. Cities run by conservative UNO mayors are favored over other cities, even over the federal government, with bizarre consequences. The UNO mayor of Managua, Arnaldo Alemán, a leader of the ultraconservatives, thus had money to initiate a highly publicized road-repair project, but ignored the desperate need of public hospitals for such things as cotton and alcohol. Managua was cheerfully decorated with Christmas lights and Nativity scenes, and work on the new cathedral was going forward, while squatter's settlements were proliferating, and nothing was done to improve Managua's deteriorating water supply.

There are plenty of goods, billboards and bright lights, hustlers, sex, alcohol and drugs — and plenty of crime. The streets have gone from being the safest of any large city in Latin America (and the United States, it could be added) to being as bad as those anywhere. It is crazy now to walk alone at night if you are a woman or a gringo. I spoke to women who had been mugged in daylight right outside their homes. You can't park on the street at night for fear of losing your tires or windshield. In 1991, sixteen taxi drivers were murdered in Managua.

During the Sandinista years, I saw this country being clubbed to death by the United States. Now, the bourgeoisie is gaudily enjoying its power, and Nicaragua is suffering even more desperately, though less visibly. The big stick of the Pentagon and the CIA has been replaced with an economic boa constrictor: unemployment. The sounds of helicopters and screaming have stopped, leaving the silence of hungry people and the weak cries of dying children.

Nicaragua had scoffed at the old Latin American realities: in place of misery, food for all, health care for all, education for all, housing for all. Life for all. Now the vultures have come home to roost.

Norma was among those retired from the army. She was angry, but what could she do? With her severance pay (which many government workers received) and her savings, she started a small restaurant in a nearby shopping center. I was impressed by her energy and resourcefulness. She had some help, but did the buying and much of the cooking, serving, and bookkeeping. She was out of the house at nine in the morning and not home till after midnight, seven days a week. The owner of the building charged her an astronomical rent and her location was not the best, but somehow she seemed to be making a go of it. I rarely saw her, except when I stopped there for a beer or a meal.

My life settled into a quiet, almost meditative routine. Norma's son Rodman, now in high school, worked at the restaurant after school. Her granddaughter Katherine was picked up from school and played at the restaurant. Another North American who lived at her house, Steve, worked at the university teaching computer science and was almost never home. Only Norma's mother, Doña Julia, spent much time in the house. She was younger and stronger than a great-grandmother ought to be, stoical, with many health problems and a great burden of work. She arrived early each day by bus from her house, prepared food, mopped the floors, washed clothes by hand, ironed, saw Katherine off to school. She and I were the mainstays of the house.

Sometimes Norma and I would have a late dinner when she came in from work. She was usually exhausted, and always there were problems. She needed to get an air conditioner installed. The woman who was cooking had to stay home to care for a sick child. The beer truck didn't make the delivery it promised. I worried that she wouldn't make it. Sandinista government workers were being replaced by conservatives, so many were starting little businesses and, with so much poverty in the country, most were having a hard time. Nine out of ten Sandinistas were said to be unemployed.

Norma told me about her plan to capture the lunch business of the workers at a nearby bank. The bank was "rationalizing"—the word for putting profits before people. It was negotiating with several hundred unionized workers about layoffs, and had already cut the workforce by 30 percent. It had been saved the inconvenience of cutting wages by a national currency reevaluation that had the effect, countrywide, of reducing wages by more than one-third in relation to prices. Now the bank wanted to close its lunchroom and commissary, further reducing the living standards of the workers. The Sandinista system had provided a lunchroom (employing about a dozen workers) that sold low-cost lunches to all workers and gave free lunches to the lowest-paid. The commissary was a consumer cooperative, providing various products to workers at near wholesale prices.

The bank was refusing to maintain these services and wanted to close or privatize them. The workers agreed to privatize on condition that they would be the ones to take over. The bank opposed this alternative—it wanted to sell concessions to the highest bidder, owing to their lucrative, because captive, market potential. Struggles like this, Norma said, were going on everywhere, with workers trying to hold on to what little they had and the enterprises trying to "rationalize" by reducing the wages and benefits of their workers. What was not being "rationalized," of course, were the profits. The incomes of owners, executives, and investors have grown enormously.

Norma expected a stalemate at the bank and hoped to step in. She said she could provide a lunch for workers that would not be much more expensive than the price they had been paying. She was thinking of a plate lunch—a small piece of meat or chicken, rice and beans, a vegetable, a tortilla, and a glass of fruit juice—for 10 córdobas (2 dollars). This price was almost as high as the same food would cost in the United States; but, given the price of food, rent, and so on in Nicaragua, Norma couldn't go any lower. She had informed the bank of her proposal, and was waiting to hear their response.

"I hope you get the business," I said. "But I see that now that you are a capitalist, your survival depends on the bank workers losing their fight with the bank. Their loss is your gain."

She smiled her tired smile, brushed her hair back and said, "Every business in the country is trying to cut benefits. I am trying to provide a good, cheap lunch for the workers."

"Yes," I said, "but 10 córdobas is a lot of money for them. The lowest-paid workers are only making about 75 dollars [375 córdobas] a month. I know you can't give them free lunches. But twenty lunches a month would cost over half their earnings."

We looked at each other, but we didn't smile.

"Welcome to the United States of Nicaragua," she said.

One Sunday morning Norma was able to stay home for a while because she had decided to open late. We sat around the kitchen table with coffee. Doña Julia was sewing a dress for Katherine, and Norma and I were talking about the new government.

The situation was quite unusual in my experience. The government was so divided that the president, Violeta Chamorro, who represents the moderate right, issued an order that her vice-president, Virgilio Godoy, who represents the ultraright, not be given an office. He has been working out of his home. Since UNO was a coalition of parties united only by their opposition to the Sandinistas, it was logical, in a way, that its factions differed primarily in their attitudes toward the Sandinistas. Both Godoy and Alfredo César, president of the National Assembly and leader of the UNO representatives, vehemently oppose Sandinista influence, especially in the army and the police. They are especially galled that Humberto Ortega, the former minister of defense and Daniel Ortega's brother, is still head of the army.

"But," Norma said, "Humberto has acted in an exemplary manner within the new government, even resigning from the Front. Some people in the Front say he has betrayed us."

"Has he?" I asked.

"Not at all," she said. "He is a man of principle. If he abandoned the Front, he would say so. His position is clear. He wouldn't violate the law in order to carry out government orders, but he is acting as head of an army that is obedient to civilian control. Doña Violeta and Antonio Lacayo work with Humberto because they trust him."

Perhaps, I suggest, they also have little choice. The army was created by the Sandinistas and originated from the guerrilla movement during the Somoza years. It is Sandinista through and through. It has cooperated with the transition and accepted a 75 percent reduction to a peacetime level. It is disciplined, and its leadership has fully committed itself to serving the new government. The Contras, by contrast, are divided and undependable. Many do not accept the existence of the Sandinistas as a legal entity. Many want revenge, want to destroy the Sandinistas. I ask Norma, "Would the Sandinistas agree to give up control over the army, when it's so important to their security and the possibility of progressive change in the future?"

"The Sandinista army is the source of whatever stability we have in Nicaragua," Norma said. "UNO won the election, so we support them. We will defend this government. On the other hand, we are the opposition, and we demand conditions that enable us to exist as the opposition. We oppose many of [Doña Violeta's] policies, we struggle against much of what the government is doing, but we support the legal process, and we believe that, bad as UNO is, the only realistic way to deal with the current situation is to support them. But César only uses the government for his ends. He is not principled. And Doña Violeta knows this. She therefore plays a very important role now, because she stands for reconciliation.

"Doña Violeta is a good person, an honest, moral person. She is a perfect Nicaraguan housewife, and as president she acts like a housewife, mother to her Nicaraguan family. Her own family is divided; her favorite son, Carlos Fernández, is the editor of *Barricada;* her favorite daughter, Cristiana, is editor of *La Prensa*."

"She must be good at handling conflicts," I say.

"No, she is good at pretending they don't exist. She's just a figurehead. She doesn't do anything or understand anything. Antonio Lacayo, Cristiana's husband, really runs the government. She just speaks for it on formal occasions.

"Let me tell you something that happened a couple of months ago. Doña Violeta had to deliver two speeches in one day. One speech was to a group of businessmen from some South American countries, here to discuss trade. The other was to welcome the new ambassador from — I think — South Korea. Well, she got the two speeches mixed up and read the entire welcome for the ambassador to the businessmen. All of it. She never noticed, and it was on television! She just smiled and stepped down when she was finished, and never knew until someone told her.

"Doña Violeta is only in politics because of her husband [Pedro Joaquín Chamorro was owner of *La Prensa* when it was a liberal voice against the Somoza dictatorship; he was assassinated by the National Guard in 1978]. She isn't really interested in government, and doesn't understand it, she's just a typical housewife."

"There's nothing typical about her," Doña Julia said angrily. "I'm a typical Nicaraguan housewife. I come from a campesino family, I have a fourth-grade education, but I can read and think! I'm intelligent! She's a typical *bourgeois* housewife. She doesn't know what life is like for most Nicaraguans, what it's like being poor, to have to feed four or five children on a few dollars a month, to live in a little house with twelve people. She's bourgeois, she's always had everything. She has good intentions, she's a good person; but when she goes to Washington and Bush pats her on the shoulder and says he wants to help Nicaragua, she believes him. She doesn't know Bush wears four faces. All she knows is how to have parties and play canasta. She's not a typical housewife."

"That's right," Norma says. "She goes to meetings and sits quietly. She doesn't talk except to express her good, motherly intentions. But she plays an important role, now, for Nicaragua."

"So you support *her,* but not her policies?" I asked.

"I support the elected government. That is the Sandinista position. We are together with her on this, and the army is there to enforce it. Many Sandinistas even agree with her on other things: for example, her economic policies."

"No," I said. "You can't be serious."

"Yes," she said. "For example, we agree on the need to cut domestic consumption in order to encourage capitalist investment. We would not go as far as they go, and we would do it differently, but realistically, we have no other choice. Nicaragua needs loans and credits, and now that the Soviet Union has collapsed, there is no place for us to go except where everyone else goes: the World Bank and the International Monetary Fund."

"This kind of realism is not what I would expect from the Sandinistas," I said. "Look what is going on now — the suffering. Look who is paying."

"We wouldn't do it like UNO. We would support the rights of workers, and maintain the basic services — subsidized basic foods, health, and education. But the austerity is something that can't be avoided. We are poor."

"But," I said, "I thought the viewpoint of the World Bank and the IMF is that Nicaragua must develop an export economy, and that would be—or is—devastating for the majority of the population. Nicaragua needs balanced development, especially small-scale business and agriculture for local consumption. This won't happen now. There is no credit for small farms."

"Yes," she said, "that's right. But, I tell you, things are different now. The people voted, and it is the UNO government they elected. They want to try the capitalist route; they are not ready for socialism. It is like the Exodus of the Jews from slavery in Egypt. The people were shown the way, but they weren't ready to return to the Promised Land. So God made them stay in the desert for forty years." She got up from the table, to get ready to leave for the restaurant.

"That is the way it is now in Nicaragua, and not only Nicaragua, but in the whole world," she said. I sensed a deep anger in her voice and a fatalism that made my skin prickle.

"We are beginning our forty years in the desert," she said.

"Does this mean that everyone who voted for UNO is going to die before socialism comes to Nicaragua?" I answered, a weak joke about her biblical reference to the Jews in the desert.

She didn't answer. She just stood there looking at me with a thin, bitter smile.

"But what about the children who will die?" I added. She shrugged her shoulders and said nothing.

After sitting all day cooped up in Norma's house, I needed exercise. There's little inducement to take walks in Nicaragua; you'll get a funny look from a Managuan if you propose a walk simply for pleasure. There are no attractive sights, no sidewalks, and almost no parks, and now there is plenty of danger from vehicles and muggers. But people do walk from necessity, so you can sort of blend in. I could cover the entire barrio, *andén* by *andén* and back, in about forty-five minutes. About five o'clock in the afternoon it was busy with people returning home, hanging out in front, walking babies, talking, and watching television.

Swimming in Xiloa were my greatest, most beautiful experiences while living in Managua. Xiloa is a lake that lies in a large, extinct volcano, a few miles northeast of Managua. Since I had a car I could stop work at about four, pick up my friend Enrique, and we could be there a little before sunset. The lake is lovely that time of day, reflecting the late afternoon light, and it is quiet because almost everyone has gone home. The water is a perfect temperature, warm, but cool when you first get in, and seems to have salts in it—it feels marvelous on your skin and has a chalky taste. You know it is clean because there are no dwellings around it, just steep, rugged slopes on one side and the park with its restaurants and picnic tables on the other. The Xiloa park was created originally by Somoza, who had a villa there. Now Xiloa has a hotel with hearts on its sign and rents rooms by the hour.

Enrique was a good swimming buddy. Usually it was just he and I, although sometimes Javier, Eduardo, and Laureano, sons of Elena Pineda, came too. (She and Enrique were somewhat tumultuously and, it turned out, temporarily living together.) The boys played near the shore, but we swam far out. We always went to the middle, slowly, because neither of us was a great swimmer. We were excited and happy and a little scared to be swimming in a volcano. There is such a feeling of depth that you think maybe there's a bottomless hole underneath you. After about thirty minutes we would decide we were at the center, paddle around a bit, and rest and look at the sky. By then the sun had usually set, but shone on the clouds overhead, coloring them yellow and red in the light, and dark and purplish in the shadows. The sky was still blue, and the evening star had begun to shine bright as a beacon. I checked out the horizon on all sides. We sensed being in the center by the curvature of the water, which was equal in all directions and hid the edge of the shoreline. We called this spot "la mitad del mundo" (the middle of the world). It felt like it. There was an almost-physical pull to stay there, as if it were a holy place. As if entranced, Enrique sometimes started to swim farther; but I stayed, circling, and called him back.

When we turned around it would be dark. The swimming began to feel like work. We swam toward the lights of a restaurant where the boys were playing. The lake usually had small waves that slapped against us as we swam. I breathed by keeping my head turned away from them, and I watched the evening star. We didn't panic, but we swam as hard as we could and in earnest.

On the drive back, everyone would be tired and quiet. We listened to a music tape; usually, Enrique wanted to hear "the brothers," meaning the Neville Brothers. They all liked the strong beat and the lyrics I translated for them. I played them songs I love and that inspire me — songs that say, "You can't stop running water, or the fire that burns inside"; "Fearless — you must be fearless"; and "Steer me right, sweet Jesus — Don't let me fall!"

I thought about driving north to visit Condega or Matagalpa, but I kept hesitating. Things were very chaotic there and it was actually less safe now than it was during the war: ex-Contras were still moving about in the mountains, still ambushing, still murdering Sandinista officials, robbing and kidnapping on the highways. The army pursued them, and sometimes engaged them in combat and made arrests, but mostly these ex-Contras got away because the government had ordered the army to avoid confrontations with them as much as possible. This tolerance was strange. One ex-Contra leader, whose nom de guerre is "Indomable" ("Indomitable," showing the influence of Hollywood!) led fifty to eighty men, and was written up almost daily for some new and rather atrocious exploit. Later I read that he was meeting with government officials and negotiating terms for disarming. For a long time he said he would speak to no one except Doña Violeta. Then he accepted a "severance payment" of 150,000 dollars to leave the country and emigrate to Miami. Soon, however, he was back and up to his old tricks.

The Contras had been repatriated from Honduras after it became clear that the United States would no longer support them. The Nicaraguan government—expecting U.S. aid—promised them protection, land, and help with housing and jobs. Many had high expectations about the role they would play in the government, army, or police. And the vast majority cooperated by laying down their arms. Their presence has been accepted peacefully, for the most part. I have spoken with some ex-Contras, though, who settled in Managua because, they claimed, there was danger of retaliation in their hometowns, where they are known. And, indeed, Enrique Bermúdez, military leader of the Contras, was assassinated in Managua, presumably because of the "large bill" he had run up against the Sandinistas (this was the expression used by a former army officer).

Although the government is attending to the needs of ex-Contra officers, giving them farms and vehicles and money, the regular soldiers have received little or nothing. I saw a sad and funny ceremony on television: Antonio Lacayo had come in a helicopter with a television crew to make a donation of government aid to a group of ex-Contra soldiers, who had been granted a section of uncultivated land in the mountains—jungle, to be precise. Lacayo gave a very upbeat speech, praising the former Contras for their patience and willingness to start a new life working in peace. Then he presented each one with a shovel, a pick, a pair of rubber boots, and a bag of seed beans. The recipients of this beneficence stood there looking like they could spit bullets. Lacayo flew back to his mansion in Managua the same afternoon.

When I and the Veterans for Peace saw Bocay, it was a perfect movie image of an old western town, with its small, wood-frame stores and horses tied in front. It has become a perfect Wild West town, a completely anarchic place. The Sandinista mayor has been assassinated, the police can do nothing, and groups of ex-Contras (now called Recontras) freely enter the town, rob everyone in sight, empty stores, and murder Sandinistas. There are reports of internationalists — that means me! — being held for large sums of ransom money, which is meekly paid.

The government estimated that about forty groups of Recontras were roaming the northern provinces. There was a widespread belief that Alfredo César, UNO majority leader in the National Assembly, and Managua's Mayor Alemán were meeting with these renegade groups and helping to arrange money and supplies for them. The army has claimed that supplies were being flown to them from Honduras, just as in the days of the war. Meanwhile, the government kept to its policy of what seemed to me foot-dragging "moderation," urging the Recontras to turn in their arms and join the peace process (even though it was obvious to everyone that the "peace process" meant unemployment). The daily news reports were of this sort: A Recontra group held a section of the Pan-American Highway south of Estelí for one and half hours and robbed more than seventy vehicles. Only a few were caught and jailed. Another day: A Recontra group attacked and took over a farming cooperative, and another robbed several cars on the Pan-American Highway.

Other groups of Recontras were known to be in the employ of returned Somocistas who wanted to use them as shock troops to regain their farms from workers' cooperatives. Almost every day there were pitched battles. All told, there were hundreds of incidents in 1991, and more than fifty people were killed. Not surprisingly, groups that called themselves "Recompas" (short for *recompañeros*) formed to defend the cooperatives and pursue the Recontras.

Years of fighting and easy access to weapons has made violence a common way to settle disputes in the countryside. When I went on trips to the north I felt surrounded by it. For example, when I was talking to some friends in Condega late one afternoon, we heard two gunshots, very nearby. We ran around the corner and saw a man lying facedown in the street in front of a house. The man who shot him was in the house with the door barred. They had been arguing about a ten-acre piece of land in the *campo*. A crowd gathered — everyone in the neighborhood. Pretty soon the dead man's wife showed up and began yelling and screaming at the crowd and at the man inside the house. She found some big rocks and threw them against his door over and over, trying to break it in. The crowd moved back and forth, depending on where she was directing her anger. The man inside, Alberto, was well known and liked in the community: a musician who led the band that played in church, a member of the town government. The dead man and his family were "Contra." After almost an hour of this screaming drama, the police drove up, restrained the woman, and took Alberto to jail. That night, his wife and kids quietly moved out of town.

The "postwar" period was producing strange alliances. I read of several cases of ex-Contras being invited to join cooperatives and doing so. I had no way of knowing how extensive these new relations were, nor did anyone else in this land of dis- and mis- and noninformation. There had also been many reports of ex-Contras and former Sandinista soldiers uniting to work together against a government that was doing nothing for either group. As Nicaragua became increasingly more bourgeois as a society, class interests were dividing some who had been strongly unified and uniting others who had been opposed during the revolution.

When an old landowner returns from Miami, hoping to take back his farm, he may find allies among ex-Contras who hope to benefit from helping him, or he may encounter a united front of armed campesinos who are working to hold onto land they consider to be rightfully theirs. The government often mediates between such groups, and a frequently applied formula balances three different kinds of rights: bourgeois owners' rights, working-class rights, and veterans' rights. One-third of the land goes to the co-op workers, one-third to returning soldiers (ex-Contra as well as Sandinista), and one-third to the old owner.

A new shift, also reflecting class conflict and the disintegration of revolutionary solidarity, was taking place in the Sandinista party. They held their first full congress in the summer of 1991, and the biggest concerns were such issues as internal democracy, privilege, and corruption in the party. To the disgust of many, the leadership shelved these issues, paying lip service to the need for reforms while "delaying" concrete actions, such as putting the national directorate up for election person-by-person rather than as a whole (if that had happened, some of the current directorate would not have been reelected).

This inflexibility doesn't bode well for the party. Many Sandinistas, as well as non-Sandinista Nicaraguans, are quite angry at their leaders—not most of the top leaders, such as Daniel Ortega or Tomás Borge, who are widely considered great and committed revolutionaries, but the lower-echelon leaders, the regional and local officers in the party who benefited personally from their position and the privileges it brought. For many years such leaders had cars, nice houses, and higher standards of living.

To take an example close to home, Norma, being an army captain and a *militante* of the party, received a car—a Russian Lada—which became her private property, and a severance bonus large enough to start a small restaurant. As well-earned and modest as these benefits are, they nonetheless stand out in her neighborhood, where most people are unemployed. And many of the more active Sandinistas are in a similar position—they received benefits that raised their personal standard of living because of their work on behalf of the revolution. This is a well-worn subject here. I remember in 1988 seeing articles, with photographs, in Monday's newspapers, showing lines of government vehicles parked at Xiloa the day before, using scarce gasoline, the articles point out, for Sunday outings. Everyone knew it was a form of corruption, minor perhaps because Nicaragua isn't rich enough for corruption to go very far; yet nothing was done, because the people who would have had to do something were the perpetrators. And the people who had no cars, who had to walk miles to get to Xiloa, or who had to try to get there by bus or, trying to hitch a ride, were breezily passed up by these serious, committed Sandinista families, were angry. Before the election and the end of the war, the "state of emergency," justified by the need for unity in struggle, was used to hold back such anger. But some people think it was this sort of corruption, and Sandinista arrogance in thinking that special privileges were deserved, that cost the FSLN the election.

Now people are more openly critical—their anger has come to the surface. A friend of mine, a painter, was not a Sandinista party member, although she was a member of the artists' union and the Solentiname painters' association. She frequently donated time and paintings to the revolution. In a small wood-frame house, about twelve by fourteen feet, with no inside plumbing and a dirt floor, in which cooking is often done with wood (for lack of money for gas), she lives with her three children and a friend and her brother and two children. Eight people.

"I don't like politics," she said when I asked her how she felt about the elections. "Of course I voted for the Sandinistas because I support the revolution, but most of them are like other people, they are opportunists. They are Sandinistas in order to get a car or a house or a job. They are not Sandinistas. Sandino wasn't like that. He wasn't looking for a house or a farm. If my country were invaded by Costa Rica or the United States, I would fight to defend it. But I would be fighting for my country, not for a farm or a house.

"Here in Nicaragua," she said, "there are many people living in cardboard houses, with nothing over their heads except plastic. You have seen those children on the street begging, without food or shoes or a place to sleep. When there are such things in this country how can people try to get a fine house and call themselves Sandinistas? They are not—they are opportunists."

Another woman I knew was a very active organizer for the revolution and the head of her barrio's CDS—the "block organizations" that were so important for handling many local problems during the revolution. Dora worked for years in her barrio, subsisting on contributions paid by her poor constituency. She is now unemployed, and lives hand-to-mouth with her brother and two children in a small house from which she expects to be evicted.

"I am Sandinista," she said, "and I always will be Sandinista, but our CDS was not a party organization. I never put on a party button and never will. We helped people who needed help. If someone needed food, we got them food; or if someone needed to go to the hospital, we got them there. We didn't care whether they were 'with the process' or not, Sandinista or not. That's what it means to be a Sandinista—to help people who need help and make a revolution."

One evening I brought Dora and some other friends to Norma's house for dinner. We got out a lot of vegetables and made a stew. Norma came home from her work at the restaurant, and we all sat down about midnight to a nice meal of beer and stew and tortillas. I thought Dora and Norma, two wonderful, bright, politically committed women, would enjoy getting to know each other. I told Norma that Dora, too, had been head of the CDS in her barrio. They had a lot in common—though Dora, I thoughtlessly added, hadn't wanted to be a party member. When I said this the air over the table instantly iced over: crack! Neither woman said a word to the other. When I looked at Norma and back to Dora I saw clearly something I hadn't noticed before. Two women with the same economic and family background, and much else in common, seemingly everything in common, now divided by class. It was a small difference, but it felt big because of the extremely difficult conditions. And this difference of class had been created within the revolution! We ate silently for about five minutes. Soon Norma excused herself and went to bed.

When I finally got my courage up to drive to Matagalpa, I spent an afternoon with veteran Fred Jacobs, whom I met in El Cedro. He had been working steadily in Nicaragua for three years and, like a lot of people since the election, was ready to go home even though no one had been found to take his place. Fred felt pretty sure that, in part, the Sandinistas' own behavior caused them to lose the election.

"Their arrogance," he said, "and the way they treated the campesinos. They were always talking *to* them, making speeches, and they did so with good intentions, with a firm commitment to making the revolution work, but they didn't apply a self-critical attitude. And they didn't listen. They were too taken up with themselves and the problems as they saw them to find out how the campesinos saw things. I think that people stopped feeling the revolution was something they could enter into and take part in. Instead it was something that was in the hands of these caudillos who were living soft in the city."

Fred described an all-day meeting he attended whose subject was how to get campesinos more involved in various projects in the countryside—health, construction, defense. Besides himself, the meeting included two local representatives of the Sandinista Front, two leaders of UNAG, and two campesinos who were heads of cooperatives.

"The meeting went like this," he said. "The first *Frente* guy talked for about a half an hour about problems. One of the UNAG guys responded and gave his analysis. Then the other guy from the *Frente,* then the other guy from UNAG. Then they talked back and forth. Then we broke for a long lunch. In the afternoon it was the same thing! The guys from the cooperatives, the only campesinos present, listened the whole time, but were never invited to speak! The very guys whose involvement was being discussed. When I left that meeting I thought, 'Those guys must be really pissed.' I'll bet they felt they had wasted their day."

When I asked him about corruption, he said he thought that had had a lot of effect on people, too. The people in the Front who worked in the *campo* had obvious privileges. "They had vehicles, they had motorcycles, and they always had plenty of gasoline. Every day they would be driving here and there and passing people on foot without giving them a ride. They were always in clean, newish jeans and T-shirts from the States. I am sure the campesinos noticed these things. They knew these guys came from poor families like them and they were benefiting from the revolution."

I asked him about donations that had come in from solidarity groups from all over the world. I had heard of some cases of officials grabbing these for themselves. "I think most donations were handled fairly," Fred said, "but many weren't. A large donation of cooking oil comes in from Denmark, say; the regional *jefe* [chief] gets a few gallons for his family, his secretary gets a gallon, the other people in the office take some, their brothers and sisters get some, and so on. The campesinos may not even see it. It is the same with donations of clothes. Most were handled well. But often they are picked through and the best things taken out. A pattern of privilege and corruption set in. It was always considered minor, or not considered, because of the war and the sense of emergency."

"And they felt they were deserving," I said. "And they *were* deserving. They were committed, they worked hard, they risked their lives, many lost their lives, and they didn't get paid much. Why shouldn't they have a vehicle? They *needed* one! Why shouldn't they have nice jeans from the States? We're talking about peanuts, here, not seaside villas or a Mercedes-Benz. Yet it's all relative, isn't it?"

"Yes, and it's something that happened to the very best, the best-educated, the most committed, those who rose in the *Frente* through their own efforts and sacrifices and courage. They gradually settled into caudillo-like roles and the positions of privilege that go with them. They became separate from the campesinos."

The observations Fred was making were repeated by many people in soul-searching discussions after the election defeat. Many Nicaraguans felt that the FSLN people were too full of themselves, didn't listen enough to the campesinos, and too often viewed the campesinos as passive or ignorant, or as potential collaborators with the Contras.

The most sensitive and interesting analysis of the election defeat was provided in a prizewinning essay by René Mendoza, in the Nicaraguan journal *Envío*. Mendoza wrote on the basis of years of experience and interviews in the rural districts of the northern mountains and also in the south near Masaya. The title of his analysis is "We Erred to Win," taken from the words of a campesino who voted for UNO and said, "We erred to win. Because we're going to win peace." Mendoza writes:

> The people have sacrificed scores of years for the hope of a more just and humane society. Their hopes have been continually postponed; only their sacrifices have not: February 25, 1990, translated a decade of wear and tear, of threats and uncertainty, accumulated hours of skipped heartbeats, into a vote. Never have a people thought so much about their vote as did most Nicaraguans. Lots of things came into it — crosses, rifles, tears, land, money, fiestas. . . .
>
> It's not good enough to state theoretically that the war and its child, the economic crisis, "caused" the Sandinistas' electoral defeat. We don't deny their dead weight on the results: the people voted with their plates empty and a pistol at their temples. Both were there, just as they were when the FSLN won in 1984. And as they will be in the future. The empire has always provoked economic crisis and

conflict in the poor countries of the Third World; nothing indicates that it will change.

The economic crisis and war conditioned not only the electoral process, but the whole course of the revolution. But they didn't determine it. Only the power of the campesinos and other popular sectors, through the struggle between classes, determines a revolution. We, in spite of everything, will determine our history, not war or empire. . . .

The FSLN lost; the empire didn't win. Many people just didn't feel represented by the FSLN. They had to "change their luck," not so much opting for a counter-revolutionary project as obliging the *Frente* to change, to recover the *Frente* as a revolutionary party, a party of the poor. That was the essence of their "punishment" vote. (Mendoza 1990, 24–25)

The article elaborates ways in which poor people felt "unrepresented by the FSLN," but first and most basic was a work-style of "bringing the line down" from the top levels to the people, rather than bringing the people's thinking upward to the leaders. "Middle-level cadres and the school that created them," he explains, "became a wall between the national leaders and the people" (Mendoza 1990, 26). This was exactly the experience Fred described with respect to the meeting he attended.

Mendoza cites another mistake: the FSLN made great and expensive efforts to accommodate large farmers and landowners, trying both to create national unity and to answer the U.S. charge that the Sandinistas were communists. While these were possibly important concerns, this "unity" policy was completely ineffective and, more important, was known to be ineffective by the poor campesinos, who had been asked to join a "unity" program that showed concern for their historic exploiters but neglected the exploited.

The article also cites the importance of religious opposition to the Sandinistas. "The most active counterrevolution in the country was the Catholic hierarchy headed up by Cardinal Obando y Bravo. They demonized Sandinismo more than Somoza did when he called General Sandino a 'bandit.' They delegitimized the revolution and legitimized the armed counterrevolution. . . . Making use of the pope and the Bible, they had no small effect on such a religious people." In Mendoza's view, the liberation church did not sufficiently counter this influence by working with the people. The Church's revolutionary leaders spoke in generalities and stayed too much in Managua. They "spoke of the poor, of justice, of imperialist aggression, but barely spoke of, much less engaged in, fights for water, health, education or economic development. [These] theologians tended to live in the past, 'reinterpreting the Bible.' They turned their backs on interpreting concrete reality, not recognizing that God is of the living. . . . Jesus is still being crucified, and in the barrios and *comarcas* [provinces] many bibles are still being written" (Mendoza 1990, 29–30).

My experience in Condega with Padre Enrique contradicts this analysis, because he did concentrate on basic needs of the campesinos and was enormously popular. He would certainly have to be considered an important worker in the revolution. But then Condega, tired and long-suffering Condega, where nearly every family had lost someone in the war, voted for the FSLN by a majority of 62 percent!

Although Tomás Borge is always full of surprises, I would never have expected to hear the most severe critique of Sandinista governance from him. Borge was the founder of the Front and a longtime member of the national directorate. My private interview with him was in January 1992. The following is a translated and edited transcription:

J.B.: Comandante Borge, my first question concerns the electoral defeat of the Sandinistas. In your opinion, what were the principal causes of the defeat? What was the relative importance of those causes which could be considered external and uncontrollable by the Sandinista Front, and what weight should be given to policies or failings in the revolutionary practice of the Front?

Borge: I believe the principal cause, even though this has been repeated many times, was the war of aggression planned and executed by the United States government. From almost the beginning of the triumph, the revolution was subjected to a severe, implacable war, one of the most intense and prolonged Nicaragua has ever suffered.

Besides the military war, we had other wars. The United States pressured multilateral financial-aid organizations to prevent Nicaragua from receiving international credit. Then in May 1985 it decreed an economic blockade of our country. Certainly, the North American government undertook the goal of defeating the Nicaraguan revolution by military means. But this was not possible. The Nicaraguan people defended themselves against a counterrevolutionary army that was larger, better-trained, and better-financed than the National Guard of Somoza. The electoral defeat of the Front in February 1990 was owing in great measure to the social and economic exhaustion we suffered for almost ten years. All of this was laid out in the objectives sketched by the Santa Fe documents,[1] which if they weren't accomplished exactly as the North Americans wished, nevertheless succeeded to a certain degree.

Certainly it is necessary to add the errors and defects of the revolution itself. We committed some errors of a structural nature, and others of a situational nature, that contributed in a substantive way to the electoral defeat. If our errors had not been added to the United States' war of aggression it would still have produced a deterioration of the revolution, but not to the degree it did. And if our errors had been committed without the war of aggression, certainly we would still have been defeated. The aggression and the errors combined and intertwined.

At the time of the triumph, we wanted to resolve with one blow the majority of the problems of Nicaraguan society, without having the objective resources to resolve them. For example, all the credits that we received and the financial aid in the form of donations and loans were used to subsidize normal life, not to accumulate investment resources that would bear fruit only later. I think this was a fundamental error.

Later, we maintained a policy of intertwining the party and the state, in such a manner that the government came to be the director of the party instead of the party being the director of the state. The government became the primary conductor of the revolution, and a revolutionary vanguard could no longer flourish. This was another error. The president of the Republic was at the same time the coordinator of the FSLN directorate. The local directors of the Sandinista Front were at the same time directors of the government. The mass organizations were converted into messengers and agents at the service of the government and were not, as had been originally intended, elements of support for governmental policies. The Front didn't lead the government, the government led the Front. I believe this was another important error.

Also, the Catholic Church exercises an important influence in Nicaraguan society. Although other churches have come to occupy a certain space, the truth is that the Catholic Church still plays a decisively influential role in the thinking of many Nicaraguans. And although from the beginning we intended to maintain a harmonious relation with the Church, the Church began to object to certain measures taken by the revolution — I'm referring here to high ecclesiastical authority — and we didn't handle this contradiction correctly. We went back and forth on this. The archbishop was flattered, then attacked, and then flattered. The FSLN directorate had an undefined attitude toward the Catholic Church. Consequently, this delicate and dangerous relationship was not handled with intelligent policies. From the beginning we established an identification of Christianity with the revolution, and the great majority of Christians understood this and identified with the revolution. The majority of Nicaraguans are Christians, and the majority are revolutionaries. So we had this identity between Christianity and the revolution that didn't translate into a relationship with the upper levels of the ecclesiastical hierarchy, which opposed this interrelationship of Christians and revolutionaries.

Another problem was that we had vertical styles of command. Not only [was this so] on the military level — in the army, the police, and State Security — but the war induced in the revolutionary leaders an authoritarian style that in my judgment did us much damage and was unnecessary. At the same time it is understandable, owing to the nature of the conflicts being produced, that within both the party and the government this style came to develop — a style not of authority, but of authoritarianism.

At the same time, we were not exemplary in our personal conduct and our style of life. That is to say, the people of Nicaragua began to notice that we, the leaders of the revolution, had adopted a style of life in conflict with what is appropriate for a revolutionary. One can't compare our life-style and conduct with the life-style of other political leaders in Latin America — there is an abyss separating us. But revolutionary peoples are so demanding that we ought to have been more like Saint Francis of Assisi in our poverty and our purity. Certainly, this was more conspicuous because of the scarcity of daily resources for the masses; when there was so much poverty and so much difficulty we ought to have been more demanding of ourselves.

We committed errors in our relations with various social sectors. I remember that at the beginning we established roadblocks on the highways, where campesinos who were coming in to sell their products were stopped. The attempt was to centralize distribution of production so that there were no intermediaries and things could be sold more cheaply to the population. But this created a contradiction with the campesinos; the small farmer who had a little corn or produce or whatever was prevented from realizing its sale, and this alienated the poor campesinos from us. At the same time, we exercised excessive control over craftspeople, impeding the natural development of their production. Also, we had an equivocal policy concerning small industries and even large ones — there were excessive confiscations of enterprises. Many of them were enemies of the revolution who became more hostile toward the revolution because of our attitude. Sometimes we appropriated property or companies without it being necessary; and, worst of all, at times we appropriated the property of poor or middle-class owners. This in my judgment was another error.

Moreover, we gave privileges to the large owners in the hope that they wouldn't be antagonistic toward the revolution. But the large owners are inclined by their very nature to be enemies of the revolution. Many of them used the excessive credits that we gave them to finance counterrevolutionary activities and to decapitalize the country. This tendency drastically increased in 1987, when certain policies were adopted to meet requirements of the International Monetary Fund.

Another point: In government offices it was necessary for us to use people who were not very advanced ideologically. . . . This was owing to the fact that within the political cadre of the party, not many had technical training. So the party cadre dedicated themselves to party tasks, which provoked a big contradiction between the political vision of the party and the conduct of the Sandinista government. We said we were Marxists, but we were timid Marxists. We never openly said we were; we kept quiet about our ideological position in order not to risk being ideologically defined in that way. But we were anyway, and with reason.

Also, we committed other errors. The Patriotic Military Service was not an error, but the way we implemented it was. We were excessively rigid and even violated the law in order to recruit more young people. At times, underage young people were inducted. At times, boys were inducted who were not obligated to go for various reasons; for example, because they were supporting their families. And even with those obligated to go into military service, sometimes excessive violence was used in recruiting them. This alienated a large sector of the youth from the Sandinista Front. Only about half of the youth went voluntarily into military service.

In the electoral campaign, instead of basing our campaign in our tradition of revolutionary struggle, we followed a traditional campaign style, like that in the United States. A campaign of images, rather than a campaign based on the great values of the Sandinista Front. In general, there was no serious consideration of a possible electoral defeat, which had its consequences.

J.B.: You are undoubtedly aware of the newly published book by Alejandro Bendana, *The Tragedy of the Campesino*, which has caused so much debate here. Based on interviews with more than forty ex-Contras, the book argues that the Contra forces were largely made up of campesinos who were alienated by the policies and actions of the Sandinistas. Bendana's argument corresponds to the claims of the Bush administration, and contrasts sharply with the claims made by the revolutionary government, who described the Contras as mercenaries, or campesinos who had been kidnapped or duped. What is your opinion of Bendana's thesis?

Borge: This book, in my judgment, is one-sided and unjust in its treatment of the revolutionary project. I mentioned the errors we committed in the application of different policies, including policies related to agrarian reform, and these errors increased in large measure the support for the counterrevolution. But one shouldn't say that the Nicaraguan campesino has been a victim of the revolution; on the contrary, we distributed more than one million, two hundred thousand hectares [about 2.5 million acres] of land among the campesinos, which means that the revolution had a vision that prioritized the campesinos. Many campesinos identified with the revolution and defended it. Add to this the agricultural cooperatives all over the country, where they defended the revolution against attacks from the counterrevolutionary forces. The book you mention presents only the sad face of our reality and doesn't include a recognition of our achievements. I want to stress to you that the agrarian policy that the Nicaraguan revolution developed was an audacious policy. I think that Comandante [Jaime] Wheelock had a correct and lucid vision of the agrarian transformation of the country, and applied the policies of the Sandinista directorate and the revolutionary government. But there were enormous limitations created by the war. Before the war reached such large dimensions, the economic achievements of the revolution and the agrarian transformation were substantial and followed a perspective that would have transformed this country in an exemplary manner.

J.B.: I would like to ask you about changes that have occurred since the election in the field of your special concern — internal security — the police, prisons, and the justice system. The Sandinista revolution was well known for its civil rights policies — its treatment of prisoners and of the National Guard, its work for the law of autonomy for the Atlantic Coast, and also for reforms meant to create a more popular, more democratic system of justice. So my question is, What are the most important changes since the election?

Borge: I think that first it is necessary to speak of what we did and didn't do. We undertook important reforms in the area of justice which were incomplete, vacillating, and basically conservative. There was a vision, a transformation of the judicial apparatus that was not completed.

I think that in the application of justice, in the jails and the penitentiary system, there were substantive changes. The prisoners received new levels of attention that gave them the opportunity to reform themselves; this culminated in the open prison farms, where the prisoners were virtually free. These experiments, certainly unique in the world, gave excellent results. Many counterrevolutionaries, ex-National Guardsmen, and common delinquents underwent a positive transformation.

In another area, that of the police forces, and the State Security forces, there were impressive successes. Delinquency diminished to almost insignificant levels. Managua was transformed into one of the safest cities in the world, without any repressive measures from the police. The Nicaraguan police are widely respected and very efficient. They are very skilled at detecting crime and at preventing it. In the area of state security, there is a fact that has hardly been acknowledged sufficiently: every attempt by the counter-revolution to engage in [underground] activities in this country failed. Never was a bomb exploded in Nicaragua, never was a terrorist act achieved in this country as a result of internal activity; of course, there was terrorism, sabotage, brutality, and destruction by the military units of the counter-revolution, but internal organs in support of those units never developed. We captured tons of explosives that were never exploded. For the first time, there was a revolution without successful acts of terrorism. All were frustrated before they could succeed. Someday this achievement by the organs of state security will be recognized.

About ten crimes for every hundred thousand inhabitants were committed here, while in the United States one could say the number is closer to ten thousand crimes for every hundred thousand inhabitants. At present we are approaching the crime levels of other countries; crime has multiplied here in a very striking manner, owing to various factors. First is that the police lack authority. The senior officers of the police are the same, but the strategic leaders of the present government are not the same; they lack the authority that we had, and — a very important factor — they lack the vocation for service that we had. Also, because of the economic crisis and for other reasons, there has been a substantial reduction in the budget for the police. And the police no longer have the same enthusiasm. The police of this country were incorruptible. I believe that now there are police who are vulnerable to corruption, and who are not infused with the same spirit they had under the Sandinista government.

Besides, the character of this government is no secret to anyone. The economic measures that it has implemented have obligated the unemployed to confront the government with social protests; they have had strikes, takeovers of factories and farms, and increasing [work] stoppages since the first months of this government. That is because the government tried to ignore the organized power of the union movement, thinking mistakenly that the social base of the Sandinista Front would be worn down. Recently, prudence and political realism among the most important government leaders have led them to seek stability in concert with the Sandinista Front; to engage in dialogue with the unions and with the revolutionary leaders of the country. This has led to a certain amount of stability. Yet this stability is threatened by the existence of armed counter-revolutionary groups. They lack the virulence or size or strength that they had before, but they are creating a certain disturbance, and in turn are causing a large number of previously discharged Sandinista comrades to rearm and confront this phenomenon.

J.B.: I would like to ask you about the current form of class struggle in Nicaragua, now that there is a new government, and now that large groups of ex-Contras and ex-soldiers of the Sandinista army are living in the countryside.

Borge: Certainly the class struggle will continue here. However, about this I have the following opinion: I believe that in the future, without ignoring class struggle, which is inescapable, the Sandinista Front must implement an ethical commitment. Not only the Sandinista Front, but all revolutions in the world — none will have the possibility of surviving or of bringing about important changes except under an moral banner. Without representing a truly elevated morality, they cannot hope to bring their people to the point of making structural changes in their societies.

J.B.: Comandante Borge, what in your opinion is the future of democracy in Nicaragua now, especially among the campesinos?

Borge: I think that the war contributed to a weakening of support from the social base of the campesinos. Not only the war, but also the way in which we applied some of our policies. There was excessive violence and injustice in the way both sides treated the campesinos. This weakened our relations with the campesinos. Now there is a huge demand for land by the ex-Contras and the discharged soldiers of the army and the police. The Sandinista Front has reaffirmed and maintained the agrarian reform, and in supporting all campesinos' demands for land, we are now in a position to regain our base among the campesinos which we lost in large measure during the revolutionary period.

Democracy exists in Nicaragua — that is, political democracy. This is an achievement of the revolution. In general, the Sandinista Front now has the freedom to organize and express itself. There have been some limitations of democracy in the struggles of the unions. But such repression has not reached the level of savagery that it has in other countries, because of the existence of a police force that continues being fundamentally revolutionary. In this country, there are distinct contradictions. One contradiction is between the Sandinista Front and the government, and it is managed above all within the framework of negotiations. It isn't like the social groups among the masses, which at times confront the government. There is another contradiction, between the Front and the ultraright; this is confrontational and has led to acts of violence, such as the bombing of the tomb of Carlos Fonseca and the events that followed. The mayor's office in Managua was burned and there were other acts of violence, acts that were stopped promptly by the good sense of the Front, which has been able to lead the masses whenever they have begun to fall into a certain level of anarchy and unnecessary and excessive violence.

But democracy is not only political. It must be thought of in a more inclusive way. We cannot speak of political democracy and nothing else. We must also speak of economic democracy, we must speak of social democracy, and in this sense there are limitations on democracy at present. More than half the population of Nicaragua is unemployed, and this cannot be the expression of a truly integrated democracy. There are many economic difficulties. There is hunger, and hunger is incompatible with democracy. Sure, the people have the right to say they are hungry, which is a crime in other countries, and here it is not, and that is a difference; if the army and police did not exist, with their revolutionary roots, and if the Sandinista Front did not exist, then probably the political democracy that I mentioned would not exist.

J.B.: My question was really about the more concrete forms of democracy, and the possibility of the growth of revolutionary forces here again.

Borge: There is a revolutionary force here that has survived, and along with it a revolutionary project has also survived. I believe that the teachings of the past, along with the intention to correct errors and the assimilation of the hard experiences we have had, will make it possible for the Sandinista Front to lead the government and to implement a kind of democracy far better than any we have had in the past.

At this point Borge stood up and said that he had to end the interview for another appointment. I was so surprised by the abruptness of his ending that, even though I had my camera ready, I forgot to ask for a photograph! I wanted to question his assertion that "the Sandinista Front . . . [might] . . . implement a kind of democracy far better than any we have had in the past." I certainly hope that it will, but its 1991 congress offered little basis for that hope. More promising is the development of independent organizations that are declaring themselves Sandinista and revolutionary.

The most powerful such organizations are the trade unions, especially those which are Sandinista-led. They have consistently fought long and hard in the postelection period for the interests of workers without property, and the gains have been truly impressive. The unions forced the government to sign a "reconciliation agreement," giving the workers the right to buy 25 percent of any privatized company (the actual percentage has varied from 11 percent to 100 percent). According to *Barricada Internacional* (May 1993), workers now control shares in 130 agricultural companies and have full control of 122. They have shares in 99 industrial or transport companies, with 100 percent control in 43. These are paper agreements, of course, and constant vigilance and strikes are needed to ensure that the government follows through. And the worker-owned companies must compete for loans under a government and banking system that is hostile to them. Still, these are impressive victories that build on the achievements of the revolution and go beyond it. In an interview in the same issue of *Barricada Internacional*, Lily Soto, a trade-union leader and a Sandinista, said: "In the past, unions fought only for jobs and salaries and had only political power. But a union that also fights for property can gain economic and social power. In Latin America, governments have privatized companies and laid off thousands of workers, leaving them in the streets with no benefits whatsoever. In Nicaragua, the same thing would have happened if we hadn't had a revolution."

The Nicaraguan women's movement is another source of activism and popular organization. The Sandinistas founded a large women's organization (AMNLAE) and passed an array of important legislation in support of women's rights: a "Law Governing Relations between Mother, Father, and Child" stressed that the father had equal responsibility for the care, nurture, and education of children; media portrayal of women as sexual objects was banned; full recognition was given to common-law relationships; divorce was allowed at the request of either partner; and so on. This legal recognition of equality and widespread participation of women in the revolution's programs created a new situation for women. Since the election, their demands have become more concrete and far-reaching. Many have been dissatisfied with the implementation of the new laws, especially those concerned with paternal responsibility. Many women have become critical of AMNLAE for having been too submissive to the agenda of the Sandinista party, particularly on such issues as abortion and lesbian rights. Such women have created a large number of independent organizations, even though most see themselves as Sandinista and socialist. New women's centers have been created, independent of AMNLAE, to discuss and take action on such issues as domestic violence, sexuality and abortion, child care, and the economic problems of women. Women have been very active in the trade unions; indeed, 52 percent of all union members are women, a percentage that coincides with the percentage of women in the population and with the name of a new umbrella organization of activists, "The 52 Percent."

An impressive example of the new activism among women is the Nora Astorga Front (named after a famous Sandinista fighter and diplomat), a group of about four hundred and fifty campesina women (and some men) who live in and around Ocotal, in the far north. They are fighting for government support for housing, for compensation due to them from the army, and education and job training, among other needs. Nearly all are single mothers. Some are ex-soldiers, some ex-Contras. Forty armed themselves and went to the mountains for military training. They have taken over the telecommunications center in Ocotal and blocked the Pan-American Highway to dramatize their demands. They have occupied a twenty-two-acre plot of municipal land and are building Barrio Nora Astorga with their own hands. One hundred and thirty-seven houses are under construction, and the Organization of American States has promised to fund the construction of a school and a health center.

Ten years of encounter between internationalists and Nicaraguans have provided a rich source of experience in cross-cultural solidarity and community development. New questions have been raised about how to share skills and material wealth in order to assist in self-development, without perpetuating old patterns of dependence and hierarchy. In my talk with Fred Jacobs, he questioned the methods and even the value of his own work in Nicaragua.

"I have a lot to rethink," he said. "The problem is how to help people without creating corruption, dependency, and loss of pride. I have control over a lot of material resources that the campesinos don't have, a vehicle, gasoline and oil, and a shed full of tools: chainsaws, come-alongs, circular saws, a lot of things. So they are always coming to me, heads down, their voices shy and even servile. Instead of being a partner, I am a caudillo on another plane than they, a guardian and dispenser of material wealth. I don't know how to overcome that sort of problem."

Fred was concerned, too, about campesinos taking things for their private use. A man was issued a donated chainsaw in order to cut lumber for El Cedro, and for several years he used it for that purpose — it was his job in the cooperative, for which he received a share of the cooperative's income — and he was given donated gas, oil, and parts. Now he has become de facto owner of the chainsaw and is using it in a private business — he cuts boards for people outside the cooperative. Another example: a man was given zinc roofing for his house. It was a donation sent down from the States. Fred later learned that the man sold the roofing to some other members of the cooperative. And once, while Fred and another veteran were repairing a well in a mountain community near El Cúa, they asked some of the men in the community to help build a stone-and-gravel area around it. The men said okay, then asked if they could be paid.

I have not lived Fred's experiences, but I felt afterward that perhaps his expectations were inappropriate. When North Americans come to Nicaragua with material aid, they are in a very idealistic mood. Their personal needs, generally well taken care of, are in the background. They are acting from moral or political concerns — to help in the development of social projects, such as a school or a water supply, that will enrich everyone in a community. People such as Fred, who come for long periods, have also put their (generally well taken care of) personal needs on hold, and they are donating time and skilled labor to Nicaragua, to the revolution. But can Nicaraguans always show the same attitude toward their personal needs? Many have made great personal sacrifices for the revolution. But at some point they, like everyone, must think about their material needs. Perhaps the man needed to use this chainsaw to make his living, and the other man needed to sell his roofing. Perhaps the men needed to be paid to work on the well; people in the States expect to be paid when they do public works. Fred got paid for his work — very little, but enough to live better than these campesinos.

These examples suggest that our perceptions and moral judgments need to be tempered by an awareness of where we are coming from. What may seem like selling out or corruption from one perspective may be a necessary act of survival from another. What may seem like a conflict of individual and community interests may simply be a matter of the survival of the individual within a community. These examples also bring up questions about solidarity and giving in connection with the self-development of a community. The questions become even more complex when one considers that the "givers" are members of an oppressor society, and their desire to control the reception and use of their "gift" may perpetuate the hierarchical relations they are hoping to overcome. The discomfort Fred and his campesino friends felt over his shed full of tools seems to exemplify this problem well.

North Americans and Europeans who travel to Nicaragua to bring material aid or to work come from societies that have traditionally exploited and adopted an ideology of superiority toward "Third World" countries. (Even the expression "Third World" carries the Eurocentric perspective of being "first.") We internationalists think we are different—we are conscious of this imperialist history and actively reject its racist assumptions. Yet we are not different in one crucial respect: we possess and control resources that others do not, because we belong to the oppressor societies. Unlike Fred, most of us have not thought very much about this. For example, many North Americans who oppose U.S. intervention in Nicaragua and support the revolution gave material aid. This is fine, yet it should be understood and accepted that charity doesn't change the social relations that are at the root of imperialism, and it does tend to promote cynicism and corruption. It is sharing the leftovers from the table of imperialism. It is not revolutionary solidarity, and it is not "development."

Even attempts to do more, to promote development, may carry cultural assumptions that are not validly applied to Nicaragua. Often there is a kind of imperialistic arrogance—that "we" know what "they" need, and can provide it *for* them. I saw a small, clear example of this in El Cedro when I was working with the veterans. A group of Germans, a work brigade, had spent two weeks there building a brick oven for baking. When their time was over, they had finished a charming, cone-shaped brick structure. A year later, when I saw it, the oven stood there pristinely, like an artifact from another era, a sculpture, never used. I don't know how it was decided to build a bread oven in the mountains, where the people grow corn and eat tortillas, but clearly the job these people did was not chosen by the campesinos of El Cedro.

A vastly larger project near León, involving the reconstruction of an entire community, also failed because it was instigated by others for the needs of the community as defined by others. At the time of the revolution, Cuatro Palos was a sixty-five-hundred-acre rice-growing plantation on the north side of Lake Managua. The land is flat and low and rich, and its location is strikingly beautiful and dramatic; Momotombo, a tall, smoking volcano lies just to the west. The prerevolutionary owner was Klaus Segleman, a German who immigrated to Nicaragua and became Somoza's minister of agriculture. The plantation included a hacienda, about fifteen shacks for workers, a few buildings for threshing and storing rice, and an airstrip for the commuting caudillo. Segleman abandoned the property and went to the States after the revolution, and the workers took over. The population grew to about a hundred families after the plantation became a cooperative.

Then a group of Swedish planners and architects, in collaboration with Nicaraguan planners and architects, initiated a multimillion-dollar project sponsored by the Swedish government. They designed what they considered an ideal, agricultural living community for Cuatro Palos. They began by researching traditional housing in Nicaragua — its design and environmental context. They studied conditions in Cuatro Palos and identified problems such as vulnerability to flooding, poor sewage disposal, contaminated water, little shade, and no good space for gardens protected from pigs running loose. The existing housing was considered small, hot and poorly ventilated, with inadequate latrines. In short, it was a typical rural village in Nicaragua.

The project members wrote and published a book complete with excellent drawings and designs surveying the results of their studies, and in the last section they set forth a grand design for an entirely new community at Cuatro Palos, with all-new houses organized in groups, each with latrines and laundry facilities and spaces for gardens and plantings, all drawn to perfection, with little people standing about shaded by large trees. The project leaders hired a professional carpenter and mason, and paid for materials, but the families themselves had to provide the labor for constructing the houses they were going to occupy.

I visited the project when it was in its "second stage." It went no further. The Swedish government had changed its funding priorities, and the Nicaraguan government had no funds for construction. A school and about 20 percent of the housing was completed, and it was obvious that the project had failed.

Most telling was a meeting I attended at which the community was supposed to discuss the results of the project with the project staff — professionals who lived in León. No one from the community came to the meeting except for the head of the cooperative, who was dragged out of his house for it. The project staff members arrived by car late in the afternoon, and very quickly went over a formal list of questions they had to answer in order to write a report. Otherwise there was no communication with members of the community. The staff left as abruptly as they had arrived, in a hurry to get back to León for dinner, appearing as alienated from the project as the people themselves. On leaving, they drove up and down the new "streets" of Cuatro Palos and waved to the people standing in front of their houses.

I found that the people liked the houses, and that each family worked willingly to build their own. But aside from the existence of twenty new houses, larger and better-designed than the old ones, the community seemed no better off. Latrines had been constructed for every two houses (presumably to save having to dig so many large holes) and were placed several hundred feet behind the houses. The head of the cooperative said, "Many have no seats or seats the wrong size. The people don't understand how to use them. Most families don't use them." One man who lived there told me, "The latrines are useless. No one uses them." What they didn't say is that Nicaraguan campesino families will not share latrines with one another, and women and girls will not use a latrine when men and boys are about, especially at some distance from their house.

All the land around the twenty new houses was bare and muddy, and pigs and chickens were running loose. The campesinos did not want to pen their pigs together. As a result, there were few gardens or plantings. The project had planted twenty-four hundred trees, but all had died because of lack of care and abuse from animals.

In some ways the community was probably worse off. It now had an internal hierarchy of co-op leaders and was divided into those who had the new housing and eighty families who did not. One old man said he preferred the old days, when the farm was run by Somoza's minister of agriculture! At least old Segleman probably had more experience at dispensing charity and was less disruptive about it than those well-meaning Swedish professionals.

Sadly, instead of providing an opportunity for people to better their lives by working together, Cuatro Palos provided a niche for professionals to put their expertise to work. The Nicaraguan campesinos were treated as more-or-less cooperative objects of manipulation. They did not manipulate well. And when the money ran out everything stopped, because only the money held it together.

Another project, more modest and effective, was initiated by two North American anthropologists in a Managua barrio. I met Michael Higgins and Tanya Coen when they were living in Managua during the spring of 1988. They invited me to visit Barrio William Díaz Romero (named after a fallen martyr of the revolution whose family still lives there). I observed such activities as construction, vaccinations, cleanups, meetings of the CDS, meetings to distribute material aid, cultural activities, and many informal activities and discussions.

Michael and Tanya work at the University of Northern Colorado. In Nicaragua they do what they call "ethnographic praxis," a method of ethnographic research that combines study with active involvement in community organizations and activities. They are scientists, but they have an open and active commitment to the revolution and to community empowerment and development.

They are aware of the issues of difference and power that affect relations between themselves and the Nicaraguans, and they recognize their complexity. In their research they do not try to be "objective observers" who take no responsibility for the consequences of their presence in the community. Since their work inevitably influences and changes the barrio, they integrate that work with the barrio's activities. They become storytellers and historians as well as reflective analysts. They become lines of communication and liaisons with the wider world, and conduits for resources. They gave talks, made a film, and wrote articles and a book on Barrio William Díaz Romero to document its history and social makeup and the wide variety of organizations and activities that take place there. At the same time, both the process of producing this work and the product itself contribute to the growth and history of the community as determined by the community itself.

What especially impressed me was their commitment and openness. Their activities were not delimited by a set research project or goal. They gathered data in a systematic way for a scientifically valid profile of the community, but they also let the people articulate their history, their present situation, and their needs. Since one of the constantly expressed desires of the Nicaraguans is closer relations with the people of the United States, Michael and Tanya helped form a network of relations between Barrio William Díaz Romero and a barrio of mainly Chicano people in their home city of Greeley, Colorado. The people in the two barrios have become linked through their own organizations. They have learned about each other, discussed common problems, and visited one another; also a considerable amount of material aid has been sent to the Nicaraguan barrio through these links.

The emphasis has been on people and on the complexity of their communities and problems, rather than on politics. Yet politics is often the subject of discussion, and political awareness in the barrios is high. The people who are involved in the exchanges between the two barrios are aware of themselves as political subjects, as actors rather than passive spectators.

One enduring aspect of the work of Michael and Tanya has been the facilitation of this growing consciousness. Although very important material results were achieved—the construction of a community center and health clinic, vaccination campaigns, environmental cleanups, many cultural activities, and so on—the growth that has occurred in skills and self-expectations are not dependent on the arrival of funding or material aid, and people in the community have learned that the political situation they live in need not be viewed passively, but can be exploited through their own efforts. Michael and Tanya write:

One of the things we learned about revolutionary action—that creates the social space for empowerment—is how ordinary it is. The issues to which these residents directed their new power were not about changing the whole world, but about getting a polluting battery shop closed or attempting to get the prices of cheese lowered. It involved long hours of work to organize and carry out a vaccination campaign or to disinfect the barrio's water system of dengue larvae. For these residents, empowerment does mean a process of local control and development. It means that they are the designers of their community within the boundaries of the power to which they have access. . . . In the processes of confronting their immediate economic and political problems, the residents of this community were aware of the forces outside the barrio that place real limits on their experiences in self-governance. . . . They were also aware that their explorations of self-governance placed them in conflict with other class interests in Nicaragua and in opposition to various international forces, primarily that of the U.S. government. The recognition of these hegemonic boundaries also made some members of the community sensitive to internal contradictions of class, gender, and sexuality in the barrio itself. . . . [T]hey were quite aware that their local actions were taking place in a much broader social arena of meanings and actions. (Higgins and Coen 1992, 159–60)

The desire to join Nicaraguans in their struggle to create a new society has motivated many internationalists in many different ways. This desire and the willingness to act and sacrifice to fulfill it is part of the best of what we are. Yet, when not informed by a consciousness of the political context and consequences, action can do more harm than good. And without long-term commitment, we cannot learn from and correct mistakes. Above all, true solidarity means a permanent personal commitment of human beings to one another's lives: a recognition that we live together in the same world.

It means working to build community—in Nicaragua, in the States, and between the two societies.

While in Matagalpa, I drive my little Honda north to Jinotega and beyond to visit the Luis Hernández Cooperative Farm. I know that the Basques, Jon and Araxo and Pulo, aren't there any longer. I want to see how the cooperative is doing after a year of the new government.

I cross the high mountains to Jinotega, then follow a dirt road toward the big eastern mountains, the same road that leads to El Cúa and El Cedro. Everything looks the same as it did on my earlier trips on these roads, but feels different. Since my blood and nerves are used to capitalism, everything feels more normal. There appears to be no wartime situation. I see the usual poor, capitalist, Central American country life: farms, people on the road, ramshackle workshops and gas stations, the Jinotega market, the storage buildings for coffee. No inspiring effort is being made to create socialism or a better world amid awkward and amateurish mistakes. Everyone is just making their private mistakes while doing what they know best: surviving. In my despondent mood, I think that even those who are unemployed and without hope must have a kind of familiar feeling, a sense of belonging to their hopelessness. In history, the term "restoration" is used to describe a period when the deposed monarchy was able to regain control of the government. It feels like that here: a restoration. The last time I visited the Luis Hernández co-op, Vidal told me they needed more families. They had plenty of land, and they could get bank loans to build more houses and buy supplies; they just needed peace and more people to share in the work. Now, with 60 percent unemployment in Nicaragua, with the "restoration," there are suddenly too many people. And I wonder, "What am I doing here now? Am I wanted?" I feel as if I'm doing my own private business, alongside everyone else.

It is still the dry season, and my little car is doing fine on the road, though bouncing and shaking a lot. Driving beyond Pueblo Nuevo is unthinkable, so a man who owns the general store lets me park behind. I tell him I'll be back before dark.

I enjoy the walk, five kilometers up the mountain. I pass through several farms. I am very moved as I come up to Luis Hernández, and a little nervous. What will I find? But it seems just like before, and more beautiful than I remembered. I look down onto the long valley stretching east to west, where I can see bits of roads and rivers. To the north it is mountains and more mountains, into Honduras.

Hardly anyone is around. Vidal is in Jinotega visiting his daughter. I walk along the path to the women's garden and find Manz at the stream washing clothes with some other women. Some of the kids are with her. When she finishes, we walk back to the house and she shows me letters from the Basques — from Araxo, really — and I give her lots of photographs. I had a photography show that included some beautiful ones from here. She likes them very much.

What is happening now? After the election the members of the cooperative voted to go private and to divide the land. Not everyone wanted to, but the majority did. Why? They were afraid that as a cooperative they wouldn't get support from the banks or the government. They were probably right. Where they were wrong is in thinking that they'd get credit as small individual farmers. It will be harder for them, I think. They won't have one another in the way they did before. I ask Manz what she had wanted. "To stay together," she says, and smiles her old smile, but she seems older and more tired to me.

The children have grown, of course, and changed. Flor seems very different, fifteen now, wearing glasses. Little Ivania sits snuggled up to me and lays her head on my lap. I think she misses the Basques a lot.

So each family now has its own parcel. It wasn't personal problems, she says, it was just what they wanted. The old individual family identity asserting itself, I think. Well, I understand it. It looks to be safer. And the projects? They, too, are over. There is no women's garden. After the Basques left, they didn't replant it. And they never got the flower project going either, or the laundry. They still own some land in common, and the water pipe and the *beneficio*. But the school is closed because the new government stopped paying a teacher. The kids have to go down to Pueblo Nuevo. Some do, some don't.

What worries them most is the Recontras, marauding and wanting land. They have been attacking Corinto, the state farm next door. Last week there was a big battle, and five Recontras were killed. People are scared here. The women and children left their houses and slept hidden in the woods by the stream. They had never done that before; they are more scared than they were during the war.

Manz and I stand outside the house and look off into the valley. "It is sad, as though a dream has passed," I think. She seems sad, but is she really or is she just sad for me? Whose dream am I thinking of? And is it really over? The Basques would be sad, but they didn't commit their lives here and they are gone. Manz smiles at me. She is still washing clothes in the stream, and it is beautiful there, and the women are together.

I think about the morning three years before when I watched the co-op

members at a meeting down by the *beneficio*. Though shorthanded, they
agreed to support Luis's family while he went to Cuba to study. Because the
revolution asked it of them. As I stand on this mountain with Manz, I
understand why I'm sad. When will people come together again like that,
work together, take responsibility for one another? When will they speak
again of "the revolution" in that way—as a process that holds them together and requires the best they have to give each other?

On my drive back to Managua the question of how Nicaragua
had changed through its revolution kept turning in my mind. What has this
revolution meant to the people here, and what meanings can we who have
observed and taken part in it in various ways draw from it? Impossible
questions, yet I end with some admittedly tentative and impressionistic
answers.

Clearly, social change doesn't lead to a terminus—it brings us to a new
level from which further change happens. Nor is it smooth and uniform—
the reality is more like a zigzag line of ups and downs over many decades.
Nor can we speak simply in terms of progress or lack of it for a society as a
whole; a society, like a person, is a complex of many relatively independent
parts, which interact yet may change independently or even in contrary
directions. Some groups in Nicaragua, for example, seem to be experiencing disintegration and "regression" after the electoral defeat of the Sandinistas, while others are continuing the self-development characteristic of
the revolution during its best years.

The revolution has not achieved the material benefits that were hoped
for. Nicaragua is poorer than before, and severely damaged by war. However, the revolution has changed Nicaraguan society in quite substantive
and lasting ways, in consciousness and spirit. Through the revolution a
hated and much-feared dictatorship was destroyed by the internal efforts of
the people themselves. This has given to many a new level of national
identity, independence, and pride. A constitution was written, one of the
most advanced in the world, and democratic political rights have been
formally established and applied on a high level. The level of political participation, not to mention political discourse and consciousness, has both
risen and spread more broadly. A program of economic rights has been put
on the social agenda, become an object of contention, and been achieved in
significant ways, even in a context of abysmal poverty. I am thinking, for
instance, about the increased ownership of land by the masses of campesinos, of property by the workers, and about the improved strength and
organization of the trade unions in all sectors—farm, industrial, health

and government workers, even prostitutes. Especially important is the increased self-organization of women, who comprise more than half the population and who are carrying on new struggles that the Contra war and the Sandinista government both stimulated and restrained. Also, the level of education, in areas such as medicine, science, and agriculture, has risen, and among many there has been a great increase in cultural creation and critical appreciation. Expectations regarding every kind of social and personal form of well-being have increased in large sectors of the population, along with the capacity to join with others in working for goals.

Such changes are hard to measure and prove, but they correspond to my experience and are affirmed by virtually all the informed people I know. These are political, ideological, and spiritual changes; they are products of revolutionary organization and achievement. Unlike changes in the levels of production and consumption, they are not dependent on the world market or on freedom from U.S. interventions, although they may be unfavorably or favorably affected by these. They are the "subjective" accomplishments of the revolution, and they belong to Nicaraguans (various among them, to various degrees) as hard-won possessions. In comparison with income levels or foreign debt, they are relatively stable and permanent, although they may deteriorate or develop further, depending on future political and economic conditions. They are the qualities that enabled Tomás Borge to say that the Sandinistas would be leading the government again and would "implement a kind of democracy far better than any we have had in the past." They do not guarantee such change, but they help make it possible.

Finally, alongside these generally positive and progressive changes, one also senses among many a high level of disillusionment, distrust, and personal withdrawal concerning political organizations, leaders, and future prospects. Many have turned away from political participation and are concentrating on individual survival. Perhaps in all individuals we can see these diverse and contrary tendencies in varying mixes and balances.

These considerations help me to understand better the old Marxist axiom that it is not outstanding individuals who make history or bring about social change, but the people themselves. Leaders are important, but they work in concert with others. And the social changes that matter and that endure are those in which the efforts of many are combined.

Holy Week is approaching, and Norma and I have been talking about going to Solentiname, a holy place of the revolution. Solentiname, perhaps the most beautiful place I have ever seen, is a group of thirty-eight islands — a volcanic archipelago — in Lake Nicaragua. It is about one hundred miles south of Granada, where you catch the boat. I have been twice before to this paradise, but Norma has never been there. Few Nicaraguans have; they speak about Solentiname wistfully, as if it were on the other side of the world. And it is a long, hard trip, overnight, crowded among feed sacks and oil drums and people camping on the deck of an old cargo boat.

Since everything closes down anyway, Norma finally agrees to take the week off. Her granddaughter Katherine and Norma and I will go. There is a small hotel there, but I bring my tent (fortunately) in case it is full.

From the shore of Granada the lake looks huge and gray and lonesome. Our boat, about the size of a tugboat, sits alone at the end of a long pier. We have to run to get on, because it is leaving earlier than expected, and is already jammed with people — families and commerciantes going for the holidays to obscure towns on the southeastern coast of the country. We lean our bags inside among rows of wooden benches. Out in the lake the water is blue and cheerful. Our first stop, in four hours, will be the island of Omotepe, with its two large, smoke-topped volcanoes. We make places on bags of grain to sit and watch the water and the gray-blue volcanoes.

Sea gulls follow us, navigating in the wind behind the boat without moving their wings. For some reason they make me think of the word "peregrinate," as if they were "peregrine" gulls. "They are peregrinating," I tell Norma in English, and explain it means to travel. Its historical meaning is "leaving the fields" (*per* means "to or from"; *ager* means "field"), leaving the land to which one's tied. In the old days, people didn't travel for just any reason, or for no reason, and *peregrinación* in Spanish means "pilgrimage," a trip to a holy place. The birds and we have left the land; we are making a *peregrinación* together, a pilgrimage.

I have a book of Ernesto Cardenal's poetry, which we read back and forth to each other. We read "On the Lake," where he described traveling to Solentiname at night in a boat like this one. He had just come from a Somoza military court. The poem travels from the fear he felt at his interrogation to the revolution in the mountains to the millions of worlds spinning and turning above him, as he lay back on bags of rice. He speaks of the "cold, black interstellar space" and the stars like a chorus of dancers around a fire and, behind that, the "zone of love." He speaks of the boat, the *María Daniela* navigating through space-time, and the earth traveling through space-time, and the revolution navigating through space-time. Learn to love evolution, he says.

It is cool and fresh and not too windy as we sit on grain bags behind the cabin. The sun is falling behind the volcanoes of Omotepe and turning the clouds red. The water is darkening, and the waves around our wake are reflecting silver and the reddish tones of the clouds. There is only a little more daylight. We read bits of poems, me carefully pronouncing the Spanish to catch its music. We eat mangos and crackers and sip rum and watch the lights of Altagracia — the main town of Omotepe — come nearer.

After a lot of off-loading and loading while the boat bounces in waves that suddenly have become much bigger, we are in the lake again in complete darkness, and Norma and Katherine go inside to lie down. I read by flashlight. The air is perfectly warm and cool at once; the stars are bright in the black sky.

Cardenal's "Oracle over Managua," a long historical poem, begins with the indigenous people on the shores of Lake Managua, whose fleeing footprints are buried under beds of lava, and moves to the lakeside squalor of modern Managua and the current history of struggle against Somoza. The poet addresses Leonel Rugama, a young Sandinista poet and former seminary student, who fought in the underground and was killed by the National Guard. Rugama used to say that "revolution is communion with the species." Cardenal sees social revolution as part of natural evolution:

> All life unites
> > unites and does not divide
> > (integrates)
> So you gave your life
> on the fifth planet of a medium star of the Milky Way . . .
>
> Let us organize hopes, Leonel Rugama.
> Possibilities that can't be dreamed by computers.
> > To bring about the Kingdom of God . . .
>
> > > (Cardenal 1983, 213, 215)

Cardenal describes the power of revolutionary struggle to heal the disintegrative effects of capitalism. Historically, capitalism has broken down the ancient unities: the traditions and communities that bound people with nature and one another. The capitalist way of life throws the individual onto his or her own resources in an indifferent world; further, it divides the individual personality by separating economics from caring relations, feeling from reason, science and technology from religious values, aesthetics from practical concerns. For Cardenal, our natural desire for love and community produces the healing power of revolutionary struggle, which germinates and reproduces "like the mustard seed" and keeps reproducing in exponential proportions:

Every living substance unites.
    What is reproduction in reality?
Every living substance: fusion with the different
        unification with the opposite . . .
As a male sperm cell penetrates the female ovum . . .
So you fought all that afternoon in that house . . .
For that City you joined the urban guerrillas . . .
    the City of the definitive meeting
of each human being with all other human beings
the City of identity and consummated community
    the City of communion . . .

                        (Cardenal 1983, 213, 214)

The creation of this ideal, or movement toward it, is a natural struggle that simply continues human evolution:

Light came from a little stick.
First came control of fire in the Pleistocene age.
The cold night changed to day in the depth of a cave!
They deciphered the sky . . . the phases of the moon.
Science was born in caves. And organization
    (the mammoth can be hunted only in cooperation)

                            (Cardenal 1983, 216)

Cardenal's poems make sudden leaps and connections. Like collages, they collect the varied sources of our experience and create new, unexpected integrations:

Revolution is not illusion
the caterpillar weaves around itself a new home
from which it emerges with colored wings . . .

                            (Cardenal 1983, 216)

In these poems the ancient unities are restored, but in a new way: "the economy of the future will be to make life more beautiful." As Marx stressed, even though capitalist development has been destructive and cruel, it has liberating potential. The old communities were often backward and oppressive, and through capitalism we have learned to use science and technology to produce abundantly. The capitalist world market provides a limited basis for world unity, and an awareness that everyone can have security and opportunity.

While the capitalist process of local disintegration and global integration still goes on in Nicaragua and in the world, and seems to have no limit,

Cardenal's poetry speaks of a deep need for community, a tendency toward socialism:

> In the midst of a general tendency for disintegration
>   there's an opposite tendency
> for union. For love . . .
>   An opposite tendency which is revolution.

> (Cardenal 1983, 214)

Katherine comes outside and calls me.

"Juan! Mamá wants you."

People are already sleeping inside. Some have hung hammocks, others are lying on the benches or have set up pallets on the deck. Norma wants me to know that after we left Omotepe she had moved my things onto a bench, saving me a small place to sleep. Katherine begins to sleep with her head on Norma's lap, who leans against the cabin wall, resting but wide awake. She has never been on a boat before, and she is also afraid of thieves. I tell her than on an earlier trip I met Byron Salas on this boat, the young soldier who fired the rocket that shot down the plane of Eugene Hasenfus. Hasenfus worked for the CIA, bringing supplies to the Contras. The downing of the plane exposed CIA activities that were in violation of congressional restrictions, and opened the Iran-Contra scandal during the Reagan presidency. In Nicaragua, Salas and his partner Fernando were national heroes. When I met him, a year or so later, I was surprised to see he was a kid. When he and his partner fired the missile launcher, he told me, they never expected to hit the plane; dumbfounded, they watched it fall like a shot bird. There were three on the plane, but only Hasenfus survived. They found him the next day, resting on a hammock. The plane was loaded with automatic rifles, boxes of hand grenades, medicine, food, boots, and some documents. Daniel Ortega gave them "Comandante Camilla Ortega" medals.

There is just enough space on the bench for me to curl up tightly on my side, feet in the passageway. I am amazed how restful it feels. I go to sleep thinking about Byron Salas, a Nicaraguan campesino who grew up on a farm downriver from San Carlos in a remote part of nowhere, a boy who confounded the president of the United States. How different worlds flow into each other like currents in a river and penetrate each other with violence and wonder.

I am sleeping soundly and as if in double time, waking only to turn from side to side, when we dock at San Miguelito and young girls walk back and forth in the cabin calling out "café," "leche caliente," "pan," and "pollo" (coffee, hot milk, bread, chicken), in strong clear voices that seemed to echo from a cosmic distance. Young girls up in total darkness to meet the boat, probably half-asleep themselves at this hour, their mothers at home resting after preparing the food.

It is light when I wake again, and the boat is running slow and quiet. Everyone else is awake. Norma and Katherine are eating crackers. Out the door of the cabin I see that the boat is following a line of barrels, painted red, that mark a channel and the long approach to San Carlos. The lake is still, and mist lies over it like a blanket. Ducks fly above the mist, their wings flashing in the early sunlight. To the south I can barely see the shoreline and, beyond it, mountains in Costa Rica. The water and mist and sky are shades of gray and blue and grayish yellow, soft and blending and quiet, as if the world were ending a perfect sleep.

The lake drains into the San Juan River and thence to the Caribbean. The estuary is miles wide and shallow, and our approach take more than an hour. Far across the way are beds of reeds and an occasional canoe with someone fishing, but mostly the estuary seems to belong to birds and fish. They say sharks — a smallish kind — are common in the estuary. Lake Nicaragua is said to have been created when a volcanic eruption raised the land to enclose what had been a bay in the Pacific; this would explain why it is the only freshwater lake in the world with sharks.

San Carlos is a Hollywood image of the Central American river town. It faces the estuary at the head of the river, a congregation of low wood-frame buildings of every color along the shore and up the hill. It is cheerful and toylike in the bright morning sun, busy, and rather metropolitan. People are gathered around little boats arriving from downriver. Women are standing in thigh-deep water washing clothes, and children are swimming and fishing.

We leave the boat and walk along a dirt road, the main street, which runs along the shore. We pass old houses and stores and the docks by the river in various stages of collapse, and watch the small traders just off the boat unpack boxes of clothes and cosmetics they brought to sell. In front of the market is the only hotel, and I know it from earlier trips; it is a large, wood-frame building, smelling of dust and sewage, its second story a labyrinth of windowless rooms, with wooden bunks and thin, worn-out mattresses. Downstairs are tables where meals are served. Some men are already drinking beer. We ask for coffee, rice and beans, and eggs and begin our wait for the *Solentiname*.

After breakfast I go to a communal washing place. Several women are washing clothes in a long stone basin; for ten cents you can stand in enclosed stalls and wash, using buckets of water. Then we walk up the hill and sit in the shade of the cathedral near the famous barracks. From here we can see Solentiname dimly to the west, looking like one island. This is where the Sandinistas attacked the Somoza National Guard when *they* had the barracks, on September 13, 1978, and you see that date painted, though faded now, on walls around the town.

At one o'clock we load our stuff onto an old wooden launch we have to take turns bailing. It's almost two hours before we reach the first islands. The happiness of being on a boat is that you have nothing to do but sense where you are; and your senses are entirely filled — by wind and sun and spray and every kind and degree of light. There's a hint of danger and the unknown, and also openness and abundance.

As we near the islands the lake grows bluer; the sun flashes and spreads a brilliant silver light, creating wide spaces and vibrating shades of silver and blue. The islands seem to answer this brilliance with a quiet intimacy. They are hilly and green, and meadows with cows and little houses are scattered along the shore. It is easy to see why the artists paint the islands the way they do, small and inviting and accessible.

Sometimes a dugout canoe comes to meet us. A woman paddles one. The launch slows and, without its completely stopping, another woman passes a baby down to her, and some bags of food, and she steps down and sits, balancing casually, and the two paddle straight and smooth to a tin-roofed hut. A white heron appears from nowhere and settles by the shore.

About a thousand people live on these islands. Rarely can you see a house from its neighbor, although every house sits by the lake. Everyone washes in the lake and drinks its water. The people plant beans and rice and corn in fields that reach into the center of the islands. They eat fish and raise pigs, chickens, and cows; some have horses. Part of the land is owned by corporations and absentee landlords, but most is owned by the families who live here. On one island, there is an avocado plantation that grows fruit of legendary size and taste. Some islands are uninhabited.

The boat takes us to the dock in front of the hotel. The hotel has space but prices have more than quadrupled, and our money will last only two days. So we follow the path to Rosa Pineda's house, a painter I knew, and then to her mother's house, who lives nearby. Francisca offers to give us our meals and let us put the tent up by her house for a fraction of the price at the hotel. We become part of her family group, most of whom are painters and artisans I already know. Her daughter Elena and my swimming buddy

Enrique are down from Managua. Rosa and her husband, Silvio, are next door, and several of Silvio's relatives are here from Costa Rica. Francisca's son José has a house nearby also, and her son Pepe and daughter Blanca and various grandchildren are also here. Francisca's house has two small rooms, a porch, and a kitchen (separate because she cooks with wood), and at night the beds and floors are covered with sleepers, but it is relaxed and hospitable. The poor have little space, but there is always enough for a few more.

From the porch you see flowering bushes and trees with leaves like lace, a grove of bananas, blue sky and water, and across the way two other green islands. Flocks of ducks pass, flying low. Sometimes a canoe goes by, as someone goes to fish or for a visit. There are no roads, telephones, or electricity. The only sounds are wind and birds and water lapping on the shore.

I borrow a machete and cut piles and piles of reeds that grow along the lake. With these I make a bed for underneath the tent, and stake the tent near the house. But in the night Norma and Katherine move up to the porch to sleep with the others—the tent is enclosed and has a floor, but Norma is afraid that snakes will crawl in.

In the mornings and afternoons Enrique and I swim together. We are the only ones who really go out into the lake, although we, too, are nervous because of sharks, and because nearly every day we see a large crocodile floating and fishing between us and a nearby island. We know that the crocodiles are shy of humans, and there's no record of either a shark or a crocodile attacking anyone here. Still, we can't bring ourselves to go out very far, and we kept a good lookout. The lake is a perfect temperature, and clean and full of fish. Solentiname feels so perfect I dream of ways I could have my own house and live here forever.

Olivia Silva is the matriarch of the family that owns the hotel. She now lives in Managua, but is staying at the hotel for Holy Week. She agrees to give me an interview. This is the third time I have spoken with her. What follows is taken from these three occasions, supplemented by some extracts from an interview by Margaret Randall (1983).

I found Olivia rocking on the porch, watching her great-granddaughter toddle about. Olivia is sixty-four years old. Born on the islands into a family of fourteen children, she is the mother of eleven. I asked her what it was like growing up here. She said, "We half-lived, because at that time agriculture gave you barely enough. There were many blights. We had a dirt-floor house, and no shoes for the children. The dampness was very bad for my asthma. We worked continually. Every year we would plant beans, lots of them, and anything over and above what we ate, we would save for a radio. And we weren't able to buy one, ever.

"When a woman was going to give birth, another would be with her. The woman who had a bit of food would help out another who didn't have anything. When I was growing up, and after I got married, there was no school.

"We always went to church, but on our own account, because there was no priest. I couldn't believe it when I heard a priest had come to this sad, abandoned place. It was like a miracle, a transformation. To be honest with you, it was our guardian angel who came to Solentiname."

In 1965 Ernesto Cardenal — forty years old and famous as a poet in Latin America — had just been ordained a priest. He was born in Granada, Nicaragua, and so grew up by the lake and by the volcanoes and islands that cluster around that town. When he decided to start a spiritual community in Nicaragua, he chose Solentiname. He bought a hundred acres of overgrown land with money he had won as a literary prize. He was surprised to find a half-finished church on the land, and at first he lived in it. He asked

A three-year-old boy paddles a dugout canoe

Doña Francisca in her kitchen

his spiritual adviser, Thomas Merton, whom he knew from the Trappist monastery in Kentucky, how the community should be run. "The rule," Merton said, "is that there should be no rules."

Two seminary friends from Colombia joined Cardenal. They had prayers and meditations and mass and vespers. They cleared the land, farmed, finished the church, and built their houses from bricks they had made themselves.

The campesinos welcomed Ernesto. Olivia said, "Priests would sometimes come by our island who might be of good character, but not with Ernesto's humility. I saw that he was such a simple little priest. I didn't think he was as intelligent as he is, being so humble."

The poverty and neglect of the people led Ernesto to take an interest in all their problems. He arranged to bring a teacher for the children, and he gave classes in the Gospels.

They modified their religious practice. Teresita, a Colombian woman, said, "We began to understand what it really meant to be a Christian. It wasn't so much the prayers and masses and communions, but love, really. Love for others. At the beginning, we had daily masses, but later Ernesto said that if we didn't want mass, we shouldn't have it. We could ask him whenever we wanted it. From then on we had only one or two a week, apart from Sunday mass. We would recite the Psalms in the morning, and read some other book."

They read the Bible and books on the economic and political situation of Latin America. The Bible study groups commented on the Bible page by page, using the method of discussion. This encouraged people to think for themselves and to apply religion to their lives. In the progressive Latin American Church these are called "Family of God" discussion groups. Ernesto tape-recorded many of the discussions and published them as *The Gospel in Solentiname.*

The interpretations became quite political. "Before," Olivia said, "no one ever read a newspaper. Somoza was thought of as some sort of king. Sometimes the men would be invited to San Carlos, where they would be given rum and a picture of Somoza."

But now they drew parallels between the Gospels and the political situation in Nicaragua. Herod was Somoza. Pilate was the gringo ambassador in Nicaragua. Jesus, born in a country filled with repression and terror, came to liberate the poor, as in Luke 4:16: "The spirit of the Lord is upon me, because he hath anointed me to preach the gospel to the poor; he hath sent me to heal the broken-hearted, to preach deliverance to the captives, and recovering of sight to the blind, to set at liberty them that are bruised." Sandino was compared with Jesus: both believed their deaths would lead to liberation. They began to believe in the possibility of change.

During this time, Ernesto was writing powerful revolutionary poetry. His famous poem "Zero Hour" had already been published. In the late sixties he met with Tomás Borge and later with Carlos Fonseca, and he became involved with the Front. They accepted him though he insisted that he was opposed to violence; and he accepted them though they disagreed. Many young people around him joined the growing struggle against the Somoza dictatorship. But they also made internal changes in Solentiname, economic and personal. This change came about through art.

Ernesto loved crafts and made little sculptures of animals and Gospel figures. He brought a loom to teach weaving and started a pottery studio. But it was painting that caught on in Solentiname. Olivia Silva became a painter and then a teacher of painting, and she told me how it happened: "Painting began in Solentiname one day when Ernesto asked for some water in a gourd, and on the other side of the gourd there were carvings. He talked to the campesino, and the man told him he would like to paint, so Ernesto said he would get him materials and whatever he needed to learn to paint. This was Eduardo Arana.

"He began to make drawings on cardboard like a child, a man of thirty-odd years, with many children, who drank a lot and lived in misery. Not poverty, misery. When he did a drawing that seemed truthful to him he painted a simple painting, but pretty, and it is now in the library of Solentiname.

"Ernesto liked his paintings and took some to Managua to sell, and brought back money. Well, the campesino could hardly believe it. Eduardo didn't have faith in painting, but Ernesto always told him, 'Paint! Paint!' And he kept painting. And Ernesto said, and this was certain, that Solentiname had much misery, but also much talent, much value; but the value of the people was choked off by the system.

"My oldest son, Alexander, worked in the community with Ernesto, and once, when Ernesto was on a trip to Managua, Alexander painted a little canvas, the palm trees and leaves quite well done, and this awakened the capacity in others. I told my daughter María to paint. She was about fifteen or sixteen, the first woman in Solentiname to paint a picture. Then my daughter Gloria began to paint, and my other daughter Esperanza, and she taught a neighbor, Marina Ortega. And so it went. We had classes and taught one another.

"Ernesto would correct them—if they lacked something, or weren't good. He was the instructor. He wasn't a painter, but he knew how to criticize painting. He gave us moral support, and got materials when we had nothing to eat or wear.

"I didn't paint, because materials were so scarce, and I didn't want to waste paint on something bad. But in 1974 a friend said, 'You must paint, get a little material and begin.' So I became excited and got a little oil and asked for help to paint a sky, and began to mess up my first canvas. Already I was liking it."

In September 1977, the FSLN attacked the National Guard barracks in San Carlos, with the participation of several young people from Solentiname. Two of them, Elvis Chavarría and Donald Guevara, were captured and were last seen being taken away in a boat, their heads covered by hoods. The National Guard bombed and strafed the community of Solentiname, destroying the buildings and scattering the people into exile in Costa Rica.

After the FSLN triumph, the community in Solentiname was rebuilt. Ernesto was named minister of culture, and through his efforts new projects commenced and the fame of the community spread. An association of painters was formed. The Ministry of Culture acted as a not-for-profit dealer. The painters donated 5 percent to the association, and with the money they built a community center. One year they donated 1 million córdobas (about 1,500 dollars) to defense. They came to be called the "Peasant Painters of Solentiname." Their paintings of nature and everyday life were extraordinarily beautiful. They have been widely exhibited, and reproductions in books and calendars have been sold all over the world.

Besides painters, there were artisans and carpenters. A sawmill was built as well as a factory for making toys, furniture, and boats. Artisans carved birds, fish, and animals out of the balsa wood that grows on the islands. Money was obtained from an Italian labor union and from various other European organizations. A small agricultural college was started. Plans were made for an artists' community, and some houses were completed. The plans included an artists' center with studios and a gallery and other facilities that, because of a lack of funding, never came to fruition. And then everything stopped after the election. Still, the economy of Solentiname — at least for many of the inhabitants — had been transformed.

But not only the economy. The artists learned about art, and began to see their art as part of world art. They organized, traveled, and participated in exhibits and conferences in Managua and abroad. But most important, perhaps, is what Olivia told me.

"The campesino who lives in misery doesn't know the love of beauty or the love of nature. Their hunger and pain is so great they don't give time or interest to contemplating a plant. They see the water and only know to drink it. But when they develop as a person, they begin to take pleasure in everything. By knowing things as the subject matter of art, one is better able to see things as they are, as lovely things, and to see that one lives in a paradise. One begins to see everything as part of a holy life, the life of God, and of the nature created by God for people."

And what now, after the electoral defeat? There is no state support for the arts. Culture is again seen as a luxury, and thus as something for the rich. There is no Ministry of Culture, and everything that was accomplished by the Sandinistas is viewed as subversive. The new government has even destroyed murals the Solentiname painters contributed to parks and buildings in Managua. The transition was shocking to Nicaragua's artists, and it threw a large and thriving arts movement into disarray and confusion. But Solentiname, and the arts movement the revolution brought forth, is not going backward. Ernesto, now unemployed, began an art gallery in Managua called "Los Cuatro Mundos" (The Four Worlds). Many painters, including Olivia, sell their works through him, but they also exhibit and sell in other galleries. The painters, now on their own, have created a new association of Solentiname painters and artisans. Elena Pineda, Rosa, Blanca, Silvio, Enrique, and others who began the association are working to open the Solentiname Gallery. Elena's house in Managua has a big porch facing onto a garden which they converted into an exhibition space and café. Two other galleries have been opened: one by a collective of women artists, another by a small group of painters. The painters have much less security now, and less exposure and support; they worry whether they can make it under the new conditions. But they are still organized, and painting, and many are selling their paintings.

The island of Fernando is large, though not the largest. It takes about three hours to walk around. Behind Francisca's house, a path passes through fields planted with corn and beans and up a hill. From the top you can see the lake on the other side and walk down to a lagoon. You pass groves of coffee trees, bananas and coconut palms, cedar from which they build houses and canoes, and other strange and beautiful trees. It is jungle wherever it isn't cultivated. A woman goes by carrying a basket of tomatoes on her head as I wind my way down the hill toward the lagoon. The path leads to the health clinic — closed since the election — and, near it, an old wood-frame house with a metal roof and a porch roofed with palm leaves. I go there to sit and talk with Gregorio, an old, skinny, bowlegged campesino who lives there alone. I had met him out walking one morning; he was on his way to the hotel, staggering under a large stalk of green bananas, and he invited me to visit him. His house looks out onto both the lake and the lagoon, where white herons stride slowly among the reeds looking for fish or frogs. Or they fly across the lagoon, croaking, their long wings flapping like sails. It is the house for me, and he "promises" to give it to me when he dies. On the hill behind, he has a grove of coffee trees and many producing fruit trees. He has a dugout canoe from which he fishes. His little house, with its hammock under the thatched porch, is just the right size. And it faces, across the lagoon, another charming house surrounded by flowers and hibiscus and poinsettia bushes, where three women from three generations live. He tells me they are good neighbors. When they bake cake in their stone oven they call him, and he brings a gift of coffee.

The best craftsman on the island is Rodolfo, whose house lies between Francisca's and the hotel. He harvests and dries the balsa, cuts it into blocks, then carves the forms of birds or fish. His animals always seem to be the most lifelike and graceful, whether it's a duck with its head turned back, beak tucked under a wing, or a parrot in flight, head and neck stretched

Gregorio posing by his harvest of drying coffee beans

forward, its wings spread. His son Ricardo sands them smooth; then Rodolfo, working in his shed with a charcoal fire, burns outlines into the balsa, marking the areas he will paint different colors. The wings, breasts, necks, and tails are separately painted bright red, green, blue, or yellow. Rodolfo also builds boats. He made Silvio's boat using solid cedar boards — a wood they call cedar, although it is harder and heavier than the cedar I know. He works under a large tree, a few feet from the edge of the lake. The wood is sawed into boards on another island. He saws and planes by hand and bends the boards to shape. For caulking he uses pitch he gets from a certain tree. Silvio's boat is long, broad, and strong and can carry a dozen people; it cost 600 dollars. Prices are higher now: for 800 dollars, Rodolfo said, he'll make me one.

We need fish, so Silvio, his son Carlos, Enrique, and I go out in the boat to catch some. Silvio takes us across to the next island and stops under a tree by an area of rocks. I hold onto a tree branch, and they turn rocks over to catch little crabs. Then we circle the island, which is small and uninhabited, to the other side, away from the wind, and throw over a weight near the shore. Each of us has a fishing line with a hook and weight. We bait the hook with a bit of crab leg, twirl it in the air, and toss it out into the water. In an hour we catch forty-five good-size fish. Silvio catches twenty-eight, almost as fast as he can, while I catch three and then stop fishing to relax and enjoy the spot. In the distance we see the crocodile floating and diving. Each time Silvio pulls a fish out of the water he exclaims, "Look, Juan, another one!" The fish are large and very colorful — some blue with dark-blue or black stripes, some green, some orange, and some yellow, with blue or black stripes and spots. Some have large humps behind their heads; some have very large mouths. I have never seen fish like these. And they are all good to eat. Carlos covers them with a cloth and pours water on them, but later when we are back they are all the same color, very dark, and their markings barely visible.

That night all the families and the visitors have a fiesta. We have fried banana and cabbage salad and beer with the fish. We play music on Silvio's boombox and everyone dances. There are kerosene lanterns and strings of decorations. The moon is full, and so bright you can easily see to walk home on the path.

In house after house there were painters. Olivia Silva was collecting a group of small paintings contributed to sell for repairs on the school. There was a meeting of painters at the hotel to talk about the sale and the painters' association. Afterward, a few of us sat around talking, and I asked them which of the small paintings they liked best, and why.

"Most important," José said, "is they should be realistic. They should show nature as it is here in Solentiname." Rafael said much the same thing: "Primitivist painting shows the riches of nature, the trees, flowers and birds, the water and hills. It is concrete. It shows reality just as it is. It isn't like the French impressionists. When I paint a cedar, I know what it is. If you can't tell it is a cedar, it isn't a primitivist painting."

"Direct experience is very important to us," Olivia said. "There is nothing you know better than your own house, right, and you can draw your house because you know it. We were born among this vegetation, and the peasant painter knows very well what the leaf of the *guácimo* is like, or the flower of the *tijuilote*."

Yet when I said their painting did not seem realistic in European terms they wanted to know what I meant. "I mean, like a photograph," and I took a color photograph out of my notebook, because I couldn't explain it. "Look at the difference," I said, and I put the photograph next to one of the little paintings. "In the photograph, the woman is big and close, and the hills behind are small and far away. In the painting, everything is the same distance, and seen from above, like in a helicopter. And yet we don't see the tops of people's heads." They laughed at that. "And in the painting, see, there are no shadows. There are only colors. Your painting, in fact, is like

Elysa Majorga, painter

twentieth-century European painting, which is thought of as less realistic, as more abstract. It is more like Paul Klee, or Picasso."

"No, it doesn't look like a photograph," Elena said. "It's a painting, it's not supposed to look like a photograph. We put our ideas into our paintings. We paint what we love. We paint the beauty in the world. But we paint it realistically, so that people will know what it is."

"What makes one painting of yours better than another?" I asked. "For example, is this painting better than that one?"

"Yes," she said. "She paints palm trees very well. Do you see?"

"Yes, it is done very carefully. The color changes; the ends of the leaves are whitish yellow, then light green, then dark toward the center. It is very well done. [But in] this [other] painting it is all the same, a flat solid green. It isn't realistic. A leaf is really many colors."

"She is just learning," Elena said. "But she does well for a beginner. Her painting is simple, but it is pretty. It will sell for less."

"Sometimes," I said, "Solentiname paintings are criticized for being so happy. Like children's paintings. Even pictures of suffering seem happy." There is a calendar on the wall, using paintings they did on religious themes, mostly about the Crucifixion of Christ, in which his suffering is emblematic of tortures perpetrated by the National Guard. Birds, flowers, and plants abound in these paintings. Probably no "Crucifixion of Christ" has ever appeared in happier surroundings than in the painting of María Guevara, one of Olivia's daughters. The bleeding body of Christ, dressed as a Nicaraguan *guerrillero,* is being carried away in a green meadow amid flowers and tall, bending plants. A blue woodpecker watches. A dove perches on the cross. Two flocks of birds, one dark, one with wings shining from the sun, cross a beautifully painted blue sky with soft yellow clouds.

"In the poetry we wrote," Olivia said, "we spoke of misery, and hunger, and children without shoes. And we have painted women who were hungry and sad, and women who had no hope. One *compañera* in Solentiname painted a very important picture of a woman giving birth without a doctor or hospital. Her husband is heating water to bathe the child after it is born, and offers her some hot water to drink. She is lying on a simple cot, and has put some rags on the ground beside her for the child. The woman painted this very small picture to show how she had her child in such poverty."

"But it is always so pretty," I said, "even when there is torture and suffering."

"What is beautiful is nature, which God has made," Olivia said. "Our painting shows the beauty of God's world, so that people will love and appreciate it, and make our world become like God's world. The revolution is inside art, both are made by love, and art is developing through the revolution. Perhaps we didn't realize this before, but the revolution *is* art.

"For me, primitivist painting and politics are equivalent," she added, "because both speak of the Kingdom of Justice, and the Kingdom of Love, where things are made for everyone. I learned to explain the reality of life from the Bible, and I don't like or understand the politics of lawyers. Politics to me means social change. I like the politics of love, and that is revolution, in which all have the right to live as persons. And it is like that in art. In painting, one creates liberation."

I have been looking at the work of the Solentiname artists for several years. There have been striking advances in style and technique. One aspect of this is in the facility with which space is organized, in design. The paintings have gained strength as constructions, as dramatic images containing a world of their own. Equally striking is the precision in the "drawing" of objects and the development of a distinctive "handwriting" by the different painters. You have only to see a single leaf to know that it was painted by Pablo Mayorga, or Yelba Urbau, or Faustino Altamirano, or Ana Julia Chavarría, or Rosa Pineda.

Often this kind of painting is described as "primitive" or "naive." These terms have gained something like official status, even in Nicaragua, as generic names for what I think can be more appropriately called "Nicaraguan campesino painting," since in origin, subject, and development it is an art of campesinos. It grew and evolved separately from various European styles, although it closely resembles in certain features some of the works of Klee, Picasso, Chagall, and Rousseau. And it should be named for itself rather than with words that denote negativity. "Primitive" has always meant culture that exists before the domination of "Western European Civilization" and that lacks the supposedly civilizing influence of European standards and traditions. "Naive" means lacking European sophistication and education. Both terms were coined by imperialists to describe cultures they did not understand or respect. It is time to throw them into the junkpile of history. Instead, we can say that these painters have had a long, historic education in struggle, community, and the process of self-liberation, and almost thirty years of artistic development — a history that is hardly "primitive" if one compares the alienation and slavish condition of most European and North American artists (forced to prostitute their art by working in advertising) with the dignity of the Solentiname painters. Their art is independent, technically developed, and profoundly connected with nature and basic values of life.

Another point. Women artists have been struggling for centuries to gain a place in the "art world." Despite enormous energy and effort, and some progress, it is still at present "a man's world." Of the artists in New York City whose works are exhibited, about 85 percent are men, even though New York is often credited with having a strong women's movement. In the new association of Solentiname painters, with twenty-seven artists and artisans, eleven are men and sixteen are women. So much for the "primitive" artists of Solentiname!

Rosa stretched a large canvas onto the side of her house, and she and Elena began painting it in the afternoons. It was to be a mural painting for the Solentiname Gallery in Managua. First they roughed in the big forms, the islands and hills, houses and trees, using blacks and grays. They discussed the composition and asked people for their opinions, until they felt it was right. Then they painted the basic colors of the sky, lake, and hills.

After Easter Sunday, when we all returned to Managua, the canvas was unfinished, but Elena rolled it up and carried it back. A few days before the opening of the gallery, Silvio and Rosa, their children, Francisca and José, and other painters and artisans arrived from Solentiname. Elena's house was as full as Francisca's had been. They brought carvings and paintings, a bag of beans that had just been harvested, two large stalks of bananas, and a half dozen live chickens.

Work on the large painting began again, while Enrique and I finished painting the iron railings of the porch and hung the exhibit. Rosa, Elena, and Ana Julia painted, and the world of Solentiname seemed to grow out of the large forms on the canvas: the shore of the lake, with its little waves, grasses, and stones; ferns and flowering bushes; herons in the water and air; the leaves of trees, in patterns reiterated in subtly changing colors to give a sense of roundness and shape; birds roosting or flying; soft bluish clouds with dark undersides that gradually lightened at the top and were outlined in a darker blue. Little by little it came alive, the women working slowly and calmly, talking and comparing and judging, serious and in fun, from morning until late at night. The painting continued even on the day of the opening. Other painters joined in. Perhaps it wasn't finished, although it looked to be. Perhaps more could be done, or done better, although it was beautiful and everyone felt satisfied.

II

Socialism and the Sacred

In 1956, Rigoberto López Pérez, a twenty-six-year-old Nicaraguan poet, wrote his mother a last letter: "seeing that all efforts to return Nicaragua to being (or to becoming for the first time) a free country without shame or stain have been futile, I have decided that I should be the one to try to initiate the beginning of the end of this tyranny." A few days later in his hometown of León, he publicly assassinated Anastasio Somoza. He was himself immediately killed, receiving thirty-five bullet wounds. As we know, he did in fact "initiate the beginning of the end" of that tyranny.

Rigoberto tried to console his mother by denying that his act was a sacrifice: "I hope that you will take this calmly. You must understand that my act is a duty that any Nicaraguan would desire to be done for his country . . . not a sacrifice, but a duty that I want to fulfill."

In 1972, Carlos Fonseca Amador, founder and leader of the FSLN, published in Cuba an essay entitled "Notes on the Testimonial Letter of Rigoberto López Pérez," which concluded: "no epistle by an evangelist . . . no decalogue by a hero or treatise on virtue contains more ethical richness than the words of Rigoberto López Pérez to his mother, affirmed with his lifeblood" (Fonseca 1981, 1:389).

The themes of Rigoberto's letter have become almost mythic in Nicaragua — the son or daughter who gives his or her life, but not as a sacrifice; the young revolutionary who wins the support of his or her mother, and often her cooperation, in revolutionary struggle; the dignity of duty, defined as working for the liberation of one's people; the ideal of the "new person," drawn from Cuba's revolution; the revolutionary motivated by feelings of great love (as Che expressed it), who overcomes egoism and fear and commits his or her life to creating a new society. For many in Nicaragua these themes have come alive in their revolution, giving it deep spiritual meaning. Christians see love of one's neighbor put into practice. Jesus becomes a model for revolutionary Nicaraguans alongside Che Guevara.

Ernesto Cardenal builds on this religious connection in a narrative poem about Rigoberto that begins by invoking the tradition of the Gospel stories:

"They told me this some time ago, someone / who was told by another, who had been told by / another who was told by a witness: . . ." In another poem, Cardenal writes that when landing in an airliner on Nicaraguan soil,

> and looking down on the earth
> I think, I don't know why, of the dead
> not all, only *them,*
>   our dead
> in the mountains, in common ditches, in lonely tombs
> in cemeteries, at the edges of roads,
> near this airport, over the entire national territory,
> with monuments, anonymous without monuments,
> all over this land, making this land more sacred.
> . . . .
> The wheels are only a few meters above the ground.
> There should be a voice on the loudspeaker saying:
>   ladies and gentlemen
> The land we are about to touch is very sacred.
> . . . the wheels have just touched down, ladies and gentlemen,
> on a great tomb of martyrs.[1]

The words "making this land more sacred" are strange and portentous to me. I come to Nicaragua from a country where by contrast nothing seems sacred, where the simulacra of the sacred, such as public prayer or the flag, are turned into a mockery by the arrogance and violence of government policies toward Nicaragua and throughout the world — continuing a long tradition of imperialist cynicism and religious hypocrisy. And I have a scientific outlook on the world; I am a marxist and an atheist. Yet seeing has become believing. I agree that Nicaragua is a more sacred land, through the sacrifices of its revolutionary martyrs. But what can that mean? Is it possible? I ask this question seriously: Can a revolutionary society that is re-founding itself and its values re-create the sacred?

In a sense, the answer is obviously yes. This transformation has occurred in Nicaragua (and elsewhere — I refer to Nicaragua because of my experience there). Yet a new conception of the sacred is called for to accommodate this experience.

Standing in the way of a new and revolutionary conception of the sacred are some traditional as well as some not-so-old philosophical ideas. According to the religious tradition I grew up in, the sacred can exist only through the manifestation of God in the world. It is not exactly that God is sacred; it is more accurate to say, following Rudolf Otto (1957, chap. 4), that God is *the holy.* Nor does this Judaic and Christian tradition consider the earth, as such, to be sacred; the sacred lies at a point of contact where the profane world is infused with the divine. It exists when things become traces and symbols of the presence of an originative power. The Word of God, when God spoke Aramaic or Greek, is a sacred text. Likewise the temple of Jerusalem, or the tablets of Moses, or Jesus himself, who is emblematic of the human being made sacred through the divine "seed."

But when the Enlightenment came along, with its critical, scientific humanism — in Western history and in my own life — the religious version of things lost its authority. Not all of its truth or importance, obviously, but the absolute seeped out of it. I can no longer see my religious heritage as more than one among several important religious traditions. And since the presence of God in the world seemed to depend on that authority, the sacred is reduced to being an appendage of a lost tradition.

I think most people in the United States now believe, or act as if they believe, that the sources of the sacred are in the past. On the one hand, the scientific understanding of the world does not permit the construction of new myths of the sacred. On the other hand, and even more powerfully, the capitalist spirit leads the sacred to be marginalized because it is incompatible with moneymaking. And since atheism and a critique of religion have been integral to Marxism, revolutionary ideologies have by and large incorporated capitalism's indifference to the sacred, viewing it as an outmoded tradition that depends on unscientific faith, that will die away when, to use the phrases of the early Marx, "the heartless world" and "its soulless conditions" are replaced by socialism (Marx 1975, 244).

My response is twofold. I believe that the sacred can and should be reinterpreted compatibly with a scientific outlook, and I think that socialists ought to worry about themselves reproducing "the heartless world" and "its soulless conditions." Socialists should respect and encourage a positive core in religious spirituality and its acknowledgment of the sacred; we should respect its valuing of community among ourselves and with nature. We should recognize that not only has capitalism depleted the ozone layer and the forests, it has also depleted our spirituality by destroying the established forms of community, of tradition, and of contact with nature, all foundations of spirituality. We need to reconstitute and nurture our human capacity to feel deeply bonded together as part of one historical struggle, on the same earth, within the same creative, evolutionary process.

I want to propose some alternative definitions of the related ideas of the sacred, the spiritual, and the religious, definitions inspired by the Nicaraguan revolution. Yet, while influenced by revolutionary Christians and liberation theology in Nicaragua, my proposals are probably rather different from what they would say, since I am not a Christian or a believer in God. On the other hand, I am hoping to avoid utopianism in its bad sense: I don't want to propose some sort of "humanist religion" in the abstract as a "model" for some equally abstract socialist society. I take the Nicaraguan case because it is a concrete experience of people who want to continue to grow within their religion, who are "rescuing" the progressive spirituality that exists in the Christian tradition so as to create a higher level of society.

Nicaraguan revolutionary Christians reject the idea of religion as based on human weakness and on the need for a higher being to resolve our limitations as a natural species. In short, they reject the conception of religion that led the young Marx to describe it as "the illusory happiness of men . . . [and] . . . the opium of the people" (Marx 1975, 244). In contrast, their way of thinking is expressed by Miguel D'Escoto (1991), in my interview with him already quoted in part in the introduction to this book:

> Humans were created in the image of God. What does this mean if not that humans are themselves creators, with the capacity for creative love? The root and true meaning of democracy is that God made us in his image to be co-creators with him. He left to us the creation of society. It is up to us, not him alone, but him through us, to create the kingdom of God here on earth. He didn't make us to be spectators, and we humans are not satisfied being spectators.[2]

Their activist interpretation of the religious project leads Christian Nicaraguans to find unity and comradeship among other activists who share a like concern for justice and community:

> I feel closer to some atheists than to many who call themselves believers because I can see the spirit of God working in them. Jesus taught this in the parable of the Good Samaritan. You know the story — a man was robbed and beaten and lies half-dead by the roadside. The well-to-do priest rides by and ignores him. Another man passes and says a prayer. But the man from Samaria, a people the Jews called "dogs" because they didn't believe in Yahweh, stopped and took the man to an inn and paid the innkeeper to care for him and said: "Wash his wounds and give him food, and in three days I'll be back to see about him." Well, the same applies here. There are many sick, wounded, and hungry in Nicaragua. When Sandinistas build a health clinic or take medicine to the sick, God is acting through them, and these are the people I want to be with. For God is love — he wants us to love one another and care for one another. He is not so vain that he cares more about prayers than about real deeds. (D'Escoto 1991)

Among the atheist Sandinistas in Nicaragua there has been a concern for unity and a respect for difference that corresponds with the openness of

Father D'Escoto. Thus, Carlos Fonseca, acknowledged to be one of the main architects of the revolution, wrote in a message to Nicaraguan students: "The Marxist perspective does not exclude respect for the religious beliefs of Nicaraguans. Marxist revolutionaries continue and enlarge the tradition of the defense of the humble people, [a tradition] which has among its principal historical precursors the first Christians, many of whom, like revolutionaries today, generously gave their lives so that one day the poor will obtain justice" (Fonseca 1981, 2:169).

I want to mention another of Fonseca's major concerns that contributed to the spiritual content of the Sandinista movement. He struggled to found the movement organically in Nicaraguan history and identity, drawing from the life and thought of Augusto Sandino. In a message broadcast during the takeover of a radio station, Fonseca connected the dimensions of Christian and Nicaraguan history, saying: "Two thousand years ago there appeared a redeemer who said that his brothers were those who did the will of one in heaven from whom proceeded justice and truth. . . . 'Brother' was [also] the term of address used by Augusto César Sandino toward those who accompanied him with their rifles against the Yankee aggressors" (Hodges 1986, 269). Fonseca also influenced the spiritual side of Nicaragua's revolution with his conception of revolutionary morality and the attention he gave to the moral quality of a "good Sandinista." The virtue he considered most important was humility. Others he stressed were sincerity, fraternity, self-sacrifice, and simplicity (Fonseca 1981, 2:257).

Carlos Fonseca's relationship with revolutionary Christians suggests that we distinguish between a religious *attitude* and religious *belief;* between having a religious orientation toward the world and accepting a specific doctrine or belief. A person with a religious attitude is bonded reverently to the world. He or she has a feeling of deep, unbreakable connectedness that implies love and a sense of responsibility toward other people and nature. This connectedness reaches across historical periods and societies and unites all who struggle for justice and new forms of community. It can exist without worship or in the absence of any particular belief system, and many who do worship or believe in traditional religions lack this quality. Jesus, Muhammad, Gandhi, Martin Luther King, Emma Goldman, and Che Guevara, who differed much in belief and religion, share a religious attitude as I define it.

According to the revolutionary Christians in Nicaragua, the biblical message about Jesus depicts him primarily as a human being with just such a religious attitude lived to an exceptional, exemplary degree. If he is divine, so are other humans for being endowed with the capacity for love and commitment to high social purpose. And except for the stories of miracles, which proliferate among all religious traditions and always need to be regarded with some skepticism, their reading of the Gospels genuinely cements Christian tradition with popular liberation.[3]

In my own rereading, I find one of the most striking characteristics of Jesus to be humility. He is never worshipped, and I believe he wouldn't have allowed it.[4] He speaks of wanting *followers*. When he tells them at the last Passover that this is his body and his blood, to take it and eat and drink, he must have meant, "what I am can become part of you just as this food does." When he was asked if the adulterous woman should be stoned, as the law of Moses commanded, Jesus looked at the ground and drew on it with his finger and finally said, "Let the one who is without sin cast the first stone."

He taught mutual love rather than worship. After washing his disciples' feet he said, "Know you what I have done to you? You call me master and lord, and you say well, for so I am. If I, then, master and lord, have washed your feet, you also ought to wash one another's feet" (John 13:12–16). Then: "A new commandment I give to you, that you love one another as I have loved you. By this shall all men know that you are my disciples, if you have love for one another" (John 13:34–35). Again, "This is my commandment, that you love one another as I have loved you. Greater love has no man than he who lays down his life for his neighbor" (John 15:12–13).

This last sentence has been perhaps the most quoted biblical phrase in revolutionary Nicaragua. Jesus is here understood to be speaking of Rigoberto, Carlos, Luis Alfonso, Claudia, and the other martyrs who gave their lives so that there could be a new society in Nicaragua.

Mutual love unites on a basis of equality. The relation of "master and lord" does not preclude equality, because the learners may become like the teacher. When there is mutual love between parents and children, to take another example, there is also inequality, in one sense, but a nurturant parent recognizes in the child one who will come to be equal, and who thus *is* equal essentially as a person.

Jesus recognized that a society founded on mutual love cannot exist with rich and poor. The liberation theologians apply this in their understanding of the historic task of Christians to create a new form of community — it has been frustrated in class societies, built on exploitation. Even the Christian Church has notoriously allied itself with the status quo and maintained a distinction between "the religious" and "the political" to hide its complicity. Obviously there can be no community in a society with rampant exploitation, where love is preached abstractly.

Jesus gave to his followers an example that directly challenged the privileged and served the poor. It is no accident that he was a carpenter and chose poor, working people to be his disciples. He lived among and taught the people. He ministered to those in need—the sick, hungry, and "bedeviled." He exposed the hypocrisy and passivity of the established teachers and religious authorities. He attacked the rich at every opportunity for their arrogance and selfishness. He taught that the Church should serve the people, and that the poor shall inherit the earth.

Most Christians in the United States speak about *believing in* Jesus as a way to gain personal salvation and peace of mind, without so much as a ripple in the fabric of our unjust society. The revolutionary Christian speaks of *following* Jesus; that is to say, putting love into practice by building community. It is because of this commitment to practice that the revolutionary Christian is revolutionary, and confronts the necessity of ridding the world of capitalism and building socialism.

Fernando Cardenal, the minister of education during the Sandinista government said:

> The Sandinista Front gave me the opportunity to commit every day of my life to work on behalf of the poor among my people, whom I see and value and for whom I have chosen, because of sacred principles and desires—religious, Christian principles of evangelism—to follow Christ and be a minister of Christ, just as he was a minister for the Father and risked his life for the poor among the people and lost his life for them. The Sandinista Front gave me the possibility of living the message with greater radicalism, with a radicalism that is not [expressed] just in words or only sporadically in writing or scattered actions, but in all of practical life. (Cabestrero 1985, 87–88)

The operative word for the relation of socialism and religion is "community" or "new society." For Marxian socialists, the struggle against exploitation and oppression requires a "new person" for building a "new society." For the religious believer, brotherly and sisterly love requires a socialist society. They share a religious attitude, and it is in their common struggle for community that new forms of the sacred are realized.

What is the meaning of "the sacred" in my naturalistic interpretation? Throughout history, human societies have upheld the sacred as a link with the originative sources of their communities and values. Sacraments, according to the Macmillan *Encyclopedia of Religion,* are places, persons, things, ceremonies, and events that "mediate the presence and power of the divine." The English word "sacrament" comes from a Latin word meaning "bond." The corresponding Greek word, *mysterion,* means "union with the divine."

Sacred *places* are places of origination, central places where society receives birth and definition, places that express the society's connection to originative powers. A temple or cathedral or mosque, often the center of a city or a region, concentrates and symbolizes the human world in relation to its source. For the Greeks, the sacred center of Delphi was the *omphala,* the navel of the earth.

The hearth, traditionally the center of the house, has been considered sacred because, as the source of heat and light, its chimney was a passage to the life-giving power of the divine. In the body, the heart is the center of the person because it is the source of blood and passion, love and inspiration, the place where God is said to enter. When God smote the breast of the Prophet and replaced the heart with a burning coal, he was giving the Prophet a connection with the divine power. All sacred places are those where the divine power has acted and been present.

Sacred *times* are observed because they reflect or reenact events in which the divine power created the basic structures of life: birth and death, planting and harvest, initiation, marriage. These are the events that mark our lives with basic turning points.

From my marxist, scientific perspective, it seems that sacred places and events were created by people in an unself-conscious, communal process of self-definition. People have given the law to themselves through these meaning-giving myths. The Word is the word they have written and cherish. The Center is chosen as the center. The Redeemer, "the Chosen One," is chosen because of the commitment, sacrifice, and love that people have decided will redeem them. They have chosen well or badly; but the point is that they, or those to whom they give authority, have chosen.

If this point of view is true, does the sacred turn out to be illusory? Certainly the imaginative forms people have given to their origins in stories and myths cannot be taken as literal truth. But the spirit expressed in these forms, the deep seriousness and importance of origins and communal forms of life, is true. In the foundation myths of our communities — in our saying, this is how we came to be, this is what we are, this is how we shall live — people express more than just stories, rules, and definitions. They are aspiring *to be,* to achieve perfection as they conceive it, and to be recognized as having ultimate value. This is a profoundly self-creative aspiration; in its historical development it clarifies and defines the idea of the good society. The sacred lies within this aspiration to be. It does not need validation by a higher being. The sacred is a monument to our highest moments of strength and purpose and self-affirmation. The higher being is our best self.

Paradoxically, the evolution of religion itself may have played a part in this reinterpretation of the sacred. Mircea Eliade has claimed in *The Sacred and the Profane* (1959) that the history written by the Hebrew and Christian authors (the Islamic may also be included) is uniquely realistic, for it advocates the actual historical occurrence of sacred events. In most if not all previous societies, Eliade says, the history of the gods and their originative acts stands apart from the known history of people. There is a separation between the profane history of ordinary life and sacred history as told in myth. The Greek poet Hesiod, for instance, called the time when the gods were active "the golden age," and human history "the bronze age."

But in the Judaic and Christian traditions, Eliade points out, mythic and human time are merged. The history of the Jews and Yahweh is not separated from actual history. The coming of the kingdom is conceived of as the historical future for Jews on earth. For Christians a specific human being, Jesus of Nazareth, is the Christ or Messiah who performed exemplary and originative acts on certain dates and in certain places in front of witnesses. A human juridical perspective — that of historical verification — is invoked. Perhaps "the star of Bethlehem" turns out to have been a predictable conjunction of planets, and the falling of the walls of Jericho corresponds to an earthquake. If so, if historical judgment differs widely from the details of a story, we accept that judgment because the worldly perspective has taught us that sacred acts and events are empirically verifiable in the human world.

This focus on real history is another reason why revolutionary Christians in Latin America have stressed their biblical tradition. They believe that the kingdom is to be created in this world, and that the task of human beings is not to await that kingdom but to create it, now, on earth. For them, the sacred is constituted by the creative and sacrificial acts of all who struggle for the kingdom. In their view, such people are expressing the originative powers of the divine.

From the naturalistic perspective I advocate, in which nature and humans are all there is, what can be meant by "the divine"? Plato said that creation is a manifestation of the divine. He thought it to be universal among humans, to be our way of participating in immortality. He saw all forms of creation — art, work, childbearing and -rearing, education, science, whatever constructively contributes to our lives in community — as expressions of the same basic creative impulse (Plato 1970, 78–94).

The filmmaker Maya Deren wrote that "human beings cannot duplicate the infinite intricacy of the living architecture of the wheat-stalk. Nature is best capable of its own forms and of the complex inevitabilities which result in such marvelous phenomena. Human beings are such a phenomenon; and the marvelous in us is our creative intelligence, which transcends nature and creates out of it un-natural forms" (Nin 1974, 4:138). Deren is speaking of the individual artist creating a work of art. Marx, however, defined the natural, creative powers of humans more broadly, as the capacity to act in concert to produce their means of life, their social relations as producers, and their culture. He defined human nature generally as the capacity for "free, creative activity" (Marx 1975, 322–34).

I see creative activity — this is in agreement with Miguel D'Escoto — as the real content of the human idea of, and reverence for, the divine. Creative life — in the broad sense defined by Plato — has a transcendent quality because creatively we go beyond the given reality toward an ideal. Also, our creativity seems to have a source outside us; it "comes" to us, and thus feels mysterious, and beyond the power of our will. It feels larger than we are and is apparently inexhaustible. The constant resourcefulness it gives astonishes us, whether in art or action or nature. We have limits in power and become tired, but it renews us. In our despair it reassures us. Also, it fills us with reverence: when we see creativity in people and in all of nature around us, we can do no other than love the world as good.

Whether we call this creative source "nature" or "the divine" seems to matter little. People who prefer "the divine" usually speak of the spiritual, instead of the creative power of nature, as that which "infuses" us. Many uses of the word "spiritual" differ only slightly from "creative." Even atheistic artists writing about their work often speak of its "spiritual" sources. Yet "spiritual" also has an otherworldly connotation; it is often used to mean a mode of being apart from, and in conflict with nature, and a belief in a spirit world. The creative is more workaday, more applicable to the variety of human activities that manifest it, and more comfortable with sex, the body, and the entire natural world. For these reasons it better suits my idea of the sacred.

Most modern religions originated as philosophies of human liberation. Modern science originated in the Enlightenment, a philosophy of liberation that was born in a struggle with institutionalized religion and, indeed, often described itself as the enemy of religion. In the nineteenth century, Marxism arose as a new philosophy of liberation, and it grew in influence because of its basis in the most advanced scientific knowledge. But Marxist critiques of religion, and efforts to create new, nonreligious societies, have stalled, perhaps partly because the scientific perspective that guided them, inherited from the Enlightenment, was a limited legacy.

Limited, but not misguided. It needs to be broadened, but not rejected. The Enlightenment project, based on a commitment to scientific truth and progress, allows no turning back. It should reject all dogma, including its own, and see its mistakes as opportunities for deeper understanding. It should become humble and worldly-wise and speak of indefinite progress and alternative paradigms instead of a single method and a final goal, but it need not abdicate its struggle for progress or abandon its faith in a higher society.

In fact, considered as the historical movement of humanistic, scientifically based, progressive thought, the Enlightenment has shown itself capable of gathering historical experience and modifying itself. Marx both attacked it and carried it forward by showing that scientific thinking is social in origin and quality, and that social conflicts divide and infuse scientific work with class and national interests. Nietzsche and Heidegger showed in their ways the shallowness of the idea of "pure, disinterested" science. More recently, feminism and "Third World" philosophies have critiqued the limitations of European, patriarchal rationality.

But there is still another dimension of concern—that of the creative or spiritual, and its product the sacred—needing scientific recognition as a valid expression of human life and a necessary element of any community worth dying for. This dimension, too, can have a form entirely consistent with the original this-worldly, emancipatory project of Enlightenment thinking.

In *History and Spirit*, Joel Kovel defines spirit in much the same way I have been speaking of the creative, as "what happens to us when the boundaries of the self give way," that is, as that part of the self which is opposed to the established way of being, ready to undermine and change it. Also, Kovel sees spirit and spirituality as inside history, rather than outside it, and as a force for liberation. He writes:

[H]istory entails an unending dialectic of splitting and the overcoming of splitting. These splits are created in domination and overcome in liberation. . . .
"[S]pirit" occurs in the motion of the dialectic, as splitting is overcome. . . . Spirit

is not opposed to matter, or the flesh; rather it is revealed, indeed created, in the freeing of matter and flesh; that is, in the overcoming of splitting. And spirit is not a by-product, or an indicator, of this overcoming; it is the lived process itself. This liberation is a spiritual project, and spirituality is emancipatory. (Kovel 1991, 7)

My central idea is this: The sacred is produced by people in our struggle for higher forms of being and society. A society maintains and venerates "its sacred" in its memory of its originative and defining history.

What follows is an example from Nicaragua of Kovel's "overcoming of splitting." It concerns the recognition and continuity of the sacred in Nicaragua, now that the Sandinistas have lost the elections and their control over state power.

Carlos Fonseca was killed in the mountains of Nicaragua by Somoza's National Guard in 1976. They were jubilant, and it was widely believed that his body had been dismembered and scattered in the woods unburied. In fact, a campesino had buried him, and his body was recovered and brought intact to Managua after the triumph of the revolution. He was reburied beside the Plaza of the Revolution across from the old cathedral, and a monument was built over his grave.

I first saw the monument in the summer of 1985. It is a modest, white, rectangular structure, at which an eternal flame burns. While I was there a group of teachers from Estelí, in Managua for a conference, came up to the monument. They stood around quietly while one of them made a statement; then each tossed a flower into the pool that surrounds the marble torch.

I saw the monument again much later—on November 8, 1991, the fifteenth anniversary of Fonseca's death. The plaza was filled with thousands of people, and Daniel Ortega spoke. He discussed the present conditions and the efforts of the Sandinistas to maintain the popular gains achieved during the 1980s. He said that the revolution had not ended, but was in a new phase. The people seemed to be in high spirits.

That night, someone bombed the monument. It was damaged but not destroyed. The reaction was tremendous. Within an hour, the area was surrounded by armed Sandinista supporters and rebuilding had begun. The monument was quickly repaired, and another rally was scheduled for the same time the next afternoon. The crowd was as large as the day before, but now there were bonfires and loud skyrockets, and the atmosphere was that of a civil war. Daniel Ortega spoke again, joined this time by the entire directorate of the Sandinista Front.

Several circles of women stood around the monument during all this, their arms locked together. They were mothers who had lost sons or daughters. Many of them belonged to the organization called "Mothers of Heroes and Martyrs." Others were women whose sons or daughters are believed to be dead, yet they have no grave to which the mothers can bring flowers. One of these mothers said, "This grave of Carlos Fonseca is also the grave of my son."[5]

In such a way as this, a sacred place is created.

Notes

Introduction

1. All Spanish-language conversations, interviews, and published sources, unless otherwise indicated, have been translated into English by the author.

Chapter 2: Sandino, Revolutionary Prophet

1. The most comprehensive history of the influences on Sandino in Mexico is provided by Donald C. Hodges (1986, 1992). Other important sources are Selser 1981 and an essay by Sergio Ramírez, "El Muchacho de Niquinohomo," which is the introduction to volume 1 of Sandino's collected writings (Sandino 1984). I have also found these books to be useful sources on Sandino's later life.

2. The Daisy Zamora poem was recorded by me at a poetry reading in Ciudad Darío, Nicaragua, in January 1986.

3. Sandino's writings are interesting for their detailed descriptions and as precious records of the man. They have not been translated into English until recently, in an excellent and fairly comprehensive edition by R. E. Conrad (Sandino 1990). All translations from Sandino's works used in the present book are my own.

4. For an excellent history of the Somoza family dynasty see part 1 of Black 1981.

5. An important, recent discussion of some of these kinds of spirit is to be found in Kovel 1992.

Chapter 4: Norma: On Sexism and Moral Change

1. A more recent study by Beth Stevens (1988) essentially confirms the point made by Professor Stoltz Chinchilla.

2. There is a very large literature on the subject of women's consciousness. Important examples are Gilligan 1982, Nodding 1984, Jagger 1983, and Ferguson 1981. Katha Pollitt (1992) provides a readable discussion of the literature.

Chapter 9: Politics and Representation

1. My understanding of the phrase "establishment media" is drawn in part from Marx's writing on ideology: "The ideas of the ruling class are in every epoch the ruling ideas. . . . The class which has the means of material production at its disposal, has control at the same time over the means of mental production, so that thereby

generally speaking, the ideas of those who lack the means of mental production are subject to it" (Marx and Engels 1975, 5:59).

The relation of the ruling power in the United States to the media — "the means of mental production" — has been studied most thoroughly by Ben Bagdikian (1992). I summarize here the framework and results of Bagdikian's research, as it directly influences the approach I use in analyzing the media.

Bagdikian's argument is that corporate power over the media is highly integrated and concentrated. For example, five New York City banks own controlling interests in the three major television networks, CBS, ABC, and NBC. The same group of banks holds controlling shares in many other media or media-involved corporations: the New York Times Corporation, Time, Inc., Newsday, McGraw-Hill, Dow Jones, ITT, RCA, Prentice-Hall, Harcourt Brace Jovanovich, Doubleday, Knight-Ridder, Westinghouse, Cox, Reader's Digest, Harper & Row, the Washington Post, and others.

According to Bagdikian's research, most U.S. media, including books, newspapers, magazines, television, and radio, are controlled by twenty-three corporations. This concentration implies an integration of perspective.

Sameness of perspective is partly a consequence of interlocking directorships among the largest corporations. Time, Inc. has directors on the boards of most major New York banks, as well as on those of more than a dozen major corporations. The New York Times interlocks with an array of the largest corporations, including Morgan Guaranty Trust. This form of integration is perhaps most striking among, again, the major banks. Bagdikian quotes from a 1978 study by the U.S. Senate Committee on Governmental Affairs: "The principal stockvoters in large banks are — large banks. Morgan Guaranty is Stockvoter Number 1 in four of its New York sister banks — Citicorp, Manufacturers Hanover Corp., Chemical New York Corp., and Bankers Trust New York Corp. — as well as Bankamerica Corp. In turn, Citicorp is Stockvoter Number 1 in Morgan Guaranty's parent holding company, J. P. Morgan and Company. Stockvoter No. 2 in J. P. Morgan and Co. is Chase Manhattan. Stockvoters No. 3 and 4 in J. P. Morgan and Co. are Manufacturers Hanover and Bankers Trust, in whose parent holding company Morgan Guaranty Trust is Stockvoter No. 1."

Bagdikian comments: "Members of corporate boards have impressive power over their corporations. They hire and fire the corporate leaders. They set corporate policy. They decide if the corporation will borrow money (or lend it) and for what purpose. They decide how the corporation will deal with the public and with the government.

"When individuals sit on more than one board they have powers that can affect all the corporations they govern. They can provide implicit cooperation that will permit two or more corporations to behave in a synchronization that would be illegal or unwise if done explicitly. This is most obvious if directors sit on boards of corporations that are ostensible competitors" (Bagdikian 1992, 27–28).

This network of a few thousand extremely rich and powerful top corporate leaders constitutes the core of what William Domhof (following C. Wright Mills) calls "the power elite" (Domhof 1974). The power elite, in turn, is the activist sector that represents the interests of the capitalist class. The common interest of these groups in the growth and stability of the U.S. capitalist system is the basis of what I call "the establishment perspective," a worldview that tends to be in general accord with the perceived interests of the establishment, produced in institutions they control, by people they hire and fire.

This may sound ominous, and I believe it is, but it is not so one-dimensional as some have concluded. There are constant intrusions, more or less disruptive, of minority voices and perspectives. There are also various forms of diversity within the establishment itself that are very important for ideological analysis. One relevant example is the opposition of the *New York Times* to the Nicaraguan Contras as a valid instrument of U.S. foreign policy, a position that marks a substantial difference between the *Times,* the mass-media newsweeklies, and the Reagan administration. A second kind of conflict occurs between the bosses of institutions and their conscientious workers (who sometimes represent minority perspectives). In 1982, for example, the *New York Times* withdrew the correspondent Ray Bonner from El Salvador because of his controversial reporting on death squad activity there and its connection to the Salvadoran military and government. Other forms of fragmentation of perspective emerge from the media's need to legitimate itself as "objective": facts and events are sometimes recognized that contradict the myths and dogmas. There are also contradictions over time, because the establishment perspective changes in response to changed circumstances.

The popular myth that our media are diverse and pluralistic fails to acknowledge the extent of monopoly control and the extent of unity on basic issues of "principle," such as consumerist values, jingoistic patriotism, "free enterprise," and (in less open forms) classism, sexism, racism, and homophobia. On the other hand, those who conclude from the monopoly of corporate control that the messages are *always* in line with corporate interest fail to recognize the fissures and conflicts that emerge within the major media. They also fail to recognize the existence of media more or less outside monopoly control of the corporate establishment — such news and arts weeklies as *The Nation, In These Times,* and *The Village Voice* — which form and express perspectives on behalf of popular interests that consistently contradict some elements — at least — of the establishment perspective.

2. For examples, see Harrison Salisbury's book on the *New York Times* (1980), esp. chap. 23.

3. The most comprehensive, firsthand study of the CDSs that I know of is Ruchwarger 1987. Michael Higgins and Tanya Coen have recently completed an intensive study of a Managua barrio, including the accomplishments and limitations of the local CDS. They give full recognition to the problems of Sandinista dominance in the makeup of the CDSs, but also show the groundlessness of the claims that they are used as means of political control. A central weakness of the CDS, according to Higgins and Coen, was a lack of government resources to back up the work of the CDSs with respect to improving conditions in the barrios. See Higgins and Coen 1992, esp. chap. 4.

Chapter 10: Managua Journal, 1991–92

1. Sante Fe II is a set of policy recommendations for Latin America prepared in 1988 for the Bush administration by the Council for Inter-American Security, a private group composed of well-known conservative "Latin Americanists." Santa

Fe I, prepared in 1980, contained recommendations that came to be implemented by the Reagan administration, such as the creation of "Radio Marti," an anti-Castro radio station. Santa Fe II recommended the continuation of support for overthrowing the Sandinista government in Nicaragua as well as proposals for policies towards Cuba, narcotics trafficking, and the debt crisis.

Chapter 11: Socialism and the Sacred

1. The poems I quote from are "El chancho que no comio Roberto" and "Aterrizaje con epitafio" (Cardenal 1983, 299, 306).

2. Compare the traditional perspective as expressed by Leszek Kolakowski: "The very phenomenon of the sacred and the very act of worship express man's awareness of his lack of self-sufficiency, of both an ontological and a moral weakness which he is not strong enough to overcome alone. . . . [T]he great prophets of atheism—from Lucretius to Feuerbach to Nietzsche— . . . did not deny human infirmity, yet they refused . . . to admit its ontological permanence" (1982, 202).

3. A good example from Nicaragua is Girardi 1989; a very interesting though more general work is Meyers 1988.

4. My son Bruce Brentlinger has pointed out to me an exception. In John 9:38 it is said that the blind man, cured by Jesus, worshipped him.

5. She said this to Sheila Tully, who is writing a book on women and grief in Nicaragua.

References

Andrić, Ivo. 1959. *The Bridge on the Drina*. New York: Macmillan.

Aristotle. 1941. *Basic Writings*. Edited by Richard P. McKeon. New York: Random House.

Bagdikian, Ben. 1992. *The Media Monopoly*, 4th edition. Boston: Beacon Press.

Bashō, Matsuo. 1966. *The Narrow Road to the Deep North and Other Travel Sketches*. Translated with an introduction by Nobuyuki Yuasa. Harmondsworth: Penguin Books.

———. 1991. *Narrow Road to the Interior*. Translated with an introduction by Sam Hamil. Boston: Shambhala.

Belausteguigoitia, Ramón de. 1985. *Con Sandino en Nicaragua* [1934]. Madrid: ESPASA-CALPE; reprint, Managua: Editorial Nueva Nicaragua.

Bendana, Alejandro. 1991. *Una tragedia campesina: Testimonios de la Resistencia*. Managua: Editora de Arte.

Black, George. 1981. *Triumph of the People*. London: Zed Press.

Bolt, Alan. 1992. *El libro de la Nación Qu*. Managua: Vientos del Sur.

Borge, Tomás. 1984. *carlos, the dawn is no longer beyond our reach*. Translated with an introduction by Margaret Randall. Vancouver: New Star Books.

———. 1986. "Poemas en la Carcel." *Poesía Libre* 18 (December): 1–9.

———. 1992. Interview by author. Transcript of tape recording, translated by author. Managua, January 14.

Brecht, Bertolt. 1979. *Poems, 1913–1956*. Edited and translated by John Willett and Ralph Manheim with Erich Fried. New York: Methuen.

Brentlinger, John. 1989. *Villa Sin Miedo: ¡Presente!* México, D.F.: Claves Latino-americanas.

———. 1990. "Nicaragua and the Politics of Representation." *Confluencia*. Part 1, 5 (Spring): 3–14; part 2, 6 (Fall): 3–18.

Brody, Reed. 1985. *Contra Terror in Nicaragua*. Boston: South End Press.

Cabestrero, Teofilo. 1985. *Ministros de Dios, ministros del pueblo*. Managua: Ministerio de Cultura.

Cabezas, Omar. 1985. *Fire from the Mountain*. Translated by Kathleen Weaver. New York: Crown Publishers.

Cardenal, Ernesto. 1974. *In Cuba*. Translated by Donald D. Walsh. New York: New Directions Books.

———. 1976. *The Gospel in Solentiname*. Maryknoll, N.Y.: Orbis Books.

———, ed. 1981. *Poesía nicaragüense* [1972]. Managua: Editorial Nueva Nicaragua.

365

———. 1983. *Antología*. Managua: Nueva Nicaragua-Monimbo.

———. 1985. *Flights of Victory. Vuelos de Victoria*. Bilingual edition with translations by Marc Zimmerman. Maryknoll, N.Y.: Orbis Books.

Darío, Rubén. 1980. *Nuestro Rubén Darío*. Introducción de Ernesto Mejía Sánchez. Selección de Jorge Eduardo Arellano, Fidel Coloma, Marc Zimmerman y Julio Valle-Castillo. Managua: Ministerio de Cultura.

———. 1982. *El Viaje a Nicaragua; e, Intermezzo Tropical*. Managua: Ministerio de Cultura.

D'Escoto, Miguel. 1991. Interview by author. Tape recording, translated by author. Managua, December 12.

Dickey, Christopher. 1985. *With the Contras: A Reporter in the Wilds of Nicaragua*. New York: Simon & Schuster.

Domhof, William. 1974. "State and Ruling Class in Corporate America." *Insurgent Sociologist* 4 (Spring): 1–15.

Eliade, Mircea. 1959. *The Sacred and the Profane: The Nature of Religion*. New York: Harcourt Brace Jovanovich.

Ellison, Ralph. 1964. *Shadow and Act*. New York: Random House.

Envio. 1983. "The Catholic Church in Nicaragua and the Revolution: A Chronology." 30 (December): 1b–23b.

———. 1989. "The Bush Administration and Central America." 90 (January): 3–7.

Ferguson, Ann. 1991. *Sexual Democracy*. Boulder: Westview Press.

Fonseca, Carlos. 1981. *Obras*, 2 vols. Managua: Editorial Nueva Nicaragua.

Fuentes, Norberto. 1984. *Hemingway en Cuba*. Managua: Editorial Nueva Nicaragua.

Galeano, Eduardo. 1985–1988. *Memory of Fire*, 3 vols. Translated by Cedric Belfrage. New York: Pantheon Books.

Gilligan, Carol. 1982. *In a Different Voice*. Cambridge: Harvard University Press.

Girardi, Giulio. 1986. *Sandinismo, marxismo, christianismo: La confluencia*. Managua: Centro Ecuménico Antonio Valdivieso.

———. 1989. *Revolución popular y toma del templo*. Milan: Asociación de Cooperación Rural en Africa y America Latina.

Heschel, Abraham Joshua. 1962. *The Prophets*. New York: Harper & Row.

Higgins, Michael, and Tanya Coen. 1992. *Oigame! Oigame! Struggle and Social Change in a Nicaraguan Urban Community*. Boulder: Westview Press.

Hirshon, S., and J. Butler. 1983. *And Also Teach Them to Read*. Westport: Lawrence Hill.

Hodges, Donald C. 1986. *Intellectual Foundations of the Nicaraguan Revolution*. Austin: University of Texas Press.

———. 1992. *Sandino's Communism*. Austin: University of Texas Press.

Jagger, Alison. 1983. *Feminist Politics and Human Nature*. Totowa, N.J.: Roman & Allanheld.

Kolakowski, Leszek. 1982. *Religion, if there is no God — On God, the Devil, Sin, and Other Worries of So-Called Philosophy of Religion*. New York: Oxford University Press.

Kovel, Joel. 1988. *In Nicaragua*. London: Free Association Books.

———. 1991. *History and Spirit*. Boston: Beacon Press.

Lorde, Audre. 1984. *Sister Outsider.* Freedom, N.Y.: Crossing Press.

Marx, Karl. 1975. *Early Writings.* Edited by Quintin Hoare. New York: Vintage Books.

Marx, Karl and Frederick Engels. 1975. *Collected Works,* 45 vols. Moscow: Progress Publishers.

Mendoza, Rene. 1990. "We Erred to Win . . ." *Envio* 9 (October): 23–50.

Meyers, Ched. 1988. *Binding the Strong Man: A Political Reading of Mark's Story of Jesus.* Maryknoll, N.Y.: Orbis Books.

Minh-ha, Trin T. 1990. "Critical Reflections." *Art Forum* 38 (Summer): 132–33.

Neruda, Pablo. 1970. *Isla Negra* [1964]. Bilingual edition, translated by Alastair Reid. New York: Farrar, Strauss & Giroux.

Nin, Anaïs. 1974. *The Diary of Anaïs Nin,* 5 vols. New York: Harcourt Brace Jovanovich.

Nodding, Nel. 1984. *Caring: A Feminine Approach to Ethics and Moral Education.* Berkeley: University of California Press.

Otto, Rudolf. 1957. *The Idea of the Holy.* New York: Oxford University Press.

Pallais, Azarias H. 1974. *En los bellos caminos del silencio.* Selección, prólogo, y notas de Jorge Eduardo Arellano. Managua: Ediciones Americanas.

———. 1986. *Antología.* Selección y prólogo de Ernesto Cardenal. Managua: Editorial Nueva Nicaragua.

Plato. 1970. *The Symposium of Plato.* Translated by Suzy Q. Groden. Edited with an introduction and afterword by John Brentlinger and with drawings by Leonard Baskin. Amherst: University of Massachusetts Press.

Pollitt, Katha. 1992. "Are Women Morally Superior to Men?" *The Nation* 255 (December 28): 799–804.

Randall, Margaret. 1981. *Sandino's Daughters.* Vancouver and Toronto: New Star Books.

———. 1983. *Christians in the Nicaraguan Revolution.* Vancouver: New Star Books.

———. 1984. *Risking a Somersault in the Air.* San Francisco: Solidarity Publications.

———. 1992. *Gathering Rage: The Failure of Twentieth Century Revolutions to Develop a Feminist Agenda.* New York: Monthly Review Press.

———. 1994. *Sandino's Daughters Revisited: Feminism in Nicaragua.* New Brunswick: Rutgers University Press.

Rich, Adrienne. 1993. "Passages from What is Found There: Notebooks on Poetry and Politics." *American Poetry Review* 22 (1): 60–65.

Román, José. 1983. *Maldito país.* Managua: El Pez y la Serpiente.

Ruchwarger, Gary. 1987. *People in Power.* South Hadley, Mass.: Bergin & Garvey.

Ruddick, Sara. 1989. *Maternal Thinking: Toward a Politics of Peace.* Boston: Beacon Press.

Salisbury, Harrison. 1980. *Without Fear or Favor.* New York: Times Books.

Sandino, Augusto C. 1984. *El pensamiento vivo,* 2 vols. Con introducción, selección, y notas de Sergio Ramírez. Managua: Editorial Nueva Nicaragua.

———. 1990. *Sandino.* Edited and translated with an introduction by Robert Edgar Conrad. Princeton: Princeton University Press.

Selser, Gregorio. 1981. *Sandino: General of the Free.* Translated by Cedric Belfrage. New York: Monthly Review Press.

Selser, Irene. 1989. *Cardinal Obando*. México, D.F.: Centro de Estudios Ecuménicos.

Silva, Fernando. 1987. Interview by author. Tape recording, translated by author. Managua, January 22.

Stanford Central American Action Network. 1974. *Revolution in Central America*. Boulder: Westview Press.

Stevens, Beth. 1988. "Women in Nicaragua." *Monthly Review* 40 (September): 1–18.

Sweezy, Paul. 1942. *Theory of Capitalist Development*. New York: Oxford University Press.

Ueda, Makoto. 1982. *Matsuo Bashō*. Tokyo: Kodansha International.

Vilas, Carlos M. 1986. *The Sandinista Revolution*. Translated by Judy Butler. New York: Monthly Review Press.

Zamora, Daisy. 1986. Interview by author. Tape recording, translated by author. Managua, January 24.

——, ed. 1992. *La mujer nicaragüense en la poesía*. Managua: Editorial Nueva Nicaragua.

Index

Parenthetical page numbers following foot-
note citations offer contextual locations in
text.

Abrams, Eliot, 246
Aburto Altamirano, Norma, 133–52, 293–
  98, 327–28, 331
alcoholism, 125, 134–35
Alegría, Claribel, 208–10
Alemán, Arnoldo, 301
Alfaro, Gerardo, 40–41
AMNLAE (Luisa Amanda Espinosa
  Women's Association), 60, 125, 169,
  316, 317
AMPRONAC (Association of Women Fac-
  ing the Nation's Problems), 136
anarchism, as early influence on Sandino,
  74–75
Andric, Ivo, 5–6
Araúz, Blanca. See Sandino, Blanca Araúz
Aristotle, 274–75
Arns, Cardinal Paulo Evaristo, 49, 51
art and politics, 9–11, 200, 338–39, 344–
  45
Artola, Aparicio, 168, 173

Bagdikian, Ben, 279, 362n. 1 (9, 267)
Barricada, 17, 49, 287, 296; Barricada Inter-
  national, 316
Bashō, Matsuo, 129–32
Basque internationalists, 249, 252
Belausteguigoitia, Ramón de, 12, 86–90
Belli, Gioconda, 207–8, 213–14
Bendana, Alejandro, 311–12
Bermúdez, Enrique, 116, 246, 300
Bible, 1, 138, 337, 345, 352, 354
Bolaños, Enrique, 283
Böll, Heinrich, 51–52
Borah, Senator William E., 78
Borge, Tomás, 38, 70–71, 92–93, 256, 273,
  279–80, 302, 337; author's interview
  with, 308–15; on poetry, 200; poem by,
  201

bourgeois, class domination after 1990 elec-
  tion, 291
Brody, Reed, 38, 39, 163, 178–79
Bryan-Chamorro Treaty, 78–79
Bush, George, 106, 169, 214, 297
Business Week, 275

Cabezas, Omar, 70, 103, 111–13
Calderón, Manuel, 38–40
Calero, Adolfo, 50
Calero, Alfonso, 116
capitalism, 4, 40, 287–93, 280, 298; de-
  structive effects of, 327, 349
Carballo, Bishop Bismark, 116
Cardenal, Ernesto, 45, 46, 139, 159–60,
  201, 209, 211, 328; in Solentiname,
  335–38; poems by, 202–3, 216, 247–48,
  329–31, 347–48
Cardenal, Fernando, 45, 46, 139, 351
Casadáliga, Bishop Pedro, 49
Castro, Fidel, 245
Catholic Church, 45–51, 221; as "church of
  the rich," 74; as oppressor of the poor,
  140; conservative-popular split within,
  46; hierarchy in, 45–46; liberation move-
  ment within, 45, 307–8
CDS (Sandinista Defense Committee), 60,
  104, 109, 137, 169, 174, 304; origins of,
  281; relation to Sandinista party, 304,
  309; U.S. media criticisms of, 281–83
censorship, 41, 116–17
César, Alfredo, 246, 295, 301
Chamorro, Carlos Fernández, 296
Chamorro, Christiana Lacayo, 296
Chamorro, Violetta, 290, 295–97, 300;
  government of, 288, 290–91
Chamorro Barrio, Pedro Joaquín, 297
Chamorro Vargas, Emiliano, 79
Chavarria, Ana Julia, 345, 346
Chinchilla, Norma Stoltz, 136
Christianity and revolution. See religion and
  revolution, religious attitude, revolution,
  sacred, spirituality

CIA (Central Intelligence Agency), 36, 39
civil war. *See* Nicaragua, civil wars in
class struggle, in Nicaragua, 39–41, 281
Coen, Tanya, 321–24, 363n. 3 (9, 281)
Cole, Brian, 76
colonialism, 75. *See also* United States imperialism
community, 4, 323, 349, 350, 351; as connection between religion and socialism, 353; sacred foundations of, 354–55, 358–59
Condega, Nicaragua, 56–65, 98–132; economy of, 99, 102–3, 106–7; population of, 115; revolutionary commitment of, 55, 308
consciousness: revolutionary development of, 21–24, 138–42; revolution's effect on, 151–52, 326–27
Contras, 2, 27, 38–41, 48, 50, 56, 57, 175, 286; amnesty for, 236; as depicted in U.S. media, 276; composition of, 163–66; danger from, 53, 108, 175–78, 181–82, 233; economic effects of, 34, 38–39; leadership of, 163, 277; psychological effects of, 63–64, 121; recruitment of, 161–65; rights violations by, 38–39, 163; terrorism by, 53, 109, 119–21, 168, 178–79, 191, 193; *vigilancia* against, 54, 108, 121. *See also* ex-Contras; Recontras
Coolidge, Calvin, 80
cooperatives: El Cedro, 228–36; Emilio Mansón, 106–7; Luis Hernández, 248–55, 324–26; Ulises Rodríguez, 66, 108
cordoba. *See* Nicaraguan economy, inflation
Cortéz, Hernán, 287
COSEP (Superior Council of Private Enterprise), 283
Costa Rica, 35
creativity, and spirituality, 356
crime, in Nicaragua, 18–21, 312–14
Cruz, Arturo, 116
Cruz, Gretel, 212–13, 214
Cuba, 21, 44, 96, 170, 175, 185, 201, 244–45, 254, 281, 326, 347

Darío, Rubén, 10–11, 199–200
de Salón, María Felicia, *see* Salón, María Felicia de
democracy, 2, 6, 266, 281, 282, 314–17, 350; and capitalism, 284; economic, in contrast to political, form of, 314–15; unreported in U.S. media, 269
Deren, Maya, 356
D'Escoto, Miguel, 6, 45–51, 350–51, 356
dialectic: between individual and institutional change, 151–52; between individual and society, 266; between leaders and popular base, 269–70; between moral values and unjust society, 96; between women and revolution, 142–43
Díaz, Adolfo, 78
Dickey, Christopher, 39, 163–64, 166
dollar, U.S. *See* Nicaraguan economy: inflation in
Domhof, William, 362n. 1 (9, 267)
draft. *See* military draft

economy. *See* Nicaraguan economy
education. *See* literacy campaign, revolution: progress in education and social well-being within
el coro de angeles, 87
El Nuevo Diario, 25
elections. *See* Nicaraguan politics: elections in
Eliade, Mircea, 1, 355
Ellison, Ralph, 244–45
Emergency Law of Media and Communications, 116
Enlightenment, the, 356–57
Enrique (Condega priest), 102, 109–10, 308; *despedida* for, 125–26; author's interview with, 114–25
Envio, 45, 306
Esquire, 278
ethnographic practice, 322–24
Evangelical Christians, 58, 166
ex-Contras, 161–62, 165–66, 235–36, 299–302, 314. *See also* Contras; Recontras
Exodus, 138, 298

feminism, in the United States, 148–49
Fonseca, Carlos, 70–71, 92–95, 280, 315, 337, 347, 351, 358–59
Francisco (Honduran revolutionary), 70–71, 95–96
freedom: and class conflict over, 281, 283–84; of investment, 280
FSLN. *See* Sandinista Front for National Liberation
Fuentes, Norberto, 244

Galeano, Eduardo, 99
Gandhi, Mahatma, 351
Garrison, C. K., 76–77
gender relations, 134–35, 137, 149–52. *See also* machismo
Godoy, Virgilio, 295
Goldman, Emma, 351
Gospel in Solentiname, The, 337

Granada, Nicaragua, 72, 186, 328, 335; historic base of conservative party, 75–76
Grenada, 16
Guardia Nacional. *See* National Guard
Group of twelve, 47
Guevara, Che, 347, 351
guerrilla warfare, 86, 93

Habbakuk, 97
Hanna, Matthew, 91
Hartman, Mary, 38
Hasenfus, Eugene, 331
Hatfield, Captain G. D., 70, 84, 85
health care, 62–63, 115, 117–18, 232–34; under Chamorro government, 288–90
Hebrew prophets, 97, 138
Heidegger, Martin, 357
Helms, Jesse, 290
Hemingway, Ernest, 244–46
Heritage Foundation, 116
Heschel, Abraham, 97
Hesiod, 355
Higgins, Michael, 321–24, 363n. 3 (9, 281)
Hodges, Donald C., 361n. 1 (2, 74)
Honduras, 71, 96, 102, 104, 161, 164, 229, 246, 300, 324

Ideology: changed throughout revolution, 326–27; of the bourgeoisie, 283; of U.S. media, 268–70, 274–75, 284. *See also* philosophy; Sandinismo
imperialism. *See* United States imperialism
INDE (Nicaraguan Institute for Economic Development), 47
inflation. *See* Nicaraguan economy: inflation in
INSSBI (Social Security and Welfare), 54
International Monetary Fund, 297
internationalism, 123–24, 317–24; in the United States, 67–68; long term value of, 317–24; motivation for, 10–11, 66–67
internationalists, 55–56, 70, 85, 252–53, 319. *See also* Basque internationalists; Coen, Tanya; Higgins, Michael; Jacobs, Fred; Jansson, Laura

Jacobs, Fred, 231, 235–40, 304–6, 317–18
Jansson, Laura, 55–56, 58, 101–2
Jesus Christ, 28, 59, 126, 138, 308, 337, 344, 347, 349, 351, 352–53, 355
Judaic tradition, 355

King, Martin Luther, 49, 351
Kinzer, Stephen, 277–78, 284
Klee, Paul, 344, 345

Knox, Philander Chase, 77
Kovel, Joel, 357–58
Kristofferson, Kris, 219

La Prensa, 36, 46, 50, 51, 133, 263, 297
labor unions: strikes of, 287, 288–89; social power of, 316
Lacayo, Antonio, 288, 296, 300
land reform, 312
Léger, Fernand, 38
Lemoyne, James, 276–77
Leon, Nicaragua, 256, 266; as historic base of liberals, 75–76
liberation theology, 307–8, 350, 352
Linder, Benjamin, 241, 243–44
literacy campaign, 142, 145–46; revolutionary significance of, 145
López Pérez, Rigoberto, 347
Lorde, Audre, 197, 200

machismo, 136–37, 149–50. *See also* gender relations; women
Magón, Ricardo Flores, 74
Marian people (*pueblo mariana*), 144–45, 146, 152
Martí, José, 96
Marx, Karl, 138, 349, 350, 356, 357, 361n. 1 (9, 267)
Marxism, 115, 348, 349, 353, 354, 357; and Christianity, 93–94, 150. *See also* Marx, Karl; philosophy
mass organizations, 309. *See also* AMNLAE; CDS
Meiselas, Susan, 275
Mejía Godoy, Armando, 128
Mejía Godoy, Carlos, 58, 128
Mejía Godoy, Luis Henrique, 128
Mendoza, René, 285, 306–7
Merton, Thomas, 201, 336
Miami, 16, 35, 39, 50
military draft, 39, 40, 117, 286, 311
Ministry of Culture, 113, 207, 211, 338–39
Miskito Indians, 38
Mistral, Gabriela, 86
Molina, Uriel, 22, 28–29
Moncada, José María, 80–82, 90–91
money. *See* Nicaraguan economy: inflation in
morality: historical progress in, 147; ideal revolutionary possessed of, 95–97, 347, 351; society-wide changes in, 151–52
Morgan, Charles, 76–77
mothering, 146–47; and Christianity, 149; and machismo, 150–52
Mothers of Heroes and Martyrs, 60, 359
Muhammad, 351

National Guard, 21–23, 24–25, 38, 46, 162, 163, 168, 277, 278, 297, 338, 358; corruption of, 141; created by U.S. government, 90; fighting Sandinistas, 103–4; repressing protest, 138, 140
naturalism, 355, 356–57
nature and revolution, 8–11
Neruda, Pablo, 12, 211
Neville Brothers, 299
new person, 94, 152, 347, 351, 353
New York Times, 15–16, 276–80
New York Times Magazine, 276–79, 284
Newsweek, 267, 270, 273, 276, 278, 281
Nicaragua, 2, 7–11; civil wars in, 38–41, 76–77; Nicaraguans' perception of, 144, 217; transoceanic canal possible in, 76–79, 84; traveling in, 51–53, 155, 216–18. *See also* Nicaraguan economy; Nicaraguan music; Nicaraguan poetry; Nicaraguan politics; Nicaraguans; Solentiname painters; United States imperialism
Nicaraguan economy: as depicted in the U.S. media, 272, 275–76; effects of Chamorro government on, 287–93; effects of Contra war on, 34–35, 102–3, 123, 308; effects of U.S. blockade on, 21, 308; inflation in, 33–36, 65, 123; mixed socialist and capitalist character of, 282–83; products exported by, 34; shortages in, 276; Somoza's ownership in, 154
Nicaraguan government (Sandinista period), 36–37; human rights policies of, 38, 280; and opposition to, 40–42, 50–51
Nicaraguan music, 58, 128
Nicaraguan painting. *See* Solentiname painters
Nicaraguan poetry, 199–214; audiences of, 200; exteriorism in, 210–12
Nicaraguan politics: elections in, 40–41, 285–86, 311; tradition of sell-out to the United States, 39, 81; traditional opposition of liberals and conservatives, 75–79, 81, 180; United States influence on, 76–79, 80–81. *See also* Sandinista Front for National Liberation; UNO
Nicaraguans, 2, 51; national character of, 7–11, 110, 144; reputation as sell-outs of their country, 74, 81
Nietzsche, Friedrich, 357

Obando y Bravo, Miguel, 39, 45–48, 50–51, 116–17, 307
Ortega, Camillo, 331
Ortega, Daniel, 16, 27, 35, 200, 209, 219, 275, 277, 285–86, 295, 302, 331, 358

Ortega, Humberto, 24, 218, 295
Otto, Rudolf, 348

Palacaguina, Nicaragua, 126–27
Pallais, Azarias H., 156, 157–60
Parrales, Edgar, 45
Pastora, Edén, 50
philosophy: author's concept of, 68; of Sandino, 74–75, 88–90; postmodern, 9. *See also* ideology; religion: and revolution; Sandinismo
Picasso, Pablo, 344, 345
Pierce, Franklin, 76
Pineda, Elena, 299, 333, 340, 346
Pineda, Francisca, 333, 346
Pineda, Rosa, 333, 345, 346
Plato, 355–56
poetry workshops, 205, 207, 210–11
police, 18–21, 142, 312–14
politics. *See* Nicaraguan politics
Pope John Paul II, 48, 50
popular church. *See* Catholic Church
Pound, Ezra, 201
prostitution, 292

Radio Catolica, 116–17
Ramírez, Sergio, 200, 209, 281, 361n. 1 (2, 73)
Randall, Margaret, 334
Reagan, Ronald, 16, 17, 50, 106, 117, 157, 214, 236, 246, 275
realism: in art, 342–45; in philosophy, 68
Recompas, 301
Recontras, 301, 325
religion: as critiqued by Marx, 349, 357; as nurturance, 146; and politics, 115–17; and revolution, 138–39, 146–47
religious attitude, 349–51, 353
resettlement communities, 57–58, 153–54, 176–82
revolution: essential location of, 247–66, 326–27; international assistance to, 123, 327–34; international significance of, 68, 123; long-term effects of, 326–27; molecular structure of, 266; and nature, 9; Nicaraguan's conception of, 247; Nicaraguan conservative's conception of, 40–42, 50–51, 263–64; portrayal of in U.S. mass media, 270–76; progress in education and social well-being within, 117–18, 326–27 (*see also* health care); and religion, 146–47 (*see also* religion); spiritual quality of, 4, 6, 9–11, 327, 344–45, 347–59; and women in, 136–37, 142–43
Rich, Adrienne, 197
Robelo, Alfonso, 47

Román, José, 71
Root, Elihu, 78–79
Rosario and Light Mines, the, 77–78
Ruchwarger, Gary, 363n. 3 (9, 281)
Ruddick, Sara, 148–50
Rugama, Leonel, 329

Sacasa, Juan Bautista, 79, 90–92
sacred: creation of, by human communities,
    358–59; revolutionary conception of,
    353–55; places and times, 354–55; tradi-
    tional conception of, 348–49
Salgado family, 14–15, 16–18, 42–45, 66
Salgado, Joaquina, 13; author's interview
    with, 21–24
Salgado, Lolín, 13, 17, 24, 35
Salon, Maria Felicia de, 232–34, 241, 289–
    90
San Albino gold mine, 75, 79–80, 92
San Juan River, 76
San Juan del Sur, 76
San Rafael del Norte, 82–83
Sandinismo, 74–75, 84, 88–89, 93–94, 96,
    112; as philosophy of history, 89; as unity
    of several philosophies, 74–75
Sandinista Front for National Liberation:
    commitment to armed struggle of, 140;
    commitment to equality of men and
    women of, 136–37, 151; as community
    of struggle, 136; condition of, after 1990
    election defeat, 302; corruption within,
    303–4, 305, 310; democracy within, 281;
    doctrinal diversity of, 93–94; failures and
    mistakes of, 304–6, 307, 309–11;
    founded by, 93; ideals and moral values
    of, 94, 314; 1969 historic program of,
    136; opposition of church hierarchy to,
    47–51; as portrayed in U.S. media, 273–
    75; respect for human rights of, 280; re-
    spect for religion of, 115–16, 351; San-
    dino's influence on, 93; relation to revolu-
    tionary government, 309; relation to
    Chamorro government, 285–86, 291;
    revolutionary commitment of, 140; top-
    down authoritarianism of, 305, 307, 310;
    women's participation in, 136–37, 142
Sandinista government. See Nicaraguan gov-
    ernment (Sandinista period)
Sandinistas, 4, 5, 36–37, 40, 103, 263,
    280–81, 286, 350, 358; but not party
    members, 303–4; during the insurrection,
    22, 24–25
Sandino, Augusto César, 12, 21, 69–97,
    112, 180, 206, 243, 277, 278, 303, 307,
    337, 351; assassination of, 90–92; birth
    and early life of, 71–73; Freemason mem-

bership of, 75; generalship of, 86–90;
    guerrilla tactics of, 85–86; marriage of,
    82–83; museum of, 160; philosophy of,
    74–75, 88–89; political education of, 73–
    75; revolutionary faith of, 89–90; spir-
    itual leadership of, 88–89; temptation of,
    81–82; as writer, 70, 83–84, 87–88
Sandino, Blanca Araúz, 82–83, 154, 180
Sandino, Gregorio, 71–72, 79, 83
Sandino, Sócrates, 72
sexism. See gender relations, machismo
Silva, Fernando, 203–5, 209
Silva, Olivia, 334–39
slavery, 10, 76
socialism, 280, 298, 349, 353
Socialist Party of Nicaragua, 93
Solentiname, 104, 211, 327–46
Solentiname Gallery, 340, 346
Solentiname painters, 342–46
Somocistas, 108, 140, 166, 207, 227, 250
Somoza Debayle, Anastasio, 17, 38, 40, 47,
    66, 92, 140, 141, 170, 207, 220, 250,
    276, 320, 321
Somoza Debayle, Luis, 92
Somoza Garcia, Anastasio, 21, 27, 117,
    153–54, 307, 337, 347; accumulated
    wealth of, 92; assassination of, 347; as-
    sassination of Sandino by, 90–92; as-
    sumption of power by, 90–92; as author
    of book on Sandino, 93; intimacy with
    U.S. embassy of, 91
Soviet Union, 2, 281; as baneful influence
    on Latin American socialism, 93
Spanish colonialism, 75
spirit: and community, 96–97; four types of,
    95–96; fire as metaphor of, 95; revolu-
    tionary, 95–97, 326–27; guides, 88, 94–
    97
spirituality: author's definition of, 355–58; a
    component of revolutionary morality,
    351; a quality of the Nicaraguan revolu-
    tion, 4, 6, 9–11, 95–97, 327
Stimson, Henry Lewis, 80, 91

Tampico, Mexico, 71, 74, 75
Téllez, Dora María, 137
terrorism, 38–39, 44, 313. See also Contras
Tijerino, Doris, 142
Time, 267, 270–76, 278, 281, 284
Torres, Camilo, 94
Trinh, T. Minh-ha, 267, 268

UNAG (National Agricultural Union),
    168, 171, 236, 249, 254, 304
unemployment. See Nicaraguan economy
UNESCO, 145

United States, 10–11, 27, 57, 67–68, 146. *See also* United States government; United States imperialism; United States media; United States military

United States government: aggression against Nicaragua, 15–16, 48, 286 (*see also* United States imperialism); Department of State of, 116; dollar diplomacy of, 80; embassy of, 69; interventions in Nicaragua by, 77–79; low intensity warfare of, 286; as source of terrorism, 182; as sponsor of Contra war, 116–17, 163, 277; support for William Walker's invasion by, 76

United States imperialism, 10–11, 27, 39, 76, 77–79, 80, 85–86, 217; and economic blockade of Nicaragua, 34–35; in the U.S. media, 274–76

United States media, 267–84; distance effect created by, 268–70; establishment economic and ideological control over, 361–63n. 1 (9, 267); ideology in, 274–75, 283–84

United States military: intervention in Grenada, 16; intervention in Vietnam, 85; threat of invasion of Nicaragua, 15–16

UNO (Union of National Opposition), 285, 286, 295, 297, 298, 306

Urtecho, Jose Coronel, 209

U.S. News and World Report, 275, 281–82

Valenzuela, Edna, 55, 66

Vanderbilt, Cornelius, 76–77

Vargas Llosa, Mario, 279–84

Vasquez, Father Miguel Angel, 174

Vega, Monsignor Pablo Antonio, 116

vegetarianism, 98–99

veterans, U.S., 219–20, 228, 229–31; Veteran's Peace Action Teams (V-PAT), 230

Villa Sin Miedo, Puerto Rico, 3–4, 113, 220

violence and nonviolence, 46–47, 48–49, 337

Walker, William, 10, 76–77

Weil, Simone, 149

Wheelock, Jaime, 312

White House, 182

Whitman, Walt, 201

Wilson, Brian, 219

women, 359; artists in U.S. and Nicaragua compared, 346; historic importance in Nicaragua of, 143; organization of, 136, 316–17; participation in revolution by, 135–37, 142; Sandinista party position on, 136. *See also* gender relations; machismo

World Bank, 297

World Court, 290

Zamora, Daisy, 79, 205–7, 208, 209, 361n. 2 (2, 79)

Zelaya, General José Santos, 77, 278

Zelayo, Franco, 140

Zeledón, Benjamin, 78, 83, 278